LEOPOLD II
OF THE BELGIANS

LEOPOLD II
OF THE BELGIANS
King of Colonialism

Barbara Emerson

With best wishes,
Barbara Emerson,
May 1979.

Weidenfeld and Nicolson
London

For Michael

Weidenfeld and Nicolson
91 Clapham High St London sw4

ISBN 0 297 77569 3

Printed in Great Britain by
Butler & Tanner Ltd, Frome and London

Contents

Illustrations and Maps

The author and publishers would like to thank the following for kind permission to reproduce the illustrations: ACL Brussels, 1, 2, 9, 16, 17, 23; Musée de la Dynastie, 3, 4, 5, 8, 10, 11, 17, 20; Palais Royal, Brussels, 6; Belgian National Tourist Office (© CGT – V.d. Bremt) 7;

Bibliothèque Royale, Albert 1, Brussels (Cabinet des Estampes) 12, 13, 25; Musée Royale de l'Afrique Centrale, Tervuren, 14, 24; Baroness van Eetvelde, 15; Musée de l'Armée et d'Histoire Militaire, Brussels, 18; British Library, 19; *Punch* magazine, 26.

Maps

Acknowledgements

I would like to express my gratitude to Her Majesty Queen Elizabeth II who graciously permitted me access to the Royal Archives, Windsor, and to His Majesty King Baudouin who allowed me to consult the archives of the Palais Royal, Brussels.

I wish to thank the archivists of the Ministry of Foreign Affairs, Brussels; the Archives Générales du Royaume, Brussels; the Archives Africaines, Brussels; the conservators of the Bibliothèque Royale, Brussels; the Musée Royal de l'Armée et d'Histoire Militaire, Brussels; the president and conservator of the Musée de la Dynastie, Brussels; the keeper of the Public Record Office, London; the librarians of the Catholic University of Louvain; the School of Oriental and African Studies, London University; the London School of Economics and Political Science; the London Library.

I would like to acknowledge my debt to Mr James Emerson for his help at all stages and for his constant encouragement; Miss Sybil Crowe kindly read the manuscript and offered valuable suggestions. Mrs Sarah Andrews did a marvellous job typing and correcting the manuscript. I am also grateful to Mr Anthony Barnes, Mr Gerry Bradshaw, Mr Cleveland Moffett and Mr George Zlatovski.

My very warmest thanks are due to my editor, Francesca George, for the many improvements she made to the manuscript.

B.E.

La Hulpe,
Belgium

Preface

'My ambition is to make Belgium greater, stronger and more beautiful', Leopold II announced on becoming king in 1865. The greatness of Belgium was the motivating force in his life; it emerged when he was in his early twenties and was a passion that never flagged. Belgium was, however, a small constitutional monarchy and the opportunities for Leopold to pursue his ambitions within Europe were very limited. This he appreciated from the outset.

It was widely held in the mid-nineteenth century that free trade made the possession of colonies unnecessary. Leopold believed differently. He argued that only the direct-link metropole-colony provided a secure market for the export of goods and capital and the provision of cheap primary products. Belgium, 'the workshop of the Continent', needed a colony or colonies. Clear in his aim, and with no support from his countrymen, Leopold set about looking for a colony. In his search he became the ruler of an enormous portion of Central Africa, the Congo Free State, and precipitated what came to be known as the Scramble for Africa.

If Leopold was in the vanguard of the opening-up of Africa, he was also the first to manifest the decadence of imperialism and its rapacious exploitation of land and people. For while it was accepted – and the king was an exponent of the view – that private enterprise should be able to make money in colonies, it was considered discreditable for the government of dependencies to be run on commercial lines and at the expense of the native population. And this was the basis of Leopold's regime in the Congo. He was the absolute ruler, without any institutions to advise or restrain him, and he ran 'his colony' as a money-making concern with a system of forced labour which reached inhuman proportions and caused widespread suffering. Leopold had hoped for a colony which would provide a market for Belgian goods – the Congo did not. However, as its primary products found a ready and expanding market in Europe, the king-sovereign made vast sums of money from their sales; these he spent on prestige expeditions to the Nile and extensive building in Belgium. In the end, Leopold's long sought-after colony was to provoke such widespread unpopularity and disgust that it overshadowed and blackened the sum of his considerable achievements and abilities.

The second king of the Belgians devoted his life, never stinting his efforts, to furthering what he saw as the best interests of Belgium. His colony was no more than a tool and it is somehow symptomatic that, although he was a great traveller, he never seems to have shown any urge to visit the Congo. Leopold succeeded in the three objectives he set himself at the beginning of his reign: he brought his small country into the ranks of the colonial Powers; he impressed on the Belgian people their military vulnerability and improved their army and defences; and he embellished Belgium in a way no other single person had done. But he died a bitter, disappointed man, unloved by his subjects and reviled abroad. The Congo was ignominiously wrenched from him in 1908, his building was unappreciated in Belgium and the notoriety of his colonial regime soured the Powers' attitude to the Belgian nation and weakened their resolution to protect her neutrality.

Leopold II was a sincere patriot and a man of first-class ability but he never understood that, however well intentioned, the ends do not justify the means.

1 L'Union fait la Force

'When men are great, however narrow the
frontiers within which they live, they always
find the means to do great things.'[1]

Leopold II.

The birth of a son, Leopold Louis-Philippe Marie Victor, to the King and Queen of the Belgians in 1835 had an importance far greater than that simply of continuing the dynasty. Belgium had been created only five years before: within the country the Orangist faction which supported the previous regime had not conceded defeat; internationally, while England accepted Belgium's existence, France still coveted the French-speaking parts of the country and Austria and Russia had not recognized the new state. If Belgium was to provide evidence of potential durability, the king, Leopold I, had to have a direct heir.

From the sixteenth century onwards the history of the Low Countries had been dominated by the antipathy between the Protestants of the northern Netherlands and the Catholics of the southern provinces. The Congress of Vienna in 1815 chose to disregard the ill-feeling and the differences between the northerners, the Dutch, and the southerners, the Belgians, and they were united under the King of Holland, William I.

To the French-speaking Walloons of the Belgian provinces the Dutch were an alien people and they bitterly resented the enforced union of 1815. The period also coincided with the rapid industrialization (which William did much to promote) of the south, based on rich coal and iron-ore deposits, and the Belgians considered that they were being exploited, through the tax system, by the largely agricultural northern provinces.[2] Although the Flemings, who constituted about half the population of the Belgian provinces, were closely akin to the Dutch of the north, the Flemish bourgeoisie preferred to speak French and did not identify with the Dutch.

To William's overhasty policy of assimilation, his unresponsive attitude towards the economic grievances of the Belgian provinces, was added his interference in the affairs of the Catholic church and the union with Holland became increasingly unpopular. By 1830 a further factor in the incipient crisis was the presence in Brussels of political exiles whose ideology owed much to the French Revolution and who manifested an aversion to William and all things Dutch. The overthrow of Charles X in France in July 1830 obviously influenced liberals in the Belgian provinces, though its importance in the sequence of events leading to the Brussels uprising has often been overrated.

In the summer of 1830 William intended to visit Brussels. Before his arrival hostile leaflets were distributed proclaiming: 'August 23rd fireworks, August 24th the King's birthday, August 25th revolution'. The king's trip was postponed, the fireworks were cancelled on the spurious grounds of bad weather, and the tension mounted. On 25 August Auber's opera, *La Muette de Portici*, opened in Brussels. The bourgeois audience left the *Théâtre de la Monnaie* humming a catchy revolutionary song from the opera. Crowds of unemployed wandering the streets on the summer's evening took up the song and were soon combining it with anti-Dutch slogans. Within a few hours a mob had formed which roamed Brussels, looting and sacking the homes of Dutch officials. The next day rioting continued in Brussels which triggered off a series of revolts throughout the provinces. Local leaders, foremost among whom was Charles Rogier from Liège, brought their contingents to Brussels and confronted a Dutch army of 12,000. Fierce fighting ensued and after a few days the Dutch troops were forced to withdraw.

The provisional government, the National Congress, set up as a result of the successful revolution, sat from November 1830 to July 1831. A constitution, in many respects the most liberal in Europe at the time, was drafted and it was decided to establish a monarchy, as republics aroused the fears of the Great Powers and their support would be necessary in the establishment of the new country. The British government in particular took a considerable interest in the creation of Belgium. It was at first distressed to see the buffer state of an enlarged Holland disintegrate but recognized that a country crippled by internal strife could no longer be effective. The new danger, which the British government clearly appreciated, was that the French would attempt to take over Belgium. When the National Congress announced that it intended to offer the new crown to the Duke of Nemours, second son of Louis-Philippe of France, the British saw their worst fears materializing and they, with the other Great Powers, opposed the choice. In his place they proposed Prince Leopold of Saxe-Coburg-Saalfeld. The Belgians and Leopold himself were agreeable and on 21 July 1831 Leopold entered Brussels and was sworn in in the Place Royale.

Leopold I's father was Prince Francis of Saxe-Coburg-Saalfeld, heir to the German dukedom of Coburg at the time of Leopold's birth in 1790. Coburg was small and as Leopold was the third son there was little for him to look forward to. He was obliged, like other younger sons of German princelings, to seek his fortune elsewhere.

Throughout Leopold's childhood and early manhood Europe was at war and, in 1806, Coburg was overrun by the French and forced to join the Confederation of the Rhine. The Napoleonic wars, however, provided excellent opportunities for young soldiers and diplomats and, having served in the Russian army, Leopold travelled with the tsar's retinue to London in 1814.

London held out a glittering prize for some fortunate young man in the form of the nubile Princess Charlotte, daughter of the Prince Regent and heiress presumptive to the British throne. Leopold met Princess Charlotte and, although she was supposed to be engaged to the hereditary Prince of Orange, she decided that she preferred Prince Leopold. They were married in 1816 and early the following year Charlotte became pregnant, to the delight not only of her husband and herself but to that of the English population to whom a healthy, happy, young and legitimately married couple made a refreshing change from the debaucheries of the sons of George III. But the son born at Claremont, the Coburg home, was stillborn and his mother died a few hours later.

Leopold mourned Charlotte personally, for he had grown to love her, and at the same time he was forced to recognize that he had not only lost his wife and child but also his role and position in society. For the next fourteen years, until his accession to the Belgian throne in 1831, he remained at the English court living comfortably, if at first aimlessly, on a substantial pension voted by parliament of £50,000 a year.

After Charlotte's death there remained no legitimate heir to any of George III's sons and to fill the void, two of the royal dukes obliged by discarding their long-standing mistresses and marrying German princesses. With Leopold's help his widowed sister Victoria was assigned one of the dukes. She became Duchess of Kent in 1819 and a year later gave birth to a girl who was also called Victoria. A few months later the Duke of Kent died, leaving Leopold's sister widowed a second time, this time however responsible for the second in line to the English throne. Victoria was fatherless and, with the decadent dukes themselves doing much to hasten their respective ways to the grave, there was the chance that a regency might be necessary. Leopold looked after his sister with brotherly affection, while the infant Victoria took the place of his own stillborn son, and he forged with her a loving bond which lasted throughout his life. Nevertheless, he was not unaware that his behaviour towards his sister and her child might affect his position if Victoria acceded to the throne while still a minor. Even if the Duchess of Kent became regent, he knew that he would wield the power behind the throne. This undoubtedly influenced his turning down the Greek throne, which was offered him in 1828. Three years later when he was asked to become the first King of the Belgians, the chances of a regency had diminished considerably and he accepted the offer.

Soon after becoming king Leopold 1 turned his mind to the question of a wife. He had little difficulty in finding a suitable princess, indeed Louise-Marie d'Orléans possessed all the attributes of an ideal Queen of the Belgians. The French had suffered a rebuff in the English refusal to allow the Belgians to have a French prince as king and Leopold hoped to go some way towards soothing Louis-Philippe's hurt pride by choosing the French king's eldest daughter as his wife and also to make a gesture of gratitude for French military help which had enabled the Belgians to expel the Dutch completely in 1831. In addition, Louise was a Catholic and this was an advantage in Belgium, as Leopold himself was Lutheran and the vast majority of Belgians Catholic. The Belgians could look forward to a Catholic dynasty without Leopold himself having to make the difficult decision as to whether or not to change his religion.

Louise d'Orléans was born in Palermo in 1812 during the exile of her Bourbon father. She was a woman of considerable intelligence with a lively, almost waspish, sense of humour and a high standard of education – her history teacher, for example, was Jules Michelet, the eminent French historian. Louise had wanted to marry the Prince of Calabria; Leopold, whom she met once before, she remembered as a cold, morose man and she told her friend the Countess d'Hulst, after meeting him again, that, although she accepted her lot, she was 'as indifferent to him as any passerby in the street'.[3]

They were married at Compiègne, one of Louis-Philippe's country houses north of Paris, on 9 August 1832, and left the following day for Brussels. The twenty-year-old French princess was ill at ease to begin with. The Count de Mérode wrote of her:

> A few days after the arrival of the young Queen I was invited to dinner. The Queen was very shy and nervous. Nevertheless, it was evident from her conversation how well and carefully she had been educated. But all this was nothing compared with her spiritual qualities which will soon be recognized and which will earn her the respect and attachment of all.[4]

If Louise was unhappy about the marriage in the early days, her husband was not. He wrote to his niece in England:

> My Dearest Love, – You told me you wished to have a description

of your new Aunt. I therefore shall both mentally and physically describe her to you.

She is extremely gentle and amiable, her actions are always guided by principles. She is at all times ready and disposed to sacrifice her comfort and inclinations to see others happy. She values goodness, merit, and virtue much more than beauty, riches, and amusements. With all this she is highly informed and very clever: she speaks and writes English, German and Italian: she speaks English very well indeed. In short, my dear Love, you see that I may well recommend her as an example for all young ladies being Princesses or not . . .

There exists already great confidence and affection between us: she is desirous of doing everything that can contribute to my happiness, and I study whatever can make her happy and contented . . .[5]

With Leopold immersed in politics and diplomacy when in Brussels and often away in the Ardennes, Louise led a lonely life at Laeken, the royal palace outside Brussels, in the first years of her marriage. With a note of probably unintentional irony, she told the Countess d'Hulst, 'The King, his dog and I live alone in the Palace.'[6] Charlotte Brontë, writing from Brussels to her sister Emily about a visit of Queen Victoria, said: 'The Belgians liked her well on the whole. They say she enlivened the sombre court of King Leopold which is usually as gloomy as a conventicle.'[7]

But the way of life suited Louise and within two years of her marriage she had changed her initial hostile opinion of her husband. 'The King makes me perfectly happy. His kindness towards me touches me deeply. I have great esteem for him and I have found in him the qualities that I admire most.'[8] She could not believe that such marital bliss could continue: 'If I could make a wish it would be to be less perfectly happy, because my happiness is so complete that it often frightens me.'[9] The price that she paid for such happiness, total self-effacement, was a high one: 'All my desires, even those dearest to me, are subordinated to his.'[10]

The queen became pregnant soon after her marriage and looked forward with pleasure to the birth of the child in July 1833. Leopold, for his part, was extremely nervous. His fears proved unfounded and his wife gave birth to a healthy boy who was named Louis-Philippe Leopold Ernest. A hundred-and-one gun salute was fired in Brussels, there were celebrations in the streets and the usually emotionless king showed his delight in his child. The baby, known as Babochon to his mother, made excellent progress for a few months then, about Christmas time, he became ill. Various, often contradictory, cures were tried, until in April 1834 Leopold sent for the eminent English physician, Sir James Clark. Clark arrived but it was too late, the heir to the Belgian throne was mortally ill and died of convulsions on 16 May. Leopold wrote bitterly: 'The saddest thing is that this child was so strong and beautiful and had he been the child of some peasant he would now be fit and well.'[11]

While Louise found some comfort for her bereavement in her religion, Leopold felt the blow more keenly. 'All this has brought back his previous misfortunes and in spite of all his efforts to remain calm and dignified, he was frequently in tears and could talk only of the little one.'[12]

However, a second child, Leopold, was born less than a year later. He was a puny, sickly baby and, though the Belgians fêted the birth, Leopold could not bring himself to feel any joy at possessing a living heir. He was afraid to pin his hopes on any child, let alone on one whose chances of survival did not appear good. After the deaths of Charlotte and his first child he had avoided emotional involvement; he had allowed himself to feel again when Babochon was born and he knew the recent pain with which he had had to pay the price. This time his emotions were anaesthetized. Describing his seven-month-old son to Victoria he simply wrote: 'He is very peculiar in his ways and very intelligent.'[13]

Two years after Leopold another child was born, again a boy. Philippe Eugene Ferdinand Marie Clement Baudouin Leopold Georges was a larger and more robust baby than his elder brother and the king immediately liked him more than Leopold, probably reckoning the child's chances of becoming king as being greater than those of his elder son. Two living sons were not sufficient to assuage Leopold's fears for the succession and he felt disappointment when his third child, born in 1840, was a daughter. (The Belgian constitution excluded women from the succession.) She was named Charlotte after her father's first wife and the fifty-year-old Leopold found himself enjoying the child – the future Empress of Mexico – who was of no dynastic importance.

In 1840 Leopold I revived the medieval Belgian title of Duke of Brabant for his elder son and Count of Flanders for Philippe. Leopold, Duke of Brabant, was the least prepossessing of the king's children. He was overly thin, with a pale pointed face and small, slanting eyes. His mother considered him, 'disfigured by his enormous nose which gives him a birdlike air'.[14] In personality he was withdrawn and often sullen while the plump Count of Flanders, known as Bijou, was outgoing and affectionate and Charlotte was 'the beauty of the family, a child so gentle and likeable, who never cries'.[15] Leopold was not a lovable child and even Louise, who tried hard, could not love her elder son as much as her two younger children.

Prince Leopold early on developed a high idea of his own importance as heir to the throne which may well have been an expression of the jealousy he felt towards his preferred brother and sister. Aged just over two he insisted – it sounds unlikely but the source is his father – that 'no nicknames should be given him … he only permits people to call him Prince or Leopold'.[16] A year later, referring to a portrait, Leopold I wrote of his son that he 'has at times an even more intelligent look … he is very original and very sly: I often called him "the little tyrant" because nobody knows so well as he *l'art de faire aller le monde*'.[17]

Today, Prince Leopold's behaviour would be recognized as that of a child manifesting symptoms of emotional deprivation but in the late 1830s it simply bewildered his father. 'He can be exceedingly violent,' the king confided to Victoria, 'which is strange because neither his mother nor father are.'[18] 'Odd' and 'funny' are the gentler adjectives used by Leopold I to describe his elder son, his most usual being 'peculiar'.[19] The tender terms in which he referred to Philippe and Charlotte are not to be found. 'He [Leopold] is unruly and [as] fractious as anything can be imagined,' wrote his unsympathetic father.[20]

Prince Leopold's mother tongue was French, though it has been claimed that he had, like his father, a German accent.[21] The Chevalier Albert de Selliers de Moranville, who was one of Leopold II's equerries from 1907 to 1909, says that, while he would not go along with this view, there was something distinctly guttural in Leopold II's enunciation of French. He also learnt German and English. The novelist, Henri Conscience, whose writing encouraged the Flemish national movement in its early days, was appointed teacher of Flemish to the royal children, but it was purely honorific and Prince Leopold never learned to speak Flemish.

Louise devoted most of her time to her children, attempting to implement the extremely high standards of behaviour and intellectual attainment that Leopold set for them. For example, the king complained to Victoria that his elder son was 'very idle about speaking', when the child was only nineteen months old.[22] Even when Leopold attempted humour it was hardly of a kind to appeal to a three-year-old boy. 'I said to him "Bonjour Mademoiselle", which shocked him a great deal and he said gravely, "Prince is a boy and not a girl".'[23] In fairness to Leopold I though, it must have been difficult for him to confront fatherhood for the first time in his late forties.

The children's life was well organized and routine. Their governor, Lieutenant-Colonel de Lannoy, drew up a draft time-table for their studies which began at 6.30 am and ended at 5 pm, with total breaks of three hours for meals and relaxation. The queen added a further hour's work from 7 to 8 o'clock in the evening.[24] On no account was the continuity of the children's studies to be interrupted, even when, for ceremonial reasons, they were taken to Brussels. Louise gave precise instructions when this happened, for example:

> April 2nd 1847. We shall leave for town [from Laeken] at 9.30 and we will take the children with us . . . We shall go first to the Palace and then to the church. The children will dine in town after the service and will remain at the Palace until 5 pm. Please arrange to take all that is necessary in the way of school books so that the afternoon will not be entirely wasted.[25]

Every month the children were subjected to an examination by their mother to ensure that they had made good progress in their studies. If they were successful, she presented them with a book from her library. Charlotte, five years younger than Leopold, and Philippe, two years younger, were nearly always rewarded for good work. Leopold was a constant problem. He was idle and only rarely showed any interest in his studies. The child's only saving grace in the classroom seems to have been artistic talent. 'He draws *so* well I think he will have great talent for drawing' his father believed, but the compliment was modified with the exasperated qualification: 'for he does nothing else all day but draws, and principally *des locomotives* with a great deal of smoke'.[26]

Unfortunately for Prince Leopold, drawing only played a minor part in his education. Increasing pressure was applied to make him overcome his laziness in his academic studies, the only one in which he showed any interest being geography. Politics, which fascinated him from an early age, was not included in his curriculum. At the age of ten he was already enjoying discussing current affairs: 'Leo is quite at home in the *salon*', said his father. 'He is extremely fond of society; let us hope that he will be gradually also fonder of study.'[27]

No improvement was manifested the following year and the king reacted by emphasizing the need for discipline to the children's governor. But Leopold's methods met with singular lack of success in persuading his elder son to apply himself more assiduously in the classroom. At the age of fourteen his mother admonished him:

> Thank you for your letter my good friend. I was happy to receive some news at last and to learn that you are all well. However, I was very disappointed to hear from the Colonel that you have again been lazy and that your dictations have been bad and careless. This is not what you had promised me and I hope that you will make a greater effort with your homework. Your father was as hurt as I by this latest report.[28]

There is something reminiscent of Winston Churchill's childhood in the unsatisfactory intellectual development of the young Leopold II. The indefatigable, extremely able man of later years was not to be detected in the unpromising child.

Louise's health had never been good and she had suffered for years from an intractable cough. It was, however, a series of emotional blows on top of her incipient tubercular state which finally killed her at the age of thirty-eight. She had never fully recovered from the death of her sister Marie in 1839 and that of her brother the Duke d'Orléans in 1842. Then in 1848 her adored father, King Louis-Philippe, was deposed by Louis-Napoleon and forced to flee to England. In addition to this her husband's frequent infidelities caused her much suffering, although she reproached herself because she was a wife 'whose health did not allow her to fulfil her wifely duties'.[29] In the late 1840s Leopold embarked upon an affair with a voluptuous Flemish beauty, Arcadie Claret de Viescourt. At first he tried to keep his visits to his *maîtresse en titre* out of the public eye, but Arcadie Claret was determined to flaunt her position. In a pathetic and moving letter to her husband at the end of 1849, Louise let him know that she was aware that he was unfaithful to her and that she accepted it: 'What more could I ask on earth than to be your friend, to be your only friend? All my happiness I owe to you: all that is lacking from my happiness is my fault, alone, and I blame only myself for all that troubles me.'[30]

During the first half of 1850 Louise fainted several times and her entourage expressed their fears for her health. She reassured them but knew that her health was worsening and warned her mother. 'Although I have no temperature, nor am I in pain, I cough a great deal and sometimes I have difficulty in breathing. You must be prepared to find me sallow skinned, thin and changed. I look frightful and much aged.'[31] In August, her father, who had never come to terms with his deposition and whose physical and mental health deteriorated in exile, died. At his memorial service in Brussels a few days later Louise again fainted and Leopold, who was not even then aware of the seriousness of her condition, felt compelled to call in her doctors. They advised sea air and Louise was installed in a large house, known as the Palais Royal, in the rue Longue at Ostend. During the month of September, pale, with an almost transparent skin, she was seen walking on the dykes with her children. Suddenly, at the beginning of October, she suffered a recrudescence and was too weak to leave her bed.

Sir Robert Carswell had come over from England to take charge of the team of doctors treating Louise and, such was the public concern in Belgium for the health of the young queen who had endeared herself to the population, that bulletins were issued daily, sometimes twice daily. Leopold remained at Louise's bedside much of the time, watching her combat great pain. He, and the ten-year-old Charlotte who was often with him, wept to see Louise in such a state. The dying woman soothed them, expressing her regret to suffer, 'only because it must hurt others to witness it'.[32] It was to her friend, the Countess d'Hulst, to whom she admitted on 10 October, 'I know that I am dying.' Her friend, shocked to hear the truth expressed by Louise herself, answered, 'It has to be admitted, your Majesty, that a further relapse could be dangerous.' 'I understand you,' replied the queen, 'I must therefore prepare myself to receive the Last Sacraments.'[33]

'My dear Leopold, we must accept the inevitable,' Queen Marie-Amélie told her son-in-law.[34] Louise had exhausted her remaining strength and was weaker than before. For several hours she was tranquil until, during the night, she was seized by excruciating pain. At five o'clock in the morning her children were called in: she kissed them one by one and said adieu. With the words, 'I hope that the people will extend to my husband and my sons that share of their sympathy and love that they have pledged to me', she fell unconscious.[35] A few hours later she was dead.

2 Duke of Brabant

*'Please advise Leo to be prudent in his
conversations. He is rather too fond of
talking.'*[1]

Leopold I to Viscount Conway, 1854.

A month after Louise's death Victoria wrote to Leopold I with sound advice: 'You should have the dear children as much with you as possible. I am sure it would be so *good and useful* for *you* and *them*. Children ought to have great confidence in their parents for them to have any influence over them.'[2] In his letters to Victoria 'Dearest Uncle' liked to give the impression of being closer to his children than was in fact the case, but his niece seems to have guessed that he was not the loving father he would have her believe.

The death of his gentle, affectionate mother had a profound effect on the Duke of Brabant and his father was unable to fill the void. Letters which have recently come to light, show the change that took place in the duke in the years immediately following Louise's death.[3] He did not find anyone in whom he could confide, or towards whom he felt real tenderness and affection. Lacking such personal relationships, Leopold became a solitary, and in his private life, taciturn young man.

Perhaps Leopold I wanted to reach out emotionally to his children but found that he was unable. From time to time the king enjoyed Charlotte's company but he did not seek out his elder son and fell into the habit of communicating with him through the intermediary of Viscount Conway, secretary of the civil list. Fairly infrequently Conway was asked to invite the heir to the throne to eat with his father, though Leopold's secretary, Jules van Praet, was usually present, and the conversation political rather than personal. Later on the king insisted that his sons should make a formal appointment before seeing him.[4]

Leopold I was certainly aware of the need to prepare his son for his future role and most diplomatic dispatches were circulated to the Duke of Brabant. Nor were any constraints placed on the duke's access to Belgian politicians or to diplomats in Brussels, although the king was not infrequently irritated by what he considered his son's indiscretions and unfortunate manner of putting himself over.

It should be pointed out though that at no time, whatever gaffes he may have committed, did the Duke of Brabant give his father cause to criticize him for usurping his authority, and the young Leopold avoided becoming too involved in those subjects the king held dear; no mean feat, one would have thought. He was a young man anxious to learn about all that was going on in the world, overly enthusiastic to promote his country. His behaviour could be both gauche and arrogant, but could his father not have adopted a more sympathetic and constructive attitude towards his heir? One feels compelled to place a share of the blame for the unattractive characteristics of Leopold II on Leopold I, since it cannot be said that contemporary views as to the upbringing of children normally led to quite such formal and distant relationships. Leopold I had demonstrated in his relationship with Victoria his ability to combine fatherly affection and didactic solicitude, and he was very fond of describing himself as the Nestor of sovereigns. After Louise's death it was incumbent on the father to make an effort at loving his son. But he did not.

The overthrow of Louis-Philippe in 1848 had been a severe political blow to Leopold I. Louis-Napoleon declared, 'The Empire stands for peace' when he made himself emperor, but Leopold was far from persuaded that a Napoleonic empire was compatible with the existence of Belgium, 'as the *gloire française* invariably looks to the old frontiers'.[5] To Victoria he wrote: 'We are here in the awkward position of persons in hot climates, who find themselves in company, for instance, in their beds with a snake; they must *not* move, because that irritates the creature, but they can hardly remain as they are, without a fair chance of being bitten.'[6]

The snake for his part, however, considered that his bedfellow was actively giving him cause to bite. It was only natural that the Belgian monarchy should regret the downfall of the Orléans dynasty in France but Louis-Napoleon felt keenly that Leopold I was not making an effort to establish good relations with France. The French emperor was well aware that he was considered a *parvenu* (there is a certain irony about this coming from Leopold I) and he was convinced that the King of the Belgians was intriguing with other European countries against him. The 1851 *coup d'état* had led to a considerable number of Orléanist sympathizers and radicals leaving France, and Belgium with its proximity, Francophonia and liberal constitution was a natural haven for them. The most prominent émigré, Victor Hugo, installed himself in an apartment in the Grand' Place in Brussels and there vented his spleen against the French emperor in *Napoléon le Petit*, published in 1852 in Belgium. Many of the French exiles were writers and, finding the Belgian press laws extremely liberal, they set up magazines and broadsheets largely devoted to attacks on the emperor. In addition, the Belgian press itself indulged in numerous articles hostile to the Bonaparte regime. Napoleon was, hardly surprisingly, furious at this propaganda against him and brought pressure to bear on the Belgian government to clamp down on the offending journals. The government's reply was that, while it deplored the attacks on the emperor and the empress, it could not do anything. Napoleon III did not accept this and took the Belgian refusal to change the law as tacit support for its press. Franco-Belgian relations were by 1853 extremely strained.

French support had been one of the props of Leopold I's diplomatic activities up to 1848 and the change of regime in France inevitably brought with it a decline in his prestige in Europe. Of this he was only too aware, and with his usual resourcefulness he set about remedying this situation. In the Duke of Brabant he had a useful asset at his disposal.

The duke came of age in April 1853 on reaching his eighteenth birthday, and to mark this Leopold I decided to take him on a tour of German states and to Austria. At Gotha they were received by Leopold's nephew, the reigning duke; they moved on to Dresden to meet the King of Saxony, then to Berlin, arriving at Vienna on 12 May.

The Countess of Ficquelmont, wife of the Austrian prime minister, who had known Leopold in London, looked forward to the visit, and in a letter to her sister gave advance warning of the real reason for it: 'I shall be curious to see the outcome of this journey for between ourselves, it is to show the Archduchess Marie-Henriette to the young Duke of Brabant and vice versa. She is sixteen and has youthful beauty, freshness and charm, but she has been educated like a boy.'[7]

The rumour was correct. The news of the engagement of the heir to the Belgian throne to the Archduchess Marie-Henriette, daughter of the Palatine of Hungary, was announced a few days later. It represented an enormous diplomatic triumph for Leopold to have acquired a Hapsburg bride, granddaughter of the Empress Maria-Theresa, for his elder son, for the connection with the conservative Austrian royal house would do much to strengthen the international position of Belgium – only sixty years before the Belgians had risen against the Austrians – and the king abandoned his usual phlegm in the round of social events celebrating the betrothal.

The Duke of Brabant seems to have made a favourable impression on Viennese society. Dolly Ficquelmont did not find him up to the standard of his father; nevertheless, he was 'an attractive young man. His nose is rather long; apart from this he is very pleasant and charming and seems very intelligent.'[8] Unfortunately Marie-Henriette was not impressed by the Duke of Brabant; her opinion was reciprocated and the couple do not seem to have hidden their views from each other. The young Leopold wrote philosophically to his brother and sister that he was resigned to his father's choice of wife for him.[9]

Marie-Henriette was attractive-looking with blonde hair, a clear pale skin, brown eyes and a short, plump body. She had spent her childhood in Hungary and her great love was riding – Magyar style – at which she excelled, shocking the Viennese court who considered it unladylike and totally unsuited to a royal princess. Her education had been slight, though she spoke English, French and Italian in addition to German. Apart from riding, she enjoyed music, her preference being for Hungarian gypsy tunes; her manner was brusque and her laugh verging on the raucous. To marry her to the Duke of Brabant, who had become increasingly serious and withdrawn since the death of his mother was, from the point of view of compatibility, catastrophic. Madame de Metternich summed up the match as being between 'a stable boy and a nun, and by nun, I mean the Duke of Brabant'.[10]

She was not the only one to feel that neither party was yet ready for marriage. When Queen Victoria heard the news, for the king had not told her of his intentions, she wrote immediately to her uncle advising him to postpone the marriage for at least a year until both bride and groom were somewhat more mature.[11] Her sound advice was not taken and Leopold wrote to explain his reasons: 'There can always be found, particularly on the Continent, men who will encourage a young man in many things for the sake of getting *hold* of him . . . With a Prince Royal the mischief of falling into bad hands becomes for all parties intense. Leo's character and turn of mind admits of what would not be advisable.' And, varying somewhat the innuendo:

> There is another consideration, our dear Albert may explain it, if young men are kept from one sort of mischief they often fall into a habit *destructive* of *health* and *mind* and *spirit*, in short everything from which habit it is difficult to break them; and the *only* means is often marriage.
>
> The next reason is our dear Archduchess herself . . . her mother, a good working woman, is a little eccentric, [and] without meaning anything disrespectful, a girl of seventeen or one of eighteen *peut-être mal gardée*, makes an *enormous* difference.[12]

Somehow his diplomatic reasons (although the young Leopold was, rather surprisingly, accused of seducing a young girl in 1853) for expedit-ing the marriage are more convincing.[13] 'The Imperial Family [ie Austrian] would not have liked the doubtful position.' 'All sorts of intrigues and grumblings are on foot, my neighbour to the south and one to the north are equally irritated. Pss. John of Saxony is particularly disappointed as she wished Leo to marry one of her daughters.'[14]

The King of the Belgians had certainly pulled off a diplomatic *coup* and, as he anticipated, no-one appreciated this more than Napoleon III who, from Paris, watched in anger the Belgian royal family flaunting its success. Napoleon had himself for some time been looking for a suitable royal wife and, being unsuccessful, had married the beautiful Spanish aristocrat, Eugenie de Montijo. That little Belgium with its Orléanist monarchy and detestable press should do better than he, was a bitter pill for the emperor.

It was a bitter pill too for the bridegroom. By forcing his son into a union with a girl to whom he was not attracted and with whom he possessed nothing in common, Leopold I curtailed any chance the young man had of finding affection and companionship in marriage. One cannot defend the king for he had himself experienced a romantic idyll during his marriage to Princess Charlotte, and even his marriage to Louise had brought him domestic harmony. The future Leopold II's unloving marriage coming only three years after his mother's death made him withdraw yet more emotionally. His personal life meant nothing to him, and, as is not unusual in such a situation, he relegated his private life to the background and threw himself into his work.

As both the Duke of Brabant and Marie-Henriette were descended from the Empress Maria-Theresa, a dispensation from the pope was needed before they could be married. This obtained, they were, in accordance with Austrian protocol, first married by proxy at the Schönbrunn Palace in the presence of the Emperor Franz-Josef, and Marie-Henriette formally renounced her rights to the Austrian throne. Four days later, on 14 August 1853, she left for Belgium.

The rigorous Austrian court etiquette demanded that she should be 'handed over' to Belgium on neutral territory and, since the German states were not considered sufficiently neutral, it was decided, with tortuous logic, to declare a part of Belgium, near Verviers on the German frontier, neutral ground for the occasion. A temporary railway station was erected in the enclave and it was planned that the train bringing Marie-Henriette from Aix-la-Chapelle would arrive at the same time as that bringing King Leopold and his three children from Brussels. The Belgian train was late, much to the king's anger; the whole scene is a burlesque and masks the pitiful plight of the young woman, who, not yet seventeen, had been obliged to leave her family, friends and country for good to marry a man she did not even like.

The Belgian wedding ceremonies had to be delayed until 22 August

as the Duke of Brabant was convalescing from scarlet fever and Marie-
Henriette was tired and unwell – probably due to emotional stress. In
accordance with Belgian law, the couple first had to go through a civil
marriage in front of the Mayor of Brussels to which the public had access.
This took place in the Palais Royal and was followed by a religious ceremony in the church of Sainte Gudule. The church was decorated with
brightly-coloured curtains trimmed with ermine; the bride was dressed
in a sumptuous white antique moiré dress embroidered with silver; the
people of Brussels cheered in the streets and in the evening there was
a concert in the Grand' Place, fireworks, and, if contemporary engravings
are to be believed, an impressive historical cavalcade representing scenes
from Belgian history, progressed through the streets.[15]

The Duke and Duchess of Brabant then went on a tour of Belgian cities
and towns followed, in October 1853, by a long visit to England to introduce Marie-Henriette to Queen Victoria. The shrewd queen immediately
saw that the young couple were not getting on and observed them closely.
The fault, the queen decided, lay largely with Leopold, and she devoted
an entire letter to her uncle to the subject of their relationship.

> I think you are not at all *aware what* a very *clever superior* person
> for her age she is. *On all* subjects I have found her *particularly* intelli-
> gent & *rightminded* ... full of *instruction* & with a *highly cultivated*
> mind. All this gives her a decided superiority over Leo & *unfortunately*
> there is no sympathy of tastes or pursuits between them. She likes
> *music*, painting & literature *extremely*, none of which Leo cares ... for
> ... On politics Leo can talk very long & very well as also on military
> matters ... She is essentially *liberal* & tolerant in her views & Leo
> unfortunately is not. Of his *religious intolerance* I think you have *no*
> idea ... All this brings me to the *conclusion* that tho it will go on well
> enough, their characters are not of a kind to find enjoyment in
> *another's* Society.[16]

The king agreed with most of her observations, though he felt compelled to rally a little to the defence of his son:

> I have to thank you for a long and most *kind* and *wise* letter from
> your dear hand. I will consider it most minutely, and I must say that
> I *agree* with *you* most *completely*. Leo is at present on many points
> inferior, on others clever enough, and will gain every month if properly
> directed. Then Marie may do an immense amount of good by showing
> Leo some demonstrative good will, and a little affection. Leo is strongly
> impressed *qu'elle dit toujours non et est fort grognon*. Leo has inherited
> from the Orleans that esprit *taquin* ... that ought to be checked. Marie
> is too young herself to be pleased with it, and it is not pleasant. Leo

must make some efforts to join in her pursuits . . . The three children, a good deal owing to Leo, have a trick of not admiring things, finding everything *ennuyeux*, which is very childish and, I trust, will wear off.[17]

The young couple themselves were firmly admonished by their older cousin for their lack of mutual affection. 'We have told them many truths which they have already acted upon. We are both touched by Leo's confidence in us & by his wish to see us often [he was already a better diplomat than husband] and his proposition to come over occasionally twice or so in the year . . . in order to keep up our *intimate relations*.'[18]

Clearly there was considerable doubt in Victoria's mind as to whether the marriage had been consummated and she assured her uncle that she had done her utmost to explain to Marie-Henriette her conjugal duties. 'You may rely upon my impressing upon dear good Marie *all* what is right with respect to Leo and I assure *you*, she is much more alive to these duties than you think . . . To ask her to obey a boy of 18, who tho' very sensible & clever, is *physically* 4 or 5 years her junior & decidedly her inferior in learning – wd be impossible. Marie (I cannot conceal it from you) does *not love* him as yet – and certainly there is nothing a woman likes less than a man who is *not manly* in his person or his accomplishments.'[19] Leo 'did not demonstrate the slightest feeling of *love* or admiration for Marie, or *any woman* – and', the queen added, was 'so very underdeveloped, delicate and boyish looking as to be *totally incapable* (I am bound to tell you this *frankly* – as I as a *woman* can judge) of inspiring love – still less respect.'[20]

Alas, as Victoria feared – 'If I were by her side constantly, and Albert at poor Leo's elbow constantly, it *might improve* but nothing short of that will do' – on their return to Brussels the Duke of Brabant once more become totally engrossed in politics while his young wife, lonely and unhappy, remained at the Palais Ducal.[21] 'I cannot help pitying her in that stiff cold family circle, she is so merry and pretty,' Princess Feodora wrote to her step-sister Victoria.[22] Mariè-Henriette tried turning to fourteen-year-old Charlotte for companionship, but while the Belgian princess was prepared to be friendly, knowing well the personality of her brother – his sarcasm, his long periods of silence, his lack of interest in people – she found Marie-Henriette 'very good-hearted but not at all high minded and with little taste for serious matters'.[23] Spurned, Marie-Henriette went riding alone most of the day and to concerts in the evening. Years later, in her last days of lucidity, Charlotte came to recognize the qualities of her sister-in-law who brought her back to Belgium and cared for her with patience, understanding and tenderness.

For many years the young Leopold's health had been giving cause for concern: the slightest cold frequently developed into a serious chest illness and sciatic pains in his leg often made him limp. In 1854 his doctors advised a prolonged stay in a warm climate – Egypt was decided upon. While there is no direct evidence as to how much the Duke of Brabant himself influenced this choice, his responsibility for it would seem to be considerable; he was little worried himself by his health but wanted to visit Egypt. He wrote to Conway, asking him to use his influence with his father: 'Give me your vigorous support. In Brussels I am thought to be a little mad, or at least flighty . . . I have only one objective, one desire, and that is to learn as much as possible about the world and its peoples. The time will come when this knowledge will be useful to me.'[24] And if possible, 'I may be able to extort from this prince [the khedive of Egypt] commercial advantages . . . I am the first [European] prince to be received by him and I think he will go out of his way to please me.'[25]

Apart from the Duke of Brabant's health, the other reason given for the proposed tour of the Duke and Duchess of Brabant was for the newly-married couple to take a delayed honeymoon. They left Brussels on 15 November 1854 and, travelling under the names of the Viscount and Viscountess d'Ardenne, they went first to Germany and Austria and then on to Venice.[26] Marie-Henriette enjoyed sightseeing and amusements; her husband did not and they were seen to have their first public quarrel in Venice when the duchess wanted a second ride on a gondola. Leopold was not enjoying his stay in Italy and wrote to his father: 'I told M. Conway before leaving that I am being sent to Italy and I am obediently complying; but do not imagine that it will transform my health and rid me of those characteristics you do not like. Something quite different would be necessary to do that.'[27]

After a few weeks in Venice, the couple went on to Trieste and from there took a steamship to Alexandria, where they landed on 2 February. The Belgian consul in Cairo, Edouard Blondeel, was there to meet them and accompanied them to Cairo, to be welcomed by the khedive. Marie-Henriette enjoyed the festivities laid on for them by the khedive but once these were over she was bored by the numerous excursions her husband made to the Nile dam and other projects. Leopold, armed always with a notebook and pen, asked incessant questions and wrote down everything that he learned. He was delighted when they took a boat up the Nile, through Karnak and Thebes to Aswan, and on returning to Cairo he was loath, after spending two months in Egypt, to continue his journey.

However, he had spent sufficiently long there to have acquired some important ideas which were to play a crucial role in his and his country's future development. Leopold had seen for himself the possibilities of commercial and colonial exploitation of Egypt and he was determined that

Belgium would be to the fore in taking advantage of the opportunities offered. Trade with Egypt promised much and the twenty-year-old national salesman had persuaded the khedive to promise, in front of witnesses, to participate in the formation of a steamship company which would operate between Alexandria and Antwerp. 'Leave it to me. The Viceroy [the khedive] will be my biggest shareholder. I hope to get out of this £100,000, maybe £200,000, that is 500,000 or a million francs. And if I play my cards carefully, I may even be able to exceed this figure.'[28]

The Duke of Brabant was aware of Blondeel's colonial aspirations (he had attempted to buy Crete for Belgium in 1838–9 and two years later had briefly looked at Abyssinia) and Prince Leopold had probably, even before he visited Egypt, considered the idea of Belgium's acquiring a colony in, or near to, Egypt. What is certain, however, is that during his sojourn there he became convinced of the rightness of trying for a territorial concession in the area. To this end he opened up negotiations with the khedive in the hope of acquiring the area of lakes in the Nile delta, the land to be reclaimed by a Belgian enterprise: 'I have offered to take charge of the project but cannot obtain any decisive answer from the khedive ... We must keep up the pressure until we have obtained what we want . . . Egypt is a gold mine and we must spare no effort in our attempt to develop it.'[29] It was clear that the duke was casting his eyes wide and was determined somewhere to find a colony for Belgium. 'One could purchase a small kingdom in Abyssinia for 30,000 francs. A second one would not cost the earth. If instead of talking so much about neutrality Parliament looked after our commerce, Belgium would become one of the richest countries in the world.'[30]

During his stay in Egypt, Leopold had met a Frenchman who was nurturing the ambitious idea of building a canal from the Nile to the isthmus of Suez. The man, Ferdinand de Lesseps, was at that time trying to raise the capital necessary for his project in France and England and no doubt saw nothing to be lost in discussing his scheme with the young Belgian prince. The Duke of Brabant was not impressed by de Lesseps: 'He's a scoundrel'[31] ('canaille', may be an intended pun on the canal builder). Although he considered de Lesseps' plan not worth supporting he hinted at the idea of the Belgians taking up the project. 'I believe that he [de Lesseps] will give up after a while and that we could take up where he leaves off.'[32] The audacity of the idea of Belgium considering, even leading, such a scheme cannot but strike one.

The voyage was by no means over when the Duke and Duchess of Brabant left Egypt. They spent Holy Week in Jerusalem as guests of the Sultan of Turkey, though the Moslem sultan was not prepared to allow Leopold to place wreaths on the tombs of the two Belgian crusaders against the Turks, Godfroid de Bouillon and Baudouin of Flanders. From

Palestine they went on to Syria to visit archaeological sites: sailing from Beirut they then headed, via Cyprus, for Tripoli and on to Athens where they were received by the King and Queen of Greece. En route for home they stopped in Sicily where they visited the palace in Palermo where Leopold's mother had been born. They then moved into Italy where they met King Ferdinand of Naples, Victor Emmanuel of Piedmont and, *noblesse oblige*, the pope.

After nine months' absence they found themselves at the end of August 1855 back in Belgium and once more involved in the world of European politics, for this was the time of the Crimean War. Franco-Belgian relations were still strained, Napoleon III himself having exacerbated things by confiscating the Orléanist inheritance worth three million French francs – known as *le premier vol de l'aigle* (a pun on '*vol*', theft or flight, in French) – which should have gone to Louis-Philippe's Belgian grandchildren. Despite this new source of irritation to Leopold I, the French foreign minister let it be known that the emperor would be favourably disposed to a gesture of goodwill from Belgium and, in view of the confiscation, it marked a diplomatic surrender by Leopold I (he was being pushed by Britain), to agree to a visit to Paris by the Duke and Duchess of Brabant.

The emperor and empress were, on the surface, welcoming to the Belgian royal couple in October 1855. At dinner at St Cloud, 'The Emperor, seated next to the Duchess, was at great pains to be pleasant with "the daughter of Caesars".'[33] One social event followed another, Marie-Henriette enjoying them far more than her husband, who much preferred to talk politics. Leopold, it is clear, was not a great social success. 'The young royal couple is very pleasing,' wrote the Austrian ambassador, immediately modifying his statement to, 'or rather it is the Archduchess who is pleasing.' She 'is charming; she does not say much but her beautiful eyes speak for her and in any case what she says is perfect. She has none of that forced banality, or cynicism that results from it, which is the curse of Courts.'[34]

While Marie-Henriette taught the French court a card game in which the losers had to blacken their faces with soot (this apparently provoked hilarious laughter), her husband attempted to use the visit as a means of persuading Napoleon III to rescind the Orléans confiscation. With great temerity and without warning anyone, the young man brought the subject up with the emperor. 'Napoleon was content to stroke his moustache and smile, saying that the subject was too serious a one to be discussed in social conversation.'[35] However, in spite of the duke's undiplomatic behaviour the visit was a success and Napoleon III seemed to have forgiven the Belgo-Austrian marriage.[36]

The business of visiting foreign reigning-houses and playing host to them in turn was an important part of the Duke of Brabant's life and in May 1856 he was in charge of the visit to Belgium of the Archduke Ferdinand Maximilian, younger brother of the Austrian emperor. Maximilian was on a tour of European capitals and, after spending some time with Napoleon and Eugenie in Paris, he came to Belgium. The archduke was known to be looking for a suitable wife and it had not escaped Leopold I that he could be a possible husband for his daughter, although Queen Victoria favoured Don Pedro, son of the Regent of Portugal, for Charlotte. Leopold I himself was equivocal; Charlotte for her part was, like her father's first wife and namesake, anxious to marry, seeing it as a means of escape from the oppressive atmosphere of Laeken. She was, therefore, very prepared to fall in love with any visiting prince, particularly a charming, romantic archduke.

Maximilian was immediately impressed by the looks, intelligence and education of Charlotte. She was beautiful in a striking way with a high forehead, her mother's long Bourbon nose, a small, well-formed mouth, a pale, clear complexion, thick dark hair and a slim figure; her only imperfection was a rather heavy chin. In addition she possessed the Coburg's determination and ambition. Her favourite author was Plutarch and she avidly devoured Auguste Nicolas's *Philosophic Studies in Christianity* which was much read at that time; in music she preferred Bach to the fashionable Strauss.

Charlotte was delighted to see her elder brother making an effort to be pleasant with Maximilian and the archduke noticed the difference in the Duke of Brabant. 'He has lost that bitterness and phlegm which were such noticeable characteristics. Likewise his health seems to have improved . . . He has fits of gaiety and laughter and is much more cordial. He looks much better and has put on weight; he boasts of fulfilling very frequently his marital rights.'[37] But behind the sociable façade the duke was viewing the archduke with a stern eye. He was sure that Maximilian was interested in Charlotte mainly because of her potential inheritance from her father, for he was, by royal standards, poor and the Belgian royal family rich.

Leopold I began life with little money. After his first wife's death his allowance from the British government had given him £50,000 a year but even if he had saved a large part of his annual income in the 1820s, this still did not constitute a fortune. However, it was well known by the 1850s that he was a very wealthy man. Where did this money come from? It would seem that on becoming King of the Belgians, Leopold was handed over part, if not all, of the shares previously held by the King of Holland in the *Société Générale*. This bank/holding-company had been founded in 1822 largely at William I's instigation (he had owned half the share capital) to provide the funds necessary for the industrial development of Belgium and it rapidly came to play a dominant role in the country's economy. Through his income from *Société Générale* shares and judicious property purchases, Leopold I's wealth had increased enormously in the 1830s and 1840s.

The younger Leopold did not like the idea of part of this carefully built-up family fortune going to the foreign princes to whom Charlotte, and future Belgian princesses, would have to be married. The Belgian civil code treated the royal family as any other, and an inheritance had to be divided among all children according to certain rules. The Duke of Brabant proposed that an exception should be made for the royal family which would permit the king's inheritance to pass only to his sons.[38] Maximilian was not aware of the duke's idea which Leopold had set out in a memorandum, but the archduke complained to Queen Victoria that Leopold 'had constantly come between him and Charlotte. He said that Leopold held such absolutist principles . . . and that he dreaded what might be if Uncle were no longer alive.'[39]

The duke's efforts to prevent Charlotte's inheriting from her father came to nothing. Negotiations between the Austrian and Belgian courts as to a financial settlement had a satisfactory outcome and the marriage took place in the Palais Royal in Brussels in July 1857. An ecstatic Charlotte left for Maximilian's château at Miramar in northern Italy.

The Duke of Brabant had not laid aside his interest in commercial expansion and colonialism on his return to Belgium and his involvement in European affairs. It saddened and irritated him to see Belgian politicians totally immersed in party political quarrels over education and taxes, with their widest mental horizons extending to Western Europe. If his ideas were to be adopted he would have to educate opinion in Belgium into accepting them, and van Praet advised him to take advantage of his position as a member of the Senate to publicize his views.

Prince Leopold had become a Senator as of right on reaching his majority in April 1853, but he had then made only a formal speech on being sworn-in. His first real speech was made on 29 December 1855 (earlier in the year he intervened briefly in a debate) when he addressed the Belgian Upper House on the subject of a regular steamship service between Belgium and the Near East. 'Our manufacturers only reach these markets second or third hand. Far from competing with other nations, we have to rely on them. Our goods, more often than not, lose all national identity before reaching their destination.'[40]

The speeches he made the following year are interesting because for the first time the Duke of Brabant turned his attention to domestic affairs. Maybe he was genuinely developing an interest in internal matters, though one cannot exclude the possibility of his having calculated that his favourite ideas would find a more receptive audience if he gave some attention to subjects Belgian politicians held dear to them. Yet in all his speeches, however domestic the topic, Leopold always managed to turn the subject to include reflections on his main preoccupation of widening Belgian horizons.

The importance of developing a sense of national pride, a separate identity, and increasing the national patrimony was the theme of his second speech, the subject of which was the arts in Belgium. The development of Brussels in general evoked his interest, and in his early reflections on urbanism one cannot help but be impressed by the stress he laid on the importance of parks and open spaces in a city. 'A large city needs plenty of air and space. It is desirable that its population should be provided with the opportunity to enjoy the advantages of the country without having to travel too far.'[41]

In his speeches on the need to make better use of the Belgian railway system and to develop the port facilities at Antwerp and Ostend, the Duke of Brabant was closer to his major interest, namely the need for commercial expansion, and from 1858 to 1861 he concentrated his energies on this subject, adding his yet more contentious ideas on colonization. 'Trading posts and colonies, gentlemen, have not only benefited the commercial interests of the people involved; it is to such establishments abroad that countries owe their greatness.'[42]

'Leopold is subtle and sly,' the king told one of his ministers, 'he never takes a chance. The other day, when I was at Ardenne, I watched a fox which wanted to cross a stream unobserved: first of all he dipped a paw carefully to see how deep it was, and then with a thousand precautions, very slowly made his way across. That is Leopold's way!'[43] Leopold I saw little of his son but the picture he painted of him was an accurate one. The fox was certainly dipping his foot in water. And deep water at that.

3 The Colonialists

'I am gathering proof and documentary
evidence which ought to convince my fellow
countrymen of the desirability of overseas
expansion.'[1]   The Duke of Brabant, 1861.

To understand the development of the future Leopold II's colonial policy
in the 1850s and 1860s it is necessary to look at his father's views on
the subject, as he inherited from Leopold I a colonial policy dating back
to the early years of Belgium's existence and a considerable body of
practical experience gained from attempts to implement this policy.

Leopold I's reason for wanting a colony (or colonies) was fundament-
ally economic, although political considerations clearly went with it. The
1830s were a difficult time for Belgium economically, partly owing to the
effects of the industrial revolution but caused to a large extent by her
having lost the world markets that union with Holland had provided,
and the use of the Dutch merchant fleet. Holland itself was a good
example of a small country which was economically prosperous through
having colonies.

The commercial bourgeoisie of Belgium, in which there was a strong
Orangist element, bitterly resented the new regime which had adversely
affected their trade and it was the danger they presented which caused
Leopold I to think about acquiring a colony in the early 1830s. Even without the Orangist problem, however, if Belgium was to succeed she would
need to find new markets for her products and fresh sources of raw
materials. Belgium was already the 'workshop of the Continent' with her
coal mines in Wallonia, integrated Cockerill steel works at Seraing, near
Liège, and rivers to provide power and transport.

While the industrial revolution had brought material prosperity to
some sections of the Belgian population it had caused, as elsewhere, great
distress in others. In 1845 one in three of the population in Flanders were
living off charity, with the concomitant danger of social unrest. To Leopold I one solution to the problem of unemployment was for those
affected to emigrate on a large scale and Belgium was, in any case, the

most densely-populated country in Europe. Some Belgians were emigrating to the United States – mainly Wisconsin and Illinois where one finds many Belgian place names – but a colony with economic and political ties to the mother country and no linguistic problems would be a preferable overflow.[2]

The political aspect of Leopold I's search for a colony was very much a desire to change the inward-looking Belgian mentality and the feeling of being a small, impotent country that could be buffeted around by the Great Powers. His ministers, politicians, civil servants and businessmen for the most part did not share his feelings. Successive cabinets refused to risk money on colonial schemes of doubtful profitability and they also feared that Belgian neutrality would be jeopardized by attempts at aggrandizement which might well conflict with the interests of the Great Powers.

As the government would not co-operate with him, the king's aim ultimately came to be to present his countrymen with the *fait accompli* of a Belgian colony. But because of his lack of support Leopold I, who was a prudent man, was forced to limit himself to trying to obtain small concessions. His first attempt (aided by Blondeel) was to try to buy Crete from the Sultan of Turkey: on failing he turned his eyes to Cuba; Lord Palmerston came to hear of it and warned him off.[3] Three years later, during the Texan republic, the Texan secretary of state offered to cede two large tracts of land to Belgium for a $7,000,000 loan. Leopold was prepared to go ahead with the deal but it was interpreted by the United States government as a violation of the Monroe Doctrine, according to which the United States held that European countries did not have the right to interfere in American affairs. The Belgian minister to Washington told the king that the United States would soon annex Texas and that for this reason alone it was not worth pursuing the idea.[4]

Closer to home, Leopold heard in 1858 that Denmark might be prepared to sell the Faroe Islands.[5] Confidential enquiries were made and the rumour proved unfounded. Various Caribbean islands and parts of Central America were looked at with keen interest by Leopold and for a time it looked as though he would succeed in establishing a colony in Saint Thomas de Guatemala, where the ubiquitous Blondeel had acquired a land concession. About a thousand Belgian colonists were sent out to Guatemala in 1845 but the climate was hot, humid and unhealthy; there was no money and no work was available. The financial resources were rapidly exhausted and some very disillusioned Belgian colonists (many had died) returned home.[6]

As there are files on fifty-one attempts to found a colony under Leopold I, one could continue the list for some time. Suffice it to say that South America was looked at and even parts of Africa were considered.[7]

The Duke of Brabant was, of course, too young to be involved in the various colonial schemes of his father in the 1840s, and few colonial ventures presented themselves for most of the 1850s. But at the end of the decade an opportunity far greater, and far more exciting than anything so far envisaged, arose to which both father and son directed their energies.

In May 1859 the British and French governments were mounting an expedition against China. For various, and not very convincing, reasons they felt that their honour had been impugned by the Chinese and they were planning reprisals. Their main objective however was to obtain commercial advantages and the opening of Chinese ports, although it had not escaped them that it might be possible to gain some territorial concessions. The Duke of Brabant thought similarly. 'If we can manage to send 4,500 Belgians to Peking, we would have to be very maladroit not to benefit from such a tactical position and from the support of our allies.'[8]

The king, like his son, on hearing of the expedition, immediately felt that here was an opportunity for Belgium to gain a foothold in the Chinese empire. He had tried unsuccessfully to send Belgian troops to the Crimea in 1855 with the French and British forces, and the Duke of Brabant had offered Queen Victoria the assistance of Belgian troops to put down the Indian Mutiny in 1857.[9] The King of the Belgians had been in no way discouraged by these rebuffs and in May 1859 he brought up the subject of Belgian participation in the Chinese expedition with the French minister to Belgium.[10] As there was no negative response from Paris, Leopold I decided to visit Napoleon III at Biarritz. The French emperor welcomed Belgian help in the form of 1,200 to 1,800 men and Franco-Belgian relations improved considerably as a result of the king's week with the emperor.

In Brussels the British minister politely asked the minister of foreign affairs, Baron de Vrière, 'if he could provide details of the project and, in particular, inform him what was the *casus belli* as regards Belgium'.[11] De Vrière replied that Sino-Belgian relations were good and that the scheme was a personal one of the Duke of Brabant's.[12] As well as British opposition practical problems arose on the French side – the French could not undertake to transport the Belgian troops to China. Then on top of this, when the Belgian cabinet came to learn of the idea it held that participation in the expedition would constitute an infringement of Belgian neutrality and that the Chamber would never vote the money necessary for such a force.

To most the affair seemed closed. Not to the Duke of Brabant. He wrote to General Chazal, minister of war: 'I am continuing my work, but I feel that a diplomatic manœuvre must first be mounted. Once we have done this, we would have every chance of achieving our ends. For the moment the words "Belgian expedition to China" must on no account be mentioned.'[13]

As well as his friendship with Chazal, in the late 1850s the Duke of Brabant came to establish a close working relationship with two men whom he had met in his efforts to acquire information to substantiate his views on the need for Belgian colonial and commercial expansion. Auguste Lambermont was a civil servant at the Ministry of Foreign Affairs: of humble background, his intellectual brilliance and pheno-menal hard work had enabled him to become a key figure in the ministry. A third close collaborator was Captain, later General, Henri-Alexis Brialmont, a talented young military engineer – he had just finished designing the fortifications of Antwerp – with an interest in colonialism. Apart from the similarity of their views, Brialmont's value to the Duke of Brabant was that he was prepared to undertake fact-finding missions abroad.

The first visible result of the work of Leopold, Lambermont and Brial-mont was the publication of an anonymous work advocating Belgian trade and colonization called 'The Sequel to the Achievements of 1830, establishments to be created overseas. The future of Belgian commerce and industry.' It appeared in the *Revue de l'Armée* at the end of 1859 and a few days later as a pamphlet, though a publication of 219 pages is hardly less than a book. The authorship was widely, and correctly, attri-buted to Brialmont and the part played by the Duke of Brabant in the conception and drafting of the document was also recognized. He personally distributed many copies.[14]

Chazal had been sent a copy of the manuscript some months before. The wise Frenchman, who had become one of Belgium's most devoted and able patriots, was shocked by what was being advocated. 'I believe that Your Highness would be wrong to give the slightest publicity to this work ... You have been carried away with strong language and have given too free rein to a youthful imagination ... Believe me, Highness, we are entering a new era when a Prince cannot be too circumspect or too prudent.'[15] Chazal's advice was discarded and, as he had feared, 'The Sequel to the Achievements of 1830' caused a political uproar when it was published. The first the minister of foreign affairs knew about it was when he read about it in the press and he was furious, as were some other ministers. Charles Rogier, the revolutionary leader of 1830 who was now a respected elder statesman and leading minister in the government, dismissed it as no more than a young man's folly.

In 1861 the Duke of Brabant began a correspondence with Baron Du Jardin, Belgian minister to The Hague. Leopold believed that Holland provided proof of the economic benefits to be gained from colonies and his aide-de-camp, Major Goffinet, wrote to Du Jardin:

> His Royal Highness the Duke of Brabant has instructed me to ask you to let him know how the special fund created in Holland for the construction of a national railway line was financed. HRH believes that the trade surplus with the colonies was responsible for a large part of the fund. Could you elucidate this point for him, preferably using official sources?[16]

The minister replied, providing the financial data asked for but, more importantly, he added a piece of information which could not fail to excite the Duke of Brabant. Holland owned part of the island of Borneo, and, according to Du Jardin, 'This possession is not financially viable. They might be prepared to cede if offered sufficient money.'[17] As the idea developed and maps were studied, Leopold's attention shifted from the Dutch part of Borneo to Sarawak, the north-westerly part of the island, rich in tropical woods and with gold and copper mines, which had been ceded by the indigenous sultan to an Englishman, Sir James Brooke, in 1842. After taking soundings in The Hague though, Du Jardin was pessimistic as to the possibility of the Dutch selling their part of Borneo and the Duke of Brabant decided that there would be more chance of buying Sarawak. Brooke's nephew in England who had inherited the sultanate was approached and, somewhat dilatorily, he came to Brussels to discuss the matter. He informed the Belgians that he had offered the sultanate to the British government; the affair was at an end. However, the attempt to acquire a colony in Borneo was not the only one in 1861. The king and duke were both actively involved in trying to found a colony in Oceania. A British adventurer, Joseph Byrne (an undischarged bankrupt who had emigrated from England), who had lived in Australia, and an Australian, called Brown, had obtained from France part of the island of New Caledonia on condition that they brought in immigrants and developed the island. They had heard that the King of the Belgians was interested in acquiring a colony and came to Brussels. There they met a Belgian who was attracted by their scheme and who drew up and sent a document to the minister of foreign affairs entitled, 'Note on the establishment of a Belgian colony in the Pacific Ocean.'[18] The minister replied that he could see no good reason to set up a station so far from Belgium and on a sea route not frequented by her ships, but the duke reacted rather differently. 'It would be interesting to find out which islands are involved ... It would be a superb place for a penitentiary.'[19]

The king was also impressed by Byrne and Brown and such royal support encouraged the Anglo-Australian pair to be more ambitious in their ideas, and they proposed to Leopold I that he should send out royal emis-

saries to Australia with the intention of seeking out free territories in
Oceania for Belgium. In particular, they suggested Belgium's taking over
the New Hebrides. Byrne duly left for the New Hebrides and two Belgian
emissaries for Australia. However, when it became evident that Byrne
could not raise the money necessary to develop the New Hebrides (the
emissaries had been specially charged not to enter into any financial commitment on the part of the king) the scheme came to nothing.[20]

Byrne was a man with an ability to bounce back after defeat equal
to that of the Duke of Brabant. Immediately after the failure in the New
Hebrides they were both immersed in a plan to colonize the Fiji Islands.
From enquiries in London it was learned that the British government
would not look amiss at Belgian efforts to colonize these islands and there
was even talk of taking over the Solomons as well. The Belgian emissaries
visited the Fiji Islands and reported back to Brussels that the natives were
very warlike and that unless a great deal of money was spent on an expedition to subdue them, there was no chance of establishing a colony. As
if this activity was not enough, the duke was working on a scheme for
a Belgian company to construct a railway network in Brazil; and writing
to Lambermont about yet another idea: 'I am specially interested in the
Argentine province of Entre Rios and the little island of Martin Garcia
at the confluence of the Uruguay and the Parana. Who owns this island?
Could one buy it, and set up there a free port under the moral protection
of the King of the Belgians?'[21]

The Duke of Brabant's work in amassing information on colonization
in no way ceased when he was taking an active part in specific colonial
schemes. He maintained a never-ending barrage of demands for facts and
figures, nearly always directed at Brialmont. At one point the captain
remarked, 'The Duke of Brabant takes me for a statistical office'; but
he continued to work for Leopold.[22] The prince expected Brialmont to
be constantly at his disposal for travelling as well as working in Brussels.
'When can you go to Paris? I am sure that in Paris you will find plenty
to support our views.'[23] When Brialmont was in London collecting data
he was also expected to do some shopping for the duke. 'Try and find
out whether there are any good geographical and historical atlases on
the colonies'.[24] In general though Leopold was prepared to do his own
book ordering. 'I would be very grateful if you could let me have the
name of your bookshop in London. My intention is to build up a library
containing all the information available on China, Japan and colonies
in general.'[25] Brialmont was also expected to place articles in the press:

I have noticed an article on 'China and Belgium' in the latest number
of the *Revue Britannique*. It was an article which originally appeared
in the *British Quarterly Review*. Do you know the editor of the latter?

A foreign article on such a subject reprinted in the Belgian press has so much more import than something written here.[26]

The duke and Brialmont were planning a book, to be called *Belgians Abroad*, and an outline was drawn up by the end of 1861. A great deal of material would be needed for what they intended to be a much more substantial work than the 'Sequel to the Achievements of 1830' and to this end the duke was anxious to visit various colonial powers and colonies to collect material.

But were there other reasons for the heir to the throne's voyages between 1860 and 1865? The obvious question is whether the king was deliberately keeping Prince Leopold out of Belgium to prevent his son usurping his authority. The answer is a clear no. There is abundant evidence that the king was opposed to his son's peregrinations. That relations between father and son deteriorated in the 1860s from coolness to estrangement is evident but the cause would seem to be the king's failing health, his general debility which caused him to lose his old vitality and enthusiasm. Colonial schemes interested him less and less. His son on the other hand had boundless energy, mental and physical, and was becoming more and more evangelical about Belgium's need to expand overseas. The king wished to see his heir studying European diplomacy which he would be forced to confront when he became king; to him colonial schemes were, by comparison, of minor importance.

The Duke of Brabant's frail health was constantly mentioned as a reason for his need to travel. One has difficulty in taking it seriously, as did observers at the time. 'What an obsession to travel,' remarked the Belgian minister to Rome. 'I am beginning to think that the dear Prince makes out that his health is worse than it really is, to provide a pretext for getting away.'[27] And according to an Austrian diplomat in Brussels, 'The Duke's travels do not go down well with the Belgians; they go as far as to say that he only limps in Brussels.'[28]

In general the king reluctantly gave in to his son's demands to travel. In 1858, however, though he allowed him to go to Berlin, he was adamant that after that the duke should return home as his wife was pregnant with their second child.[29]

> He wanted to go to Sweden and Norway but it [he] could never have managed to be back in proper time. Besides it makes such an odd impression that so near her confinement he leaves Marie and little Louise *en l'air*. People who are always on the look out for dreadful events say that there has been a blow up between Leo and Marie, and that he left her in disgust.[30]

The king could not think up any overriding objections in 1860 and the young Leopold was able to set off. As before he diplomatically visited Vienna first and then made his way via Bucharest to Constantinople. The sultan laid on for the Duke of Brabant lavish receptions and dinners, illuminations, fireworks and sightseeing expeditions. It does not appear that Leopold was given much time for serious talks and researches. In fact his father gave an extraordinary reason for his son's presence in Turkey. 'The diplomats are much puzzled by it and would be astonished to learn that the real reason for his journey was because he lost his hair. How far the Orient will remedy the evil is difficult to guess.'[31]

The Duke of Brabant returned to Belgium via Athens and it was while there that he bought a piece of marble from the Acropolis. A photograph of himself was inset, under which was carved, 'Belgium must have a colony. Souvenir of Athens presented by the Duke of Brabant to M. Frère-Orban, Minister of Finance.'[32] Walthère Frère-Orban, a young politician the duke knew well, did not share his imperial sentiments.

Two years later the prince left for Spain where he hoped to find evidence in the archives of the profitability of Spanish colonies. He had to return home after his ship was damaged in a storm in the Bay of Biscay but on his second attempt reached Seville, where he spent a month researching. After paying a visit to the Queen of Spain, he was about to embark for North Africa when news arrived saying that his father was seriously ill. The duke was obliged to return to Belgium though by that time the king had recovered from his abdominal operation and the heir to the throne was able to leave Belgium again at the end of October 1862.

The duke had earlier in the year intended to make his way to Egypt but this time he avoided sailing in the Bay of Biscay. Instead, he went overland to Marseilles from where he took ship to Algeria; here he spent some time studying French exploitation of their colony. On leaving Algeria, he once again found himself in a storm at sea and was five days late in arriving in Egypt. Naturally, the duke went to see the Suez Canal works and this time he visited Sinai. After leaving Egypt he returned home via Spain and Portugal, ending his journey with a three-day visit to Napoleon III in Paris. In May 1863 his father wrote to Victoria: 'We expect now Leo who has been flying about in an absurd manner.'[33] This time falling hair does not seem to have been a problem; on the contrary, the king complained: 'He has a great beard which is however to give way to discipline.'[34] (Beards were forbidden in the Belgian army and the duke was an officer.)

Apparently unperturbed by his father's mounting objections to yet another voyage, and his declining health, the duke was planning to visit the Far East. 'We have no great luck with our eldest son,' complained Leopold I to his niece. 'Leo is now more selfish and fantastical than ever ... he makes use of it i.e. his *delicate* health, to be constantly moving about, what the French call *de vagabonder*.' 'He *shams illness* because he wishes to set off for Ceylon and India in October.'[35] The king opposed the voyage for all manner of reasons, the danger of cholera, the possibility of shipwreck, the strain on his son's weak lungs of hot humid weather. None of this deterred his son who left Belgium as planned in late 1864. Once more he halted in Egypt, but only for a few days; his only stop after Egypt was Aden and by the end of December he was in Ceylon.

After fulfilling his official engagement of opening the Colombo to Kandy railway, the duke sailed to Madras and then to Calcutta. The British Raj took charge of his stay and explained tea-planting to him, but he was also received by local potentates. From India Leopold sailed to Rangoon and then on to Singapore where he studied British trading methods. He spent some time in Sumatra and from there he left for Hong Kong and Canton. By now he had accumulated cabin trunks full of notes on all that he had seen: he would have liked to have remained longer in China but pressures were brought to bear on him to return home as quickly as possible. He arrived in Brussels at the end of May 1865, leaving almost immediately for England to thank his cousin Victoria (who found him much improved) for the treatment he had received in her colonies. This duty accomplished, he was forced to confront the situation in Belgium. It was obvious that in the none too distant future he would be king.

Leopold I had been in poor health for the past five years, though he did his utmost to dissimulate his frequent pain. He had an intense dislike of doctors and very unwillingly allowed them to operate on him. The king was convinced that they were only interested in charging him large sums of money for unnecessary surgery and he preferred to be left alone in his sickness and be cared for by Arcadie Claret de Viescourt, who was now his nurse rather than mistress.

By the autumn of 1865 Leopold I's health was failing fast. Victoria sent Doctor Jenner over and insisted on receiving a daily bulletin from him. The Belgian public was also informed daily of the king's state and writing to his mother-in-law Leopold showed some of his old spirit. 'I hope to be better soon, although the papers kill me off every morning.'[36] He forbade his family to visit him and did not always admit his doctors to his bedside. 'If Uncle took the necessary nourishment prescribed', Victoria felt, 'he might pull through.' He was to take 'brandy every hour and broth every two hours ... All this reminds me too painfully of beloved Albert's terrible illness!'[37] The king's only solace was to have a pianist playing in an adjoining room and to listen to readings of novels.

On 9 December Leopold I's strength declined hourly. He lived through the night but his doctors announced that death was imminent. The ministers were brought from Brussels to witness the death and the royal family was summoned. According to Baron Beyens, who was given the account by van Praet, an eye-witness, on seeing Marie-Henriette, the king held out his hand to her and called out, 'Do not leave me!' 'Sire,' she said in German, 'do you regret the sins you have committed? Do you regret the scandals you have caused?' The king sighed and replied, '*Ja.*' 'Sire,' she continued, 'in the name of the love you bear the memory of the Queen, would you not wish to draw closer to her and be converted to the religion that was hers?' The king seemed to reflect, to hesitate. Finally the reply was heard: '*Nein.*'[38] The Protestant chaplain was brought in and spoke to the dying man. 'Yes, may God pardon all my sins,' Leopold said in a still intelligible voice. The king kissed his sons and his grandchildren; with his hand still holding that of his daughter-in-law he several times ambiguously whispered 'Charlotte'. He then lost consciousness and died peacefully at a quarter to twelve on 10 December 1865.

His body was embalmed and, dressed in his full uniform of a Belgian general and enveloped in the mantle of a Knight of the Garter, laid in state at the Palais Royal in Brussels. Crowds passed by the catafalque night and day and the whole country went into deep mourning. On 16 December he was given a state funeral and buried in the vault at Laeken, alongside Louise.

It was now, the new king pointed out to Queen Victoria, up to them to maintain the Coburg reputation.[39]

4 La Politique de Pourboires

*'Belgium is a ripe pear which one day will fall
into our mouth.'*[1]   Napoleon III.

Leopold II became King of the Belgians on 17 December 1865, six days
after the death of his father. Mounted on a charger, dressed in the uniform
of a general and surrounded by foreign rulers and princes, the new king
left Laeken and was welcomed at the gates of Brussels by the mayor,
Jules Anspach, and the municipal council. There Leopold made a short
speech and to cries of *'Vive le Roi!'* went on to parliament. After being
sworn in (there is no coronation ceremony in Belgium) he addressed
parliament:

> Gentlemen,
>   Belgium like myself has lost a father! The unanimous homage that
> the nation renders to his memory worthily responds to the sentiments
> it cherished for him in life.
>   If I do not promise Belgium either a great reign like that which wit-
> nessed the foundation of her independence, or a great King like the
> one we are mourning, I promise her at least a Belgian king in heart
> and soul whose whole life belongs to her ...[2]

The new king's speech was much appreciated. The Crown Prince of
Prussia described the scene to his wife, Queen Victoria's eldest daughter,
who in turn told her mother. 'Fritz was delighted with Leopold's speech
and said that the ceremony of taking the oath was very fine and striking,
and that Leopold had been enthusiastically received.'[3] Not everyone
though was happy with the way the ceremony had been conducted. The
minister of the interior, Alphonse Vandenpeereboom, in his diary, reveals
a difference of opinion between the new king and his ministers as to the
role to be played by the queen and the royal children in the inaugural
ceremonies. 'It seems that the Duke wishes to keep a good distance
between the Queen and himself. He does not want her to enter [Brussels]

with him nor to sit on the throne at his side for the oath of allegiance. The ministers were much much in favour of the latter. The King, the Queen and the children together on the throne would add a great deal to the ceremony.'[4]

However, this was a minor point. The accession of the Duke of Brabant – who had never been very popular with the Belgian people – was marked with much acclaim. As he rode through the streets of Brussels after leaving parliament, handkerchiefs were waved, flowers were thrown before him. This was not lost on foreign observers. Lord Clarendon, the British foreign secretary, told Sylvain van de Weyer, the Belgian minister in London, 'I consider the impressive events of these last two days as not only the consecration of 1830 but the strongest guarantee for the maintenance of peace. From this point of view it is an important European event.'[5]

According to the constitution the king could have formed a new cabinet but Leopold II decided to maintain the existing, rather worn-out Liberal government under the aging Charles Rogier. (It should perhaps be pointed out that there was no prime minister in Belgium at this time. One minister in the cabinet was always *primus inter pares* and one speaks for example of Rogier's, Frère-Orban's, d'Anethan's cabinets, though there is no constitutional basis for so doing.)

Rogier was in no way flattered when Leopold asked him and the other ministers to continue with their existing portfolios. He remarked that the king would have liked to have formed a new government only he knew that he could not. Leopold II called his first cabinet meeting on 20 December 1865 – the king could, if he wished, preside at cabinet meetings. He flattered his ministers, affecting modesty himself. 'I have until now kept out of politics and as a result I am very ill-informed. I intend to be a constitutional monarch as I am convinced that Belgium owes its prosperity and international security to the constitutional regime which it practises so well.'[6] At the first few cabinet meetings the king appeared nervous and unsure of himself in front of his ministers. He never argued with them, 'but listens attentively and seems very anxious to do his best'.[7] Within a couple of months Vandenpeereboom was changing his opinion:

Little by little the King is revealing his true personality. He has excellent intentions, is talented and possesses tact and judgement. He has seen a lot and knows a great deal but he is artful and devious, if not two-faced at times. He conceals his thoughts and argues obliquely in order to expose the inner thoughts of anyone opposing his views.[8]

At the same time as making a great effort to be friendly and affable with his ministers, for Leopold was by now learning the value of charm, he was anxious to be on good terms with foreign rulers, in particular with Queen Victoria, and in July 1866 paid her a visit. Leopold had been in England in March 1866 (for the funeral of his grandmother, Queen Marie-Amélie) and had talked briefly to his cousin, but there were important matters which he wished to discuss in detail with her. The timing of his visit in fact gave it even greater significance, as it was during his stay in London in early July 1866 that the news was received of the Prussian victory over Austria at Sadowa. Leopold, realizing that the position of Napoleon III would be severely weakened by a much strengthened Prussia and fearing that Belgium might be annexed to France in an attempt to redress the shift in the balance of power, took the opportunity to press the British government personally to guarantee Belgian neutrality.

Prussian ambitions in Europe had been evident since 1862 when army bills were passed almost doubling the size of the Prussian army and Bismarck, who had become prime minister, made his famous speech in which he declared that 'the great questions of the day will not be decided by speeches ... but by blood and iron'.[9] Prussia's first victim was Denmark which, in the face of an Austro-Prussian alliance, saw the duchies of Schleswig and Holstein swallowed into the German Confederation in 1864. The implications of the Schleswig-Holstein fate had not been lost on the future King of the Belgians.

With tension mounting between Berlin and Vienna in 1865 Bismarck felt it necessary at this juncture to assure himself that, in the event of an Austro-Prussian conflict, France would remain neutral. He began by letting drop to the French first secretary in Berlin in September 1865 that he was prepared to see France extending her boundaries, 'wherever in the world the French language is spoken'.[10] This was of course ambiguous and did not necessarily mean Belgium. Nevertheless, French-speaking Canada and Switzerland seem less obvious targets for Napoleonic ambitions, which were in any case known to be for the *frontières naturelles*, that is, up the Rhine.

What upset Napoleon's calculations was that when Prussia and Austria came to blows, Austria was so overwhelmingly and quickly defeated. As a result, in the negotiations which followed, while he was officially a principal interlocutor, in reality Napoleon had no leverage at all and Prussia was able to absorb twenty north German states in the North German Confederation under the Hohenzollern monarchy and to force Austria to withdraw from the German union, without France's being able to object or extract anything for herself. Bismarck adopted a high-handed attitude towards the French emperor which did not go down at all well. Napoleon, and French public opinion was very much behind him, considered that he was owed something for having remained neutral in July 1866 and because of half-promises Bismarck had made him at Biarritz in September 1865. Bismarck described Napoleon as being like an inn-keeper who has his hand out for a tip (*pourboire*).

As early as 1865 rumours had been circulating in Europe that Napoleon III was looking for an opportunity to annex Belgium. In June 1866, before the outbreak of the Austro-Prussian war, Lord Clarendon told the Belgian minister in London that Bismarck had offered France the coal-mining region of Wallonia bordering France, and after the Austro-Prussian war the Belgians were even more aware of the kind of deal France and Prussia were planning at their expense.

Exactly which country in July 1866 suggested a French take-over of Belgium is not clear; the sources are French and German and their respective claims to veracity at that time are extremely weak. Bismarck claimed that the French made the first move: Count Vincent Benedetti, the French ambassador to Berlin, in *My Mission to Prussia*, claims that Bismarck proposed that France annex Belgium and, according to a French dispatch of July 1866, Bismarck told Benedetti:

> Your position is quite simple. You must approach the King of the Belgians and tell him that the inevitable political and territorial aggran-dizement of Prussia is most disquieting and that there is only one way to protect yourselves from dangerous eventualities; that is to unite the destinies of France and Belgium. Assure him that the monarchy would be respected and that Belgium would have an important role to play in a France which had recovered her natural rights.[11]

Benedetti was under orders to ask for Rhenish Bavaria up to Mainz, the Grand Duchy of Luxemburg and Belgium, but Bismarck made it clear from the outset that no cessions of German territory would be considered. Hence the major subject of the proposed deal was French annexation of Belgium as regards which Bismarck foresaw only one major obstacle. 'I cannot hide from you the difficulty I will have with the King [of Prussia] who will undoubtedly be subjected to pressure by England against the arrangement.'[12] This minute was only made public after the First World War. In 1870, when the Benedetti proposals were published in *The Times*, Bismarck told the Belgian minister, 'I have always opposed such schemes [the Benedetti treaty] and will always do so.'[13]

In August 1866 Napoleon III for his part was protesting vehemently that France had no designs on Belgium and the King of the Belgians believed him, attributing the annexationist ambitions to Prussia. He con-sidered Bismarck, 'a dangerous fool'.[14] Writing to Queen Victoria in Sep-tember 1866 he waxed lyrical: 'The French Emperor suits us admirably. I hope he will regain his health. As for Bismarck, we are perfectly well aware that he is continually offering us to France.'[15] Leopold was un-aware that the infamous Benedetti 'treaty' had been drafted, in the ambassador's own handwriting, only a few days before – dictated by Bismarck according to Benedetti. Article IV states,

> His Majesty the King of Prussia, on his side, in case H.M. the Emperor of the French should be led by circumstances to cause his troops to enter Belgium or to conquer it, shall grant armed aid to France and shall support her with all his forces military and naval in the face of, and against, every Power which should in this eventuality declare war.[16]

Whoever was the instigator of the plan to annex Belgium, one thing was clear: Leopold II would have to strive hard if his country was to survive the designs of his powerful neighbours.

The British government's attitude caused him considerable concern. Lord Clarendon, the outgoing foreign secretary, counselled Jules Devaux, Leopold's secretary, 'fortify your country morally and materially so as to make its absorption more difficult!'[17] Devaux found English opinion distinctly indifferent to Belgium's difficult position: 'The more frank openly declare that it matters little to them into how many states the Continent is divided.'[18] Furthermore, the change from a Liberal to a Conservative administration in July 1866 boded even less well for Belgium. British foreign policy had undergone a change in 1864 when, after years of Palmerstonian interference in Continental affairs, Britain withdrew to a position of almost complete isolation. Lord Stanley, who became foreign secretary in July 1866, was a non-interventionist *par excellence* and it was made abundantly clear to Leopold II that Belgium could not count on active support from Britain.

One cannot help but sympathize with the young king. Leopold knew only too well that the guarantees of Belgian neutrality signed by the Powers in 1839 had been made for the general peaceful well-being of Europe and not for the sake of Belgium. His powerful neighbours, France and Prussia, had strong reasons to disregard the exiguous country which separated them and Britain was virtually saying that she no longer felt a commitment to help Belgium in the event of a violation of her neutrality.

If Napoleon III was looking for a compensation after the Austro-Prussian war, the failure of his Mexican policy following soon after this made him yet more determined to find a source of French aggrandizement in Europe. The danger for Belgium mounted. For Leopold II the Mexican affair compounded increased political vulnerability for his country with personal tragedy.

The disastrous French involvement with Mexico began in 1861 when Benito Juarez, who the previous year had become President of the Mexican Republic, suspended payment of the interest on his country's foreign debts. A combined English, Spanish and French expedition sailed to Mexico with the declared intention of bringing pressure to bear on Juarez to meet his country's commitments. The English and Spanish contingents, however, withdrew soon after arriving in Mexico, when it became clear that the French had broader aims. Mexican exiles in Europe had led Napoleon III to believe that a French force would be welcomed in Mexico as an army of liberation. In fact the Mexicans offered strong resistance but, heavily reinforced, the French force pushed forward and in 1863 Juarez was forced to leave Mexico City. Napoleon saw his scheme taking shape and decided that the next step was to establish a suitable European monarchy in Mexico.

To the French emperor the Archduke Maximilian seemed an ideal choice for the throne of Mexico. He had met Maximilian in 1855 and had been impressed by the young Hapsburg who had gone on to prove himself an able Governor-General of Lombardy-Venetia in the late 1850s. The Italian successes against Austria in 1859 had destroyed this job and Maximilian was now unemployed. While Maximilian hesitated about accepting the Mexican throne, Charlotte his wife was full of enthusiasm for the proposed Mexican empire, as were her father and brother Leopold. The only voices which spoke up against the Mexican involvement came from the two wise women in England, Queen Victoria and Queen Marie-Amélie.

A Mexican loan was floated in both France and Britain (it was a complete failure in London) and France promised to provide military and financial aid for the new monarchy. A new French commander was appointed and a rapid campaign in various parts of Mexico was launched early in 1864 to prepare the country for the new emperor and empress. In 1864 Maximilian and Charlotte (from then onwards frequently referred to by the Spanish form of her name, Carlota) arrived at Vera Cruz.

At this point the real difficulties of the Mexican enterprise began to emerge, since it coincided with the almost certain victory of the Northern States in the American Civil War and the United States now made its hostility towards Maximilian's regime felt by helping Juarez carry out armed raids on Mexico from across the border.

For a time Napoleon refused to desert Maximilian, even though he himself was beset by problems at home. The French legislature was becoming progressively more restive as the expense of the Mexican affair continued to mount and the loans floated in Paris on even more onerous terms, went nowhere near meeting the financial needs of Mexico. Gradually Napoleon III also came to realize that the hopes he had placed in his fellow emperor were far too optimistic. He found Maximilian wanting in decisiveness and not up to the difficulties of his position. Maximilian's position became yet more precarious and after the end of the American Civil War, the new president, Andrew Johnson, showed himself determined to enforce the Monroe Doctrine once more by officially recognizing Juarez as the lawful ruler of Mexico. When Napoleon protested to Washington at this step the American government lodged a counterprotest against the setting up of a monarchy in Mexico. Napoleon had little choice in the matter and was forced to recall his expeditionary force.

Maximilian had been forced to renounce his rights to the Austrian throne on becoming Emperor of Mexico and had no place left for him to return to in Europe. His only hope was to make Napoleon III change his mind and to this end he sent Charlotte to Europe to plead for the Mexican monarchy. Charlotte's ship arrived at Saint Nazaire in Brittany in August 1866. Much to her annoyance there was no official reception, only the news of Austria's defeat at Sadowa. Soon after disembarking and, sensing that she was none too welcome in France, she dispatched a curt telegram to Napoleon: 'I have arrived at Saint Nazaire today, charged by the Emperor with the mission of discussing with your Majesty various matters. I beg to assure Your Majesty of my friendship and to believe what a pleasure it will be to see Your Majesties again.'[19] At the same time she sent telegrams to her mother-in-law in Vienna and to her brother in Brussels informing them that she was unable to visit them owing to the unfriendly attitudes of their governments. Leopold II was irritated by his sister's gesture as Belgium was not involved in the Mexican venture.

Napoleon III replied to Charlotte saying, 'I have just returned from Vichy and am ill and forced to stay in bed so that I am not in a position to come to meet you. If, as I suppose, Your Majesty is going first to Belgium, you will give me time to recover.'[20] Charlotte's answer to this polite refusal to see her was to telegraph announcing that she would be arriving in Paris the following day.

Eugénie called on the Mexican empress at her hotel in Paris and tried to put her off seeing Napoleon. Charlotte refused to withdraw her demand to see the French emperor and Napoleon III finally gave in and agreed to an interview. The Emperor, who was painfully aware of his discreditable role, wept profusely as she described the situation in Mexico: in his physically debilitated condition he was a pathetic figure. There was nothing that he could promise: 'We have done our best by Maximilian but all we can now do is to help him escape from his present danger.'[21]

Charlotte saw Napoleon III twice more, yet could not elicit anything from the French emperor. At her final interview she became hysterical and stormed out shouting, 'How could I have forgotten who I am and who you are. I ought to have remembered that Bourbon blood flows in my veins and I ought not to have dishonoured my forebears and myself by treating with a Bonaparte.'[22] Afterwards she wrote a long vindictive letter to her husband which shows strong signs of paranoia; 'He [Napoleon III] has hell on his side and we have not ...'[23]

Charlotte's mind was cracking in Paris; she went on to Rome and it was there that her persecution mania publicly manifested itself. She had for some time feared that she was being poisoned and in Rome she would only drink water. She herself took it from the Trevi Fountain and she ate nothing but oranges and nuts, carefully examining the peel and shell to see if they had been tampered with. The pope, Pius IX, agreed to see her and during her second audience she threw herself at his feet and, weeping, told him to have all the members of her entourage arrested as they were trying to poison her and that she was being followed by spies of Napoleon. The pope was having his breakfast when the empress burst in and, with distinctly unroyal etiquette, dipped her fingers in his cup of chocolate and licking them cried out, 'This at least is not poisoned. Everything they gave me is drugged and I am literally starving!' Charlotte refused to leave the Vatican, 'I shall sleep here in this room, I cannot leave.'[24] However, the pope managed to have her removed to a convent without incident soon afterwards and her brother, the Count of Flanders, was sent for. Philippe accompanied his sister to Miramar in northern Italy where she had lived with Maximilian in the first years of their marriage, and he saw for himself her condition. Joan Haslip, in her book *The Crown of Mexico*, suggests that Charlotte's introverted character was 'the result of a lonely, unhappy childhood'. 'There is little doubt', she says, 'that this proud reserve, this iron self-discipline, contributed to her final mental breakdown.'[25] According to legend pregnancy may have been a further contributory factor to Charlotte's derangement. If she was pregnant by a man other than Maximilian (and after ten years of marriage they had no children) then guilt and physical discomfort could certainly have done much to aggravate her fragile mental stability. Rumour has it that Colonel van der Smissen, leader of a contingent of Belgian volunteers in Mexico, was the father and that the child later became the French General Weygand. There are many other variations to the story, one that Maximilian was the father and that she was afraid of Franz-Josef's reaction to a potential rival heir to the Austrian throne. All possess some degree of plausibility, but there are also good reasons for scepticism.

Maximilian's own behaviour burdened as he was with Mexican problems was far from what might have been expected in the circumstances. Though informed of his wife's state of mind, he spent most of his time alone in his study, refusing to discuss the deteriorating situation with his advisers, most of whom realized that his one hope was to abdicate and leave Mexico. In a desperate attempt to assert his authority he tried to defend Queretaro against the increasing republican forces. In June 1867 they captured the emperor and a few days later he was executed by firing squad.

It was decided not to tell Charlotte of her husband's death, as her periods of lucidity were becoming fewer and her paranoid behaviour more marked. Franz Josef had disclaimed Austrian responsibility for her, and rumours reached Belgium that the empress was being cruelly treated. Yet the Austrians did not wish to relinquish her as she was a rich woman since her father's death. They finally gave in and Marie-Henriette made the journey to Italy to bring back her sister-in-law to Belgium. After spending a few weeks at the château of Tervuren, a few miles east of Brussels, Charlotte showed signs of improvement.

> My sister arrived in a dreadful state [Leopold told Victoria] but her stay at Tervuren has done her a great deal of good. She looks much better and is regaining confidence in those around her. The isolation and treatment at Miramar did her much harm. My sister lived there in a perpetual trance and there was no-one she knew with her ... My wife hardly ever leaves her and takes her on outings to see people.[26]

Charlotte even regained her taste for reading and asked for Froissart's *Chronicles* and recent English novels.

In view of the amelioration in the empress's condition it was decided, at the end of 1867, to tell her about Maximilian's death. 'We hear', wrote Vicky, Queen Victoria's eldest daughter, to her mother, 'that poor unhappy Charlotte has been informed of Max's death. How sad one feels for her! How difficult it must have been for Leopold and Marie to weigh every word they say.'[27]

However, within a year Leopold was forced to admit to his cousin in England:

> The poor Charlotte goes from bad to worse. She wishes at all costs to fill the throne of Spain. It is necessary at Laeken [where she had been transferred] to shut all the doors and exercise a close watch over her. My poor sister imagines that Max is not dead and that he is shut up in England; she writes to him without ceasing and has sent him some presents. The lamentable state of Charlotte makes us extremely sad.[28]

The presence of the mad Empress of Mexico cast a shadow over the Belgian royal family throughout Leopold II's reign. She was installed at the château of Tervuren and then at Bouchout close to Laeken and, oblivious to all that went on, outlived her contemporaries. She died in 1927 at the age of eighty-six after being insane for sixty years.

It came as something of a relief to the European powers when a plan for a seemingly reasonable and possible French compensation emerged at the beginning of 1867. French public opinion, reeling from the failure in Mexico, was demanding an initiative by the emperor in Europe to restore France's prestige and, with rather indecent haste after his Mexican fiasco, the emperor's eyes fell upon the Grand Duchy of Luxemburg.

The Grand Duchy had since 1815 been part of the German Confederation; Prussia maintained a garrison in the fortress and in 1842 it had joined the German customs union, the *Zollverein*. However, the Congress of Vienna had made the King of Holland ruler of Luxemburg. Even though the Luxemburgers had not risen with the Belgians against the Dutch in 1830, when in 1839 the treaties delimiting Belgium were drawn up, the north-western, French-speaking part of Luxemburg was given to Belgium and the Grand Duchy was reduced to half its former area. At the same time, to offset this loss, the Dutch king was given part of Belgian Limburg.

The Belgians felt that they had been badly treated by the Powers in 1839 and that all Luxemburg ought to have formed part of Belgium, but they were impotent to press their demands. Suddenly, in 1866, the Luxemburg question was reopened. The German Confederation, as reorganized after Sadowa, had ceased to include Luxemburg. Secondly, the King of Holland was willing, indeed eager, to sell the Grand Duchy as he was short of money. The prospective buyer in 1867, however, was not Belgium but France.

Secret negotiations between France and Holland began in February 1867. A few weeks later rumours about the proposed deal reached Leopold II who immediately wrote to his cousin in England: 'Would you be so kind as to tell Lord Stanley that the French are currently intriguing in Dutch Luxemburg. I sincerely hope that Bismarck is not thinking of letting the Emperor Napoleon acquire it.'[29]

In not objecting to the proposed deal Bismarck had given his tacit approval, and the British government for its part had not been outraged on learning of it. Virtually single-handed, the thirty-two-year-old King of the Belgians tried to prevent its fruition and to acquire Luxemburg for Belgium. He pleaded his case with Victoria in numerous letters and went to Paris in an attempt to persuade Napoleon to desist. The emperor told him that Bismarck had encouraged him to buy Luxemburg.[30] Napoleon III had again put his faith in the chancellor's word. As in 1866 he was deceived.

At this point Bismarck changed his mind and decided that he was not prepared to abandon Prussian privileges in Luxemburg without some compensation. Fear of French expansion would also be a convenient tool for forcing the recalcitrant southern German states into his confederation. At the end of March there was a leak in the Prussian press, almost certainly planted by Bismarck. The news caused the desired outburst of German national sentiment. In The Hague the Prussian ambassador told William that the sale would lead to hostilities with Prussia and the Dutch king withdrew his offer to sell. Napoleon III for his part was not ready for war with Prussia and the war scare that the Prussian reaction had produced was over.

Nevertheless, the fate of the Grand Duchy remained to be settled. To Rogier, the Belgian chief minister, belonging 'for all his white hair to that audacious generation that had accomplished great things in spite of Europe', it represented his last opportunity to regain what had been lost nearly thirty years earlier.[31] If the Grand Duchy were made part of Belgium, France should be satisfied by the evacuation of the Prussian garrison, and the strengthening of Belgium, while the exclusion of France from Luxemburg would be welcomed by England and Prussia.[32] The king gave his willing backing to Rogier, not unaware that the acquisition of Luxemburg would be a highly auspicious beginning to his reign. He pointed out to Victoria that, lacking the *Zollverein*, Luxemburg could not survive economically on its own. He added: 'I feel that I should tell you, but only you dear Cousin and your Government, that we would be prepared to pay a large indemnity to the King of Holland.'[33]

The queen herself was favourable to the Belgian cause but her private secretary expressed doubts as to the wisdom of the young king's methods.

> I must say it [a letter of Leopold II's] alarms me a little lest he should be *overactive*. You know my opinion coincides with the Queen's, that the simplest and the best arrangement would be the transfer of Luxemburg to Belgium and the transfer to the former of the neutrality guaranteed to the latter by the great Powers – But this object will not be achieved, in my opinion, by any appearance of overeagerness on the part of Belgium to effect it.[34]

The British foreign secretary, Lord Stanley, had from the outset reservations about a Belgian take-over of Luxemburg, and Lord Cowley from Paris advised, 'For heaven's sake do not encourage the idea of giving Luxemburg to Belgium. It would raise a storm here which we shd. never allay.'[35] To arrive at a solution acceptable to the European powers therefore, Britain proposed a conference of the signatories of the 1839 Treaty.

The Belgians were optimistic as to the outcome. However, when the Austro-Hungarian delegate, Count Beust, circulated a proposal that either Luxemburg should remain under Dutch control and that Prussia should renounce her right to the garrison; or that the Grand Duchy should become part of Belgium, in which case Belgium should cede to France the strip of territory and fortresses along its border which France had lost in 1815, there was an immediate outcry from the Belgians. There was simply no question of a territorial trade-off as far as they were concerned.[36]

Walthère Frère-Orban, the minister of finance, who was by then *de facto* the strongest man in the cabinet, opposed any policy which risked annoying France or Prussia. The king, still relatively inexperienced in diplomacy, did not dare to oppose Frère-Orban and was wary of aligning himself with Rogier's nationalistic impetuosity. Leopold had to content himself with bombarding the ever-patient Victoria with letters arguing the case for Belgian absorption of Luxemburg. He was afraid of a diplomatic rebuff and did not want it to appear that Belgium attached too great importance to Luxemburg in case the Powers should veto the union.

Thus at the Conference of London the Belgian delegate, under orders from Brussels, did not take a strong line. And Belgium did not gain Luxemburg. Instead, the Grand Duchy was neutralized, remaining under the control of the King of Holland: the Prussian garrison was to leave and the fortress was to be razed. General satisfaction with the result was expressed throughout Europe. The French were pleased that the Prussian presence was removed and the Germans congratulated themselves on having thwarted the French. The Belgians for their part congratulated themselves on not having given Napoleon III any cause for complaint against them, though years later Leopold expressed his regret that a stronger stand had not been taken in 1867.[37]

Nevertheless, the solution to the Luxemburg crisis was a further blow to France. Napoleon III had learned that Bismarck would rather fight than allow him to gain even a '*bicoque*' (shanty) like Luxemburg. Henceforth, there was no more talk of a friendly agreement to redress the balance of power and to appease French public opinion.

The Belgian railway crisis of 1869 was, like the Luxemburg affair, caused by the desire of France to strengthen her eastern frontiers. Unlike the earlier crises, however, it was not initiated by Napoleon III but had its inception in certain financial plans of Belgian railway speculators.

The Belgian railway system was in 1868 a mixture of private and state ownership, though in the eastern part of the country the main lines were entirely in private hands, namely the *Compagnie du Grand Luxembourg* and the *Compagnie du Liègeois-Limburgois*. Both these companies were heavily in debt and, when the board of directors of the *Compagnie du Grand Luxembourg* had failed to interest the Belgian government in their line, both companies separately opened negotiations with the French *Compagnie de l'Est* in Paris.

The *Compagnie de l'Est* had, a year earlier, concluded an agreement with a private company operating in the Grand Duchy of Luxemburg, according to which the *Compagnie Guillaume Luxembourg* had ceded to the *Compagnie de l'Est* not only a line running from the Swiss border to the city of Luxemburg but, in addition, a line which crossed the Belgian frontier and ran almost to Liège. It was clear that if the French company made similar arrangements with the two Belgian companies their railways would serve as an extension of this system and the *Compagnie de l'Est* would dominate the stretch of territory which flanked the Rhine from Switzerland to the Dutch border.

The Belgian government was kept informed of the negotiations taking place in Paris and preliminary arrangements for the cession of the two Belgian lines were completed without any hitches early in December 1868. Then, out of the blue, the Belgian minister of public works announced that the proposed deal could not take place without the consent of the government, adding that such consent would never be given.[38]

It was assumed that this announcement would put an end to the talks taking place in Paris. In this the Belgian government was mistaken and the Belgian railway company representatives in Paris assured the French that their government would give way as soon as the agreements were ratified. The continued pressure from Paris forced the Belgian government to take a stronger line and Frère-Orban drew up a bill for submission to parliament stating that Belgian railway companies could only cede lines with the permission of the government. This bill, intended as a warning to the negotiators in Paris, was rapidly passed through both Houses.

With the passage of the law the dispute over railway rights, like so many other seemingly non-political questions in this period, was transported to the higher ground of diplomatic controversy as the French government could no longer hide behind the *Compagnie de l'Est*. Napoleon himself claimed:

> The truth is that M. Frère-Orban has premeditated all of this, that he went expressly to Berlin, and that the matter was concerted with Bismarck. The Belgian government is demonstrating its illwill towards France, and public opinion is convinced ... that Belgium would not be so arrogant were not Prussia behind her ... Must war arise out of this conflict? I do not know. But it is necessary to act as if it will arise.[39]

Leopold II had again been sending off a stream of worried letters to Queen Victoria and, as in the Luxemburg affair, she did her utmost for her cousin by expressing her concern about Belgium's situation to the foreign secretary, Lord Clarendon, insisting that the government make clear its willingness to uphold the Belgian guarantee. Clarendon had no desire to make such a statement as he feared that intervention in the railway dispute might well lead to British involvement in the ever-evolving duel between France and Prussia. Clarendon, in fact, blamed the Belgian government for having allowed the railway question to become one of European interest and British action was limited to putting pressure on the Belgian government to accept the French offer of a mixed commission to investigate the matter.

When the Belgians duly accepted the proposal, and Frère-Orban went to Paris to negotiate, the French saw it as a complete surrender and refused to consider Frère-Orban's suggestion that French trains could use Belgian tracks, the lines remaining in Belgian hands. It looked as though the talks would break down and Frère-Orban prepared to leave Paris. His parting shot was to hint that an international conference might be called to settle the matter. The English bogey did not frighten the French who knew that Clarendon was reluctant to become involved in the issue. On the other hand when Bismarck stated that he was prepared to enter into talks this changed everything. An international conference, the French realized, would vote against them. The alternative was war against Belgium. And from this Napoleon III shrank away since it would undoubtedly place France in the wrong in the eyes of Europe and might well involve her with the Great Powers. The French government gave way.

Napoleon III had suffered yet another diplomatic defeat. He, and French public opinion, albeit incorrectly, believed that Prussia had instigated the Belgian railway affair and moved a step further forward towards the battlefield.

5　1870

'When wine is opened it has to be drunk.'[1]

Napoleon III, 1870.

The crisis that precipitated the Franco-Prussian War was Bismarck's plan to make Prince Leopold of Hohenzollern-Sigmaringen king of Spain. The Spanish throne had been vacant since 1868 when the long-expected revolution deposing the eccentric Queen Isabella had taken place. The provisional government which took her place began looking for a suitable king to replace the fallen Bourbon monarchy; after failing to obtain any of the three princes they would have liked, Prince Leopold was proposed to them.

Prince Leopold was the second son of Prince Charles Anthony of Hohenzollern-Sigmaringen, the Catholic branch of the Hohenzollerns which had remained in south-western Germany when the younger branch had left to attain such dazzling success as kings of Prussia. Leopold II's connection with the prince was through his brother Philippe who had in 1867 married Prince Leopold's sister, Marie. The King of the Belgians thus inevitably found himself drawn into the acrimonious diplomacy that ensued.

The Hohenzollern family were not averse to leaving their principality and Prince Leopold's elder brother had recently become King of Roumania. The prince himself, however, was an officer in the Prussian army and a man without political ambition.

Quite what part Bismarck played in the early stages of the affair in the autumn of 1869 is not clear, but there is abundant evidence to show that from February 1870 onwards he was pushing Prince Leopold's candidature. Both the prince and his father opposed the idea on the grounds of the unsettled conditions in Spain – the fate of Maximilian was fresh in everyone's mind – and the opposition to be expected from France. So did the King of Prussia but Bismarck looked at things from a different standpoint.

For Germany it is desirable to have on the other side of France a country on whose sympathies we can rely and with whose feelings France is obliged to reckon. If during a war between Germany and France conditions prevail such as those under Queen Isabella when there was a prospect of an alliance of the Latin Catholic Powers it would even become possible for French forces to be relieved by Spanish and thus made available for use [ie against Germany].[2]

King William's marginal comments on the memorandum show that he was unconvinced and throughout the prolonged discussions he never concealed his anxieties about Bismarck's policy. But so great was the chancellor's authority that finally Prince Leopold, with his father's consent, accepted the invitation in June 1870.

Hitherto the secrecy of the negotiations had been carefully guarded. Napoleon III was to be caught by surprise; the plan was to rush the election of Prince Leopold through the *Cortes* and to confront the French emperor with a *fait accompli*. At this point, however, two hitches occurred in the plan. In the first place, as a result of an error by a cypher clerk in the telegram sent by the Spanish negotiator in Berlin, the leader of the provisional Spanish government, General Prim, had concluded that the talks would continue for a few more weeks. It was sweltering in Madrid and Prim, not wishing to fall foul of members of the already weary *Cortes* by prolonging its sitting, prorogued it until the following November. The second error arose because Don Eusebio di Salazar, the Spanish negotiator, knew nothing of this and arrived in Madrid exultant over his triumph and unaware of constraints on telling his friends. It is hardly surprising that on 2 July articles found their way into French newspapers announcing that the Spanish crown had been offered to a Prussian prince and had been accepted. The news caused a sensation in Paris. In the cabinet, at court, in the press and in the street there was but one opinion: the candidacy was a menace to the security of France and the secrecy in which it had been enveloped was an insult.

The King of the Belgians and his sister-in-law had, it was said in some newspapers, proposed Prince Leopold, and *La France* asserted that the king had gone to England to persuade Queen Victoria to support the candidature.[3] King Leopold, it was claimed, was in the pay of the Prussians: the whole plan was seen as a Bismarckian attack on France.

In France, in spite of the bellicose state of public opinion, Napoleon III himself – by now a chronically sick man in frequent pain – was not convinced that it would be necessary to go to war with Prussia and on 8 July he called in the Belgian minister to Paris and asked him to pass on to the King of the Belgians a message. Could Leopold II use his influence with the Hohenzollern-Sigmaringens to persuade Prince Leopold to step down? Leopold II immediately wrote to the candidate and he also asked his brother to do what he could.

I believe that you would do well to write immediately to your father-in-law. Tell him that it is your duty to make clear to him that world peace depends on the wisdom of his son. Add, that what is happening at the moment inevitably reminds you of Mexico. Are we to see a similar tragedy afflicting your wife's family!!!![4]

On 12 July Prince Charles Anthony, Prince Leopold's father – who had been deterred until then by scruples about loyalty to a pledge given to the Spanish government and by a feeling that it would be dishonourable for a Hohenzollern to yield to the menaces of France – withdrew Prince Leopold's candidature. Napoleon believed that the crisis was over. 'The country will be disappointed,' he said, 'but what of that.'[5]

The French emperor had in fact played Bismarck at his own game and forced him to climb down. Bismarck was so downcast that he seriously considered resigning. However, the French prime minister in addressing the legislature on the subject did not convince the deputies of the extent of the French diplomatic success. Parliament, members of the cabinet and the Empress Eugénie who, according to Prince Metternich, looked ten years younger at the prospect of war, pressed for more.[6] The foreign minister, with Napoleon's approval, then instructed Benedetti to extract from the Prussian king assurances that he would never again authorize Prince Leopold to renew the claim.

Napoleon was taking a calculated risk in relying on King William's well-known abhorrence of war when he sent Benedetti to Ems. William listened to what Benedetti had to say but rejected the demand for assurances. The French ambassador persisted until the king finally lost patience with him. He raised his hat and resumed his walk. Benedetti asked for another interview which irritated the king sufficiently that, contrary to normal practice, William decided to make public details of his conversation with Benedetti. He sent a telegram, setting out what had been said, to Bismarck to release to the press. The famous Ems telegram, which was meant as a counter-gesture to the French gloating over the withdrawal of Prince Leopold's candidature was, as is well known, edited by Bismarck such that it omitted how courteous and correct the king had been with Benedetti and insinuated that the French ambassador had been snubbed and that all relations with France had been abruptly terminated. It had the desired effect. France mobilized on 15 July and declared war on Prussia four days later.

It had been clear for some time that war between France and Prussia was imminent and Leopold II had been putting pressure on the British government to state that England would intervene if Belgian neutrality were violated. He went over to England in May 1870 to see William Gladstone, the prime minister, and Lord Granville, the foreign secretary. According to the Prince of Wales, who saw him, 'he rushes around in all directions and fatigues himself to death'.[7] Certainly Leopold had a tendency to confuse motion with action, but in 1870 he found himself, at a moment when his country's very existence seemed jeopardized, obliged to deal single-handed with foreign affairs.

Elections had taken place in Belgium in 1870 which resulted in an inconclusive majority for the party in power, the Liberals. The government tottered on until 2 July when it resigned. Some Liberals had defected to the Catholic opposition but from the point of view of the Catholics they could not be relied on in the long run. Fresh elections were obviously necessary. They were called for at the beginning of August. Meanwhile, the Catholic Baron d'Anethan formed a government and, for internal party reasons, he had to include a well-known anti-militarist in his cabinet. The political crisis could not have come at a more inopportune time. It weakened the international diplomatic position of Belgium and had a distinctly detrimental effect on mobilization when the moment came.

None of Leopold's efforts to persuade England to ask for renewed guarantees of Belgian neutrality from the potential belligerents came to anything before war was declared. And even after hostilities had broken out, Granville assured the king that any additions to the 1839 treaties would be superfluous. Then suddenly, at the end of July, the British government changed its mind.

On 22 July Bismarck called in the Belgian minister at Berlin, Baron Nothomb. 'Do you know Benedetti's handwriting?' the chancellor asked him. Nothomb replied that he did and Bismarck handed him the draft spoliation treaty. At the same time, Bismarck gave a copy to *The Times*.

The publication on 25 July of the infamous proposals caused a sensation throughout Europe, in particular in England. Public opinion was outraged at such evidence of French duplicity and in both Houses of Parliament speeches were made affirming England's firm adhesion to the treaty of 1839. Gladstone spoke in high-sounding tones of what was at stake:

> Is there a man among you who does not feel that, if Belgium were to disappear through the lawless desire of aggrandizement of any of its neighbours, the day that witnessed it would also be the knell of public right and international law in Europe? Would England stand aside as the passive witness of the most odious crime that had ever

sullied the pages of history and thus make herself the accomplice of the crime?[8]

In view of the changed circumstances, the British government drew up a treaty which both France and Prussia were asked to sign. It reaffirmed Belgian neutrality and stated that Britain would declare war if either state violated Belgium during the current struggle or in the year following its conclusion. It was signed by the French on 9 August and the Prussians two days later.

Ever since his accession Leopold II had been pressing for a larger and better equipped Belgian army. To many members of the government, and the public, the international guarantees of 1839 took the place of men and arms but the king himself firmly believed that if Belgian neutrality was to mean anything it had to be clear that it was not worth while violating it. If a belligerent knew that he would tie up a sizeable part of his forces in confrontation with the Belgian army, then the albeit marginal size of the Belgian army would be critical. The Prussian army in 1870 numbered 360,000 and that of France 250,000; a force of 80,000 to 100,000 would be necessary to deal with the Belgian army, thus virtually eliminating the Prussian manpower superiority. And in theory Belgium had 100,000 men to put into the field.

As regards weaponry the Belgian army was well equipped, possessing since 1867 an Albini system breech-loading gun of the same Wahrendorff type as the Prussian army.[9] Yet as soon as mobilization took place its serious lacunae elsewhere were revealed. In terms of equipment it was short of gun-carriages to transport the artillery, though even if the carriages had been there they would have served little purpose as only half the required number of dray horses was available.[10] The cavalry maintained 4,245 horses, expecting to buy a third as many again in time of war. This proved impossible as French buyers had recently scoured the country and bought up all the horses suitable for military use.[11] The minister of war was relieved that the campaign took place in the summer, as beds were in short supply and many men had to sleep on straw.[12] The only commodity of which there was plenty – and there is something distinctly Belgian about this – was food.

However, the most serious weakness of the Belgian army in 1870 was the shortfall in men that mobilization revealed. In theory it should have been possible to muster an army of 104,999 men, 95,374 of whom ought to have been available immediately.[13] In reality, the report of the minister of war reveals that 72,613 men were mobilized in the middle of July, and after calling in all reservists, the maximum figure reached was 83,350 on 20 August.[14] It was quite a blow to expectations. On 17 July Leopold had been optimistically assuring Queen Victoria, 'At the end of this week I expect to have 60,000 men guarding the roads between France and Prussia and 20,000 to 30,000 defending Antwerp with 4,000 cannon.'[15] It emerged that many of those who had done their military service in the 1860s could not be traced as neither the army nor the communes had bothered to keep track of these men's names and addresses.

The system of military service in Belgium consisted of calling up one man per 420 inhabitants by ballot.[15] If the man so chosen did not wish to do his military service, and if he could find and pay a replacement, then this other person could do it for him. This system, the *remplacement*, led to a standing army of dubious quality in any case, and when in July 1870 many men without even rudimentary military training were added, the quality, as the commanders recognized, left much to be desired.[17]

The army was divided into two corps, a defensive army based on Antwerp and a mobile army of observation under General Chazal. The latter was in the early stages of the conflict based at Louvain but after its defeats at Wissemburg and Worth, the French army was seen to be moving in the direction of the Belgian frontier and Chazal moved his army towards Namur and Charleroi. As a result of further Prussian victories at Rezonville and St Privat, the French found themselves surrounded at Metz and it became clear that the war would be decided close to the Belgian border. Chazal therefore established his headquarters at Namur where he could make use of the Namur–Marche–Arlon railway line and send troops deep into the province of Luxemburg. All roads, and even paths, across the frontier were marked with white flags on which was written '*Belgique/Belgïen*' and people living in the towns and villages in the area were told to fly the national flag from their houses.[18] Men were quickly recruited to man the frontier posts to prevent foreigners from entering the country but despite this, many French from the areas where hostilities were expected to take place crossed the border by successfully claiming to be Belgian.[19]

It was intended that if either army crossed the frontier all railways and bridges would be destroyed. Leopold's brother, the Count of Flanders, who was serving under Chazal and who was responsible for the corps of engineers, was far from happy about this policy.[20] He seems to have feared that if his men had nothing to do they might create a little explosive action to relieve the tedium. He need not have worried for the war was soon over. Napoleon III, with General MacMahon, marched north from Chalons (where they had tried to regroup their forces prior to falling back to defend Paris) hoping to swing down to Metz from a position north of the German forces. Some officers advocated invading Belgium to facilitate this move but they were overruled. The Prussian intelligence learned of the move and immediately informed headquarters at Bar-le-Duc. With great speed the Prussians moved north and trapped the French at Sedan, twelve miles from the Belgian border. After a hard-fought, bloody battle, Napoleon III and his forces surrendered on 2 September 1870.

After his capitulation to the Prussians, Napoleon III was anxious to avoid the humiliation of appearing before his fellow countrymen and, as he could not yet be taken into Germany because all the railway lines were blocked with troops, he sent a telegram to Leopold II. 'Obliged to pass through your country on my way to Germany.'[21] Considering his position, the emperor's turn of phrase was distinctly arrogant and Leopold was irritated by Napoleon's assumption that he could enter Belgium. 'My first reaction was one of considerable annoyance at what seemed to me a violation of our neutrality. The details I have since received have assuaged my feelings.'[22] The reasoning which led Leopold to allow Napoleon III to cross through Belgium was that as he had capitulated at Sedan, the emperor was no longer a belligerent. In the end Leopold did what he could to facilitate Napoleon's passage.

Chazal and some Belgian officers awaited the fallen emperor at the frontier post of Beaubru. Napoleon arrived on the morning of 3 September escorted by his aides-de-camp and some Prussian officers. The Belgians asked the French and Prussians to leave and, escorted only by Belgians, Napoleon was taken to the Hôtel de la Poste at Bouillon. The hotel, frequented mainly by commercial travellers, was a far cry from the splendours of the Tuileries or St Cloud; his room was simple and he was obliged to go down to the dining room for dinner in the evening. The emperor cut up a piece of meat but he did not eat anything and after only a few minutes he excused himself from the table. The officers who stayed up talking far into the night could hear Napoleon sobbing in his bedroom; all he asked for were cigarettes, which he chain smoked, and tea.[23]

The following morning the emperor was taken by train to Verviers, close to Liège. At the station he asked a Belgian officer to buy him some newspapers, but not French ones. The train to Verviers was late and he was seen standing on the platform holding a newspaper named somewhat ironically – L'Indépendance Belge.

Chazal considered it likely that there would be hostile scenes at Verviers and he took the precaution of addressing the crowd that had gathered. 'Gentlemen, His Majesty the French Emperor is about to appear before you. He is on his way to Germany as a prisoner of war and, for the moment, he is our guest. In the name of Belgium ... I ask you to treat him with the respect his misfortune warrants.'[24]

Silence followed and Napoleon appeared; walking unsteadily he held on to Chazal's arm for support as he approached the train. He mounted the steps and came to the window. Suddenly all hats were raised and a spontaneous cry went up from the Belgian crowd, 'Vive l'Empéreur!'

It was the last time in his life that Napoleon III was to hear it. (A diplomatic rumour which made the rounds in late 1870 had it that Leopold II might become King of the French.)[25]

The Prussian victory was welcomed in Belgium, not least by Leopold II. However, where the king differed from the vast majority of his subjects was in the lessons derived. To the Belgians the Franco-Prussian War proved that their neutrality was meaningful in a war between the Great Powers; they did not need to pay much attention to military questions and certainly not to maintain a larger standing army than they had done in the past. To Leopold the war had demonstrated the fragility of international guarantees and the inadequacy of the Belgian army. He feared that in a future conflict, strategic considerations could well outweigh international honour and he pressed for a large army. Leopold died five years before being proved right.

6 In Memoriam

*'It is necessary to lay eggs all over the place
... Some at least are sure to hatch.'* [1]

Leopold II.

In 1857 Marie-Henriette had become pregnant. 'My dear cousin,' Leopold wrote to the prince consort, 'the wise and practical advice you gave me at Osborne four years ago has now borne fruit.' [2] A daughter was born in February 1858 and named Louise. The following year they had a son who was baptized Leopold. Five years later, in 1864, a third child was born, Stephanie, clearly not of the sex Leopold would have liked.

During the 1860s Leopold II's relations with his wife were reasonably cordial but it would seem that their common interest in their children was their only bond. The fundamental reason why their marriage never succeeded was their lack of compatibility, although the onus for the failure of their relationship is usually attributed to Leopold. Marie-Henriette, who had been a warm and lively young woman, gradually adopted an aloof manner and withdrew into herself; at thirty-six Queen Victoria found her 'much altered and much aged'. [3] Her life was, without doubt, an unhappy one, but she must herself bear some of the blame: her lack of interest in Belgian affairs and her duties as queen put a further strain on the royal marriage, and as Leopold placed kingship above all else he could never be satisfied with a wife who openly preferred horses and concerts.

The acrimonious relations which later developed between Leopold and his two elder daughters were another manifestation of the supreme importance he attached to royal duty. Louise and Stephanie have written supposed autobiographies. Both are appalling books, self-justifying, self-indulgent, and the prose largely purple. They describe loveless childhoods in rigorous conditions. Maybe some of what they say is true, though Louise came to be a mythomaniac in later life and Stephanie's book was ghost written for her – indeed when she saw what had been produced on her behalf she tried unsuccessfully to withhold publication and one is wary of attaching much credence to the contents of either book. There are letters in existence which show Leopold II as a loving father to his daughters when young, while from their autobiographies he emerges as an ogre; at best as uninterested in them.

Apparently he did care, but certainly the focus of his paternal attentions was his son who, after his father's accession to the throne in 1865, became Duke of Brabant. Prince Leopold was a lively, intelligent and mischievous boy, not unaware of his position. After a public appearance he returned home, repeating to all whom he met, 'They cried, long live me!'[4] He was however a weak child and liable to frequent illnesses.

At the beginning of 1868 rumours began to circulate that all was not well with the heir to the Belgian throne, although no-one could say exactly what was wrong. Then, in August 1868, it was formally admitted that the Duke of Brabant was ill, the official bulletin adding somewhat ominously, that 'there were hopes of recovery'. Sir William Jenner was called over from London and felt compelled to tell Leopold and Marie-Henriette that their child stood no chance of recovery. In the knowledge that the child's illness was fatal it was decided that he should receive the Last Sacraments; apparently the child was not upset on being told this and received the communion calmly. 'Poor Leopold and Marie look sadly dejected – and Brussels makes a most melancholy impression,' wrote Vicky to her mother after a visit to Belgium in December 1868.[5] For some time the Duke of Brabant's condition did not change. In pain, with a persistent cough, each morning on waking he would burst into tears at the thought of confronting another day. On 21 January 1869 his condition worsened and he died peacefully the following day.

Leopold II was not able to restrain his tears at the church during the requiem mass. Still weeping he followed his son's coffin down into the royal crypt at Laeken, where the child was to be buried alongside his grandfather, Leopold I. The king fell on his knees, threw flowers over the coffin and sobbed uncontrollably. Such distress had never been witnesed in Leopold II. The wound never healed. Edmond Carton de Wiart, Leopold's secretary 1901–9, recollecting in the 1950s, said that time and time again the king repeated that it was the death of his son that had caused him to direct all his energies to acquiring a colony.[6] The desire for territorial aggrandizement which he had cherished as a young man became, after 1869, his sole aim and ambition, his obsession. He had failed to provide his country with a son; instead he would bequeath Belgium a colony.

The change was not obvious immediately as Leopold was pursuing several colonial schemes in the late 1860s on which he had embarked before his son's death, but during the 1870s he came to devote less and less time to, and to show declining interest in, other subjects.

Leopold had returned to Belgium from his six-month voyage to the Far East only months before becoming king in December 1865, and the colonial potential of Asia was, at this time, to the fore in his mind. A trade convention on terms favourable to Belgium was signed with China in November 1865 and the Duke of Brabant was in contact with the Belgian consul in Yokohama with the intention of establishing commercial relations with Japan, which at that stage had relatively few contacts with Europe.

Lambermont for his part was engaged upon studying the possibilities offered by Formosa. The Baron thought that it might be possible to acquire a territorial lease on the island and to set up an international commercial company to develop trade between the Far East and Europe.

China had held a particular fascination for Leopold since the 1850s and he had in no way been deterred by the Belgian failure to take part in the 1860 Anglo-French expedition to China. In 1866 he wrote: 'My dream is to create a world-wide Belgian company with headquarters in Brussels which would, in time, become for China what the East India Company became for the Indian subcontinent.'[7] However, in the face of the refusal of the Chinese authorities to open up the Celestial Empire to Western trade and influence – the Belgians lacked the means of compulsion possessed by the British and the French – the scheme was stillborn.

Nevertheless, the king revived the plan in 1868, with the variant that this time he was thinking in terms of an international company which would finance railways and mining enterprises in particular. Leopold offered to contribute 25,000 francs and commercial firms, banks and wealthy individuals, such as Krupps, Barings and Baroness Burdett Coutts, were approached. The money was not forthcoming and the project was abandoned in 1869.[8] The king did not give up and at a conference organized by the British iron and steel industry in Liège in 1873 Leopold called upon Belgian and British industrialists to interest themselves in China and he proposed the creation of an Anglo-British agency in China to obtain commercial concessions. Nothing came of the idea, although Cockerills, Belgium's largest iron and steel producer, began exploring the Chinese market.

Just as the attempt to gain a foothold in China was a revival of earlier ideas, Leopold II turned again in the late 1860s to the island of Borneo which had interested him at the beginning of the decade. The Dutch government again turned down his offer to buy their part of the island and for a while Borneo was forgotten. Some years later he directed his sights to another part of the island, namely the north-east corner which belonged to the Sultan of Brunei. He tried to enlist Queen Victoria's help and his ever-patient cousin asked her ministers whether there would be any objection to a Belgian colony in Borneo.[9] As happened on so many occasions, and concerning different parts of the world, the British government, while not seeking further territorial expansion itself, did not want other countries establishing colonies close to theirs.

A new source of interest to Leopold was the Portuguese possessions in Africa. Portugal had acquired her colonies in the sixteenth century at the zenith of her power but by the nineteenth century she lacked the resources to exploit or administer them. Perhaps with an eye to the imminent opening of the Suez Canal (in which he was a considerable shareholder) Leopold became interested in East Africa, and in 1868 he sent an envoy to Lisbon to take soundings as to the Portuguese reaction to a possible company to develop coffee production in Mozambique. The authorities in Lisbon insisted that such a company would have to have a Portuguese controlling interest and the idea was dropped.[10] The following year a similar idea, this time concerning Angola, was mooted. It met a like fate.[11]

The most serious colonial scheme of these years was undoubtedly that concerning the Philippines. The attempt in 1841 to buy the archipelago had failed as the Spanish government had not been prepared to sell, but by the late 1860s the situation had changed. Disorder was rampant in Spain following Isabella's abdication in 1868; Cuba was in the hands of a revolutionary junta, the Philippines were close to insurrection and financial chaos reigned, while an article in the *Economist* of 14 August 1869 discussed the possibility of the United States buying Cuba and the Philippines also being put up for sale.[12]

At this stage Leopold was still trying to interest his fellow countrymen in his colonial projects, and in January 1870 he submitted his ideas as regards the Philippines to his chief minister, Frère-Orban, and to Jules Malou, a leading Catholic politician and financier.[13] Both were opposed to doing anything: the king was not put off and, assuring Frère-Orban he would not ask for either financial or diplomatic help from the Belgian government, he set about opening up negotiations with Spain. One of his military aides, Captain Donny, drew up a draft contract according to which a private company would be created which would take over the economic development, administration and defence of the archipelago in exchange for a considerable loan to Spain. At the end of ninety years Spain could reimburse the money borrowed and the Philippines would revert to her.

A lawyer, Jules Le Jeune, was sent to Madrid in the spring of 1870 to put forward the plan. He reported that the Spanish government did not dismiss the idea out of hand but that they were not prepared to commit themselves to any schemes concerning the Philippines.[14] The matter lapsed for a while.

Affairs went from bad to worse in Spain. At the end of 1870 Prim was assassinated; Amédée de Savoie, the king, was unable to establish order, the Carlists rose and, after a brief civil war, Amédée abdicated and a republic was proclaimed early in 1873. A new Belgian minister to Madrid was appointed at this time, Jules Greindl, a young diplomat enjoying the full confidence of Leopold II, but at the same time a man of considerable intellectual stature and independence who refused to go along blindly with his sovereign's schemes.

Greindl did not consider the earlier idea of a private company feasible. To him, either the Belgian government had to buy the Philippines, or 'the colony had to become an independent state under the sovereignty of the King of the Belgians, Spain being compensated financially by the new state'.[15] The next step as Greindl saw it, would be to find out whether a suitable indemnity could be found; such a sum could not be raised in Belgium and it was decided to try in England. Leopold and Greindl visited London separately in the spring of 1873 to take soundings in the City, and the bankers Baring Brothers were approached. They were not, however, prepared to lend money to the King of the Belgians without a guarantee from Belgium itself. Barings' view was that the proposals were not sufficiently developed and thought out for them. They would need the agreement of Spain and that of the inhabitants of the Philippines; they would need to know the sum and terms required; unless these conditions were met they refused to co-operate. Leopold was not surprised. He accepted the setback but remained optimistic as to the long-term outcome.

Possession of the Philippines would open the door to trade with China and Japan and Leopold was not prepared to forgo any opportunity to acquire such a colonial prize. In 1874 he turned again to his original idea of a commercial company to develop the archipelago, and Greindl was now aided by a Belgian businessman who was more enthusiastic than himself about the idea. The Spanish were not convinced, and the following year a variant on the scheme was proposed. But by this time order was returning to Spain. Alphonso, Isabella's son, had become king, the Carlists were defeated, and the new government did not wish to divest the country of the Philippines. In August 1875, Leopold finally decided to let the matter drop.

However, even before accepting that the Philippines project had failed, Leopold had, in July 1875, called in the British minister to Belgium, Sir Savile Lumley, to sound him out as to what the British reaction would be if the Belgians established a colony in New Guinea. Taking care to point out that the Belgian government was in no way associated with his ideas – he had given up trying to interest the Belgians and his schemes were by this stage all personal ones – the king set out his case with his usual skilful phraseology. He 'wishes to establish colonies with a view to distract his subjects' minds from religious disputes and to establish a merchant navy. If England did not want New Guinea he thought of going there.'[16]

Lumley was guarded in his reply to the king's question. 'I told His Majesty that I had to admit my total ignorance about New Guinea but, in view of its position so close to the Equator, I feared that the climate would not be favourable to settlers from Belgium.'[17] Leopold then turned to blatant flattery, saying that, 'He was aware that his people lacked the drive and the robustness of the English' and Lumley realized that the king had already given a great deal of attention to New Guinea.[18]

The Foreign Office told Lumley to discourage the king. It was pointed out that emigration would not distract the Belgians from religious disputes, 'see Spain and Ireland', and, although it was not planned for the immediate future, 'Australia intends to annex New Guinea.'[19] Years later Leopold II, reminiscing with a British diplomat, said, 'the Foreign Secretary of the day had answered *"Do not go there"*; and he relinquished the idea'.[20]

The British government was involved in another project of Leopold's in 1875. Early in the year, after international arbitration, Delagoa Bay on the east coast of Africa was attributed to Portugal and the Transvaal, which had contested this, found itself without an outlet to the sea. President Burghers of the South African Republic visited Europe a few months later to try to raise the capital and find a company prepared to construct a railway linking the Transvaal and Delagoa Bay. The consul-general of the Boer Republics to Belgium was told that Burghers would be welcome in Brussels and towards the end of 1875 and again in February 1876 he visited the Belgian capital, where he met businessmen interested in the railway project. With the discreet backing of the king, Cockerills entered into detailed discussions, agents were sent to the Transvaal and the post of Belgian consul in Pretoria was created.[21] The long-term hopes of the consul, Baron de Selys Fanson, were as ambitious as those of his sovereign, namely to use the railway project as a foothold for eventually acquiring the colony. However, the independent republic was rapidly collapsing; bankrupt and surrounded by the hostile Bantu, who attacked in 1876, it was in that year annexed by the British.

While the Transvaal project was still only in its early stages, in the autumn of 1875, Leopold was writing: 'Tongking would suit us well. The population is dense … and the people very friendly. A Frenchman … took control over I don't know how many towns with only a few men …'[22] Tongking (now Vietnam) was ruled by the King of Annam. Although independent, in fact his title was conferred by the Chinese emperor, and periodic missions had to be sent to Peking bearing tribute in acknowledgement of China's suzerainty. In 1862 he had been compelled by the French to cede the three southern provinces of his kingdom, known as Cochin-China; after the Franco-Prussian War France resumed her forward policy in Annam and in 1874 secured further rights, among them that of navigating the Red River in Tongking. Clearly Leopold II would need the support of France, whose influence in the peninsula was supreme, and in 1876 it appeared that, after an unsuccessful, unauthorized raid into the interior of Tongking by a French officer, France was not interested in the hinterland.

Leopold's diplomatic tactics in dealing with Paris were not all of a very friendly nature. He reminded the French in several different documents that 'France's last act with regard to Belgium was the Benedetti treaty. It would be a good way of wiping the slate clean.' He also pointed out to the French government, 'if they let us go where they do not want to go themselves, they would avoid the possibility of having one of the Great Powers as its neighbour.'[23] He was again thinking in terms of a private company which would administer and develop the country, but nowhere is anything said as to where the necessary finance would be found – presumably Leopold was prepared to use his personal fortune, as he did later for the Congo.

Negotiations were a closely-guarded secret and Baron Beyens, the Belgian minister to Paris, was told by the king to use a special messenger for their correspondence. Beyens for his part, as with Greindl a few years earlier, was far from convinced of the feasibility of the project, but he possessed the great advantage of being a close friend of Léon Gambetta, president of the French Chamber. For a time it looked as though the French were going along with Leopold's plan and talk of their moving into Cambodia rather than Tongking encouraged the king to persist. When in 1878 it began to look as though the French were going to take over Tongking, Gambetta promised to ensure that part of it would be ceded to the King of the Belgians. In 1881 when he became minister of foreign affairs the occupation looked imminent. Leopold was watching anxiously from the sidelines. Suddenly the carefully constructed diplomatic house of cards collapsed: Gambetta's ministry fell and he himself died a few months later. The scheme for the Belgians to occupy Tongking met the same fate.

7 Ecce Homo

*'To be a great person is not necessarily the
same thing as being a good person.'*[1]

Leopold II.

'The Coburgs are late developers,' Leopold I had remarked, but it was
not true of his son: the distinguishing features of the Duke of Brabant
became with the passage of time more marked; in old age they were exaggerated. Leopold II possessed an extremely strong personality. He knew
what he wanted and would stop at nothing to attain his ends. With this
went exceptional intelligence and enormous mental and physical energy.
From his agile and ever-fertile mind ideas and schemes flowed. Many
seemed extravagant to those around him but Leopold was always in
complete earnest and his overwhelming determination to carry them out
resulted in many being realized. Setbacks in no way deterred him: he never
took a defeat as final. His tenacity and obduracy exhausted not only individual men but entire governments. Even with his own prodigious
energy, though, he needed men to work for him, and at his pace. His
youthful off-putting manner disappeared and he developed considerable
charm. Numerous accounts exist of men called in by the king and presented
with tasks that they considered impossible and/or outrageous. They
usually left his study fired with the enthusiasm to carry out his schemes.
He was a delightful conversationalist when he wanted to be – and in his
correspondence solicitude for the person to whom he was writing
is ever present. He couched his summonses in the guise of politely-worded
invitations to dinner, he always knew what ailment to ask about and
the names of wives and children. At the same time he never let his rank
be forgotten, though the emphasis varied. To Bismarck he made it clear
that he was a Coburg, a German prince; Jules Ferry, the French prime
minister, was left in no doubt that he was dealing with Louis-Philippe's
grandson; British statesmen were made aware that he was the son of the
queen's favourite uncle. Leopold II made as much use as he could of his
royal relations, in particular Queen Victoria, but he had none of his

father's genuine *esprit de famille*. Nor did he care about the Belgians as people; 'I am King of a small country and small-minded people,' he said derisively.[2] They for their part did not feel any personal attachment to him. As Duke of Brabant his political ideas and unattractive personality had not made him popular in the country and though in the early part of his reign he did achieve some degree of popularity, it was more because he incarnated a certain conception of the monarchy, and hence the country, that was pleasing to the populace. His very kingly person gave status to Belgium which was appreciated, but he made no attempt to be liked personally by his people. 'Popularity — I've had it and lost it. It's like the tide . . . except that not even any foam remains . . .'[3] A more appropriate title for Leopold II would have been King of Belgium rather than King of the Belgians, for it was Belgium and not the Belgians he worked for.

In the devious world of international diplomacy Leopold was probably no worse than many other men. Where he was worse was in being cruel, unfeeling and vindictive. For, and this is by far and away the most serious charge levelled against Leopold II, in his latter years he obstinately refused to act — as was in his power, and there was no shortage of evidence — to put an end to large-scale atrocities that were taking place in the state he personally controlled.

How much one can blame his unhappy childhood and marriage is debatable; to some extent certainly, but it does not by any means absolve him. He was callous and ruthless. Time and time again he discarded men who disagreed with him or whom he felt were no longer of use to him; 'He treats men as we use lemons, when he has squeezed them dry he throws away the peel,' wrote one of the victims of Leopold's temper, Auguste Beernaert, his chief minister for ten years.[4] Banning and Brialmont suffered the same fate as did General Chazal, who devoted his life to serving Belgium and who helped Leopold when a young man. In 1886 when the fortifying of the Meuse was being debated, Chazal adopted a position in opposition to that of the king. Some months later the old man – he was now over eighty and had been in retirement for some years – found that he was not receiving his pension. On enquiry it emerged that the king himself had stopped it.[5]

Leopold's acerbity was feared by many. His irony and cynicism of which his father and sister had disapproved became accentuated and his treatment of people, if not cruel, was distasteful. The Crown Prince of Germany, the future Kaiser William II, records that at a dinner celebrating Leopold's silver wedding, the Count of Flanders, Leopold's brother Philippe who had become completely deaf, was discussing in unflattering terms with his neighbour some of the guests. It was the end of the meal and the guests had stopped talking and were waiting for the king to rise.

A court official, the Countess of Grünne, tried to make signs to the count to stop talking. He did not notice and continued. The countess looked imploringly at the king, hoping that he would move. He did not. Instead, he turned to the crown prince and said: 'Can you see how the Countess de Grünne is pleading with me to give the signal that dinner is over? I have no intention of doing so. I am letting my dear brother continue speaking. In that way I learn all sorts of things that otherwise no-one tells me.'[6]

Clearly the desire for money played an important part in the life of Leopold II; he certainly enjoyed being known as one of the richest men in Europe. But it was not money in itself that interested him. It was the power it conferred that he sought. Leopold needed financial resources to explore the Congo, later to build railways and to launch expeditions to expand its frontiers. And when the Congo began making a profit, he used the greater part of this money on buildings in Belgium. This was not done with personal glory in mind, for the benefactor of numerous public edifices was not disclosed during Leopold's lifetime. His artistic taste may well have left a great deal to be desired, though his constructions have stood the test of time better than many others. The physical improvement of Belgium was an end in itself, but it was also a means in that it contributed to increasing Belgium's international standing. However great his failings, Leopold II was undoubtedly a public-spirited monarch of his country.

In his personal life Leopold II, like his father, lived very simply. At Laeken the royal family made use of very few rooms and the king was content with his bedroom, study and drawing room. His bedroom was austerely furnished with a simple wooden bed and plain linen. The only personal touch was the souvenirs from his travels which he displayed there. His study was similarly furnished, with a large desk which photographs show piled high with papers. There was no heating and Frère-Orban had special fur-lined clothes made for his audiences with the king. When foreign visitors entered the study they sometimes noticed busts or pictures of distinguished compatriots. The American ambassador once remarked to a member of the court that he had been much impressed by seeing two busts of American statesmen. He was told that the king kept a stock of such things and brought out whatever was appropriate.[7]

After he had become king no more was heard of Leopold's weak chest, though his sciatic leg was never cured and he limped throughout his life. He was an impressive-looking man, well over six feet tall and broad shouldered (his frame had filled out in his twenties). The enormous nose that his mother had so despaired of was less overpowering now that he had a long thick beard. Nevertheless, in the early years of his reign medallists touched up his profile for coins. He had absolutely no interest in clothes. One of his costumes, which can be seen at the Musée Royal de l'Armée et d'Histoire Militaire in Brussels, is threadbare.

Leopold attributed his good health and vigour as an old man to the regime he had practised throughout his life. He rose at 5 am winter and summer, dressed, drank a large glass of warm water, '*ma boule d'eau*' he called it, and then went for a walk by himself.[8] By 6 am the first mail had been delivered to Laeken. This he read and dealt with as many letters as possible. At 7.30 am the *grand courrier* arrived and now, assisted by a secretary, he dictated replies, memoranda, signed decrees and went through his engagements for the day. This done, he sat down to breakfast. During the first years of his reign it was often taken in company with Marie-Henriette. Everything was laid out on the table and no servants were present to serve. Leopold drank tea, never coffee, ate five or six eggs, bread, a whole pot of marmalade and some fruit from the royal greenhouses.[9]

After breakfast – it would still not be 9 am – the king set out on another, longer walk, this time accompanied by an aide-de-camp, to whom he dictated his correspondence. The aide-de-camp could not, of course, write down his instructions. The memoirs of Leopold's various secretaries, aides-de-camp and equerries abound with accounts of how tired, footsore and out-of-breath they became trying to keep up with the king – even when Leopold was an old man and the men in question were young. About 11 am, his walk ended, Leopold drank another two glasses of warm water. He then sat down for a little to work and after that took more exercise, in the greenhouses or on horseback if he was at Laeken; in the streets round the Palais Royal if he was in Brussels. The socialist leader Emile Vandervelde remembers as a young man seeing the king taking his exercise in Ixelles. He does not seem to have excited much attention. If acknowledged, he lifted his hat and said 'Good day.'[10]

Visitors and members of the royal family joined the king for lunch which consisted of steak or mutton, frequently Leopold's favourite vegetables – spinach, endives and new carrots – and then cold meat. Fruit from the royal greenhouses was the usual dessert. The king's preference in wine was for claret. At lunch and dinner he drank two or three glasses but he would never permit champagne as he considered it an extravagance. For a large part of his life he smoked a cigar after lunch and dinner.

Lunch was over in half an hour, often twenty minutes, and even that time was not used for relaxation. Leopold usually talked politics and at extremely busy times read telegrams and documents at the table. One of his favourite expressions – the king used the English – was 'Time is money'; and immediately after leaving the table he would set out from Laeken for the Palais Royal where he saw his ministers and the many other men who played a part in his life. This over, he returned to Laeken for dinner which was served at 6.30 pm. There was soup followed by chicken or game; fruit again and perhaps a few chocolates. During various economy campaigns of the king's, the number of courses was reduced. Leopold enjoyed food but he was more a *grosse fourchette* than a gourmet.

After dinner Leopold retired to the drawing-room to read *The Times* which was specially delivered to him and ironed before he read it. It was, until the last years of his reign, his oracle (he cancelled his subscription in protest against attacks on him, and he had it bought at the Gare du Nord instead), but, contrary to what has often been claimed, it was certainly not the only newspaper he perused. He read practically all the Belgian newspapers, including those hostile to him, the *Daily Telegraph* and sometimes Indian newspapers. In his papers there are wads of newspapers which had been sent to Ostend or Ciergnon, in the Ardennes, with his mail. In addition, members of his staff and various contacts cut out articles in the foreign press of interest to him and these, it is clear from his references to them, he read.

It is perhaps superfluous to say that Leopold retired early to recuperate his energies for the following day. When Cousin Bertie, the Prince of Wales, proposed doing something in the early evening, Leopold replied, '*Ich bin aber so müde*' (but I am so tired).[11] It should however be pointed out that he worked a seven-day week and even on holiday in the Ardennes or Ostend, his day followed a similar pattern. Although a large number of his papers are missing, those that are available are voluminous, indeed daunting, in number. He wrote thousands of letters, memoranda and notes, to say nothing of his comments in writing on much that was put before him. His handwriting is virtually illegible. With practice one can get the sense of what is written but it would be presumptuous to claim that it is possible to read it word for word.

Leopold worked in French, though he was far from rigorous in his syntax and use of accents. He had an easily recognizable style and was aware of this. One of the qualifications demanded of his secretaries was to be able to imitate it, as the king liked to be given a draft of formal letters. This he almost always altered, and in anything written by himself it is extremely rare not to see erasures. In some cases, when it would be inappropriate for the king to write, Leopold himself prepared a letter for his secretary to copy out and sign. Many of his collaborators were anglophone and to them he wrote in English. He certainly spoke fluent English but his letters in English were drafted for him, though his grasp of the language was sufficiently good that he invariably changed quite a few expressions prepared for him. On one occasion he asked for a list of ending salutations in English, in order of friendliness. Leopold wrote on anything; in the margins of letters he received, on the back of documents, on envelopes and not infrequently on scraps of cheap paper that somehow fell beneath his hand.

Not all Leopold II's energies were devoted to *haute politique* and one of his ministers, Vanderpeereboom, reproached him: 'The King continues to be preoccupied with small things.'[12] Certainly Leopold read through meticulously every document to do with colonial policy and anything emanating from the Ministry of War, for example, individual appointments and army pay. On another level, travel arrangements fascinated him: he studied time-tables and worked out suitable train connections and hotel arrangements, not only for himself, but for those around him.

After the death of their son Leopold made an effort to be amiable with Marie-Henriette and in 1871 she was again pregnant. A third girl, Clementine, was born in 1872 but from then onwards the king and queen only saw each other when they were obliged to for ceremonial reasons. Leopold, realizing that there was little chance of having a son himself, transferred his attentions to his nephew Baudouin, elder son of his brother Philippe, who had been born a few months after the death of his own son.

As regards his daughters Leopold's one positive action was to attempt to change the laws of succession. Belgian law is straightforward on the subject. An inheritance must be divided among all children. In the late 1850s Leopold, then Duke of Brabant, had tried to have the law modified in its application to the royal family and now that he found himself only with daughters, he was even more determined that his personal fortune should not go to the foreign princes to whom he would be obliged to marry his daughters. The *chef du cabinet* of the time, Jules Malou, and most of the ministers, were prepared to go along with the king in changing the law in 1874.[13] A bill was drawn up ready to be put before the Chamber and Senate when Malou, after reflecting on the subject, changed his mind. He was not prepared, he decided, to tamper with one of the fundamental principles of the *Code Civil*.

> The law of succession is based on very strongly held and honourable human feelings, namely parental affection for children. The law is there to ensure that children cannot be cut off by their parents. The legal restrictions, combined with the principle of equal shares, ensures that the rights of the individual are upheld. The equality of all before the law is a fundamental principal of the law of this country.

Then, in an attempt to lighten the tone, with a *reductio ad absurdum*, he added:

In 56 years there might be a princess, a great-grand-daughter of a
Belgian king. If she loses her parents early on in her life, I am sure
that she would find a place in a Brussels orphanage. Later on she might
find a room for herself and work in a shop. Or she might even open
her own shop called *The Dynastic Heritage* ... The Princess X,
Fashions and Accessories.[14]

The king's riposte in the margin was, 'I prefer to see that happen rather
than that a Belgian prince should find himself in such a position. Perhaps
a cobbler in Brussels with the sign *Due to the improvidence of my ances-
tors*? Between the two ills let us choose the one least harmful to
Belgium.'[15]

Without Malou's backing the bill would not be accepted by parliament
and Leopold had – for the moment – to desist.

While all this had been taking place, arrangements were being made
to betroth Louise who was now sixteen. She says in her autobiography,
'I was praised on all sides in verse and in prose, with or without music,
and it seemed that I was "a flower of radiant beauty". I was quite taken
with the phrase.'[16] That is as may be. She was certainly presentable
enough, lively in personality and attractive looking. Prince Philip of
Coburg – whose grandfather, a brother of Leopold I, had married an Hungarian princess of the Kohary family – wanted to marry her; so did one
of the Hohenzollerns. But whereas Leopold did not want to become too
closely associated with Berlin, the idea of having a daughter at the Viennese court appealed to Marie-Henriette and, although he did not rank
high in the Almanack of Gotha, Philip was very rich. There was little
else to recommend him: he was dissolute, lacking in affection and ugly.

Louise was a romantic adolescent and she greatly enjoyed her wedding
as she was for once the centre of attention. 'The chants and prayers
carried me to heaven, although I by no means forgot the ritual of my
marriage and that I was the cynosure of all eyes'.[17] A few hours later
she saw things rather differently. 'Whilst all Brussels was dancing amid
a blaze of lights and illuminations, I fell from my heaven of love to what
was for me a bed of rock and a mattress of thorns.'[18] The apposite metaphor seems unintentional.

The marriage was a total failure. Louise loathed her thirty-one-year-
old husband with his unsalubrious tastes, and the family residence where
they lived, a damp castle in Hungary full of Gothic furniture and little
sanitation. 'Mon dieu! when I think of all this, the stuffed birds, the unhealthy books, the dirty jokes and the daily miseries of life – I am at a
loss to know how I endured it.'[19] Fortunately for Louise they spent a
fair amount of time at Vienna where she enjoyed court society. She was
witty and charming and attracted men, though admiration made it all

the more difficult for her to put up with her boorish and sometimes brutal husband.

One man who liked her was the Archduke Rudolph, heir to the Austrian throne, and it was because of this that he was prepared to consider marrying Louise's younger sister, Stephanie. Leopold had not been very happy about Louise's marriage from a political point of view and he was determined to make a more advantageous match for his second daughter. Stephanie was quieter than Louise and tolerably good looking in a rather mousy way. Louise claims that the idea of marrying Stephanie to Rudolph originated with her. In fact it was by a process of politico-religious elimination of European princesses that Stephanie was chosen and the fortune of her father was not a drawback, even though Charlotte had not been a good advertisement for the Belgian Coburgs.

The strange and beautiful Empress Elizabeth of Austria passed through Brussels in 1878 to look over the young princess. She was not impressed but she was so self-absorbed that she could not be bothered to object.[20] Rudolph, whose taste in women was more exotic and sophisticated than a fifteen-year-old schoolgirl could offer, actually responded positively: 'Stephanie is nice-looking, sensible, good and very distinguished.'[21]

The idea of his daughter becoming future Empress of Austria gave great pleasure to Leopold II, indeed no better match could be imagined. The wedding took place in April 1880 in Vienna. It was a cold, miserable day and the overly decorative dress did not flatter Stephanie. 'The only one who looked radiant was King Leopold.'[22] His second daughter suffered in much the same way that Louise had. Rudolph's womanizing and heavy drinking in no way abated and he continued to spend his time with his radical friends. The empress referred to Stephanie as 'that tiresome lout of a girl'.[23] Franz-Josef was concerned solely with matters of state. Stephanie was lonely and unhappy, though Rudolph treated her with affection. In 1883 she had a child and there was naturally disappointment when it was a girl, though in itself it was not too serious in a young woman. However, when doctors announced that Stephanie would not be able to have any more children, her position in Austria slumped. Rudolph continued to be kind and she tried much to his annoyance, to persuade him to lead a less debauched life. She could not turn to Louise for support since her more attractive sister enjoyed flirting with the crown prince and Louise's husband Philip was Rudolph's closest friend. When in January 1889 Rudolph and his mistress, Mary Vetsera, committed suicide it was Philip who found the bodies.

Stephanie of Belgium was incidental to the tragedy of Mayerling, even though she was Rudolph's wife. Franz-Josef and Elizabeth reproached her for not having exercised more control over her husband and blamed her for his death. Leopold and Marie-Henriette immediately took the train to Vienna to be with their daughter. It has been claimed that as soon as Leopold arrived he began trying to sell Congo shares. The story is almost certainly apocryphal although he did conduct Congo financial business while in Vienna. What is true is that Leopold saw Rudolph's suicide more as a dynastic slight than a personal tragedy for his daughter.

A more serious death in the family followed three years later when Prince Baudouin died of influenza at the age of twenty-three. Leopold was predisposed to look favourably on whoever was his heir (though the Count of Flanders never actually renounced his rights) but he seems to have been genuine in his liking for Baudouin. Nevertheless, Baudouin's death was above all a blow to the Belgian monarchy and Leopold felt it keenly. At the time of Baudouin's death he had been looking around for a suitable wife for his nephew: Princess Wilhelmina of Holland was a strong candidate in Leopold's eyes and the king was also thinking of his youngest daughter, Clementine. Coming on top of the death of his son and his disappointment at having three daughters, Baudouin's death embittered Leopold yet more. His cynicism increased; his hardness and lack of feeling became more marked. The older Leopold II emerged.

8 First Steps towards Africa

'I intend to find out discreetly whether there is anything doing in Africa.'[1]   Leopold II.

Central Africa began by being no more than one of the king's numerous colonial projects. Nevertheless it was Africa which finally provided the young, able, super-abundantly energetic, constitutional monarch of a small European country with the necessary outlet for his talents.

Interest in the Dark Continent in the nineteenth century originated largely in England where the Evangelical Revival led to pressure to abolish the slave-trade in the British empire and elsewhere. At the same time Africa became the focus for missionary zeal – as typified by David Livingstone. He spent more than twenty years in Africa spreading the Gospel and exploring all the territory north of the Boer colonies, discovering the Zambezi, the Victoria Falls and crossing the continent from coast to coast before embarking on his final journey. This took him through Tanganyika (where Stanley found him in 1871) to the river Lualaba, the latter being, though Livingstone did not know it, the upper reaches of the Congo.

Another product of Victorian England was the explorers, such as John Speke and James Grant who, starting from the Indian Ocean, arrived at the northern end of Lake Victoria and discovered a river into which the lake poured its waters; following this northward they met Sir Samuel Baker who had come up the river from Egypt – they had discovered the White Nile. Sir Richard Burton was also active in the same area, and he for his part was convinced that other sources of the Nile would be found. In West Africa Mungo Park's earlier exploration of the river Niger and basin was completed by English travellers. Between 1850 and 1870 other tracts of the Sahara and the region around Lake Chad were investigated by Germans, while an Anglo-German expedition penetrated the Sudan. The French were increasingly active in West Africa and in the early 1870s the Marquis de Compiègne et Marche, starting from Gabon on the west coast, discovered the river Ogooué which he established, despite competition from the Germans, as 'La Ligne Française' into the centre of the continent.

The discoveries of the explorers and the work of the missionaries created interest in Europe, not only among geographers, scientists, philanthropists and religious groups: it attacted the attention of a much wider public – Livingstone's funeral in 1874 was virtually a state occasion crowned by his burial in Westminster Abbey. The discovery of diamonds in the Transvaal in 1867 and the explorers' accounts of the mineral and agricultural potential of the continent caused businessmen to take notice and the opening of the Suez Canal in 1870 made access to East Africa much easier. The entrepreneurial spirit, and cupidity, of capitalists in Europe was stimulated; they were looking for new markets for the products of their industrial economies, for new sources of raw materials, and they possessed steam power which could make such trade realizable. It was clear that Africa was about to be linked to the world economy dominated by Western European countries.

There was no more assiduous follower of African exploration than Leopold II. In 1867 he joined the Société Géographique de Paris and was a subscriber to numerous journals emanating from France, England and Germany. There was, however, still very little Belgian interest in Africa. A small group of Antwerp businessmen organized a geographical conference in 1871, but no ripples of curiosity about Africa resulted from it.

The situation in France was quite different. French interest in exploration and colonies in the 1870s was not only a reaction to the loss of Alsace-Lorraine; France had been active in Africa for some years. The Société Géographique de Paris had been founded in 1821 and had been promoting since then voyages of discovery; after 1870 the aims of the Société were widened to include commercial interests.[2]

In August 1875 an international conference was held by the Société Géographique in Paris to which Leopold II contributed 1,000 francs. For this modest outlay he was able to send a representative, Emile de Borchgrave, and to gain access to the latest information and thinking on Africa, the Dark Continent dominating the conference. De Borchgrave was told to focus his attention on the group debating economic questions and that concerned with deciding where in Africa it would be most useful to send expeditions.

Africa was increasingly in the news at this time. The Sultan of Zanzibar visited England in July 1875 and The Times published an article describing how he and the Khedive of Egypt intended to create a vast Moslem empire in Central Africa. Then in August, Savorgnan de Brazza, a French naval officer of Italian parentage, set off, with financial backing from the

French admiralty, to explore the upper reaches of the Ogooué. Simultaneously, a German expedition was preparing to strike eastwards from the mouth of the Congo: Leopold knew that Africa would not remain *terra incognita* for much longer.

The king had been following for some time the progress of Verney Lovett Cameron in Africa. Cameron, a Scottish naval lieutenant, had been sent out by the Royal Geographical Society in 1872 to find Livingstone – the story of his being beaten by a Welsh-born American named Henry Morton Stanley, is too well known to bear retelling. On reaching Udjiji on Lake Tanganyika Cameron learnt that the missionary was dead; nevertheless he decided to push on and to take up Livingstone's work in trying to resolve the problem of the Lualaba river, and to establish whether it was the upper reaches of the Congo. In March 1875 his letter spelling out his aims was read to the Royal Geographical Society.

Thus when in November 1875 Cameron arrived at Benguela on the Angolan coast, having crossed the continent and identified the Lualaba as the Congo, the King of the Belgians was not taken by surprise. He was extremely interested and when he heard that Cameron could not afford the fare back to Europe he offered to pay it himself, the first outward manifestation of Leopold's interest in Central Africa.[3] By this time, however, the Royal Geographical Society had paid for the explorer to return to England.

Cameron had hoped to follow the Congo downstream, but at Nyangwe he was prevented from going down river any further by the hostility of the Arab slave-traders. His failure was to some extent due to his own lack of forcefulness and he struck south from the Lualaba through Katanga into Angola. At the end of December 1875 Cameron announced that he had annexed the Upper Congo Basin for Britain. He was repudiated soon afterwards by Disraeli's government. Britain did not want Central Africa.

In letters to *The Times* published in January 1876 describing his expedition, Cameron raved about the beauty of the countryside, the abundance of the crops, the mineral resources of Katanga; at the same time he described the horrors of the slave-trade. When Leopold visited London in May 1876 the first person he talked to was Cameron: two important pieces of information had emerged from the Scotsman's experience, firstly England was not interested in the Congo and secondly, in leading a crusade for suppression of the slave-trade, Leopold could create a role for himself in the movement that was opening up Africa.

Work had been going on in Brussels since August 1875 to build up as complete a dossier as possible for the king on the subject of Africa.

Baron Lambermont, according to his secretary Jean Guillaume, was summoned by his master:

> I have just got back from the Palace. The King said to me, 'I would like to do something in Africa; I have had this in mind for several days and would like you to help me ... You must know exactly what the explorers have done there and together we shall see what we can make of it with a peaceful humanitarian objective – my only concern and aim.'[4]

However, as Jean Guillaume was writing more than forty years later, one may reasonably question whether the beginnings of Leopold's interest in Africa were quite as clear cut and as rapidly arrived at as his account would have one believe. Nevertheless, whatever *ex post facto* simplicity is attributed to the king in 1876, the important point is that Guillaume, Lambermont and Emile Banning, the key figures at the Ministry of Foreign Affairs, were all involved in assembling information on Africa.

Early in 1876, Banning, who was officially archivist at the ministry, published a series of articles in *L'Echo du Parlement* on Africa, lauding the contribution of recent discoveries to science and commerce, and pointing out that all the signs indicated that the European powers would soon become interested in acquiring territory there.[5] For many years it was widely believed that Banning was Leopold II's intellectual mentor in African matters and that the king conceived his African plan, and the Conference of Brussels, after reading the articles in *L'Echo du Parlement*. The king's papers for these years are not available – Leopold's last secretary claimed that they had been destroyed as the king did not like piles of 'old papers' cluttering his offices, although some Belgian historians believe they still exist.[6] One cannot today do more than surmise, though in view of the king's interest in colonies over a period of twenty years one would think that he had little to learn from the articles, or maybe even that he had a hand in the writing of them.

Similarly, it is not known exactly when Leopold II decided to call a geographical conference in Brussels to discuss the future exploration and 'civilizing' of Africa. Even if the idea had come to him soon after the Paris conference he would clearly have to wait for a reasonable interval of time before convening another one. His ideas as to the role of such a conference seem to owe something to the German explorer Georg Schweinfürth, who wrote, that 'If the slave-trade was to be abolished it would be necessary to set up large negro states under the protection of the European Powers'.[7] De Brazza, who was advocating international co-operation in exploration, also seems to have contributed to the king's thinking and the international financial formula that de Lesseps had used successfully in financing the Suez Canal added a further element.

As the political and moral centre of gravity as regards African affairs lay in England, Leopold decided to visit London himself to sound out his ideas. Travelling *incognito* he was in London for a few days in mid-May 1876, then returned to Belgium for a further few days before again visiting England from 30 May to 12 June.[8]

On 30 May he got down to work immediately and saw Cameron at his hotel, Claridge's. After this he had dinner with the Prince and Princess of Wales, and the next day went to see Lady Burdett Coutts, patroness of the English Protestant missionaries, and again saw his cousin Bertie. A dinner was given at the Belgian legation at which General Wolseley, a popular hero of the time, was presented; Leopold also met Sir Henry Rawlinson and other prominent members of the Royal Geographical Society.[9] He then took the train up to Scotland to pay his respects to Queen Victoria at Balmoral. 'I have sought,' he told his cousin, 'to meet those most interested in bringing civilization to Africa. There is an important task to be undertaken there, to which I would feel honoured to contribute.'[10]

Leopold also went to Germany, though this visit seems to have been in a rather lower key than that to England. The Germans were attracted by the king's plans, and in both Berlin and London Leopold was held in high esteem as a disinterested philanthropist.

As he had received the agreement in principle of the British, French (the Belgian minister, Baron Beyens, encountered no opposition in Paris) and German governments, Leopold II decided that the moment was opportune to call a conference. The idea had clearly been germinating for some time but the first indication that it was to take place in September 1876 is to be found in a letter of 21 June.[11]

The Geographical Conference of Brussels was in all respects the work of Leopold II. The overall aims came from him (with drafting help from Lambermont) and he personally supervised arrangements down to the smallest detail. He made sure that the invitation cards were ready on time and, knowing Victorian sensibilities, he made sure that no *faux pas* were committed towards the English. 'The names must be correctly spelt, just as I have written them. G.C.B., F.R.G.S., K.C.B., M.P. These letters must, as applicable, be written after the names.'[12]

There were few men, the king knew well, who did not appreciate an invitation to stay with royalty and so Leopold wanted as many as possible of the delegates to be lodged at the Palais Royal. Unfortunately the palace was not equipped for this, being used mainly for offices: the king himself supervised the necessary furnishing arrangements and the staff found themselves sleeping in the linen cupboards. 'Put the archives temporarily in the main corridor ... pack up my library with great care ... You may call upon the services of a remover for this. Packing cases can be placed wherever there is space, including the stables in the rue Ducale, in the Palace cellars and if need be in the old linen room at Laeken.'[13] For the English delegates a special steamer was to be provided at Dover, and on their arrival at Ostend a special train would be waiting to take them to Brussels. At Ostend, and the frontier posts where the Continental delegates – Russian, Austrian, Italian as well as French and German – would pass, there would be no customs formalities.

On the evening of 11 September the king gave a dinner at the Palais Royal. He mixed with the guests and his constant questioning, despite his own considerable knowledge, was undoubtedly flattering and he created a favourable ambiance for the conference which was to begin the following day.

In a carefully thought-out speech, the King of the Belgians opened the Geographical Conference of Brussels. He began:

> Gentlemen, allow me to thank you very warmly for the eagerness with which you have responded to my invitation. In addition to the satisfaction which I shall derive from hearing the problems in which we are interested discussed, it will also give me great pleasure to meet the distinguished men whose work in favour of civilization I have followed with interest over the years ... Needless to say, in bringing you to Brussels I was in no way motivated by selfish designs. No, Gentlemen, if Belgium is small, she is also happy and contented with her lot. I would not, however, go so far as to say that I would remain indifferent to the honour which my country would derive from any important step forward which might result from this meeting.[14]

Quite how convincing the king's disclaimers of personal colonial ambitions were, one cannot say. Probably most of the delegates believed him as his recent colonial projects had been secret and known only to the governments of the countries with whom he had been dealing.

But the king did not speak only in polite generalities. He outlined the work before the conference, namely, the designation of operational bases in Africa on the coast of Zanzibar and at the mouth of the Congo: what routes should be opened up in the interior and where medical and scientific stations should be established from which to abolish the slave-trade: creation of a central international committee and national committees which would arouse and channel interest in Africa through the international committee.

Leopold knew exactly what decisions he wanted the conference to arrive at. He stepped down from the rostrum, literally and metaphorically, on 12 September 1876 hoping that he had created the optimum conditions for his proposals to be accepted. The conference was very well stage-managed: a distinguished Russian explorer, Pierre Semenov, was made chairman; while the Belgian delegation was told by Lambermont to keep a low profile and let the foreigners shine.[15]

The king's proposal to set up scientific and medical posts was immediately adopted. Their location, though, called for discussion and two groups were set up. That under Sir Henry Rawlinson came up with an extremely ambitious scheme covering the breadth of the continent from Zanzibar to the Angolan coast. From this axis three other lines of stations would extend in the direction of the Nile, Zambezi and Congo. The second group, under Semenov, had more modest ideas. Roughly following Cameron's route, they proposed setting up three stations, at Udjiji, at Nyangwe on the Lualaba and at Bagamoyo, near to Zanzibar. A compromise between the two schemes was adopted.

A special committee was constituted to discuss the king's third proposal. It reported to the conference suggesting that an international commission and national committees should be set up but Leopold, who was taking part in the concluding session, pointed out that they had not clearly defined the functions of, and relations between, the two bodies. The committee went back to work and returned with a more detailed proposal. An international commission, under a president, and composed of the presidents of the main geographical societies represented at the conference, would be created. The commission would direct, by means of an executive committee, the enterprises to be undertaken and manage the funds. The executive committee would be composed of the president, four members (chosen in the first instance by the conference and later by the international commission) plus a secretary-general and treasurer designated by the president. The role of the national committees would be to keep the international commission informed as to what was happening in their respective countries and to interest as many people as possible in explorations, not to mention money-raising.[16]

Sir Bartle Frere, President of the Royal Geographical Society, proposed the King of the Belgians for the post of president. This was greeted with great applause. Leopold said how flattered he was; he would accept but only for a year as the presidency ought to be rotated among the various countries.

The Brussels Geographic Conference was a brilliant success for Leopold II. Europe recognized him as leader of the crusade to bring civilization to Africa. The International African Association (its initials in French are AIA and it is in this form that it is usually known) had been created with the King of the Belgians at its head and with wide powers.

It has been claimed that Leopold had purely philanthropic motives in setting up the AIA. It is difficult to go along with this in the absence of any evidence that he had abandoned his earlier colonial aspirations, indeed he was writing in 1877, 'I do not want to miss the opportunity

of our obtaining a share in this magnificent African cake.'[17] Emile Banning had been advocating the creation of Belgian stations in Central
Africa and the pursuit of purely national ends. His sovereign was in agreement with Banning's long-term aim to ultimately acquire a colony, but
the king was a more subtle mind. His tactics were to create an innocuous-
seeming international structure for the opening up of Central Africa
behind which he could pursue his own ends. He had learnt from his previous attempts to find a colony that the Powers, Britain in particular,
were not disposed to allow Belgium to have a colony. Furthermore, there
was simply not sufficient interest in Belgium for national stations in
Africa to be supported.

On the other hand, it seems overly harsh to describe the AIA as 'a
spurious exploring and scientific organisation'.[18] Leopold II wanted the
AIA to work, to undertake expeditions that would increase knowledge
of Central Africa. He intended to dominate it but he also wanted it to
be genuinely international and functional, and if the member countries
of the AIA demonstrated that they preferred to undertake exploration on
a purely national basis, for their own ends, for that one cannot blame
the King of the Belgians.

Immediately after the closure of the conference Leopold set to finding
suitable men with whom to work and to seeing that the various national
committees were formed as planned. Lambermont continued to collaborate with him, but the Belgian government dissociated itself from the
king's initiatives. Leopold was in no way disappointed by this attitude,
for it gave him greater freedom of action than having to manœuvre within
the limits of official Belgian diplomacy. He did, however, ask to be permitted to second individual members of the foreign service for his personal use.

It had been expected that the secretary-general of the AIA would be
of a different nationality from that of the president. Jules Greindl, who
was again in Madrid, was therefore very surprised when he received a
letter from Lambermont in October 1876 offering him the post of secretary-general. He replied saying that he did not feel himself qualified for
the job, adding that he was surprised that as a Belgian he had been asked.
Lambermont, the king's spokesman, replied that on the contrary it was
indispensable to have a Belgian.[19] A first step had been taken to strengthen
the king's position within the AIA.

A Belgian national committee was set up with the Count of Flanders
as president. In France the *Société Géographique de Paris* met on 16
October and began forming a national committee under the presidency
of Ferdinand de Lesseps. He immediately launched a fund-raising drive.
The Germans for their part in December 1876 formed the *Deutsche Afri-
kanische Gesellschaft*; in Holland Prince Henry became president of the

national committee.[20] No American delegates had been able to attend
the Brussels conference but opinion in the United States was sympathetic
towards Leopold. The king paid considerable attention to the American
national committee, no doubt hoping for substantial financial backing
from rich American philanthropists. At the beginning of 1877 he was considering a visit to the United States later in the year when he hoped to
'set up a movement in favour of opening up Africa'; more specifically,
he asked an American judge, 'Do you think that a lottery for 3,500,000
dollars could be arranged? Two million dollars for the African enterprise,
one million to be divided among the winning numbers and half a million
to cover organization expenses, publicity etc.'[21]

However, in England the situation developed quite differently from
how Leopold had hoped. The British delegates led by Sir Bartle Frere,
Sir Henry Rawlinson and Sir Rutherford Alcock had been among the
most enthusiastic at the conference and they returned home determined
to establish an English national committee. Formation of this committee
was entrusted to the Royal Geographical Society and the subject was discussed at its meetings in November 1876. But at this point the Foreign
Office stepped in. Alcock was called in by the permanent under-secretary,
Lord Tenterden, who drew his attention to what he, Tenterden, considered to be the inadequate provision contemplated for protection of
the AIA's operations. Alcock rather lamely replied that he hoped no protection would be required. The point though had been made.

Worse though was to come. A few days later a memorandum by Sir
Henry Thring, legal counsellor to the Home Office, raised more important objections. The Prince of Wales had promised Leopold that he would
become president of the English national committee – he and his wife
had stayed with Leopold at Laeken in August 1876 so he knew the king's
aims personally. However, Thring was not only opposed to the prince's
accepting the presidency, he also cast doubts as to the wisdom of any
British participation in the AIA. In particular he objected to the abolition
of the slave-trade as one of the association's aims.

1. It would seem to be clear that the repression of such trade is a
matter for state interference and not within the province of any private
association.

2. Again the establishment of stations throughout Africa is in effect
the establishment of factories such as laid the foundations of British
power in India, and must of necessity involve grave commercial questions and interference in disputes incidental to all trading transactions
in uncivilized countries.

3. It is quite conceivable that an international association, of which
the majority would necessarily be foreigners, might, without any hos-

tile intention, be disposed to favour views which would be disapproved of alike by the English [community], and by their delegates on the Association.[22]

Leopold watched events in England – a national committee was set up in Scotland in October 1876 – with anxiety. In November 1876 he wrote to Lambermont telling him to pay particular attention to England and in November 1876 he sent the baron on a mission to England to chivvy Frere and his colleagues. The Foreign Office took a quite different line with Lambermont than that with Alcock, and told him that they had no objection to the setting up of a British national committee. Leopold was not deceived; he realized that the British were reneging. The Prince of Wales' secretary wrote to General Ponsonby, Queen Victoria's secretary, on 27 December: 'The Prince had a most despairing letter yesterday from the King of the Belgians who had heard a rumour that this country intended to decline having anything to do with his African association. It is quite true that HRH thinks that in its present form England cannot join.'[23] Having appealed to Cousin Bertie without success, Leopold then turned to Queen Victoria, reminding her of her continued support for his African endeavours. 'As Bertie promised me his support, I have launched this project almost everywhere. It has been well received on the Continent but suddenly the English who were initially enthusiastic, have become hesitant because of Bertie's legal adviser ... I have already stated that I am ready to accept any modifications.'[24]

All effort was in vain. The Royal Geographical Society decided that it could not become involved with an international body whose objectives were other than those connected directly with geography. The British opted out of the AIA. Leopold was bitterly disappointed but in the long run the British withdrawal vastly strengthened his own position as a separate force in the movement to open up Africa.

9 Henry Morton Stanley

'Here lies the Congo kingdom, great and strong,
Already led by us to Christian ways;
Here flows Zäire, the river clear and long,
A stream unseen by men of olden days.'[1]

Camoens, *Lusiads, translated by Sir Richard Burton.*

On 17 September 1877 the news broke in Europe that H.M. Stanley had arrived at Boma, at the mouth of the river Congo, having crossed equatorial Africa at its widest part, the first white man to do so. From a village on the Lower Congo he had written, on 4 August 1877, a letter addressed 'To any Gentleman who speaks English at Embomma' (Boma).

Dear Sir,

I have arrived at this place from Zanzibar with 115 souls, men, women and children. We are now in a state of imminent starvation ... There are no provisions in the country that may be purchased, except on market days, and starving people cannot afford to wait ... I beg you not to disregard my request ... The supplies must arrive within two days, or I may have a fearful time of it among the dying. Of course I hold myself responsible for any expense you may incur ...

Yours sincerely
Henry M. Stanley
Commanding Anglo–American Expedition
for Exploration of Africa

He added, with the superfluity that earned him a ridicule he could never understand: 'P.S. You may not know me by name. I therefore add, that I am the person that discovered Livingstone in 1871. H.M.S.'[2]

It was 999 days since Stanley had left the Indian Ocean, in the course of which he had walked, or been rowed, 7,000 miles, circumnavigated the two great lakes, Victoria and Tanganyika, and followed the Congo river from one of its sources for 1,600 miles, shooting cataracts, sometimes having to transport his boats overland and repeatedly fighting for his life against hostile tribes. He had lost every white member of his expedition and 173 Africans.

Publication of the explorer's arrival caused a sensation in Europe. But it did not surprise Leopold II. Ever since Cameron had shown in 1875 that it was possible to cross the continent, Leopold had believed that Stanley's expedition, of which he was aware, stood a good chance of emerging at the west coast.

The first Europeans, the Portuguese under Diego Cam, had arrived at the mouth of the Congo in 1482. Three years later Cam returned to Portugal, taking some Congolese hostages who were suitably impressed by Lisbon, so that when they returned home they persuaded their king to receive a Portuguese ambassador and, more importantly, to accept Christianity. The King of the Congo was converted in 1492, the country followed, and in 1534 a cathedral was built in the capital which was renamed San Salvador. Later in the sixteenth century an incursion by fierce tribes of uncertain provenance overwhelmed the kingdom and the Portuguese came to the aid of the Congolese king. In gratitude he ceded to Portugal the strip of territory from the mouth of the Congo to the river Cuanza. This seems to have marked the apogee of Portuguese influence in the Congo. Whether as a result of the cession or not, they moved south and occupied Angola and embarked on the construction of the city of Sao Paulo de Luanda. Their interest in the Congo declined and the Congo never became a Portuguese colony, although it maintained diplomatic, cultural and religious ties with Portugal.

However, the dominating factor in relations between Europe and the Congo for nearly four centuries was the slave-trade.[3] This had existed before the arrival of the Portuguese although they came to play a leading role. It has been estimated that 13,250,000 slaves were exported from the Congo between the arrival of the Portuguese and 1885.[4]

Because of the cataracts 200 miles from its mouth the economic potential of the Congo river system was limited. At the beginning of the nineteenth century the most important commodity was ivory, as it was valuable and did not deteriorate in transport. Though subject to Portuguese government monopoly, a certain amount was sent by the north-westerly flowing rivers in order to by-pass Portuguese territory. From here it passed along numerous side routes, through the forest and down streams which flowed towards the Atlantic, to the European trading factories scattered along the coast north of Angola.

Leopold II was in no doubt as to what he wanted in the long run and even if the AIA had succeeded in becoming a viable organization, it constituted only the first stage in the king's plan. But exactly how to go about attaining his ends, Leopold was not sure. After the Brussels Conference he was thinking in terms of establishing trading posts in Africa, and in the early months of 1877 considered the Cameroons as the most likely location.[5]

At the same time he knew that Stanley was descending the Congo river, the great blank on the map of Africa. Three weeks before the international commission of the AIA was due to meet he wrote: 'It seems to me that the first thing we should do is to find out for sure whether Stanley has reached the Lualaba.'[6] (The river was not then known as the Congo.)

When the first, and last, plenary session of the international commission took place on 20 June 1877 its major decision was to authorize the executive committee to send out expeditions to Africa with a view to establishing stations. It put off until a later stage the abolition of slavery and concentrated its energies on choosing a flag, a blue background with a gold star at the centre. The choice, according to Stanley, representing bright hope in the African darkness.[7]

The international commission which was supposed to be the 'parliament' of the AIA thus handed over control of the association to the executive committee. The national representatives on the international commission were 'rotten boroughs' from the outset, but they could have asserted their constitutional rights. They did not do so and Leopold, re-elected president, could from now onwards ignore the international commission. He again protested that he would only remain president for a little while longer, being convinced that 'it was not in the best interests of the African mission for control to remain for too long in the same hands'.[8] He could afford such utterances as he had retained the sanction of internationalism and had taken complete control over the AIA.

The executive committee then set about sponsoring expeditions to Africa. All expeditions under the auspices of the AIA were organized by the Belgian national committee, hardly surprisingly as it was the only one to contribute any appreciable sums. Leopold himself provided most of the money. The first expedition led by Louis Crespel, Ernest Cambier and Arnold Maes left for Zanzibar in November 1877. Crespel and Maes died soon after their arrival in Africa, but Cambier reached Lake Tanganyika and founded a station at Karema. A second expedition under Emile Popelin and Theodore van den Heuvel set out in 1879 but this and two later ones failed. The leaders were for the most part unskilled in the work to be carried out and little or nothing was accomplished at great loss of life and suffering. Emile Storms, who led the last one in 1882 (they all set out from the east coast), did manage to reach Karema and succeeded, without too much hindrance, in establishing another post on the lake. The value of these expeditions lay in their diverting attention from the work being pursued from the west coast.

Leopold II was an astute judge of men and he appreciated the importance of having the right men to lead African expeditions. All that he

had read about Stanley led him to believe that he was the man he needed
to work for him in Africa. The explorer was still on his way back to
Europe when the king wrote to the Belgian minister in London:

    1. I would like to see Stanley as soon as he has been fêted in London.

    2. If Stanley appeals to me, I shall provide him with the money neces-
sary for him to explore fully the Congo and its tributaries, and to establish stations there.

    3. According to circumstances, I will endeavour to transform these
stations into Belgian settlements, either afloat or on land, which would
belong to us.

    I believe that if I commission Stanley to take possession in my name
of any given place in Africa, the English would stop me ... I am therefore thinking in terms of entrusting Stanley with a purely exploratory
mission which will offend no-one and will provide us with stations,
staffed and equipped, which we will put to good use once they
have got used, both in Europe and in Africa, to our being on the
Congo.'

In a relatively short letter the king had set out his African design. It was
now a matter of sounding out Stanley.

The explorer arrived in Italy at the beginning of January 1878 and from
Genoa took the train to Marseilles where the local geographical society
was to give a dinner in his honour. As he stepped from the train he was
greeted by Greindl and General Sanford, an American who had been us
consul in Brussels for some years and who, though now retired, was a
close collaborator of Leopold's. Stanley was not interested in working
for the AIA. His aim was to hand over to England the fruits of his exploration and he was en route for London, where he hoped the government
would declare annexation of the Congo so he fobbed the emissaries off.
'I am so sick and weary that I cannot think with patience of any suggestion
that I should personally conduct it ... at present I cannot think of anything more than a long rest and sleep.'[10]

The Royal Geographical Society of London which in previous years
had treated Stanley as a journalist and not a *bona fide* explorer, fêted
him. The press made him into a popular hero and he was invited to lecture
throughout the country. But the British government was not interested
in annexing the Congo. From February to May 1878 Stanley remained
in England, writing his two-volume account of the crossing of Africa,
Through the Dark Continent, and awaiting a summons from the Foreign
Office. He dined out practically every evening in the hope of influencing
people. He put his case before the Prince of Wales who by way of reply
pointed out that Stanley's decorations were placed in the wrong order.[11]
By the end of May he was disillusioned with England and English society;

his manuscript now at the publishers, he decided to accept the invitation of the King of the Belgians.

Stanley was now thirty-seven; a highly ambitious, able, resilient but complex-ridden man. Despite his success as a journalist and an explorer he could not overcome his feeling of shame about his lowly origins. He was an illegitimate child and had passed much of his miserable childhood in a workhouse in North Wales before emigrating to America at the age of seventeen and, whereas immigrants who made good were socially acceptable in the United States, in Victorian society his behaviour seemed crude and his accent transatlantic. Though Stanley tried pathetically hard to become an English gentleman, he was ill at ease in the society that wined and dined him and he never gained the acceptance he so dearly wanted.

The King of the Belgians was outside all this. He recognized the talents of the Anglo-American, his determination and endurance, his genuine belief that the opening up of Africa by Europeans was for the benefit of Africans; he detected Stanley's taste for spectacular feats, his need for constant praise and, not least, his acceptance that to undertake the sort of tasks he found challenging it was necessary to have a rich and influential sponsor.

Leopold was naturally delighted when he learnt that Stanley was coming to Brussels in June 1878. His ideas for using the explorer had developed during the previous few months.

> I believe that it would be a good idea to enter into an agreement with this able and enterprising American and to undertake to provide him with $100,000 a year for five years. With such money he could set up a base on the Congo and from there spread out in all directions on, and around, this great river.
>
> If Stanley accepts my offer and thinks that such a plan is feasible, I might well increase my subscription to the International Association by 50,000 or maybe 100,000 francs.[12]

Stanley for his part arrived in Brussels with his ideas for the Congo basin clearly formulated. He wanted a railway and finance company to be created, a *Société Internationale de Commerce*, to build a railway from Matadi to Stanley Pool, that is to by-pass the cataracts and open up the Upper Congo. He envisaged this commercial venture as being under the patronage of Leopold II. Alongside this he saw the AIA as a philanthropic organization which would independently establish 'stations' up the Congo.

The king approved of Stanley's idea for a railway company but it was not something that could be achieved in the immediate future.[13] Leopold was concerned at this stage with raising money for the establishment of bases along the Congo for, even with this increased contribution, money would have to be found elsewhere.

Four million was contributed by two subscribers, of whom one was probably the Belgian banker Léon Lambert, a son-in-law of the French Rothschilds and friend and banker of Leopold. Greindl was instructed to try and raise the rest in France, Holland and Germany.[14] The response in Paris was encouraging, but when the Dutch *Afrikaansche Handels Vereeniging* was approached the scheme foundered. Leopold II attached great importance to the participation of the Rotterdam-based company as it was already established and trading at the Congo mouth. However, representatives of the *Afrikaansche Handels Vereeniging* rejected the proposed *Société Internationale de Commerce* and insisted that, financed by grants, a syndicate should be set up (*un comité à fonds perdus*) to undertake a purely fact-finding expedition, staffed by engineers, before deciding on any capital investment.[15] Sanford laid the Dutch proposal before Stanley. The reply was clear.

> He is not disposed to go on the preliminary expedition as proposed by the Dutchmen ... it is impossible, he says, for these unacclimatized, untried specialists to go down without disaster unless the way be prepared for them ... and he lays great stress then upon a smaller, permanent expedition ... He would want to be engaged for this for five years at £1,000 per annum.[16]

In the end a scheme agreeable to all concerned was worked out. The compromise was that only one organization was to be set up. However, it was to send out, not merely a reconnaissance expedition as the Dutch wanted, but one which would establish permanent stations, these to be available for use for commercial as well as for philanthropic ends. The *Comité d'Etudes du Haut Congo* (CEHC), as the new syndicate was to be called, was formed on 25 November 1878. It was a commercial organization with a capital of 1,000,000 francs, Leopold II, through Lambert, being the chief subscriber with 265,000 francs, followed by the Dutch with 130,000. The two British subscribers, James Hutton, head of a Manchester firm trading in West Africa, and William Mackinnon, a Scottish shipping magnate, each contributed about 30,000 francs.[17] Colonel Maximilien Strauch, who had replaced Greindl as secretary-general of the AIA, became president, Leopold, honorary president.

After spending July in Paris where, to his chagrin, he was more warmly received than in London, Stanley returned to England. He had not committed himself to Leopold in June 1878 and tried again to arouse public opinion in England. He wrote bitterly in his journal:

> I had hoped to have inspired Englishmen with something of my own belief in the future of the Congo. I delivered addresses, after-dinner

speeches, and in private have spoken earnestly to try and rouse them to adopt early measures to secure the Congo basin for England. Even as late as October, November and December ... I continued trying to impress upon them that some day they would regret not taking action, but it was of no use. I do not understand Englishmen at all ... My reward has been to be called a mere penny-a-liner.[18]

In December he abandoned all hope of England and returned to Brussels. Leopold had been anxiously watching Stanley's efforts to persuade the British government to annex the Congo and was much relieved when on 10 December 1878 the explorer signed a contract with the *Comité d'Etudes*. The seemingly simple task assigned to Stanley was to construct three stations between the Lower Congo and Stanley Pool and to explore the commercial possibilities of the Upper Congo. If these studies yielded a satisfactory result, the subscribers to the CEHC would form two companies, one for the construction of a link between the Lower and Upper Congo, and the other to establish navigation and develop commerce on the Upper Congo. A shroud of secrecy enveloped the *Comité d'Etudes* and the national committees of the AIA were not informed of its creation.

Preparations for Stanley's expedition began immediately. Suitable Europeans had to be chosen, goods of every kind – prefabricated houses, wagons, barter ware – obtained. It was not until June 1879 that the cargo ship left Antwerp, arriving in July at the Congo mouth. Stanley himself had left Brussels on 10 January as he was going first to Zanzibar to recruit African porters. It would have been more convenient to use west coast natives and, even before Stanley had signed his contract, Leopold had written to the British prime minister, Benjamin Disraeli, about recruiting in their west coast possessions. Disraeli had replied in guarded terms: 'I myself know nothing of Mr. Stanley except from his public acts ... and it seems that our colonial authorities would not much care to assist Mr. Stanley in making engagements of the kind suggested ... with men belonging to tribes subject to, and protected by, England.'[19]

The Sultan of Zanzibar, although subject to not inconsiderable influence from the British, was nominally independent and so worth cultivating in the circumstances. Stanley took with him a miniature of Leopold set in brilliants and a service in gold plate to offer to the sultan and gold watches for the American consul and the leading Hindu merchants, in his own words 'to secure the cordial co-operation of everybody'.[20]

Obfuscation was the order of the day and Stanley left Brussels by train for Marseilles, travelling under the name of 'Monsieur Henri'. At Marseilles he boarded ship for Suez where his own ship, the *Albion*, was waiting to take him down the Suez Canal and on to Zanzibar. His work there successfully completed, he sailed up the east coast and docked at Aden. There a letter from Strauch was awaiting him telling him of the Dutch firm's bankruptcy and summoning him to Brussels. Stanley refused to comply, explaining that his Zanzibaris might well rebel if left in limbo on board ship. Instead, he agreed to meet Strauch at Gibraltar, en route for the Congo.

One might have expected that the financial failure of one of the chief subscribers would have jeopardized the whole undertaking. On the contrary, when Stanley met Strauch he learnt of vastly more expanded plans for his expedition and he was told to obtain territorial concessions.

> It is not a question of Belgian colonies ... It is a question of creating a new State, as big as possible, and of running it. It is clearly understood that in this project there is no question of granting the slightest political power to negroes. That would be absurd. The white men, heads of the stations, retain all power. They are the absolute commanders of stations populated by free and freed negroes. Every station would regard itself as a little republic. Its leader, the white man in charge, would himself be responsible to the Director-General of Stations, who in turn would be responsible to the President of the Confederation.
>
> ... The work will be directed by the King, who attaches particular importance to the setting-up of stations ... the best course of procedure would no doubt be to secure concessions of land from the natives for the purposes of roads and cultivation, and to found as many stations as possible.[21]

The explorer was in general agreement with the aims of the new directive but did not consider them realizable in the immediate future. In his opinion it would take quite some time after establishing stations before confederating the native tribes and, furthermore, his expedition, possessing only limited resources, could not take on more ambitious schemes than had already been agreed to.

Leopold II feared that too much emphasis was still being laid on the philanthropic nature of the enterprise, and in a note of August 1879 one finds distinctly firmer views set out. It is not known whether the document, a copy of which can be found at the Ministry of Foreign Affairs in Brussels, was communicated to Stanley. 'When three stations are properly established, it will be possible to constitute them into a Free State to which may be added further stations and settlements beyond the immediate limits of the Congo.'[22]

The bankruptcy of the Dutch plus the rapid depletion of the financial resources of the CEHC enabled Leopold in November 1879 to propose a new scheme. The subscribers, he held, could not be expected to provide yet more money; he himself offered to provide the new capital on condition that the *comité* as originally constituted was dissolved. The new capital would be used for the establishment of three stations on the Congo and a portion of their trading profits would be divided among those subscribers who accepted the king's proposal. The distribution of profits, increased annually by five per cent, would continue until the original sums had been redeemed. The scheme was agreed to: the *Comité d'Etudes* ceased to exist and Leopold took over sole charge of the Congo enterprise. In addition, his magnanimity was duly noted and appreciated by the shareholders. Stanley, however, was not told of the demise of the CEHC.

Not satisfied with having dispatched Stanley to the Congo to work for him, Leopold was looking around for other suitable men to further his ambitions, and in August 1879 de Brazza and Noël Ballay, another French explorer, visited Brussels at the king's invitation. He invested them with the Order of Leopold and discussed Africa with them. He then proposed to de Brazza that he should return to Africa under the auspices of the AIA. The Frenchman refused. But worse, while in Brussels he had been informed of Stanley's aims, and repaired to Paris where a French expedition was rapidly organized. De Brazza left for West Central Africa four months later in December 1879.

The front of internationalism which enabled Leopold to woo de Brazza also led him to make overtures to an Englishman whose career he had followed for some years and who seemed ideally qualified to further the king's schemes in Africa. Colonel Charles Gordon, Chinese Gordon as he was known from his exploits in the Far East, had in 1879 recently resigned from his post as governor-general in the Sudan. Leopold's idea was to employ Gordon to set up a chain of stations beginning on the east coast, and William Mackinnon, one of the British subscribers to the CEHC who knew Gordon, was asked to approach him. The colonel's commitment to the abolition of slavery was well known and, to tempt him, it was suggested that Zanzibar would provide an ideal base for such operations. Gordon came forward with the alternative idea of his entering the sultan's service and striking a blow at the slave-trade by extending the sultan's effective authority into the hinterland. Leopold saw Gordon on a number of occasions early in 1880, but Gordon remained convinced that the AIA's lack of international status must necessarily involve obtaining a concession from the sultan and the use of his flag.[23] This the king refused to contemplate.

Leopold had failed to enlist either de Brazza or Gordon. All his hopes in 1880 rested with Stanley.

10 The Race for the Congo

*'The time will come ... when this river will
become an international question. Happy
that nation which will soonest avail itself of
what I have disclosed.'*[1]

Henry Morton Stanley.

Stanley arrived at the mouth of the Congo on 14 August 1879, 'with the
novel mission of sowing along its banks civilized settlements, to peacefully conquer and subdue it, to remould it in harmony with modern ideas
into National States within whose limits ... justice and law and order
shall prevail, and murder and lawlessness and the cruel barter for slaves
shall for ever cease'.[2]

Fine words by the explorer, but was Stanley aware of his patron's
ulterior motives in financing the expedition? At the beginning of the year
the explorer had written, 'The Belgians strike me as being a peculiarly
innocent people. Innocent in the sense of not being suspicious of other
people's penetrative power.'[3] He seems to have included their king in
his judgement but in August 1879, that is after the Gibraltar instructions,
he wrote in his diary:

> The King is a clever statesman. He is supremely clever, but I have
> not had thirty opportunities of conversing with him without penetrat-
> ing his motives ... He has not been so frank as to tell me outright what
> we are to strive for. Nevertheless it has been pretty evident that under
> the guise of an International Association he hopes to make a Belgian
> dependency of the Congo basin.[4]

Though he knew what Leopold wanted, he was aware also that the king
was entirely dependent on what he, Stanley, could do for him. 'Were I
in his place,' the explorer reflected, 'I would certainly want greater
security from my principal agent than a bare promise.'[5] But whatever
imperialistic designs Leopold might entertain, the Anglo-American held
the real power. He knew it: Leopold also. 'We must equip Stanley from
top to toe and give him staff and supplies in abundance,' ordered the
king, 'otherwise we are lost.'[6] When the barrage of letters from Brussels

began to reach him at Vivi in December 1879, Stanley realized that his employer could do no more than exhort him.

Only a week after landing at Banana Point, at the mouth of the Congo, Stanley was leading his men up-river. He describes the first, easy stage of the ascent of the river, the flotilla gliding along the three-mile-wide estuary to the beating of tom-toms, the mangrove swamps on the banks, the creeks from which native canoes suddenly darted out, the hot, humid, enervating air. The explorer's style in his two-volume work *The Congo and the Founding of the Free State*, may be heavy and luxuriant: so is the atmosphere of the Congo.

From Boma, the chief entrepôt of the Lower Congo, the expedition passed by the various national trading posts, French, Dutch and Portuguese, on the north bank, to Mussuko. By 26 September they were at Vivi where, after several days of palaver with the native chiefs as to the price of the ground to be conceded, a station was founded. It took several months to erect the station as work began in the hot and continued through into the rainy season; several Europeans collapsed and were incapable of supervising the building. Finally, by the end of January 1880 the station possessed headquarters, houses, all painted inside and outside, stables for the mules, a garden and roads from the landing place to the headquarters and from there to a source of drinking water. To celebrate Stanley gave a dinner – he had a personal supply of wines with him – for the Europeans in his expedition and local chiefs. The first toast was to His Majesty the King of the Belgians, the second to Queen Victoria and a third to the President of the United States.[7]

Leopold was little interested in hearing about festivities at Vivi. He wanted Stanley to advance faster. Stanley replied explaining about the climatic conditions, the difficulties of the terrain and his meagre manpower resources. (It is now clear that it was above all his lack of porters, and other auxiliary personnel that caused his slow progress.) Not that the explorer considered speed critical: talk of de Brazza's approach from the north did not frighten him. On 6 February 1880 he wrote to Strauch: 'I beg leave to say that I am not a party in a race for the Stanley Pool, as I have already been in that locality just two and a half years ago and I do not intend to visit it again until I can arrive with my 50 tons of goods, boats and other property, and after furnishing the second station.'[8]

Stanley was determined to set up the stations and make trading agreements as originally agreed. He signed the first commercial treaty at Vivi on 13 June 1880, according to which the *Comité d'Etudes* was given the sole and exclusive right to cultivate any part of the Vivi district, excepting that required by natives, and to trade in it.

However, from the point of view of ascending the river, the expedition was not coming up to expectations. In the summer of 1880 Leopold was alarmed to learn that it was progressing only at an average rate of twenty-two miles a month and de Brazza was outstripping it. He immediately ordered Stanley not to attempt to found any more stations nor to build any more roads but, with a light caravan, to head as quickly as possible for Stanley Pool. Stanley retorted: 'Double our power and we will double our speed; treble the working power and our progress will be three times quicker.'[9] He was still only at the Bula River, not far upstream from Vivi, in November 1880 when the Count Savorgnan de Brazza announced himself. Stanley invited him into his tent, offered him lunch and, despite his poor French and de Brazza's rudimentary English, they managed to make themselves mutually understood. De Brazza described the course he had followed up the Ogooué, striking south towards the Congo, following the line of its tributary, the Lefini, to Stanley Pool, where he had left one black soldier and two black sailors, before descending towards the coast. De Brazza's lack of candour with Stanley at this meeting as to the real nature of his activities at Stanley Pool featured prominently in the feud they were later to pursue.

As he left the camp de Brazza pointed at the mountain, Mount Ngoma, which loomed above it and remarked: 'It will take you six months to pass that with your wagons. Your force is too weak altogether for such work as you are engaged in; you should have at least 500 men.'[10] To Stanley the taunt was a challenge. The rock rose sheer from the water so that there was no room to pass between it and the river, but Stanley noticed a narrow track made by animals some twenty feet above ground level, and this he decided to enlarge. By means of ropes attached to poles the rocks above were pushed over, so that on falling they formed a sort of causeway. On these smaller stones could be laid to provide a foundation for his road. The work advanced at the rate of a few yards a day and it took nearly a month to complete 400 yards. The nine-foot wagons, with their load of boats and boilers, were then safely rolled across between the cliff and the river raging just below.

They were now above the worst of the cataracts and it was possible to launch boats on the river. While the land party continued to cut a road through the forest, the heavier material was conveyed by river to a new camp at Isangila. Stanley himself then returned to Vivi to collect the rest of the material. Six weeks later he was back at Isangila and on 21 February 1881 founded a station there.

Above Isangila the river was relatively smooth for eighty-eight miles to Manianga, where another series of cataracts began. Manianga was also less than 100 miles from Stanley Pool and therefore a suitable place for the third station. Work began at the beginning of May 1881 but proceeded slowly. The river banks at Manianga rose steeply on each side to rocky escarpments devoid of life and vegetation; the climate was un-salubrious and one by one the Europeans, including Stanley, succumbed to sickness.

The explorer had been told to establish two stations between the coast and Stanley Pool; he had set up three. He had been told to carry his steam-boats overland and launch them at the Pool; this he was doing and he had already covered two-thirds of the distance. He was also to establish friendly relations with the natives and to make treaties with the chiefs for the cession of land; this too had been accomplished without firing a shot. But instead of thanks for his services, and appreciation of his diffi-culties, all Stanley got were warnings that he was losing the race with de Brazza and orders to press on ever faster.

Worse, additional demands were being made on him. Previously the goal had been Stanley Pool, now he was being told to create stations on the Upper Congo and to establish regular communications with Nyangwe, 1,200 miles higher up the river. It was on the unfortunate Colonel Strauch, who relayed Leopold's instructions, that the explorer vented his fury and frustration. As regards sending provisions to Nyangwe Stanley was clear, 'I answer: never!'[11] He went on: 'My health is so fearfully battered with the endless, wearisome work ... always some-thing new, always by each mail some new divergence from the straight, simple path, some new change of plan, some additional weight to carry ...'[12] Another long volley followed ten days later:

> Your letters prove that you and I are working at cross-purposes, you with the nervous enthusiasm which characterises you, I unremittingly and ungrudgingly with a certain kind of love for my work ...
>
> You, probably engrossed with a hundred other things, thoughtlessly imagine that these objects so desirable to you may be done at the mere bidding ... You furnish ideas, baggage, goods, and Europeans in abun-dance, but the very means that realise your ideas ... you forget. You awake in me admiration at your perseverance, astonish me with the scope of your ideas ... and I know not what to think.[13]

Nevertheless, despite his defence of his adherence to his original in-structions, in the summer of 1881, immediately after establishing the station at Manianga, Stanley moved his equipment twenty miles further upstream to Mpakambendi and from there proposed to make a rapid advance to Stanley Pool with a small escort, the main body of the expedi-tion to follow at a later stage. This was a new departure, as in the past he had kept the whole expedition together, consolidating each move for-ward before embarking on the next.

After ten days' march the explorer and his men arrived at the Pool and encamped. They had been there for only three hours when they learnt that de Brazza had signed a treaty with a native chief, Makoko, ceding to France a strip of territory about nine miles long on the north shore of the Pool.[14] Stanley moved on to Malima, a few miles beyond the French camp (today Brazzaville), where the native chief knew nothing of any treaty and told Stanley that in any case Makoko was only one of a number of chiefs and had no right to sell their land. However, during the night the tom-toms were heard beating, a native crier announced that there must be no truck with the white man, and that any African speaking to, or trading with him would be punished. Fearing an incident, which could well prejudice future negotiations with native chiefs, Stanley decided to retreat.

While the party was falling back from Malima, a messenger from a chief on the other side of the Pool arrived offering to conduct Stanley and his men to a place where the chief would pay a visit. The chief duly came but used the opportunity to extort as much as he could from the explorer. Stanley handed over two asses, a dog, a large mirror, a gold-embroidered coat and jewellery. A few days later the scene was repeated and Stanley asked for concessions in return. None was forthcoming. The native population had come to appreciate the power it could wield over Europeans.

Stanley was rapidly running out of barter goods. Finally, by a successful ruse, he frightened the most important chief in the area south of the Pool. By the end of the year Stanley felt confident enough of the situation to begin constructing a station. The main building was to be a blockhouse as well as a residence and, made of logs a foot in diameter, it was designed by Stanley to be impregnable. There were also to be storehouses, barracks for the Africans, stables and a garden. The work advanced well and was hastened by the arrival in January of the first batch of a hundred new recruits. A week later a caravan from Manianga brought up part of the goods Stanley had ordered for trading. By the end of February the block-house was complete and the Europeans moved into their 'palatial' new quarters.

On 5 March 1882 trading began.

> The goods are now on exhibition in the magazine. The barred windows are crowded by curious natives. Native imagination, fired by the brilliant display of cloths of all colours, silks, satins, ribbons, fancy jewellery, cutlery, pottery, crockery, glass ware, guns, swords, machetes ... etc. etc. will report that my wealth exceeds calculation! Who would have expected such a result as this three months ago? Over £500 [worth] of goods were sold by us before night.[15]

It remained only to give the station, the most important yet founded because of its position linking the Upper and Lower Congo, a name and, by general consent of the Europeans, Leopoldville (now Kinshasa) was deemed appropriate.

While at Leopoldville and feeling that he had done well by his royal patron, Stanley received a letter, dated 31 December 1881, from Leopold.

I take advantage of a safe opportunity to send you a few lines in my bad English. I have at heart to thank you for your exertions and to tell you again what I am expecting from them. Belgium desires no territory in Africa, but it is indispensable you should purchase for the *Comité d'Etudes* as much land as you will be able to obtain, and that you should place successively under the suzerainty of that *Comité*, as soon as possible and without losing one minute, all the chiefs from the mouth of the Congo to the Stanley Falls.

Brazza in a very short time has placed under his dependence the chiefs around the Stanley Pool. Should we not do the same for the *Comité*? ... If you let me know you are going to execute these instructions without delay I will send you more people and more material. Perhaps Chinese coolies.

I am desirous to see you purchase all the ivory which is to be found on the Congo, and let Colonel Strauch know the goods which he has to forward you in order to pay for it and when. I also recommend you to establish barriers and tolls on the parts of the road you have opened. It is but fair and in accordance with the custom of every country ...[16]

Three months later Stanley sent a long, exasperated sounding reply:

Sire,

You possess an excellent memory, an uncommon intelligence and an exceedingly penetrative intellect. It will not be difficult for you to recall to mind the expressions I used in personal conversation with you . . I said then as I say now that whatever intelligence, activity and zeal I might boast of was at your service to further the interests you have at heart ...

We suffered considerable loss because by procrastination we were unable to compete with de Brazza, the men being delayed until it was almost too late ... Of what use is it to erect stations, and give the command to buy ivory if in one week our stock is exhausted?

Much of the letter is one of Stanley's familiar diatribes against the men sent out to him, many of whose contracts were soon to expire: 'Your Majesty has ... also an opportunity of converting your entire force into Belgians this year ... They will be good for Belgium, but not for Africa ...' Leopold's suggestion of Chinese coolies for Africa was tactfully ignored but the explorer firmly opposed tolls. 'The mere rumour of such a course in Europe would bring general condemnation on our heads, and

I beg that the utmost caution be taken to prevent such ideas getting abroad.'[17]

But again, after complaining about the demands from Brussels, Stanley obeyed them and set off for the Upper Congo. A fifth station was founded at Mswata, sixty miles above the Pool. Another party set out to explore the river Kwa, an important tributary of the Congo, in the course of which a large lake was discovered and named Lake Leopold II. However, by the time it had been circumnavigated, supplies had run out and the men were in a state of exhaustion. Stanley again fell prey to fever and at Leopoldville had to be carried ashore, barely conscious.

It was now obvious to all, including the explorer himself, that he was too ill to carry on and must return to Europe. He was therefore taken downstream by bearers and arrived at Vivi on 8 July 1882. The fever had by now abated but Stanley was suffering from acute gastritis. He handed over command in the Congo to a German, Doctor Peschüel-Loesche, a scientist with some experience of African exploration, and sailing from Luanda, arrived back in Europe at the end of September 1882.

The explorer was under the impression that his contract with the Comité d'Etudes in 1879, for three years' service in the Congo, had superseded the one with Leopold for five years that he had made the previous year. Strauch, however, informed him that the five-year contract was still operative and, with a distinct lack of sympathy, told Stanley that he had to return immediately to the Congo. The sick man explained that doctors had told him that it would be suicidal to return to the tropics in his present state of health, and he refused to comply. Strauch no doubt told Leopold of this interview, for the next day, when the king met Stanley, he used more subtle phraseology. ' "Surely, Mr. Stanley, you cannot think of leaving me now, just when I most need you?" My powers of resistance failed me [said Stanley] and in a weak moment I assented to depart once more for the Congo, on or about November 1st.'[18]

Leopold was extremely fortunate that Stanley was prepared to return to the Congo, and so soon. Had he refused Leopold's whole Congolese enterprise would have been wrecked. The situation in October 1882 was a critical one.

De Brazza had returned to France in June 1882 brandishing the Makoko Treaty and, despite his fatigue and ill health, was determined to persuade the French government to ratify the treaty. Leopold again invited de Brazza to Brussels and in September 1882 the explorer arrived, though quite why he came is difficult to see. The king still appears to have held out hope that de Brazza might agree to work for him. 'De Brazza seems to think that Stanley is working for Belgium and Britain. We must explain to him that Belgium wants absolutely nothing, that our

Comité is an international one.'[19] But the visit had for Leopold a distinct, though negative, value. Lambermont warned his sovereign after talking to de Brazza : 'In the political field, de Brazza recognizes only three parties involved : Portugal, Britain and France.'[20]

The struggle for the Congo was between Leopold and France: the public feud between Stanley and de Brazza begun in October 1882 encapsulated it. De Brazza, as part of his campaign for ratification of the Makoko Treaty, talked a great deal to the press and in demonstrating the superiority of French claims and exploration methods, he attacked Stanley. 'I never was in the habit of travelling on African soil in martial array like Mr. Stanley ... and I never needed to resort to barter, because, travelling as a friend and not a conqueror, I everywhere found hospitable people.'[21] Stanley was, naturally, riled by the accusations and retorted : 'I am an American, therefore free of all political leanings and interested in Africa solely as an unhappy continent.'[22]

The quarrel between the two explorers was given wide coverage in the French and British press. Leopold was watching it carefully and had good cause to be alarmed; the French attitude was summed up in an article in Le Voltaire: 'Monsieur de Brazza's undertaking is as pacific as that of Mr. Stanley but it is French and for that reason we give it our strong support.'[23]

So far Leopold II had been trying to gain control over the Congo basin by means of commercial domination, the treaties that Stanley had negotiated being seen as forming a sound base for the operations of the large trading company the king envisaged. It was essential for the successful exploitation of the Congo that these bases should not fall into the hands of a European Power; however, in October 1882 Leopold realized that his project could not withstand political threats – an enterprise which could be accused of being commercial could not defend itself against those who claimed territorial sovereignty. The forthcoming French ratification of the Makoko Treaty demonstrated to Leopold that by claiming to be setting up purely a trading operation, he was placing himself in an extremely vulnerable position.

He changed course and from October 1882 onwards set to establishing sovereign territorial rights in the Congo. A reason had to be given for the new-found necessity to make native chiefs surrender land: Leopold promised free trade (he had previously been seeking trading monopolies). To make it possible to open up the Congo basin and to guarantee unimpeded commerce to all countries, the king had to control the territory in question. To achieve his new ends he set up the Association Internationale du Congo (AIC) which took over from the defunct Comité d'Etudes. Leopold financed and directed the AIC.

The necessity to send Stanley back to the Congo immediately was therefore clear. De Brazza was not planning to return to Africa in the near future and it was imperative that advantage should be taken of this to gain as many territorial concessions as possible before the French tried to expand from their base at Stanley Pool. In addition to establishing sovereignty in the Lower Congo, where he had already set up stations, Stanley was to include the Upper Congo, as far as the Stanley Falls.

In December 1882 the American found himself once more at the mouth of the Congo. He had recovered his health and was all set to undertake his new task. 'But alas! What dismal news was borne to me as I made myself more and more acquainted with the state of affairs in the expedition!'[24] His German replacement had left for home some time before, the commander of the Vivi station had disappeared, that of Leopoldville had abandoned his post for a holiday by the sea, the captain of the steamer *Belgique* had been dismissed, the *En Avant* had been robbed of its steam-valve and lay idle, rust-blistered and covered with slime at Leopoldville.

Stanley's first task was to organize an expedition to the Niari–Kouilou valley, an obvious region of expansion for the French. Captain Grant Elliott, an Englishman who had succeeded Peschüel-Loesche, duly headed north and established a station called Stephanieville (after Leopold's second daughter). Following the course of the river Niari, Grant found that it joined the Kouilou and this he descended, founding a station, Franktown, en route downstream. Elliott then had to choose either to retrace his steps or to press on into the unknown towards the Atlantic. Knowing the importance to the association of linking the Congo with the sea, he continued on. His two companions fell sick and Elliott went on alone in the hope of finding help; he was within a few miles of the coast when he too collapsed.

Meanwhile Stanley had dispatched a second expedition under a Belgian, Victor Vandervelde, with orders to take possession of the mouth of the Kouilou and the adjoining coastline. Vandervelde moved quickly and by the end of February 1883 had signed treaties securing the territory on both sides of the river mouth and founding a station, Rudolphstadt (after Stephanie's husband). He then mounted the river in the hope of meeting up with Elliott's party. En route treaties were signed with chiefs on either bank which gave the AIC control over all the lower reaches. At the confluence of the Kouilou and the Lumani another station, Baudouinville, was founded.

By this time Vandervelde was running out of supplies and returned to the coast, just in time to forestall a French gunboat which, on de Brazza's advice, had been sent to seize the mouth of the Kouilou.

On learning that a white man lay sick upstream and suspecting that it was Elliott, Vandervelde again ascended the river, concluding yet another treaty as he went, and eventually found Elliott. The Englishman soon recovered and the two returned to Rudolphstadt, from where Elliott immediately set off again, establishing another station, Grantville (his own Christian name), midway between Kouilou and Loango and setting up a series of posts all along the coast, which effectively secured all the outlets between the Ogooué and Congo rivers and the Atlantic. Only Loango, which the commander of the French gunboat had claimed, was excluded.

Stanley sent a third expedition under another Belgian, Edouard Hanssens, to establish a line of communication between the Congo and the Niari which would be linked up with the route opened up by Elliott. Starting from Manianga in February 1883, Hanssens reached the upper Niari by the end of April and founded Philippeville. By means of these three brilliant strokes, Stanley turned the tables on de Brazza: not only was the Kouilou–Niari route several times shorter than that of the Ogooué but without control of this valley, along which a railway could be built to the Stanley Pool, the French territory at the Pool lost much of its value.

After ratification of the Makoko Treaty in November 1882 the French government had voted 1,250,000 francs for a new expedition led by de Brazza. However, it was February 1883 before the French reached Africa and de Brazza saw immediately that Stanley had beaten him. In an attempt to undo as much of the damage as possible, de Brazza made his way to Stanley Pool where he summoned the native chiefs from both sides of the Pool and, invoking the Makoko Treaty, persuaded them to place themselves under French protection. This was no more than a gesture, but it served to establish a French claim to the left bank of the Congo which could later be exchanged for the Niari–Kouilou valley. There was no attempt at effective occupation of the left bank.

As he had successfully accomplished the first part of his task, Stanley then set about establishing stations on the Upper Congo. The explorer was delayed for several weeks at Leopoldville as he found the station in a dilapidated state and, worse, there had been skirmishes with the natives in the surrounding area. In May 1883 he was able to leave and in the *En Avant* ascended the river to the Stanley Falls, 1,200 miles above the Pool. He had to return to Stanley Pool three times for supplies and it took him almost a year to make the necessary treaties with native chiefs and to set up three stations at Bolobo, Equator and Stanley Falls.

Stanley started on his journey down to the coast from Leopoldville at the end of March 1884. His five-year contract with Leopold had almost expired and he looked forward to returning to Europe. Leopold had been well served by his agent who had, in little more than a year, established a dominance over the Congo basin that placed the king in a strong position to combat the difficulties he faced now that the Great Powers had become involved in Central Africa.

11 The Diplomats Take over

'We have no doubt that the English
government will not [sic], by a stroke of the
pen, declare that our works and properties
belong not to us but to Portugal.'[1]

Leopold II, 1883.

For much of the period during which Stanley was working for Leopold
in the Congo the European Powers were preoccupied with a series of
international crises: the Eastern Question involved them all; in Egypt
France and Britain were wrestling for domination; France was taking
over Tunis; Britain faced problems in Afghanistan and South Africa. For
some time this state of affairs worked to Leopold's advantage; however,
at the end of 1882 the dismantling of the Dual Control in Egypt and the
virtual British take-over of the country marked too great an assertion
of British power for the French to stomach and they were determined
to prevent any further such occurrences. When in 1883 it appeared that
the British were again – this time using their weak ally Portugal – extending their power in Africa, France could not stand back and permit it.
As the part of Africa in question was the Congo, Leopold II found himself
deeply involved with the two great colonial Powers.

The Portuguese had since Cameron's crossing of Africa become increasingly aware that interest in West Africa was growing in Europe, and
from 1877 onwards they pursued a more active policy towards Angola
and the surrounding territory than had previously been the case. Many
more missionaries were sent out to make the Portuguese presence felt
and in Lisbon the government was favourably disposed in 1879 when
the British ambassador proposed an Anglo-Portuguese agreement on
West Africa. However, in 1880 there was a change of government in England and the new Liberal administration was loath to become involved
in Congo negotiations as there were many more urgent matters to deal
with at home.

But by the end of 1882, after the ratification of de Brazza's Makoko
Treaty by the French assembly, the situation had changed radically. The
British, fearing that worse was to come, decided to support Portugal's

claims to the Congo basin. 'The point of view of the Foreign Office was that the creation of foreign, and especially of French colonies, was detrimental both to general considerations of humanity and also to British trade ... In order to keep out France, we were glad to put forward Portugal.'[2] Such was the explanation of Sir Charles Dilke, a junior minister at the Foreign Office who was considered pro-Portuguese. Leopold's association was not thought of as a possible alternative to Portugal as the AIC appeared to the British government too weak to withstand a potential French take-over.

The British were prepared to recognize Portuguese sovereignty along the west coast of Africa between 5° 12′ and 8° south. In return for this, the Portuguese were to guarantee free navigation on the Congo and the Zambezi and the introduction of a liberal tariff in all Portuguese African colonies, with most favoured nation status for Britain. There was also to be due consideration for all rights enjoyed by British subjects by virtue of treaties with native chiefs; British subjects were to be on the same footing as Portuguese as regards the ownership of land, missionary operations and taxation and the Portuguese were to abolish the slave-trade and slavery.

There was an immediate outcry against the proposed treaty both in England and abroad. Philanthropists and the commercial community in England objected on the grounds of Portugal's toleration of slavery and oppressive, corrupt, colonial administration, and traders pointed out that Portugal had maintained a consistently protectionist policy.[3] On the Continent, Portugal had for a long time been looked on as a British satellite and it was widely held, particularly in France, that Britain was trying to establish a veiled protectorate over the Congo basin.

For Leopold the recognition of the Portuguese claims to the Congo basin would mean the destruction of all his work in previous years. He wrote to Queen Victoria and also raised the matter with the Prince of Wales who was then in Brussels, and his cousin agreed to speak to Lord Granville, the foreign secretary. Leopold was delighted when a concession, albeit a minor one, was made:

> My dear Bertie,
> A thousand thanks for the excellent news you sent me. By intervening you have rendered me personally a great service, as well as the cause in which I am interested ... Perhaps you would be so kind as to tell Lord Granville how grateful I am to him, and I take the liberty of asking you to continue keeping an eye on things.[4]

Nevertheless, the British royal family could only perform a limited amount for Leopold and he turned to William Mackinnon, the Scottish businessman who had been one of the founders of the *Comité d'Etudes* and who had considerable contacts in Whitehall, to James Hutton, a Manchester businessman with West African trading connections who was also President of the Manchester Chamber of Commerce, and Sir John Kirk who had been British consul in Zanzibar and who had immediate *entrée* in the Foreign Office. While Mackinnon wrote letters to Gladstone and members of his cabinet and visited civil servants, Hutton ranged the powerful Manchester Chamber of Commerce, and others in important industrial cities, against the treaty.

Hutton was also successful in channelling the opposition of the various Protestant missionary societies to that of Catholic Portuguese ones. In addition the Anti-Slavery Society also lent its support and Hutton took care to keep the issue before the public in the national and local press.

A letter from him was published in *The Times* on 3 April 1883, the day the House of Commons was debating the Anglo-Portuguese Treaty. Many members of the Liberal party spoke against the government. The radical, Jacob Bright, urged the House 'to protect the interests of the English and of England, and not by an unfortunate Treaty [which] puts a hostile tariff on the struggling merchants of this country.'[5] A vote on the motion was taken at the end of the day; the government, which in theory had an overall majority of seventy-two, was defeated.

After reading the Hansard report of the debate, Leopold was yet more convinced that his one hope of saving the Congo for himself lay in offering free trade and allied guarantees to the various interested parties. He knew that he stood little chance of having the AIC's claims recognized by the other European Powers. They were contemptuous of the association and, in the case of France and Portugal, flatly stated that it was out of the question for the territorial pretensions of a private company to be recognized by a government. Leopold therefore decided to try and persuade the United States to recognize the AIC, hoping that if he were successful this would strengthen his position *vis-à-vis* the European Powers.

General Sanford, who had been deeply involved in Leopold's schemes for some years, was the ideal man to undertake negotiations, and at the end of November 1883 he arrived in Washington, although President Chester Arthur had been studying the AIC's claims as early as May 1883.[6] The king sent a letter by Sanford to the president in which he claimed, distinctly prematurely, that 'Entire territories ceded by sovereign chiefs have been constituted by us into independent States.'[7] He went on to put forward the case for the legality of the territorial rights, citing Borneo, where the British North Borneo Company governed a large territory under charter, and Liberia. The latter example was designed to appeal to American opinion as it was a private American society which had conceived and carried out the founding of a Negro republic in Africa. Leopold let it be understood that the association would play a similar role in the Congo where it would act as an agent, until such time as the independent state could rule itself. Emphasis was also laid on the abolition of slavery, another aim designed to find favour in the United States, and Leopold also made the most of the fact that Stanley was American (although Stanley only took out American citizenship in 1885).

As he had been in the diplomatic service for many years, Sanford had first-class contacts in Washington, both in the State Department and in Congress. He drew up memos, paid calls and gave excellent dinners.[8] The fruits of his work were seen immediately, as in his annual message to Congress on 4 December 1883, the president included a reference to the Congo which closely followed a draft prepared for him by Sanford. After describing Leopold's association as a philanthropic society with no political objective, Arthur declared that the United States could not 'be indifferent to this work nor to the interests of American citizens engaged in it'.[9]

Although nothing was said about recognizing the association, it was clear that the matter was being seriously considered by the administration. Recognition would have to be passed by a resolution of both Houses of Congress and Sanford successfully approached Senator John Morgan, chairman of the Senate Foreign Affairs Committee, who took it upon himself to have the subject examined by the committee. The documents used by the Senate committee show a total confusion in the minds of Americans between the AIA and AIC, the two ambiguous words international association often being used. The Senate Foreign Affairs Committee, and the secretary of state for foreign affairs, who provided much of the briefing, believed that it was the philanthropic AIA that had made the treaties with the chiefs and neither Sanford nor Leopold went out of their way to put the Americans right. It was a rather incoherent debate that took place as to what was happening in the Congo, and the Americans did not pose any too difficult questions. Territorial rights acquired by individuals, or groups, had been the means by which some of the first settlers had established themselves in the United States and the Senate, on 11 April 1884, voted a resolution recommending that the flag of the association should be recognized as the 'flag of a friendly government'. However, the United States still counted for little with the European Powers in questions of this kind, and the recognition of the AIC, despite Leopold's hopes, was barely noticed in Paris and London.

The Anglo-Portuguese treaty had, meanwhile, on 24 February 1884, been signed. Britain had taken into consideration Leopold's interests, indeed Granville had maintained a consistently friendly attitude, and had ensured that the AIC posts remained outside the Portuguese zone. Even so, passage between these posts and the sea would henceforth entail traversing Portuguese territory.

Before becoming effective, the Anglo-Portuguese Treaty had to be ratified by the British parliament and the other European Powers and at this juncture Leopold applied himself yet more assiduously to organizing opposition to it. It was obvious to those involved what he was up to. 'The King is agitating to upset the treaty in the House,' the head of the Foreign Office African Desk, Percy Anderson, informed his colleagues.[10] Anderson suggested that the best way of combating the king would be to show up the true character of Stanley's work by publicly revealing the real nature of the treaties made a few years before. 'The King of the Belgians' Co. is a gigantic commercial monopoly.'[11] Granville himself, who so far had behaved in a gentlemanly way towards Leopold, wrote to the king politely threatening revelation but Leopold was not to be blackmailed. He knew, soon after the signing, that the other European Powers were prepared to oppose the treaty and that the tide had now turned in his favour. France began the international opposition to the Anglo-Portuguese Treaty by delivering a protest on 13 March. She had the greatest interest in seeing the treaty destroyed and Leopold thus decided to ally himself with France.

What the French, with their pathological fear of British expansion in Africa, feared most from Leopold was that the British would take over from him. The French ambassador in Brussels, in March 1883, had warned the Quai d'Orsay: 'It is not impossible to foresee the day when the International Association, left to the personal resources of the King of the Belgians or losing in him its only support, would surrender to some British company the fruit of its efforts.'[12]

In September 1883 Stanley had had a letter published in *The Times* in which he once again called upon the British government to declare a protectorate over the Congo, and the AIC employed many Englishmen.[13] Early in 1884 Leopold was interviewing General Gordon as Stanley's potential successor. The general was persuaded to work for Leopold; the Foreign Office was greatly irritated by what it considered poaching and retaliated by threatening to withdraw Gordon's pension rights. Leopold offered to compensate the general if this occurred and earned a stiff rebuke from Queen Victoria for meddling in British affairs.[14] When Gordon went back on his promise and agreed to go to the Sudan for the British government, Leopold was furious. (Gordon left debts of nearly £600 as a result of his trips to Brussels. After his death the following year Leopold called upon his executors to pay them.[15])

Although France had done most to obstruct the AIC, she was also in the best position to defend it and in April 1884 a marriage of convenience was solemnized. On 23 April 1884 Ferry received a letter from Brussels in which an astonishing offer was made to France. Leopold offered the French the right of pre-emption (*droit de préférence*), that is first option, on the association's territories if at any time in the future the king decided to divest himself of what he had acquired in the Congo.[16] The French prime minister replied immediately and assured the king – as well he might in the circumstances – that France would respect the stations and territories to which the association claimed title.[17]

Leopold had no intention whatsoever of allowing himself to get into a position where he would have to cede AIC territories and he felt satisfied with his offer, which cost him nothing, and in return for which he obtained quasi-recognition from France. Ferry for his part was convinced that Leopold did not possess either the financial or the military means to maintain the territories acquired by the AIC and he looked forward to extending French possessions in the Congo basin. The British government held much the same view as the French and was extremely alarmed when it came to hear of the *droit de préférence*. Leopold tried to reassure Granville: 'The hypothesis of our handing over [our territories] is contrary to our intentions and totally improbable ... Your Lordship is well aware that our main preoccupation is to conserve all that we have done in the course of the last six years.'[18]

The foreign secretary does not seem to have been satisfied by the king's reply. The following day an irate Foreign Office memorandum was circulated: 'The K of the B has bound himself to give the refusal of all the possessions of the "Assoc" to one of the most exclusive and protectionist Govts in the world. It is therefore incumbent upon all Govts that value freedom of trade to abstain from recognizing the Assoc its treaties and its flag.'[19] And the same day *The Times* published an article, clearly officially inspired, attacking the AIC.

If England was the Power most affected by the French right of preemption to the Congo, Germany nevertheless had an interest in the matter and Bismarck at this juncture stepped in. Germany had in 1884 joined in the race for colonies, one result of which was that a petty squabble with England developed over Angra Pequena, a small area on the southwest coast of Africa. In previous years Anglo-German relations had been cordial with Bismarck supporting England in Egypt. With France, Germany was on friendlier terms, backing French colonial policy in all areas except Egypt, to take their minds off Alsace-Lorraine. However, there was no Anglo-German estrangement and the outstanding territorial disagreements over Fiji and Samoa were of a minor order.

The rapid deterioration in Anglo-German relations which took place in the early months of 1884 arose because the British failed to realize that Bismarck had changed his policy with regard to colonies. He had been consistently opposed to their acquisition by Germany and when in December 1883 he sent a note to the Foreign Office asking what claims the British had to Angra Pequena (a German trader was asking for a German protectorate to be declared there), his enquiry lay unanswered for six months, as the Foreign Office handed the dossier over to the Colonial Office who in turn asked the government of Cape Colony to annex the coast. The colony's officials were quite willing to comply but reluctant to provide the money necessary to administer the territory. They procrastinated in their exchanges with the Colonial Office and the Foreign Office, the latter considering the matter out of its hands, did not want to force a decision.

Bismarck became increasingly suspicious of British intentions, knowing that in the past they had disclaimed the title to Angra Pequena. When in January 1884 London once again rejected his request for a united commission on the Fiji claims and in February he learnt that the British were keen to annex Togo, Bismarck found such disputes which in the past could be dealt with amicably, a source of mounting irritation. With the signing of the Anglo-Portuguese Treaty on 26 February, Bismarck felt that the British had gone too far in their creeping expansion in Africa and would have to be called to task.

The active stage in Bismarck's policy began on 24 April, when he announced his decision to annex the German settlement at Angra Pequena. A few days later, on 29 April, Germany protested against the Anglo-Portuguese Treaty. Bismarck took exception to the commercial privileges the treaty accorded to British subjects and having studied the terms of the United States' recognition of the AIC, signed a few days earlier, he decided to find out more about this association which promised free trade.

Unlike the Americans, Bismarck immediately saw certain contradictions in what the AIC was claiming and the treaties with native chiefs conferring exclusive rights on the association; he also noticed the apparent mix-up in the names. In addition, the chancellor felt sure that the AIC did not possess the means necessary to provide adequate guarantees. The German minister in Brussels could only obtain information from the Palais Royal and this did not satisfy Bismarck. He therefore arranged for an article to be published in the *Norddeutsche Allgemeine Zeitung* on 6 May in which some pertinent questions about the AIC were posed. After pointing out that the association operated under various names, the writer demanded to know its composition and constitution. What was its authority to conclude treaties and who would carry them out? Was the association correctly incorporated and who was the *Rechtssubjekt*? Colonel Strauch was the president: by whom was he appointed and to whom was he responsible?

Leopold recognized the article as an official enquiry, and a fortnight later an article appeared in the same paper, replying to the first. It was written by Victor Gantier, a Belgian journalist living in Berlin, who was in constant contact with Leopold at this time and it illustrates the state of the king's thinking.[20]

After tracing the history of the association, the article stated that a line of stations was nearly complete and that in a few years' time they would extend across Africa from the Atlantic coast to the Indian Ocean. It went on to explain that the 'founders of the stations who had formed an association under the name of the AIC planned to link up the territories into an independent state'. Regarding the treaties signed with the native chiefs, the rights conferred by them were to be used to the benefit of all nations and as to the financial position of the association, the writer pointed out that among its members was 'one who furnished the necessary funds'. In conclusion, he claimed that the association 'was a purely temporary body and would disappear when its work was completed'.[21]

Leopold had begun employing the words 'free States' to designate the territories of the AIC in November 1883, when negotiating with the United States.[22] At the beginning of 1884 he moved from the plural to the singular and spoke of the 'new State'. When he saw that Bismarck was seriously considering recognizing the 'new State' he decided that he would have to have a clear idea as to what it comprised and he sent the chancellor a document setting out his territorial aspirations. In addition to the Congo basin he claimed certain provinces 'of Central Africa, abandoned by Egypt, where the slave-trade continues to flourish. To allow these [provinces] to be incorporated into and administered by a new State would be the best way to get at the root of the trouble and eradicate it.'[23] In addition, he asked for territory stretching as far east as Lake Tanganyika.

Bismarck was astounded at the grandiose pretensions of the King of the Belgians. He had never been convinced by Leopold's philanthropic image and felt his intuition vindicated. Alongside the section dealing with the repression of the slave-trade, he noted '*Schwindel*'.[24] The chancellor thought that Leopold was essentially a speculator who was investing his own money in the Congo with the intention of selling out at great profit at a later stage. He decided for the moment to ignore the territorial claims and merely announced on 23 June in the Reichstag that he would support the creation of an independent state in the Congo, if he could obtain in advance a treaty according commercial liberty to German citizens. He would go no further than opposing the Anglo-Portuguese Treaty.

On 27 June Leopold submitted a document in response to the chancellor's statement. It was, however, rather different from what Bismarck had expected. The king did not mention the German demand that guaranteed freedom of commerce to German citizens in the event of alienation. At the same time the territorial claims became yet greater and vaguer, Leopold promising that the exact frontiers would be announced later.

The chancellor was furious at the one-sided demands and did not bother to answer. Leopold was puzzled when a month later he had still not received a reply from Germany.[25] Bismarck said of the king: 'His Majesty displays the pretensions and naive selfishness of an Italian who considers that his charm and good looks will enable him to get away with anything without his ever being asked for anything in return.'[26]

It was the German banker Gerson von Bleichröder, who had for years been on friendly terms with Leopold, who reopened the negotiations at the beginning of August 1884. Von Bleichröder pointed out to the king where he had erred in his approach to Bismarck and advised Leopold to submit a revised treaty, incorporating an alienation clause and containing strictly delimited and more modest boundaries to the new state.[27]

Fortunately for Leopold, the only man capable of drawing reasonable frontiers was with him at Ostend in August 1884. Stanley had returned to Europe two months before and was the king's guest, staying at a hotel at Leopold's expense (a special cook was employed to prepare an English breakfast for the explorer) and dining each day at the Chalet Royal. Stanley was about to return to England when on 7 August the king called him in to his study and pointed to a large map of Central Africa pinned to the wall. The explorer was ordered to outline what he considered the reasonable frontiers of a Congo state.[28] Stanley excluded territory east of Lake Tanganyika and the Sudan which Leopold had earlier included – the inspiration to aspire to the Sudan had come from General Gordon some months before. Nevertheless, with bold strokes he outlined a large area from 4° north to Lake Tanganyika in the east and as far south as the sixth parallel. Roughly, territory within a 600–9000-mile radius of the stations occupied was included.

This map was immediately dispatched to Bismarck at Varzin. At the end of the month the chancellor called in the French ambassador and showed it to him.

> Prince Bismarck showed me a map King Leopold sent him on which were represented the boundaries of the territory where the Belgian association aspires to form a sovereign state: it is an immense quadrilateral including the whole sweep of the upper Congo, that is the whole course of the river from the cataracts on the West to the great lake region on the East, we might as well say all Central Africa, the very core of the continent.
>
> It is indeed vast, the Prince-Chancellor said to me, but it is not for us to bridle those ambitions, seeing that the Company guarantees our trading freedom and that the benefit to us from application of this principle increases with the size of the Company's operations. I do not know just what this Belgian Association is, nor what will become of

it, but … it is always useful for diverting troublesome rivalries and claims that we could handle less easily ourselves. We can give it our backing to clear the way.[29]

The chancellor was at this stage engaged upon 'the cementing of the Franco-German *entente*' and as the French for their part saw no objection to the proposed frontiers, as they were convinced that before too long they would be able to exercise the *droit de préférence* and take over the Congo basin, Bismarck was therefore able to write to Leopold on 4 September. It was an eight-page letter in the chancellor's own handwriting.[30] The chancellor was of the view that there was really nothing to be lost by Germany's conceding to Leopold what the king asked for and on 8 November 1884 the German empire formally recognized the AIC. It did not seem to Bismarck to matter much whether an eccentric European monarch was able or not to indulge in his fancies in tropical Africa. For once the chancellor was wrong.

12 The Conference of Berlin

'Leopold II set sail straight into the winds of Anglo-French rivalry in Africa. An ever watchful helmsman, in the end, against heavy odds, he steered his frail craft majestically into port.'[1] Jean Stengers, 1969.

The idea of calling an international conference to resolve the Congo question originated with Portugal. Granville realized in early May 1885 that the Anglo-Portuguese Treaty was unacceptable to the Powers and consulted the Marquis du Bocage, the Portuguese prime minister, as to how to go about modifying it. The latter replied by proposing a conference as the best means of doing so.[2] The British foreign secretary opposed the idea and in his reply at the end of the month maintained that an international commission would be better suited to the task. However, Portugal had, without informing the British, sent a circular to the other Powers on 13 May, proposing a conference. Though this appears to be pure duplicity, it may have been more a case of 'flying a kite' rather than a deliberate attempt to cross the British government.[3]

Bismarck immediately responded to the suggestion and sounded out the French as this was the time when he was nurturing the Franco-German *entente*. On learning that Ferry was in agreement, Bismarck then took the initiative and developed the idea. His reason for doing so was to avoid Portugal, and hence England, controlling such a conference. When Granville learnt that the idea of an international conference had been taken up by Bismarck, he accepted defeat as regards the Anglo-Portuguese Treaty.

Leopold was watching anxiously from the sidelines, waiting for signs to guide him. By the end of June, the day fixed for ratification of the Anglo-Portuguese Treaty had passed: he could relax a little as one battle had been won. Now that an international conference was proposed, he had to prepare his case and work out the strategy to follow. Germany's recognition of the AIC, just seven days before the conference met in Berlin on 15 November 1884, strengthened Leopold's position enormously.

France, in agreeing to the calling of an international conference, had stipulated that she would attend only on condition that the question of territorial rights in the Congo basin was excluded from discussion. Bismarck agreed to this and as a result the agenda was restricted to three main headings. The first basis was to secure free trade in the basin and mouths of the Congo: the second was to establish freedom of navigation on the Congo and the Niger, the inclusion of the latter being made at the request of France. There had been considerable commercial rivalry between England and France on the Lower Niger and France hoped that with the backing of Germany, she could gain ascendancy over England in this area. The third basis was to define the political obligations of the Powers concomitant with the occupation of new territories on the African coast.

Invitations had been sent to thirteen countries: Austria-Hungary, Belgium, Denmark, Great Britain, Holland, Italy, Norway, Portugal, Russia, Spain, Sweden, Turkey and the United States. Although there was no more interested party than the AIC, it had no official representative since it did not have any international status, being recognized only by Germany and the United States. However, Auguste Beernaert, the chief minister in the Belgian government, was prepared to go along with the king's schemes and named Lambermont and Banning as the principal Belgian representatives; Leopold also sent General Sanford to Berlin to report on the conference for him. The fact that the Belgians were much more knowledgeable as to the Congo than any of the other representatives was quickly recognized and Lambermont was appointed *rapporteur* to the conference. In this position, he was able to guide the proceedings in the direction he wished. Africa was not at this stage sufficiently important for the Powers to send their top men from home and each country was represented by its ambassador to Berlin.

As it had been the first to recognize the AIC, the United States could be counted on to give its full support, although its ambassador to Berlin, John Kasson, was totally incompetent. Fortunately, he was assisted by Stanley, whom Kasson invited to assist the American delegation as technical adviser. This placed Leopold in an embarrassing position, for Stanley was still employed by him and his presence at the conference might appear as an attempt by the king to influence proceedings in favour of the AIC. Furthermore, the explorer was not known for his discretion and more than once had embarrassed his employer by his speeches and writings.

Bismarck approved of Stanley's attending and hence Leopold gave his permission, though on condition that he complied strictly with Sanford's instructions, a difficult task as Sanford disliked Stanley intensely and wanted to keep him out of the public light.[4] Bismarck on the other hand was looking to Stanley as a popular figure to arouse colonial enthusiasm in Germany now that he had decided to go for colonies, and he invited the explorer to dinner and arranged for a series of banquets in his honour in various German cities, where Stanley had a great success describing Africa and the opportunities which awaited Europeans in the Dark Continent.

The delegates met at Bismarck's official residence in the Wilhelmstrasse, where the last great international congress had assembled six years earlier. Sitting at a large horseshoe-shaped table whose open end overlooked the garden, the representatives could remind themselves of their immediate task by looking at a large map of Africa. From this derived the myth that the Berlin Conference partitioned Africa.

At two o'clock Bismarck opened the first session and accepted the chairmanship. He stated that the purpose of the conference was to promote the civilization of Africa by opening up the interior of the continent to commerce. He then attempted to define the three specific goals facing the delegates. The conference, he said, would not concern itself with questions of sovereignty, but it was extremely unclear as to exactly what the chancellor intended. The Foreign Office thought that Bismarck's 'speech is extremely vague and it leaves it doubtful whether the Conference is to do more than register a few platitudes about freedom of commerce and navigation'.[5]

The German chancellor had conveyed the impression that he placed the Niger and the Congo on the same footing and as soon as discussion began the commercial expert of the Foreign Office, Joseph Archer Crowe, set about demonstrating that the French could not hope to exploit the Lower Niger. He was successful; the move to internationalize the Lower Niger collapsed when Bismarck gave his support to Britain. Bismarck increasingly saw that Germany's goal of free trade coincided with Britain's and diverged from France's; to achieve the most liberal extension of free trade on the Congo, he supported Britain on the Niger. The Franco-German *entente* had begun to crumble.

The rot had set in for the French and when the delegates turned to the Congo, the British and Germans proposed a wide delimitation of the 'conventional', geopolitical, river basin. The French and the Portuguese were forced into a defensive position and had to fight hard to get the line pushed away from their spheres on the west coast. The *Economiste Français* complained that France 'has everything to lose and nothing whatever to gain from the proceedings of the Conference'.[6]

To free-trade Britain and Germany it was clear that the Congo risked falling into the hands of the protectionist French and Portuguese, and that the political vacuum which had been created must be filled. Thus, in December 1884, the British who had so far been hostile to, and disparaging of, the AIC, suddenly changed course. Sir Percy Anderson, the

Foreign Office African expert who, rather than Sir Edward Malet the British minister to Berlin, decided British policy at the Conference of Berlin, was firmly francophobe. He feared that France's expansion in Africa would cut off potential markets and increase her political and military power, and to win German support against France he was prepared to follow Bismarck's lead in making the AIC into a state, in the hope that with sufficient guarantees it would keep the Congo open to free trade and frustrate French ambitions.

In London there was considerable disagreement among senior officials as to the wisdom of this course of action. Sir Julian Pauncefote, the legal adviser, agreed with Anderson, but T.V. Lister, the assistant under-secretary held: 'It is one thing to "assist the Assocn. in its endeavour to become a State" and another to recognize it as being one. It is, I imagine, usual in recognizing a new state to have a clear idea of its boundaries and even perhaps some proof of the validity of its claims to its territories.'[7] Pauncefote tried to find a compromise: 'It might be provisionally recognized for all practical and necessary purposes as an *inchoate State*. It would be a new feature in the practice of Nations, but I do not see any great objection to it under all the circes.'[8] The weary Granville had had enough of the controversy and noted 'I agree'. On 4 December Malet wrote to Lambermont telling him that he was authorized to draw up with Strauch a treaty recognizing the flag of the AIC as that of an independent state. Nothing was said as to the frontiers of the proposed state. It represented a major success for both Bismarck and Leopold II and the other countries represented at the conference (with the exception of Turkey) followed suit now that both Germany and England had recognized the new state.

France had from the outset insisted that territorial questions should be excluded from the conference as she hoped that as long as her territorial disputes with both Portugal and the AIC were kept on a bilateral basis she could take advantage of her strength *vis-à-vis* her two weak rivals. Bismarck had already undermined the French position by recognizing the AIC: in December 1884 he went much further – and in so doing destroyed what remained of the Franco-German *entente* when he called upon France and the AIC to begin solving their outstanding territorial disputes. In this he kept to the letter of his promise but his action was clearly contrary to the spirit of the understanding.

This represented an exciting new opportunity for Leopold to exploit. He applied himself yet more assiduously to keeping his men in Berlin up to scratch; Lambermont and Sanford were bombarded with instructions from Brussels and as usual, when it suited him, Leopold was solicitous for the personal well-being of his advocates: 'The Berlin climate is very severe. I am most grateful to you for braving it.'[9] Certainly they worked hard for him – Sanford alone sent twenty-two dispatches to Brussels between 20 November and 24 December 1884.[10]

The question of sovereignty in the Congo basin was, Leopold realized, of greater importance than proclamations of free trade, simply because whoever exercised power could, if so desired, cast aside trade restrictions – as indeed happened later. Lambermont therefore concentrated his energies from the middle of December 1884 on dealing with French and Portuguese pretensions in the Congo. Portugal was claiming, as it had done in its negotiations with England, all coastal territory between 8° and 5° 12′ latitude south, which would assure it of control of the Congo estuary and would necessarily cut off the association's territory from access to the sea. France for her part, on the basis of the Makoko Treaty, was claiming sovereignty over both banks of Stanley Pool and the valley of the Niari–Kouilou, which Stanley had annexed in 1883 on behalf of the AIC and which had been recognized by France in the pre-emption agreement of April 1884. As Sybil Crowe says, in her study of the Berlin Conference the AIC was caught 'like a nut between the jaws of a nutcracker'.[11]

But neither England nor Germany wished to see the AIC squeezed out of existence. Nevertheless, for different reasons they could not openly support it; they stood by as a stern reminder to the French and Portuguese that they would have to arrive at a settlement with the association which would satisfy them as being fair. With his usual diplomatic acumen, Leopold saw that his bargaining position had been strengthened and at the end of November 1884 he circulated among the delegates at Berlin copies of the map showing the new state's frontiers as recognized earlier in the month by Germany and which included the whole of the disputed valley. He modified his claims a little in the middle of December and agreed to cede the right bank of the Niari–Kouilou in exchange for financial compensation, but the French were not prepared to accept this and maintained their demand for the whole valley. Then on 24 December Leopold outlined audacious new frontiers for the state. These excluded the whole of the Niari–Kouilou valley, but, in compensation, extended the territory claimed by the AIC as far south as Katanga on the watershed between the Congo and the Zambezi – a move which Leopold called in a Belgicism, which in this case is also a euphemism, an 'ajoute'. Despite this enormous increase in territory – and it represented a movement towards the south of more than four degrees of latitude – Leopold considered Katanga insufficient compensation for the loss of the Niari–Kouilou and renewed his demand for financial compensation too.

Stanley was with Leopold on 24 December and wrote to Sanford:

I saw the King. He is pale, probably from confinement indoors, otherwise charming, and polite as usual and in no way dispirited, so far as I can judge. It will be difficult for him to make a concession from what he asks on the ground that he might be asked to do more. If no compensation is made then the King will be obliged to leave the Congo, and the responsibility for such an act must rest on those who rob him ... When the preference treaty was signed the British Foreign Office was very angry. Where is their consistency now, if they drive the King to sell out to France?[12]

Stanley went over to London to put pressure on the British government to support Leopold against the French. Granville lent a sympathetic ear but said 'he was not going to war for the Congo with France'.[13] Lister, whose antipathy towards the AIC had not abated, would have nothing of Leopold's threat to pull out: 'We must not expect to frighten France by threatening to leave the Congo.'[14] The British were prepared to give general backing to Leopold but Stanley found that they were not prepared to support his every claim.

The same was true of Bismarck, who, in an attempt to salvage what remained of the Franco–German *entente*, assured the French that they were wrong in thinking that he had become the association's protector. It was rather that he did not like the Portuguese system of colonial administration. But what gave the French strong leverage over Leopold was their knowledge of the penury of the new state. The king was in desperate need of money as he had almost exhausted his personal inheritance (and that of his sister Charlotte, whose money he controlled). It was clear that the new state would need enormous financial resources, far beyond Leopold's means. The Belgian stock market was not capable of raising the sums necessary and the Belgian government would not be pleased to be asked to help. The king was looking to Paris.

Jules Ferry knew that he could force a hard deal and he laid the blame for the delays in reaching a settlement on the association whose territorial claims, he said, increased almost daily. During negotiations in January 1885 the new state finally conceded the Niari–Kouilou in return for the left bank of Stanley Pool. Ferry refused to pay an indemnity, but in its place accepted that a lottery should be held in France in the name of the association, aimed at raising at least 6,000,000 francs. As regards the frontier on the right bank of the Congo, the French were prepared to draw a line northwards from Manianga, rather than from Vivi further downstream which they had previously demanded, thus increasing the new state's territory in the north to the watershed of the Niari. Ferry had promised to support the association in its negotiations with Portugal which were to decide the southern frontier of the new state, but instead he informed the Portuguese that France had conceded the right bank of the Congo down from Manianga and advised the Portuguese to claim it, an increase in their claims far below 5° 12′ south.

Clearly possession of an outlet to the sea was indispensable to the new state and in February 1885 the Portuguese were prepared to renounce the right bank of the Congo at the estuary as far as Banana. The coastal strip to the north, the enclave of Cabinda, they claimed on the grounds that it figured in the Portuguese constitution as an apanage of the crown. They also demanded the left bank of the Congo up to Nokki. The association was extremely anxious to possess Nokki as otherwise the left bank of the river as far up as Isangila would become useless because of the cataracts.

The Portuguese were distinctly erratic negotiators and while hotly disputing Nokki they suddenly extended their claims up to Vivi, accompanied by the dispatch of the Portuguese fleet to the Congo mouth. French and British gunboats appeared on the spot before the Portuguese and the plan aborted. The Powers were distinctly exasperated by Portuguese diplomacy; they wanted the dispute settled quickly and Portugal was told to abandon her claims on the right bank as far as Banana and to make Lunga the southern limit of Cabinda. On the other hand, she was given the left bank up to and including Nokki. The association was to possess the left bank from there upstream, the inland boundary of its possessions, and those of Portugal to the south of the Congo, running eastwards along the latitude of Nokki, to the intersection of this line with the river Kwango, and from this point following the course of the Kwango southwards. A convention with France was signed on 5 February 1885 and one with Portugal on 15 February.

Meanwhile, the Conference of Berlin had been discussing the three bases. The Congo basin, geographical and conventional, was defined as including the coast of Africa between the mouth of the Zambezi and the Somali coast; this area was to become a free-trade zone. In addition all powers in the area were to seek to improve native conditions, to protect missions, to allow liberty of conscience and to suppress the slave-trade. The second basis, namely the question of securing free navigation on the Congo and the Niger, owing to its technical nature, had been referred to a commission, but nothing could disguise the fact that France's insistence on including the Niger had completely failed to undermine the British position there. As regards the Congo, the Berlin Act provided for the setting up of an international commission to oversee navigation and if necessary to raise loans for its expenses, a situation Leopold was determined to avoid. The attempt at defining the political obligations of colonial powers in future occupations of the African coast failed. Malet reported home: 'Dangerous generalizations had been avoided, and international duties on the African coast remained such as they had hitherto been understood to be'.[15]

On 25 February 1885 the Berlin Act was signed. This done, Strauch on behalf of the AIC then signed documents by which the association pledged itself to adhere to the act and which accorded recognition to the new state. Leopold was not present at Berlin to witness the culmination of his years of striving. He had been forced to make concessions to France and Portugal but these were very minor compared with what he had gained – a large sovereign state established in a key position at the mouth of the Congo and backed by a vast hinterland. At the end of the signing session and at mention of the king's name the audience rose and applauded loudly. Though never present at the Conference of Berlin, Leopold II had dominated it. It is only fair to admit that he could not have succeeded without Bismarck's support, but the result of the conference was an immense personal triumph for Leopold.

The Berlin Conference has frequently been blamed for much that happened later in Africa. It is said that the frontiers agreed to were artificial and took no account of tribal boundaries. But such boundaries were unknown at the time and it was necessary to devise a settlement to prevent an international free-for-all which would have led to incidents, if not to war. No Great Power was prepared to see another seizing a large area, such as the Congo. Thus the settlement reached at Berlin, in placing it in the hands of a neutral who was regarded as a sort of international trustee, was in the circumstances the wisest. Whatever happened subsequently in the Congo does not detract from the highly creditable work of the diplomats at Berlin.

The speeches at Berlin vaunting the virtues of Leopold II were read with surprise, if not amazement, in Belgium where knowledge of the king's activities during the previous nine years was minimal. The vast majority of Belgians had no wish to become caught up in the sort of grandiose colonial ambitions that the Powers were manifesting. Leopold was therefore obliged to tread carefully and, when the chief minister called upon parliament to ratify the Berlin Act, nothing was said of the king's position. One deputy proposed a congratulatory vote to the king. This was passed but with a distinct lack of enthusiasm. The Chamber was indifferent to its monarch's international starring role; in the Senate there was even opposition to the ratification.

This represented no more than a preliminary sally into the arena of Belgian politics, for the king was confronted by a far more difficult task. Article 62 of the Belgian constitution stipulates that the King of the Belgians is permitted only to become sovereign of another state with the approval, by at least a two-thirds majority, of parliament. The press in general took the view that there was no objection to the king's becoming head of the new African state, provided that it was strictly personal and that there was no chance of Belgium's becoming entangled. Naturally, in some newspapers Leopold had articles placed supporting himself.

Although Beernaert, the chief minister, was prepared to go along with the king's wishes, many deputies and senators were known to be opposed. Leopold wrote to Beernaert advising him how to deal with parliament. The king understood the shrewd Belgian mentality: 'The best way of winning over the leaders of the left to the idea of my becoming sovereign of the Congo is to tell them that the Government is assured that the new state possesses revenues sufficient for its needs.'[16] In a further letter the king expanded his ideas; the revenue would come from three sources; a special fund constituted for the purpose, export duties and taxes. The special fund would be provided by Leopold himself and would amount to a million francs a year. Duties and taxes would bring in a further 500,000 francs.[17]

Leopold, with help from Lambermont, Banning and Beernaert, wrote a letter to parliament requesting permission to assume sovereignty over the Congo state. 'I cannot back down from the pursuit of a task in which I have taken an important part and I am sure that you consider, as I do, that it can be useful to the nation. I request of you, Gentlemen, the necessary consent.'[18]

The letter was immediately followed by a resolution tabled by Beernaert beginning, 'The King is authorized to be head of the State founded in Africa by the International Association of the Congo'. Subsequently, the words 'the King' were substituted by 'His Majesty Leopold II'. The significance is clear, the personal union was to be limited to Leopold II while in the original version it would have applied to his successors. No plans were made as to what would happen on the king's death.

The resolution was debated by the Chamber on 28 April and voted with only one dissident. The deputy Xavier Neujean was not convinced that such an arrangement was feasible. 'What strikes me most is the enormity of the work to be done and the limited resources available ... Are there not sometimes forces stronger than good intentions?'[19] Beernaert was prepared to admit in the Senate that the undertaking might well appear beyond the capacities of any individual, however 'exalted and powerful', but asked his colleagues to support their king. Without manifesting any real approval they permitted the personal union.

This hurdle over, Leopold applied himself to the easier task of choosing a title. For a time he considered calling himself 'Emperor of the Congo' but eventually decided to settle for the more restrained 'King-Sovereign'.[20] The name of the state, and the title of its head, were notified by a royal decree of 29 May 1885, on which date the *Etat Indépendant du Congo*, the Congo Free State, came into existence. It is frequently known by its French initials, EIC, and this form will be used in future references.

The birth of the new state was announced in the Congo itself on 1 July by the governor, Sir Francis de Winton, but there remained an important issue to be resolved before a similar announcement could be made in Europe. The Berlin Conference had granted the new state the option of declaring itself neutral and that if it did so, the other Powers were bound to guarantee its neutrality. This facility Leopold used to resolve an outstanding problem of the delimitation of frontiers. Territorial conventions had been signed with Germany, France, Portugal and Belgium; Britain in particular had not recognized any frontiers of the state.

Leopold first cleared with Bismarck that Germany would raise no objections to the frontiers agreed to by France in February 1885. Bismarck had had more than enough of Africa and was prepared to allow Leopold to do as he liked. On 1 August 1885 the sovereign of the Congo Free State dispatched a notification of the state's neutrality to the Powers. As expected, it was accepted without demur in Paris and Berlin; it was towards London that Leopold was looking with apprehension.

In December 1884 the Foreign Office had refused to recognize the territorial limits claimed by Leopold, considering them 'some bold lines drawn through almost unexplored regions', and there was no reason to believe that the British government had changed its mind.[21] The Conference of Berlin had expressly stipulated that paper annexations were not to be accepted and, furthermore, the British government would be aware that it did not have to accept Leopold's declaration of neutrality unless they acquiesced in the frontiers.

To Leopold's great surprise the British government sent a letter on 1 September acknowledging receipt of the declaration without comment, which represented tacit agreement. The key to the king's unforeseen success was that the declaration arrived in the month of August when all the high-level officials in the Foreign Office with competence in the subject, in particular Anderson, were on holiday. An assistant clerk had to deal with the matter and, appreciating that it was a question of frontiers, he called in a cartographer who had been a member of the British delegation to the Conference of Berlin. The cartographer was aware that various maps had been drawn up at the end of the conference, however, he extrapolated and assumed that they corresponded with the contents of the Berlin Act – which they did not; they had been affixed to facilitate understanding of it. The assistant clerk accepted the cartographer's view that Leopold's maps were in line with the Berlin Act and drafted a minute advising acceptance of the king's declaration. When Anderson returned and realized what had happened he was furious about 'this stupid blunder'. 'The King based his neutrality circular on article 10 of the Berlin Act. The acknowledgment speaks of "limits" laid down in article 10. No limits were laid down in this article.'[22]

Anderson's ire was nothing compared with that of another Englishman a few years later when he discovered that Katanga formed part of the EIC. Cecil Rhodes appreciated far more than Anderson could ever have done what the British had handed over to Leopold II.

Leopold was now absolute ruler of a country of over 1,000,000 square miles. It had a population of about 10,000,000 people and possessed waterways navigable by steamer thousands of miles from the sea and was already known to be rich in groundnuts, palm oil, gum, ivory, rubber, copper and timber.

For Leopold to have acquired all this – with no support from his country and in competition with far more powerful rivals – was an extraordinary feat, explicable only by the king's qualities of will-power, perseverance, imagination, intelligence and skill in negotiation. It was an immense achievement.

13 King of the Belgians

*'The Belgians get on their high horse when I
give them my advice. But am I not well
qualified to voice an opinion on questions
affecting Belgium?'*[1]   Leopold II.

During the first two decades of Belgium's existence political differences had been reduced to a minimum in the knowledge that the newly-created country could not afford the luxury of internal political dissension when her international position was precarious. However, Unionism, as this state of political truce was called, became more and more difficult to sustain, and in the 1850s two political parties emerged. The Liberals derived their strength essentially from Walloon and Bruxellois business and professional men, free-traders and free thinkers, and an important aspect of their policy was their anti-clericalism, though this was more an attitude of mind than a programme. The Catholic party, as the name indicates, stood for the maintenance of the privileged position of the Catholic church in Belgium. It was essentially conservative and its following was greater in the country areas than in the towns. The party was particularly strong in Flanders.

For many years the Catholics made no real effort at political organization and it was largely due to their indolence as regards wooing the electorate that the Liberals were able to establish themselves as the party of power. The Liberal ministry formed in 1857 under Charles Rogier lacked cohesion from the outset. There were substantial political disagreements within the party and personal antipathy among leading members of the Cabinet but, *faute de mieux*, it survived the 1860s. By 1870 the Catholics had set up a party organization; the Liberal party was yet more internally divided and the ministers clearly exhausted men.

In the elections of 14 June 1870 they suffered a significant defeat and found their seats in the Chamber reduced from seventy-four to sixty-one. The Catholics won fifty-nine and the dissident Liberals – radicals who had broken away from the official party – four. While the Catholics held fewer seats than the Liberals, it was obvious that the government had suffered a considerable defeat. However, it was far from clear which party would be called to the Palais Royal. The king was no admirer of any political group in Belgium though he found the Liberals somewhat less obnoxious than the Catholics. The clerical party, while to the right of the Liberals in terms of domestic policies, was strongly anti-militarist. In Antwerp there had been strong opposition, known as *Meetingisme*, to the fortifying of the city in the 1860s, and the Catholics had taken advantage of this anti-governmental feeling and had come to adopt a pro-gramme calling for a general reduction in military expenditure. A party campaigning on this ticket in 1870, with war between France and Prussia looming on the horizon, hardly found favour with Leopold II.

For a week after the election results had been declared in June 1870, the king did not call upon anyone to form a new government. In the news-papers there was talk of a new Liberal ministry or a coalition but the Catholics firmly dismissed such ideas, holding that they should be asked to form a government. Leopold finally sent for the Count de Theux, the elder statesman of the Catholics.

Theux declined the king's invitation to lead a cabinet on the grounds of age, advising him instead to send for Baron Auguste d'Anethan. Leo-pold interrogated d'Anethan for some time as to what his party's plans were, particularly as regards the military question, before proposing a deal acceptable to the Catholics and himself.

Leopold II's constitutional weapon was the sovereign's right to dissolve parliament. The June elections had only concerned the lower house, the Chamber of Representatives, and the Liberals, who had a majority in the Senate, could obstruct legislation desired by a Catholic government. Leopold knew that the Catholics were anxious for fresh elections for both houses to be held, confident that they would win an overall majority in both houses. D'Anethan was prepared to go along with the king's mili-tary policy in return for the promise of elections, and he set about forming a cabinet (though Leopold himself reserved the right to choose the minister of war). Two hardline Catholics, Victor Jacobs and Prosper Cor-nesse, considered that d'Anethan had sold out to the king but even so, they accepted ministerial office.

Lest the Catholics should let political power go to their heads, Leopold made it clear that they would have to act with circumspection and in co-operation with him. He drew up a long note, which he passed to d'Anethan, ordering the *chef du cabinet* to see that it was signed by all ministers.

> The new administration will exercise the utmost economy in the use of governmental funds, at the same time taking great care not to disrupt the functioning of established public services. [An obvious reference

to the army.] It will study the best way to make use of our increasing financial resources; it will extend public works programmes but at the same time will seek means to reduce taxes on basic food stuffs.[2]

However, within a few days there were more urgent matters, for on 19 July the Franco-Prussian War broke out and the king made it clear that he would himself control Belgian policy. 'I must insist once again that no instructions are sent from the Ministry of Foreign Affairs without having received my approval.'[3]

New elections in August 1870 confirmed Catholic popularity and the party found itself with a comfortable majority in both houses. Leopold was rather surprised to discover in d'Anethan a sympathetic personality and one who clearly wished to restrain the extremist elements in his government. Nevertheless, the king lacked full confidence in his chief minister and their relations became increasingly strained in 1871 over the military reforms Leopold wanted. Whether or not d'Anethan agreed with the king – and he probably did – he found himself confronted with strong opposition in his cabinet, particularly from Jacobs and Charles Woeste, a young ultramontane neophyte possessing great eloquence and force of character. The Catholic party was at this time split into two camps, the liberal Catholics who found themselves condemned by Pope Pius IX, and the ultramontanes who attached supreme importance to the encyclicals from Rome and who considered that pontifical authority was superior to that of the state. As some provisions of the Belgian constitution were antagonistic to Roman Catholic theology of the time, there was obvious political conflict.

Woeste, Jacobs and Baron Kervyn de Lettenhove, the minister of the interior (known today outside Belgium for his excellent edition of Froissart's *Chronicles*), the leading ultramontanes were active not only in parliament but also dominated the Catholic press. The king thought that d'Anethan ought to control his cabinet more firmly and frequently admonished him. The ministers under attack resented Leopold's constant interference in governmental policy and expounded their views yet more in the press. Leopold was unperturbed when d'Anethan warned him that he was becoming unpopular in the country because of his insistence on the need for the country's being able to defend itself. In lofty tones he replied: 'You speak to me of my popularity; it simply doesn't arise here. I assure you, my dear Minister, that between popularity and duty I do not hesitate to choose. Popularity bought at the expense of serving the best interests of the country would impose a burden on my conscience that I could not support.'[4]

Over the following few months the situation deteriorated yet further. Woeste and Jacobs had taken up the Antwerp demand to demolish part of the city's fortifications; Leopold naturally opposed this but more, it was the time when he became convinced of the need for personal service in the army, an idea which was anathema to right-wing Catholics. The king was therefore seeking to rid himself of his distasteful ministers at the first possible opportunity. He did not have to wait long. In November 1871, d'Anethan made an injudicious public appointment by nominating as governor of the province of Limburg a man whose name had been mentioned in connection with a financial scandal – though the man concerned, Pierre de Decker, had been proved innocent.

The Liberals were determined to make political capital out of the nomination. Not only did they attack the government in parliament, they also encouraged the general public – for the vast majority of the population was at this time unenfranchised and their only means of making their views known was to protest in the streets – to demonstrate against the government. In Brussels the scenes became violent and the mayor, Jules Anspach, made only a half-hearted effort to see the civil guard restore order, partly because the Brussels guards' sympathies were anti-Catholic. In view of the lack of control exercised by the government, Leopold demanded the resignation of the minister of the interior who, he considered, should have prevented the demonstrations getting out of hand. D'Anethan stood by Kervyn; trouble in the streets broke out again and the cry *'roi de carton'* (cardboard king) was hurled up at the palace. Leopold was certainly not this and was determined to show his people as much. He therefore demanded the resignation of the entire cabinet. The resignations were handed-in in poor grace and with much resentment. Charles Woeste in his *Mémoires* reproached Leopold 'for having set an unfortunate precedent that the Catholic party could not quickly forget'.[5]

As long as he could form a government from the majority party, the king was acting within his constitutional rights and he turned again to Theux, who was by now seventy-seven. The old man was prepared to lend his name to the cabinet but was not prepared to bear ministerial responsibility, for at this time the *chef du cabinet* also held a portfolio. In a demonstration of his talent for choosing men, Leopold went outside the parliamentary ranks of the Catholics, and persuaded Jules Malou, a brilliant businessman and banker who had helped him in 1870, to leave the *Société Générale* and become minister of finance. In 1874 Theux died and Malou, who for two years had been *de facto* chief minister, then headed the cabinet. His shrewd financial brain and support of military expenditure made him a man able to work with the king and under him the Catholics remained in power until 1878. By this time the Liberals had plastered over their own internal divisions, while the split in the Catholic party was being well aired in the press. The Liberals were as a result carried to power in the elections of 1878.

Frère-Orban formed a government determined to establish the supremacy of the lay State and to eradicate the encroachments made by the Catholic church in previous years. The area in which its power and influence had increased most was education: this was therefore chosen as the political battlefield. The Catholics considered that the church had the power to organize schooling and to receive subsidies to finance it and the law of 1842 seemed to confirm their interpretation. Maurice Maeterlinck, one of Belgium's most distinguished writers, described his schooling in the 1860s: 'Lessons were principally given over to prayers, to simple catechism, to religious history and geography and a little elementary mathematics.'[6] Those of liberal disposition were none too happy with this state of affairs. However, the maintenance of some form of Unionism was still too important at this stage for them to risk arousing too much political acrimony.

In 1878 though the Liberals had received a clear mandate from the electorate and Frère-Orban was determined to make use of his large parliamentary majority to introduce lay primary education. He began by appointing a minister of public instruction. In the speech from the throne in November 1878 the king announced that education entirely provided out of public funds would be placed under the control of the government.

However, the bill introduced in January 1879 was not purely an attack on the existing system. Primary education was far from being available to all children and the Liberals proposed substantially extending the number of primary schools in Belgium. The state would ensure that every commune had at least one primary school; education would be secular and provided by teachers trained in state colleges (up until then Catholic colleges had provided the majority of staff). Frère-Orban and his colleagues wanted to go further and ban all religious instruction in the schools but at this stage Leopold intervened and insisted that priests or ministers of religion should be able to give non-compulsory classes, outside normal school hours.[7] A similar reform of secondary education was also proposed, though it did not excite passions in the way that the new primary legislation did.

The Liberals were well aware that there would be an enormous outcry by the Catholics but they were in no mood for compromise. Undoubtedly they provoked a largely unnecessary political confrontation and wasted the country's resources in their insistence on the building of state schools in every village and town. Even if large numbers of Belgians did not regularly go to church, they were essentially Catholic and the majority favoured educating their children in the Catholic faith.

Not all Liberals approved of the bill and it was passed by only one vote in the Senate. Malou described it as the '*Loi de Malheur*' (the law of unhappiness), and it is by this name that it has gone down in history.

The hierarchy called upon Leopold to refuse to sign the bill but, as a constitutional monarch, he had no choice other than to give the royal assent. This he did with obvious reluctance and pleaded with his people for a cooling of passions. 'Let us try and recreate that vital and wise state of mind which led to the foundation of Belgium ... Let us work together in a spirit of generosity, moderation and thought for the future. The King is imploring you as the future of our dear and noble Belgium depends on your sagacity.'[8]

He met with no success and the country embarked on a bitter internecine feud. In pastoral letters the bishops fulminated against the heathen government; a prayer was added to every mass, 'Lord deliver us from godless schools and faithless teachers'. The sacraments were to be denied to any Catholics sending their children to the new state schools, or to any Catholics teaching in them, unless there was an overriding reason for this. All available buildings were taken over as temporary classrooms and an enormous effort was put in hand to raise money for establishing new schools. In many parts of Flanders, Catholic teachers took a stand against the dictates of the clergy and the debate split families. The more militant Catholic employers dismissed employees for not conforming with the bishops' orders, tenants were thrown out for similar reasons.

A Catholic boycott spoilt Leopold II's plans for celebrating the fiftieth anniversary of Belgium's creation in 1880, the *Cinquantenaire*. However, the peevish behaviour of the Catholics was matched by that of the Liberals and Frère-Orban himself was much too emotionally involved in the issue to behave in a manner that might have been expected of a nineteenth-century rationalist. Disregarding the efforts of the new pope, Leo XIII, to cool the political temperature in Belgium by telling the bishops to modify certain of their stances, Frère-Orban chose to break off diplomatic relations with the Vatican in 1880. Leopold opposed the rupture on diplomatic grounds because for him the issue was not worth the unpleasantness it caused. Marie-Henriette, on the other hand, who normally eschewed politics was, as a devout Catholic, extremely upset.

Behind the fiery front, all was far from well in the Liberal party itself. Frère-Orban was a representative of the already old-fashioned liberals of 1830, men believing in political freedom and the duty and right of the patrician class to govern in the best interests of others. The vote had in 1830 been given to a small number of men, the *cens*, paying high taxes. Some extension of the franchise had been granted and the middle classes were by 1880 somewhat better represented.

The radicals, who formed a loose alliance with the Liberals, had for many years been campaigning for universal male suffrage. Frère-Orban consistently opposed this, but on coming to power in 1878 he had had to make a deal with the radicals: they would support him on educational reform in return for which there would be electoral reform. The government introduced a bill making concessions as regards local and provincial elections; as to national elections, they were intransigent. Paul Janson, the Radical leader, saw his bill overwhelmingly defeated in parliament. He concluded that the right-wing Liberals were no longer worth courting and the split between Frère-Orban's supporters and the radicals was exposed for all to witness. This added to the excesses of the educational legislation which, apart from its political consequences, had overstrained national finances and alienated many moderate men from the Liberal party. The result was a Catholic landslide in the 1884 elections.

Malou was again summoned by the king. While personally a man of moderation, he was forced, for internal party reasons as Woeste and Jacobs had done much to win the election, to include them in his cabinet. All hope of restraining the Catholics from taking their revenge on the Liberals disappeared with their presence at the Ministry of Justice and the Ministry of Public Works. The cabinet at once demanded that the king should dissolve the Senate, which still had a Liberal majority, and, had they been men of compromise, they would have taken note that the electorate again returned a Liberal majority. They were not. Leopold, appreciating that the *Loi de Malheur* would be repealed, wished for a return to the *status quo ante*, that is, the law of 1842, which seemed to have satisfied the Catholic population. Woeste and Jacobs, however, insisted that the Catholic party should take advantage of its parliamentary majority and make no compromise. The king counselled prudence. He told his *chef du cabinet*: 'Accept a few amendments ... True firmness entails thought for the future.'⁹

It was sound advice, though not untinged with personal interest, since at this stage, summer 1884, Leopold was involved in the delicate negotiations preceding the conference of Berlin and was fearful lest the impression be put about internationally that Belgium was disintegrating. Malou for his part did not see any chance of working with the moderate Liberals – his party simply would not stomach such a move – and he found himself a prisoner of the right wing. Modification of the Catholic bill, he told the king, was out of the question.

The bill duly went through the Chamber, only to be thrown out by the Liberal majority in the Senate. Riots broke out in Brussels, the largely anti-clerical people of Brussels applying what pressure they could to persuade the government to withdraw the bill. Leopold did not like the proposed legislation any more than the mob did. Nevertheless, their actions were counter-productive as far as he was concerned. Violence was not the way to run the country and, if the elected majority wanted the law, he would sign the bill placed before him.

The Liberals in the Senate gave way and let the bill through. Others were not prepared to give in so easily. There were well-attended demonstrations in towns throughout Belgium and a large number of mayors, practical men used to implementing laws, gathered together in Brussels and had an audience with the king in which they asked him to mediate. Aware of his impotence, he told them: 'I am obliged to act in conformity with the wishes of the majority of the population as expressed in Parliament.'[10]

While on the one hand highly polarized, the political mood of the country was also, in some respects paradoxically, volatile and in the local elections of 1884 showed a desertion to the Liberals. Leopold, who up until now had, reluctantly, considered himself hamstrung, spotted his opportunity to force his government into a more conciliatory position. The electorate had demonstrated – albeit in local elections which are not necessarily typical of voters' views in national ones – its desire for moderation, and the king could take the initiative.

There was nothing original about Leopold's action in October 1884. He told Malou to dismiss Woeste and Jacobs. The *chef du cabinet* would not, or could not, comply (even though Woeste and Jacobs offered to resign), and handed in his resignation. Leopold was delighted. He immediately sent for the only man in the Catholic party in whom he had any confidence, Auguste Beernaert. The king's move met with sufficient general approval in the country for Leopold to be able to get away with changing governments. After the excesses of the two previous governments moderates in both parties were anxious for a period of stable government. Only by following a policy of appeasement would this be possible. Leopold counselled: 'After 1878 the Liberals behaved as though there were no longer any Catholics in Belgium. The Catholic party would do well to remember that there is a large number of Liberals in the country.'[11]

Many Catholics were, not unnaturally, furious at the king's intervention. The constitutional powers of the monarchy were, in theory, those of guidance in an ambiguous situation and not to remove legitimate cabinets distasteful to the sovereign, but for the second time Leopold II had rid himself of a Catholic cabinet which he did not like. His high-handed treatment of Belgian politicians served him ill in the long run, as it made them wary and suspicious of his political actions.

14 The Age of Democracy

*'Freedom from internal strife is above all the
result of a wide distribution of economic
wealth.'* [1]   Leopold II.

During Leopold II's reign the Belgian economy passed through a period
of brilliant success. It was the age of the chemist Ernest Solvay, the
financier Edouard Empain, the Coppées in coal-mining and the continually innovatory Cockerill firm in the steel industry. But it was also a time
of considerable social disturbance and the working class saw things rather
differently from the glossy picture given at the international fairs – so
fashionable at the time – extolling the wonders of Belgian industry and
commerce.

After passing through the doldrums of the 1830s and 1840s, the Belgian
economy embarked on a period of spectacular growth in the 1850s and
1860s. Independence had brought with it a determination on the part of
the entrepreneurial class to show what it could do without Dutch support; the period also coincided with increased world production of gold
and the industrialization of France and Germany whose expanding
economies provided the main outlets for Belgium's major exports, coal
and iron.

The Belgian government's foresighted decision in the 1830s to undertake a massive programme of railway investment had stimulated the
economy at a difficult time, since virtually all the rails, rolling stock and
constructional material were produced within the country. The railway
network set up – the densest in Europe – provided the necessary infrastructure for the development of Antwerp as a port and generated considerable entrepôt trade. [2]

Whatever indicators one chooses to take, the impressive picture of Belgian industrial expansion is the same. [3] On the other hand, as Belgium
depended more than any other Continental country on trade, this
exposed her to the full vicissitudes of international trade cycles, and when
the world economy entered a period of contraction from 1873 onwards,

its effects were immediately felt in Belgium. It was the banking world which suffered the first impact in 1875–6, and by 1877 a fall in world prices took place, leading inevitably to wage reductions and un-employment. At this unpropitious moment an agricultural crisis de-scended on Europe, caused by the wheat exports from North America and the Baltic which, due to their large-scale production and the improved means of transport, undercut the prices of European producers. Germany and France were both less dependent on foreign markets and could afford to adopt a degree of protection. Britain was in the same trading position as Belgium but its agricultural population was by then relatively small. Belgium faced the worst of all worlds.

If life was hard enough in the rural areas, in Belgian towns and cities it was appalling. Economic success had been achieved because wage rates were significantly lower than in industrial rivals. Working-class living conditions were squalid. Most habitations were one room to a family, they were packed close together and frequently lacked even the most basic sanitation. Many people went hungry and even those who did not lived mainly off potatoes or bread. There was no factory legislation; men, women and children (as young as six-year-olds) worked long hours in unregulated factories. Contemporary studies provide ample evidence of the sufferings and deprivations of the Belgian working class and peas-antry. Certainly in other countries the situation was far from ideal, but it was distinctly better than in Belgium.[4]

In addition to discontent caused by economic factors, Leopold II, on ascending the throne in 1865, faced agitation aimed at ameliorating the political position of the Belgian masses. A meeting of Marx's *Inter-nationale* took place in Liège in 1865 and several socialist newspapers and groups were set up as a result; the following year the Belgian socialist lawyer Edmond Picard published a workers' manifesto in which he called, in the first instance, for a massive increase in the franchise. Social ques-tions could not by this stage be ignored and in his speech from the throne in 1866 Leopold announced that the government would take steps to improve the lot of the working class. This was in keeping with his speech in the Senate as Duke of Brabant. Throughout his life the king's attitude to social questions changed little: he favoured the alleviation of misery in a spirit of benevolent paternalism – no more.

The ensuing legislation conferred the right to strike and the workman's *livret*, a form of report book which had to be handed to employers and in which the employer could write what comments he chose about the employee, was abolished in 1873. It seemed easier to remove legal dis-crimination against workers than to take positive steps to protect them, and all attempts at factory and mines regulation in the 1870s failed.

It was obvious that parliament as then constituted would not go very far in social questions. The leaders of the working-class movement therefore concentrated most of their political energies on campaigning for suffrage reform. They fairly soon realized that neither of the two established parties would take up their cause (the Paris Commune had scared many parliamentarians) and they decided that it was necessary to form a separate political party. A Flemish socialist party was founded in Ghent in 1877. Two years later it fused with a similar Walloon group, only to split up soon afterwards. Before long groups covering much of the left-wing political spectrum were organized throughout Belgium.

As happened elsewhere, the appellation socialist with its Marxist, republican and anti-religious associations frightened off many working men and middle-class sympathizers. The left-wing leaders came to appreciate this and in 1885 the Belgian Workers' Party was founded.[5] A brochure published earlier in the same year, The People's Catechism by Alfred Defuisseaux, which graphically described working-class misery and called for universal male suffrage, sold 200,000 copies in French and 60,000 in Flemish, an enormous circulation for the time.[6]

The following year, when the economic situation had deteriorated yet further, proletarian anger could no longer be contained. Riots broke out in Liège in March; for days desperate miners roamed the streets, breaking windows and destroying whatever they found before them. The civic guard was sent in and its brutality only served to increase the fury of the masses. Finally, order prevailed in Liège only for trouble to break out in the coal-mining regions of the Borinage and in Hainault. Here factories were set on fire, the town of Charleroi was looted; glass works in Hainault were easy prey to destruction and even farms and a château in the area were sacked and destroyed. This time the army was sent in to deal with the situation. About twenty people were killed and many hundreds injured. The king's attitude was summed up in a note to his chief minister: 'As to repressive measures, I think that it is necessary to pass a law giving the government power to arrest the ring leaders and suppress their writings and a further one to make the possession of firearms without a permit, illegal. We also need more gendarmes.'[7]

The ruling classes in Belgium were shaken by the civil disorder they saw erupting around them. Their eyes were opened to the misery of many. 'We were not aware of the extent of the crisis [the people] were going through. Everyone agreed that something had to be done to remedy the situation,' wrote Woeste.[8] The year 1886 marked a turning point, for from then onwards the government would have to concern itself actively with social questions.

It also coincided with Beernaert's becoming chef du cabinet. There was work to be done by the Catholic government and also, assuming some extension of the suffrage would have to be granted, there were votes to be gained by the Catholic party's becoming the champion of the working class.

Auguste Beernaert came from a bourgeois Flemish family. A large, well-dressed, urbane man, with an enormous nose to delight cartoonists, he looked very much the successful barrister he had been at the Brussels bar before being wooed by the Catholic party to stand for parliament. He did not possess the political drive and Catholic militancy of Woeste but was a man of moderation, a conservative who accepted the need for change. Once in parliament he was ear-marked by Leopold II as one of the more sympathetic Catholics since he had already, in the 1870s, shown interest and support for the king's African schemes. He had been a member of the Belgian committee of the AIA and vice-chairman in 1878. On becoming *chef du cabinet* he did much to help Leopold in winning the necessary parliamentary approval to become sovereign of the Congo Free State, and he was prepared to collaborate further in Congolese matters. This undoubtedly formed the basis of their relationship. Leopold's dependence on Beernaert enabled the chief minister to be firm and frank with the king in a way none of his predecessors had been, and they mutually appreciated their respective ironical turns of phrase.

In an attempt to reduce unemployment in 1886, a massive programme of public works, mainly road building and local railway-line construction, was voted. The king very much approved, though he seems to have been more interested in the roads from the point of view of urbanism rather than their employment-creating function. He considered being out of work a sign of laziness.[9]

At the same time a Commission on Work, modelled on British royal commissions, was set up. It heard evidence from many sources and in 1888 published its findings in four large volumes. On employment in general it had little to offer; however, it came out in favour of abolishing the truck system, factory legislation and obligatory accident insurance. By this time, though, the government had already embarked on such a programme. The first reform, ending the infamous system of payment in kind practised in the arms industry in Liège, in the port of Antwerp and elsewhere in Flanders, went through without much trouble as did the creation of work and industry councils made up of employers and employees whose function would be to prevent strikes and lock-outs. Women and children were protected by a law of 1889 which forbade the employment of children under twelve years of age and limited adolescents to a twelve-hour day.

Previous Catholic governments had all fallen foul of Leopold on the subject of defence and in choosing Beernaert the king had hoped that his chief minister would be able to control the anti-militarist wing of the party. Since 1870 when the Franco-Prussian War had revealed the short-fall in good soldiers for the Belgian army, Leopold had been convinced of the necessity for personal service (ie to abolish the *remplacement*) and greater expenditure on defence. He was not a military man himself and he had never seen active service as had his father. He took no interest in the finer points of military discipline and dress, whereas Leopold I had immediately spotted an epaulette out of place on a guard at the Palais Royal. Even colourful military manœuvres failed to impress his son, who made a point of arriving in time for the closing ceremonies, and no more. Though Leopold II frequently wore the informal dress uniform of a general its state of upkeep would never have passed muster on the parade ground. He irreverently referred to the distinguished *képi* that was part of his uniform as '*mon bonnet*'.

Leopold's view of military matters was that of a politician, and he knew European statesmen sufficiently well to be sceptical of the value of the guarantees of neutrality if Belgium fell in their path. He was fond of re-peating that if Belgium was not a barrier it immediately became a passage, and he continued throughout the 1870s to make speeches on defence, when practically everyone else in Belgium was more occupied with other matters. He tried to appeal through his countrymen's business spirit:

> In the past, vessels from all over the world came in their thousands to the ports of Ghent and Bruges ... It was the apogee of our com-mercial and industrial prosperity ... I am convinced that in Flanders today the will and the necessary skills are to be found to make it poss-ible to relive those glorious days.[10]

One man who shared the king's point of view was Henri-Alexis Brial-mont, one of his mentors of the early 1860s when Duke of Brabant. In *La Belgique Militaire*, Brialmont continued month by month, year in, year out, to expose the military vulnerability of Belgium and to propose what should be done. The French were fortifying a line along the Vosges and the Germans were rebuilding the defences of Strasbourg and else-where; it should be made clear to both, *La Belgique Militaire* held, that Belgium also was prepared to defend her territorial integrity. To do this a line of forts along the Meuse and the Sambre was necessary. In particu-lar, Liège with its railway lines into Germany and France, six bridges over the Meuse and many industries needed to be defended.

The military issue came to the fore in Belgium in the years 1886-7 for external reasons. The Balkan crisis of 1886 provoked a war scare through-out Continental Europe and Leopold, who visited the aged German emperor in October 1886, returned home much impressed and discon-certed by the magnitude of German military expenditure. Both of Belgium's powerful neighbours had become increasingly suspicious of each other's military preparations and their respective presses took delight in stirring up old enmities. In January 1887 the German minister in Brussels warned Beernaert that the French were thought to be likely to attack Germany: was Belgium in a position to defend her neutrality in such an eventuality? The French waxed strong on how Belgium was to all intents and purposes a German satellite. England, the defender of Belgian neutrality in 1870, seemed anxious to avoid all involvement, and in articles widely considered to be Foreign Office inspired, if not actually written there, it was argued that, if foreign troops passed through Belgium, this would not constitute a violation of Belgian neutrality.[11]

Soon after the opening of the 1886–7 parliamentary session an independent deputy proposed the introduction of personal military service. Leopold was delighted and optimistic as to the outcome, as many Liberals had come to favour it. Woeste and Jacobs, as would be expected, led the opposition to the proposal. Beernaert did not take up a position publicly on the subject. He could not push this issue too strongly, but there was a chance that he could use it to demand some concessions from the anti-militarists. He judiciously threatened to resign, knowing that the right could not form a government. His point made, he then announced his *quid pro quo* for not forcing the personal service issue. The right would have to support the fortifying of the Meuse.

In the debate on the forts in the Chamber that followed, Frère-Orban criticized the proposals, holding that unless the army was almost doubled in size, there would simply not be enough men to defend the forts adequately. They would be 'useless' ineffective and dangerous'.[12] Beernaert disputed this contention and claimed that Brialmont's new designs would not entail a larger army. Leopold did not share this opinion and decided to try yet again to rally the Catholics to personal service.

His seemingly original tactic was in fact borrowed from Bismarck who, several years before, had successfully done a deal with the pope in which the pope persuaded the Catholic Centre party in Germany to vote for the military expenditure the chancellor wanted, in return for which Bismarck agreed to end the *Kulturkampf*. Leopold therefore wrote to Leo XIII asking for his support over personal service; he for his part would guarantee that anyone wishing to enter the priesthood would be exempt. Leopold's offer to the pope was hardly a tempting one and Leo XIII had no desire, nor incentive, to become involved in Belgian domestic problems. With elegant Roman diplomatic phraseology he refused to intervene.[13]

The king could only hope that the Belgian parliament could be persuaded. He personally canvassed deputies and rallied several to his way of thinking. He pleaded with Beernaert to use all his influence to push through the military reforms. In the end the credits for the forts were passed by a large majority, though not all the forts Leopold and Brialmont considered necessary were constructed. The project for personal service, however, was rejected by sixty-nine votes to sixty-two, with four abstentions. It was an enormous disappointment to Leopold, mitigated somewhat by the fact that he was at that moment taking part in Queen Victoria's Golden Jubilee celebrations in England and rather enjoying himself.

As a constitutional monarch he ought, strictly speaking, to have accepted parliament's rejection of personal service. However, Leopold I had established the precedent that in military matters the king had the right to exercise greater influence than in other areas. His son, and later heirs, have maintained the same position. Therefore, in August 1887, when Leopold II was due to inaugurate a statue to two fourteenth-century Flemish heroes, at Bruges, he informed Beernaert that he wanted to talk about personal service. If he could not, he would not go. To the petulant note stating the king's position, the *chef du cabinet* replied with his usual discretion:

> I do not think it advisable for Your Majesty to make any direct reference to this question at Bruges. But I have no doubt that Your Majesty's words will, as always, be patriotic ... On the other hand, it would be most regrettable if Your Majesty did not go to Bruges where he is sure to find a very warm welcome. Your absence would certainly give rise to unfavourable speculation.[14]

By return of messenger the king told his chief minister: 'As to Bruges, dear Minister, it is impossible for me to go there and make an empty speech. If I go it will be to speak openly and seriously.'[15]

It was, Beernaert knew only too well, an extremely sensitive political issue in Catholic Flanders and the Bruges incident well illustrates the power of the king *vis-à-vis* a cabinet with a substantial parliamentary majority behind it. Banning suggested sugaring the pill by making the speech in Flemish,[16] but although Leopold made a few drafting changes he gave the speech he wanted – in French. His closing words were: 'The Lion of Flanders must not sleep. Liberty is born with and dies with independence. This lesson is written on every page of our history.'[17]

The Catholic government was successfully keeping the electorate happy with its policy of social appeasement. The non-voters, however, while they appreciated the reforms, were not content with them. They were increasingly vociferous in demanding to participate in governing the country. Belgium was gradually rising from the economic nadir of 1886 and working men were more able to devote their energies to political action. In August 1890 at least 100,000 people demonstrated in Brussels in favour of universal male suffrage and the issue dominated the press. The progressives in the Liberal party supported large-scale extension of the vote, seeing in it the only political salvation of the demoralized Liberal party, although Frère-Orban remained intransigent in his opposition. Many Catholics came to accept that some degree of enfranchisement was necessary for social stability and the electoral success of the progressive Liberals in 1890 convinced Beernaert that resolution of the issue could not be delayed. To do him justice, however, one should add that he believed that the small electorate – 137,000 men out of a total population of about 5,000,000 – was a vestige of the political theory of an earlier age. Furthermore, England, France and Holland had all extended the franchise. Belgium alone maintained the *cens* of 1831.

Qualification for voting had been included in the 1831 constitution and, for more than a minor extension, constitutional revision would be necessary. For this to take place there had to be a two-thirds majority in both Houses. Strictly speaking if parliament expressed its wishes in this way, the sovereign should be obliged to give the royal assent, but Beernaert knew his master well and took pains to ensure that he was behind the government. He was greatly surprised to find that he encountered little difficulty with the king. The explanation came a few weeks later when Leopold announced to Beernaert that his support for the extension of the franchise was dependent on the constitutional reform which would grant the sovereign the right to extend Belgian territory, control over royal marriages and, most importantly, the right to hold referenda. A further proposal according to which the police would come under state rather than communal control was immediately discarded.

When the king's demands became public they caused a political uproar. The first did not excite too much interest as the Congo was not at that stage an issue in Belgium. Leopold's desire to control royal marriages was simply a desire to preserve the national patrimony and his own fortune intact and it was not a national issue. It was the third, the idea that the sovereign should be able to hold referenda that was original and audacious. Writing from London the king claimed: 'that Lord Salisbury attaches a great deal of importance to the royal referendum ... He has been thinking of introducing it in England and hopes eventually to borrow from Belgian legislation.'[18] There is nothing on paper to substantiate this surprising assertion. What was not new, however, was the king's determination to do a deal. Years of diplomacy and politics had made the notion of the trade-off in all that he did, second nature. That the idea of royal referenda – and one imagines that they would have to have a broad voting base to be credible reflections of grass-roots views – should be advanced in a parliamentary democracy which was tentatively feeling its way towards a limited extension of the franchise, is somewhat unexpected. As is still widely held, and it was one of the tenets of nineteenth-century political thinking, the concept of referenda is antagonistic to the principles of parliamentary democracy. Another line of opposition in Belgium in 1891 was, to use the double metaphor of the time, that it smacked of Caesarian Bonapartism.

Leopold was proposing the referendum *ante legem*, the sounding out of the people before parliament voted on an issue, but this egregious idea caused such an outcry that he declared himself prepared to abandon it and substitute for it the referendum *post legem*, to be used in cases where a major bill had been passed by a narrow majority. Many could not see why the king was prepared to create such a fuss about what amounted to a tarted-up version of the power of veto – which he already possessed.

Nevertheless, the king deployed his considerable energies to pushing his proposition as he realized that a great deal of persuasion would be necessary to win acceptance for the referendum. This was no easy task since if the left considered it an extension of democracy, this would frighten the right and *vice versa*. Favourable articles were placed in the press – one in the *New York Herald* was reprinted in most Belgian papers on Leopold's instructions – and the king took pains to give dinners for parliamentarians. All was in vain; Leopold was isolated. His brother Philippe wrote to Queen Victoria:

> Our good Leopold is somewhat excitable by nature and sometimes lacks simplicity. This idea of direct consultation with the electorate is an unfortunate idea which, if adopted, would do more harm than good. Unfortunately there is no one here whose advice Leopold is prepared to take. He does everything on his own which can sometimes be dangerous ... Naturally, the person of the King will not emerge without suffering a loss of prestige.[19]

Beernaert counselled dropping the idea of the referendum, pointing out the opposition it had aroused in many quarters. The king was aware of this but remained as tenacious as ever. It was, he insisted, simply a matter of putting it over properly.

After preliminary discussion in parliament, it was decided to set in motion the steps for constitutional reform. This entailed setting up a *Constituante*, a specially-elected parliament, and elections were duly held in July 1892, the political balance changing little as a result. A commission of thirteen was chosen from the *Constituante* to undertake detailed examination of the various proposals and to work out the compromises which would enable the necessary two-thirds majority to be obtained.

Discussion centred on the suffrage. The left-wing Liberals and radicals pressed hard for universal male suffrage; the right hit back with all manner of forms of plural voting. The masses had suffered more than enough of parliamentary procrastination. A general strike was called, during which violent demonstrations took place in the streets. The *Constituante* took note and rapidly came to a decision. However, what emerged was far from what the working class had hoped for. Every male citizen over twenty-five was to have the vote: in addition, what Disraeli had described in 1866 as 'fancy franchises' when similar ones had been proposed in England, were added. Those occupying a property which fell into the taxable bracket, *censitaires*, were to have a second vote: those having successfully passed secondary school examinations and civil servants, *capacitaires*, were to have an extra vote, as were heads of families. No-one however was to dispose of more than three votes. Voting was made obligatory to ensure that the moderates, frequently the politically indifferent, were not swamped by militants.

The politicians were naturally more interested in the subject of electoral reform which affected them directly than the extension of the powers of the monarch. Beernaert's advocacy of the royal referendum was lukewarm; it was obvious to his colleagues and they told him firmly that it was a non-starter.

Leopold II's pride and obstinacy would not permit him to accept this defeat, even though his other two demands went through without too much trouble. In place of the referendum, he demanded that the Senate should be reformed in such a way as to make it a brake on the democratically elected Chamber. The qualifications for voting in senatorial elections were to be tightened up and the requirements for standing similarly. In the end this minimal reform of the Senate was made as a sop to the king.

Leopold then turned on Beernaert and blamed him for having suggested the royal referendum to him in the first place. 'In proposing and persuading me to adopt the referendum, you gave me bad advice. The referendum which I did my utmost to defend is, of all the proposals I have approved over twenty-seven years, the one which has done me the most harm; it has almost overthrown the monarchy.'[20] Woeste also claims that the idea originated with the *chef du cabinet*.[21] But even if – and it seems doubtful – Beernaert was the originator, Leopold had taken the project over and claimed it as his own. It was, to say the least, less than generous, to turn on his minister in this way.

Beernaert had suffered a defeat at the hands of the right in the degree of extension of the suffrage. He believed that the age of democracy had arrived whether the ruling classes liked it or not. The masses would not be satisfied with the fancy franchises; political stability was his aim and he tried to redress the balance in favour of the proletariat by proposing proportional representation. He knew that Woeste among others would raise objections, but Beernaert had genuinely come to believe in the need for political democracy. There was, nevertheless, an element of fatigue, the signal that he considered his task to be done and wanted to hand over to someone else. Even so, Leopold II, who favoured the simple majority system, was, it is said, extremely upset when he heard that Beernaert had been jettisoned by his party.[22]

It marked the end of a political era in Belgium. In the elections of October 1894, thirty-four socialists were elected to parliament, though the Catholics still had an overall majority since the socialists had taken votes almost entirely from the Liberals. Plural voting enabled the bourgeoisie to maintain its dominance in parliament – 850,000 voters had one vote while the plural voters amounted to 1,240,000.[23] Despite this, the government had to give serious consideration to the working class and during the next few years important social legislation was passed.

Paradoxically, however, the extension of the suffrage strengthened Leopold's hand. Although the legislature increased in stature in that its power base was broadened, on the other hand the sizeable number of socialists weakened the hegemony of future governments – all Catholic as the Liberals were in disarray. They were obliged to be highly circumspect in the policies they adopted, thus shifting the balance of power in favour of the monarchy. No chief minister after Beernaert was able to stand up to Leopold II.

In the years before the extension of the franchise Leopold's interest in Belgian domestic politics had been declining, the Congo and other international projects increasingly occupying his time. From 1895 his financial independence curtailed whatever vestiges of involvement in Belgian politics remained, though his personal interest in military affairs and urbanism lasted until his death.

Town and country planning was a subject of increasing interest to Leopold. As Duke of Brabant he had only been able to exhort the Belgian government and the Brussels' authorities to pay more attention to the physical aspect of the country, but when he became king he was able to play a more active role. All projects concerning Brussels and Ostend were scrutinized by the king and, because of his intervention and pressure, the government was constrained to spend more money than before on urban development.

Early on in his reign Leopold also began using his own money to finance and maintain projects. In 1873 he bought about two acres at the lower end of the avenue Louise for a garden; it was the first of many with which Leopold endowed Brussels. His next scheme (though he insisted that his name should not be mentioned) was to create a large park outside Brussels in Forest to provide recreational facilities for the densely-populated commune of St Gilles. On the opposite side of Brussels the château of Laeken was enlarged (it was subsequently heavily damaged by fire in 1890) and Leopold acquired a large amount of land in the commune to extend the royal park and to create a public park. But Leopold's major contribution to Laeken was the building of magnificent greenhouses in the château grounds. He was an enthusiastic and knowledgeable horticulturist and imported many tropical plants, until by the time of his death he possessed the most extensive private botanical collection in the world.

In 1897 the château of Tervuren was destroyed by a fire (his sister Charlotte escaped unhurt), and Leopold decided to build a new château as a museum of Congolese art approached by a wide, tree-lined thoroughfare from Brussels. The avenue de Tervuren was considered sumptuous and excessively wide at the time; today it is one of the few beautiful and efficient roads leading into a capital city. At the Brussels end of the avenue it was decided to build a monument commemorating the fiftieth anniversary of the founding of Belgium, the *Cinquantenaire*. In 1880, the year of the anniversary, the country was too involved in the schools war to celebrate; temporary exhibition halls were eventually constructed in the 1880s but much to Leopold's disappointment there was insufficient money to build a triumphal arch linking the two buildings.

Outside Brussels the king particularly enjoyed the seaside town of Ostend and the Ardennes and he was keen to develop their amenities to attract tourism. In Ostend he pressed the local authorities to develop the town as a holiday resort and he himself bought land for the Marie-Henriette and Stephanie Parks; he also tried to extend the town by developing the dunes. In the Ardennes he demolished and rebuilt his château at Ardenne as a luxury hotel, complete with a golf course and a special railway station, but it was not a success.

In the first years of the twentieth century, with the influx of money from the Congo, the king's passion for building found full expression[24] so that today a glance almost anywhere in Brussels, indeed in Belgium as a whole, and one can see the stamp of Leopold II.

15 Sovereign of the Congo Free State

*'There is no other example, at least in
modern times, of a state whose history can
be so much identified with a single man.'*[1]

Jean Stengers, 1970.

Leopold's first task once the Belgian parliament had given its assent to his becoming King-Sovereign of the Congo Free State in April 1885, was to find the money necessary to administer the country. And while he had his work cut out to prevent the infant state from collapsing, he was at the same time seeking to extend its frontiers – above all to the Nile – by expeditions and diplomacy and pursuing projects for trade and/or colonization in China, Morocco, Persia and Russia. For even after he became its sovereign, the Congo was at no stage his sole preoccupation and though it is necessary for the sake of clarity to consider Leopold's projects separately the enormous diversity of schemes he was involved in at any one time should be borne in mind.

To win parliament's approval, Leopold had insisted that the EIC possessed adequate financial resources, but he knew that his assertion was not true and that he had to find large sums of money, and quickly. He had by 1885 spent about 10,000,000 francs out of his personal fortune on his African enterprises. Even allowing for his successful investment of the 15,000,000 francs that his father had left him, his own and Charlotte's money would not go very far in administering the vast colony. The difficulty of the king's position was heightened by the fact that the Conference of Berlin had expressly forbidden the new state to impose import duties for twenty years. While direct taxation was permitted, in reality this was meaningless as the native population was virtually outside the cash economy. The only tax allowed which could raise revenue was the imposition of export duties. Other sources of revenue, such as the registration of land sales and postal taxes, were negligible.

Most colonies relied on subsidies from the government of the colonial power concerned in their early years. However, the Berlin Conference seems to have assumed that Leopold would continue to subsidize the EIC until such time as private enterprise generated sufficient revenue-raising economic activity, even though it was unrealistic to expect one man, albeit a rich one, to bear all the costs himself.

Leopold was counting on money from France. At the Conference of Berlin the French government, after refusing to pay an indemnity for the Niari–Kouilou, had agreed as compensation to allow the king to launch a lottery worth 20,000,000 francs in France. (Lotteries were forbidden by law in Belgium.) This commitment had been made in a personal letter from Jules Ferry to Leopold in February 1885.[2] However, Ferry's ministry fell soon afterwards and the succeeding government was unsympathetic to expansionary policies either by France or others. Louis de Freycinet, the minister of foreign affairs, informed Leopold that the offer of a lottery had been a personal gesture of Ferry's and that the new government did not feel bound to it. 'M. de Freycinet seems personally well disposed towards us, but he says that France is not legally obliged to honour the promise.'[3]

By September 1885 Leopold was exceedingly worried by his perilous financial situation and its effect on the Congo. He had previously always spent part of the summer at the Chalet Royal in Ostend, but in 1886 Leopold did not feel able to allow himself the luxury of a holiday by the sea. He had already borrowed from banker friends such as Gerson von Bleichröder and the Rothschilds. Friends they may have been to lend the money, but they were above all professional financiers. On being approached for a further loan Charles de Rothschild replied: 'I am obliged to inform you, Sire, that in accordance with the rules and customs of my bank, regretfully it will no longer be possible to extend to Your Majesty the facilities hitherto offered.'[4] Leopold was therefore forced on to the open market and a syndicate composed primarily of the *Société Générale de Belgique*, the *Banque de Paris* and the *Länderbank* of Vienna was set up to float a 100,000,000-franc interest-free loan on behalf of the EIC, with prizes awarded by lottery from time to time. (Premium bonds are a later example of the same principle.) However, the bankers' terms were too onerous for the market and Leopold had to let the project drop for the moment. The following October, 1886, he planned another loan issue but its terms did not satisfy the banking world.

In no way discouraged Leopold tried again in 1887. This time he aimed for 150,000,000 francs (in 100 franc shares) as he now realized that the scale of operations necessary to develop the Congo as he wanted was greater than he had previously thought. Moreover, he was hoping to finance a railway project in the state. A loan of 150,000,000 francs, part of which would be reinvested, would produce an annual income of about 1,000,000 francs which, together with the king's subsidy, would be sufficient for the EIC to survive. For such a sum it would clearly be necessary to go to the international market, though the issue could be made in Belgium. For this, there would have to be parliamentary approval. Strictly speaking it could be done by royal decree, but such a course of action would lay itself open to adverse criticism and if the loan was to succeed in foreign countries it would have to be seen to be popular in Belgium itself. In the end the project was passed by both chambers, though they added the rider that their permission was given, 'subject to the formal and categorical condition that the legislature is in no way implicated, either legally or financially, because of the union of the two crowns under the same monarch'.[5]

It was evident to Leopold that there was no greater enthusiasm for colonies in Belgium now than twenty years before and, this being so, the lukewarm attitude of the parliamentarians would not help in persuading the financial world of the desirability of the loan. The king once more turned to France. As part of a frontier settlement relating to the northern boundary of the EIC with the French Congo, the French government agreed to a Paris issue.[6] There remained a crucial technical obstacle, namely that loan-lotteries were forbidden on the Paris *Bourse* (an exception had been made for the *Credit Foncier*). The matter was referred to the *Chambre Syndicale des Agents de Change* which set about studying the matter. It showed no inclination to hurry, much to Leopold's annoyance. He pressed the Belgian minister in Paris and the Belgian banker, Leon Lambert, to extract a decision from the chamber. All was to no avail. It was not until the middle of May 1888 that the chamber came to a decision, favourable to Leopold if unpopular in some financial quarters in France.[7]

In the meantime Leopold was grappling with the problem of raising the loan in Belgium, where the bankers he had approached to handle the issue showed no interest.[8] Part of the problem was the king's own fault as he was trying to float the first part of the loan, 10,000,000 francs, at 92% of par. He tried to persuade the Austrian railway company to buy the shares at 85% and to sell at 92%. Leopold was told firmly that he was overstating the issue price and would have to lower his sights. Other bankers told him the same but the king refused to reduce his demands. Instead, he decided that the EIC itself would issue the loan with the 'moral support of a broadly based committee of which the national bank would be the mainstay'.[9] This formula, however, would not provide the necessary reserve fund which such a loan was obliged by law to have. In any case, the EIC would not constitute a sufficient guarantor in the eyes of potential investors. Beernaert told the king that his ideas were impracticable and that the only possible situation would be for the loan to be issued by a syndicate of bankers. He himself set negotiations in motion but the king would not go below 90% of par.

Leopold was convinced that the financiers wanted to underprice the issue. Beernaert intervened with the bankers, who were sticking at 82·5%. He asked for 85%; agreement was reached on 83%. The king was forced to accept what the market would offer or fail completely.

The subscription was opened on 6 March 1888. At first it was a great success and the issue was rapidly sold out. Then a fortnight later, the shares fell by two francs and the bankers advised Leopold to intervene to support the price. Over the next few months the price oscillated dangerously, falling to 72% in January 1889. The following month when he was in Vienna for the funeral of his son-in-law, the king tried unsuccessfully to get the shares quoted on the Austrian stock exchange.

The price rose to 84% in April 1888 and when it again fell Leopold bought nearly three million francs' worth of shares at 83%. The time for the second part of the issue was fast approaching, and it was obviously indispensable, if it was to be a success, that the new issue had to be priced somewhat below the old stock. A rate of 84% had been fixed for the second issue. A few days before the issue day, the old shares fell below this figure. Leopold for once panicked, and started buying his own shares to force the price up – financially highly unethical behaviour. He wrote a desperate letter to Beernaert:

> I entirely share your opinion that we are heading straight for disaster ... Will you kindly call a meeting of the bankers tomorrow and ask them to support the market for two days. The enormous sacrifices which I have made so far do not permit me to assume this task alone ... I cannot keep buying shares at 84 when the syndicate then buys them back from me at 74, as well as financing the EIC.[10]

Of the new issue of 600,000 shares, that is, 60,000,000 francs, only 260,000 were subscribed. Leopold learnt the hard way that the financial world did not have confidence in his Congolese enterprise and this failure contributed to the king's alienation from such circles.

Although the financing of the administration fell to Leopold II it was expected that the economic infrastructure, as well as the commercial development of the country, would be taken care of by private enterprise. And as the latter was dependent on the former, it was particularly important to set in motion the building of a railway to by-pass the Congo cataracts.

The king was aware of this and as early as 1883 he told Strauch to broach the subject to Mackinnon. Leopold was thinking in terms of an Anglo-Belgian-French railway company – French participation being necessary to placate their ever suspicious attitude towards his activities. Mackinnon was asked to sound out potential investors. The reaction of

Hutton and others interested in trade with the Congo was positive. However, they envisaged the creation of a British chartered company to implement the scheme. When Leopold learnt of this he politely let it be known that there was no question of such a company's being either British dominated or registered.

Other preoccupations forced the king to let the idea drop for a while, then in 1885, after the Conference of Berlin, he turned to Stanley to take fresh soundings in England. With Hutton's co-operation a set of proposals was drawn up and submitted to Brussels in September 1885. At this stage Leopold was still optimistic about raising money himself which would enable the EIC to have a large say in such an enterprise, but when financial resources were not forthcoming he gave the go-ahead to Hutton and his friends.[11] They then formed a syndicate and, without any difficulty, received promises of participation amounting to £400,000.

They would build 150 miles of narrow-gauge railway from Vivi to Isangila which would cost, with the necessary stations and stores, £1,000,000. In return for this investment they expected not only to benefit from the ensuing trade generated but to be given land concessions, including mineral rights, and to be able to establish industries. The state authorities were to give the company every protection and assistance, but in the event of the EIC's being unable to maintain its authority, the company would be empowered to exercise authority and jurisdiction in its own territories.

The terms were exacting, almost exorbitant, and were part of the reason why Leopold was so anxious in 1885 to raise the money himself. Even after he failed he treated the British syndicate with scepticism. 'I think the English will want to sign something tomorrow' (21 December 1885), he told Strauch. 'We must try to satisfy them ... while remaining prudent. Perhaps one could sign that one is in agreement in principle [and] ... give a provisional concession to the syndicate.'[12] The syndicate was not taken in and their 'political' leader, Stanley, whose relations with Leopold were at this time strained, used the opportunity to send a mildly blackmailing letter to the king. 'The principal promoters of it [the railway] are holding aloof and withdrawing their promises. Mr. Hutton is despairing, and urges me to appeal once more to Your Majesty to resolve all doubts upon the subject of my present and future relations with the Congo State.'[13]

The king with his usual tact reassured the explorer, but four months later the EIC came forward with amendments to the agreement signed on 21 December 1885, the most important of which was that any dispute which might arise would be settled according to EIC law – as yet not promulgated – and not British law.[14] Acrimonious discussions followed and in September 1886 the state authorities informed the syndicate that acceptance of the draft agreement would compromise the sovereignty of the EIC, and that certain terms, the constitution of a monopoly, infringed the Berlin Act.[15]

The real reason for dropping the English was that by now there were Belgian capitalists interested in the railway project, who were resentful that the concession had been awarded to foreigners. Whether, when the amendments were demanded in April 1886, the Belgian group led by Captain Albert Thys had already made its views known is not certain. There are no documents showing double dealing at this stage, though this does not, of course, preclude conversations having taken place. Duplicity or not, Leopold was understandably greatly pleased about the Belgian offer.

Thys, the leading figure in the Belgian group, had distinguished himself at the military academy by his study of Africa and in this way he found himself chosen as an equerry to the king in 1878. He shared his master's colonial views and after the creation of the EIC in 1885, Leopold let Thys remain nominally on his staff while permitting him to devote all his time to Congolese matters. The king, as ever a good judge of men, appreciated the value of the dynamic thirty-seven-year-old's ability, his great strength of personality and determination.

Thys persuaded Leopold that a survey should first be carried out to determine where exactly a railway was most needed in the Congo, to make a technical feasibility study and to estimate potential receipts. Such a survey, he calculated, would cost 1,000,000 francs, and to show his resolution Thys set about raising the money himself, calling first on bankers. A typical reaction was: 'All those in the King's entourage are no doubt distinguished diplomats and officers like yourself. But, my dear Captain, however devoted and intelligent they are, they know nothing about business.'[16] Thys, as tenacious and energetic a man as the king, tried everyone he could think of – it was said his friends crossed the road when they saw him approaching with a subscription form always in hand – and he eventually raised the 1,000,000 francs.

The *Compagnie du Congo pour le Commerce et l'Industrie*, the CCCI, later known familiarly in Belgium as *la Douairière* (the Dowager), was created to take charge of the operation, and in May 1887 a party led by Thys sailed from Antwerp to the Congo. From the point of view of railway engineering the project, to construct a railway from Matadi to Stanley Pool, was a difficult one to study, let alone to build. The terrain up-river was appalling: sheer mountains, deep ravines and impenetrable scrub made the task of cutting even a path a major effort. The engineers were unused to the tropical heat, storms and mosquitoes and one by one they succumbed to fever. Replacements were found and at the end of eighteen months the task was finished. Thys himself had returned to Brussels in March 1888 where Leopold, impressed by the man's faith in the future of the Congo, appointed him administrator-general of the

interior for the EIC. Strauch the incumbent was dismissed without ceremony.[17]

The technical report of the survey team confirmed the estimate of
25,000,000 francs for the construction of a railway from Matadi to Leopoldville and Thys installed himself in an office in the rue Bréderode,
an unprepossessing street behind the Palais Royal in Brussels, from where
he set to finding the money. He worked tirelessly to convince the world
of finance that the project was a good investment. He saw Mackinnon
and the Scotsman demonstrated considerable generosity of spirit, considering the treatment the British syndicate had received, in helping to
raise 5,000,000 francs in England. Some German bankers provided
2,000,000 francs; the American railway magnate Collin Huntingdon,
who wanted to build the line himself, came forward with a subscription;
Rothschilds contributed and in Belgium Thys raised nearly 8,000,000
francs. But, above all, Leopold persuaded Beernaert to ask parliament
for approval of a 10,000,000 franc loan from the Treasury and the
Chambers agreed.

On 31 July 1889 the *Compagnie du Chemin de Fer du Congo* was
formed. That 71% of its capital came from Belgium could not but please
the king. A few months later a contract was signed with the EIC officially
granting the company the concession and stipulating that the work
should be completed within five years. It was in fact finished in 1898 and
proved a tremendous asset to the Congolese economy. Unfortunately the
exciting story of the construction of the railway – known subsequently
as the OTRA Co. – cannot be told here; it has been well recounted by
René Cornet in *La Bataille du Rail*.

Thys was determined that the CCCI should do more than build a railway
in the Congo and he used his first trip to the Congo in 1887 to study
the commercial potential in general of the country. A study in depth was
undertaken by Alexandre Delcommune, and within a few years three
more companies were formed by Thys for general trading, a second for
the purchase of ivory and rubber, the *Société Belge du Haut Congo*, and
a third for raising beef with which to feed Europeans. In addition, while
Thys was in the Congo in 1887 he looked into the functioning of the EIC
in order to report back to Leopold. He was not impressed either by the
efficiency of the administration or by the way Europeans were treating
Africans, which he considered unjust.

Undoubtedly, the running of the Congo was not easy in conditions
of considerable financial stringency. Under the king-sovereign there was
a cabinet of three in Brussels consisting of the administrator-general for
foreign affairs and justice, the head of the department of finance, and
the administrator-general for the interior, who dealt with territorial

Leopold I (*top left*), his wife, Queen Louise (*top right*), his daughter, Princess
Charlotte (*below left*) and his son, the Duke of Brabant, later Leopold II

The Duke and Duchess of Brabant

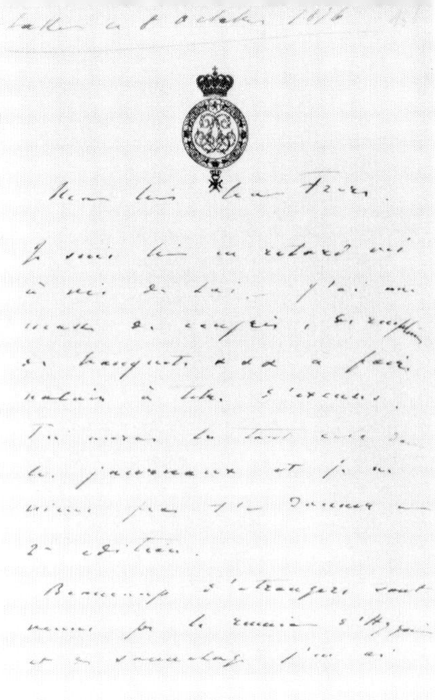

A letter from Leopold II to his brother

The royal palace at Laeken

The children of Leopold II: Louise (*top left*), Leopold Count of Hainault (*top right*), Stephanie (*below left*) and Clementine

Leopold's collaborators: Emile Banning (*top left*), Baron
Lambermont (*top right*), Colonel Strauch (*below left*) and
Baron van Eetvelde

Belgian politicians: August Beernaert (*left*), Walthère Frère-Orban
(*above right*) and General Brialmont

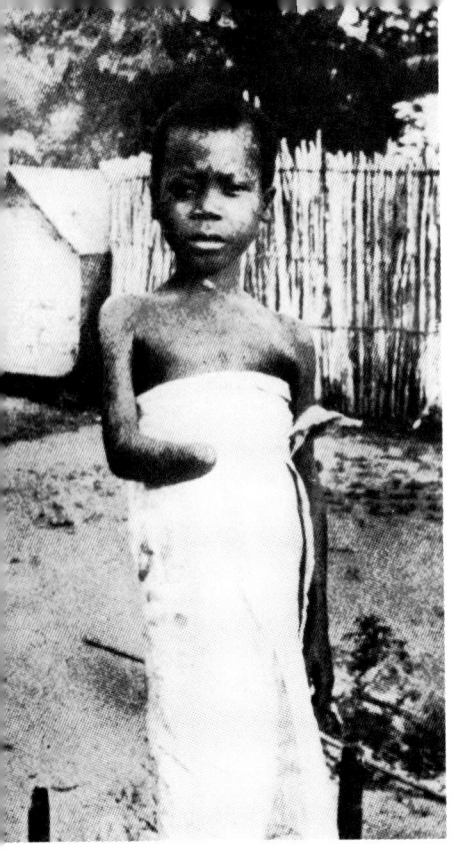

Child mutilated by Congo
soldiery

H.M. Stanley

Leopoldville 1882

The Cinquantenaire, Brussels

The greenhouses at Laeken

The Congo Museum, Tervuren

Leopold II as seen in a satirical
magazine

The Royal Python attacks the
'Rubber System', *Punch* 1906

organization, that is, the setting up of districts and administering them, industry, agriculture, communications, the *force publique* and military supplies. (The administrators-general became secretaries-general after 1894 and the higher post of secretary of state was created.)

In the Congo itself, at Boma the capital, there was also an administrator-general who came to be called governor-general. The administrative machinery was highly centralized and was directed from Brussels. Leopold's power was absolute, to a degree virtually unheard of in the late nineteenth century.

There were only 430 European (of whom 130 were Belgian) administrators in 1889, many without previous colonial experience. Added to the enormity of the task of organizing the new state was the antipathy of the missionaries already there who resented the new officials. In the first years expenses – about 2,000,000 francs a year, rising to 3,000,000 in 1889 – were ten times greater than receipts, the sole revenue coming from export duties.[18] Exports were worth about 2,000,000 francs a year, composed of mainly, in value terms, ivory from the Upper Congo and palm oil from the Lower Congo.[19] As there was no reason to believe that such a state of affairs would change radically in the near future and as he was unable to raise loans on the open market, Leopold knew that he would be compelled before too long to ask the Belgian government for assistance.

It was much easier to approach the ever vigilant Belgian parliament in 1890 than five years before. In the intervening period the Belgian people had learnt a great deal about the Congo. They read encouraging reports in the press, the successful flotation of the railway company, and the formation of other commercial companies promised well. Then, in the spring of 1890, Stanley, the most famous explorer in the world, delivered a widely reported encomium.

> What does the greatness of a monarch consist in? If it is the extent of his territory, then the Emperor of Russia is the greatest of all. If it is the splendour and power of military organization, then William II takes first place. But if royal greatness consists in the wisdom and goodness of a sovereign leading his people with the solicitude of a shepherd watching over his flock, then the greatest sovereign is your own.[20]

The year 1890 also marked the twenty-fifth anniversary of Leopold II's accession to the throne. The festivities culminated in a garden party for 2,500 given by the king at Laeken: the magnificent greenhouses were thrown open; Marie-Henriette, elegantly dressed, was at his side; the personable twenty-one-year-old Prince Baudouin was there in his captain's uniform. The Belgian *Bourse*, whose relations with Leopold had hardly been warm during previous years, gave a splendid reception for the king, decorating the great hall of the stock exchange with pictures of the Congo. The cabinet was there and many high-level foreign diplomats who were in Brussels for the Anti-Slavery Conference. The president of the Congo companies presented Leopold with a richly-bound album containing 40,000 signatures from the world of commerce and industry in Belgium and other countries. The year marked what was probably the zenith of Leopold II's reputation.

The following July Beernaert made public the king's will. There seems little doubt that Leopold had always intended that the Congo should eventually become a Belgian colony. However, the reason for publication of his will at that moment was that it was a dramatic way of drawing attention to the financial sacrifices he had made and the advantages that Belgium would derive from them. When he asked for a loan of 25,000,000 francs to continue his work, parliament could hardly refuse. He received the money he sought, interest free. Five million francs was to be paid immediately and the balance in annual instalments of 2,000,000 francs. At the end of ten years Belgium would be entitled either to be repaid in full, or to annex the EIC. Meanwhile, the state undertook to supply full information on its economic, financial and commercial situation and not to contract any new debt without the consent of the Belgian government. Even so, the loan constituted no more than a stop-gap measure: in the long run the EIC would have to become economically viable.

Later that year an opportunity to acquire some revenue-producing resources occurred and Leopold naturally jumped at it. The abolition of the slave-trade in Africa had been one of the avowed aims of the European Powers for some time. It stemmed largely from the ivory trade in East Africa which was run by 'Arabs'. (The description is inexact as the so-called 'Arabs' were very often half-caste, Swahili-speaking, Arabized Africans, but the conventional terminology will be maintained.) In the early part of the nineteenth century they had been based in the Zanzibar region but they had gradually extended their trading zone and political influence into the hinterland in search of fresh sources of ivory. The ivory had to be transported to the coast and as the tribesmen of the interior were not prepared to be hired as porters and to make the long, arduous journey to Zanzibar, the Arabs took to making them slaves. As well as providing porterage, the Africans could also be profitably sold.

In the past the Arabs had avoided letting the missionaries see their slave-trading operations, but by the late 1880s they conducted them openly and paraded their African captives in full view. Furthermore, greater European activity in Africa meant that there were more witnesses of slave-trading. Increasing numbers of reports reached Europe describing the process of capturing slaves, the brutal treatment of them and the widespread misery caused to African tribes by the Arabs. It was believed that the slave traffic was increasing, though it is impossible to know whether this was true or not. By 1888 the British government was being urged to take action not only by the Anti-Slavery Society but also by missionaries and an articulate section of the Victorian population, which was outraged by what it read in the press.

A separate attack on the slave-trade, also in 1888, came from the French Cardinal Lavigerie, Archbishop of Carthage and founder of the Catholic missionary order of 'White Fathers'. Lavigerie's missions were threatened by Arab hostility, and some had had to be abandoned. To prevent further erosion, he decided to arouse European public opinion to end the slave-trade by force. He delivered rousing sermons in Paris and Brussels (which greatly pleased Leopold) in which he depicted the horrors of the trade which, he claimed, was depopulating Africa at the rate of 400,000 people a year, to say nothing of the suffering it caused. He presented the slave-trade as a desperate human problem which all Christians should urge their governments to solve.

Lord Salisbury was genuinely sympathetic to the anti-slavery cause. He was also not averse to the kudos to be gained by the British government's taking the lead in this humanitarian field, and he proposed that the signatories of the 1885 Berlin Act should get together and work out what step should be taken to abolish the slave-trade. It was decided that Belgium should be asked to call the conference as, if the initiative came from Britain, the French and Portuguese would probably interpret it as hostile to them.

The Brussels Anti-Slavery Conference met in November 1889 and continued sitting until July 1890. A forked slave-yoke was on display for the edification of the plenipotentiaries and much horrifying information about the slave-trade had been gathered by the Belgian Ministry of Foreign Affairs. It was a lively and distinguished gathering. 'It is hard work,' Sir John Kirk, the senior British delegate, reported, 'all the dinners, receptions and balls.'[21] Lambermont was chosen as president and the proceedings were naturally followed closely by Leopold II.

As soon as the delegates settled down to the main purpose of the conference the wide divergence of views as to how the slave-trade should be suppressed was exposed. The British insisted that only the maritime slave-trade should be dealt with; the French opposed this. The Germans wanted to restrict the arms trade; the British were against it. So it went on. The only extensive and detailed plans for an all-out attack on it came from Leopold. He proposed that the Powers should establish fortified posts in their territories in the interior to stop slave raids and to serve as bases from which flying columns could intercept and pursue caravans. They would also serve as centres of refuge and civilization where natives could be organized to defend themselves. Roads and railways would have to be built inland from the coast, and steamboats should operate on navigable rivers and lakes, thus replacing human porters. Laws should be passed authorizing stringent punishment for man-hunting and man-dealing. Caravans should be supervised when they formed at the coast and inspected on their arrival and departure in the interior.

Hardly surprisingly, none of the Great Powers was prepared to undertake such vast commitments. Leopold cannot have expected their reaction to be otherwise, indeed, it was what he wanted. For though there is no reason to doubt that Leopold II genuinely wished to stamp out the slave-trade in the Congo, he was also prepared to use the subject for other ends. Through Lambermont he asked the conference to authorize the EIC to levy import duties in the Congo, to provide him with the means to attack the slave-trade. It seemed a perfectly reasonable request to all the delegates except the Dutch as it would adversely affect the trading of the Dutch *Afrikaansche Handels Vereeniging* established in the Congo. Agreement had by now been reached on a wide range of subjects, though the resolutions were rather watered-down, and the Dutch intransigence threatened to wreck this work. Leopold himself immediately launched a campaign against what he described as the '*caprices*' of the Dutch.[22] He wrote several letters to Queen Victoria enlisting her support. 'The bastion of the slave-trade is, alas, in the Congo State and import duties are needed by the State to combat it'.[23] He asked Stanley to write a letter to *The Times* advocating import duties; and he initiated a press campaign against the Dutch.[24]

France then threatened to join up with the Dutch unless the Congolese export duties, which had been considerably increased, were lowered. The Dutch for their part left the conference in a huff. It was decided therefore that a general act should be signed, excluding the contentious subject of import duties. This was done in July 1890 (the Dutch finally signed at the end of the year) and discussion continued in Paris on the import duties. Agreement was reached in February 1891. Leopold could levy a ten per cent maximum *ad valorem* import duty across the board.

So far it is possible to go along with Leopold II's efforts, albeit unorthodox, to raise money for the EIC. By the end of 1890 he had in his pocket a 25,000,000 franc loan and the revenue from import and export duties. They were not enormous sums but with the expansion of trade, both taxes would become an increasingly large source of revenue. But Leopold was not satisfied with what he had obtained. He nurtured extremely ambitious plans for the state – he wanted to expand into the Arab-dominated eastern Congo, into Katanga in the south-east and the Nile valley in the north-east. If he was to succeed in his aims he would need much greater financial resources than he now had at his disposal. And so began the domainal policy that was to lead to his moral and political downfall.

Expanded trade would in time, Leopold knew, produce more revenue. But he was not prepared to wait and the sums he could expect were not of the order of magnitude he had in mind. What could be simpler, more immediate and more lucrative than for the state itself to engage in trade? In particular, the quantity of ivory being collected was increasing considerably in the later 1880s. Why, Leopold reasoned, should the newly-established commercial companies of the rue Bréderode reap the benefits of his investments? To the king it seemed only fair that he too should profit from the fruits of his labours. In September 1891 he issued a decree ordering the district commissioners in the Aruwimi and Ubangi-Uele basins to secure all the ivory they could on behalf of the state. The decree was followed by orders in October 1891 and May 1892 from the vice-governor of the state prohibiting natives from hunting elephants or harvesting wild rubber unless they handed the produce over to the state. Anyone buying such rubber would be considered guilty of receiving stolen goods. And all trading was then forbidden in the Uele valley.

The effect of the decrees was to create a state monopoly in the two most important products of the Congo. Leopold argued that it was merely an 'extension' of a decree of 1885 which had asserted that all 'vacant' lands belonged to the state. This earlier decree had not at the time seemed unreasonable, but its expanded interpretation was contested, for in 1892 it was assumed that all lands were vacant if they were not actually occupied or cultivated by the native population. In reality the forests where elephants were hunted or rubber was tapped might be a long way away from a village. None the less, the natives believed them to be 'their' lands. Apart from this, by instituting a monopoly, the state was able to buy at a price below the normal market one.

There was an immediate outcry from the commercial companies who had only recently invested in trading stations along the Congo and its tributaries. But it was not only those whose material interests would be damaged who were outraged by the king's action. Lambermont objected and according to Woeste, Leopold, 'never forgave him for having differed from his way of seeing things'.[25] Camille Janssen resigned as governor-general; Hubert van Neuss, the administrator-general for finance, argued against as did A. J. Wauters, the influential editor of the *Mouvement Géographique*. Beernaert was opposed and threatened to resign. There was talk of the entire cabinet doing so.[26] Emile Banning was disillusioned with the king, and bitterness as well as reasoned objections enter into his protest. He drafted a memorandum on the subject which he laid before Leopold.

The doctrine of State ownership of land as it began to emerge in about 1890, and has developed since, is the exact opposite of the regime [of free development of trade]. The [new] doctrine should not be allowed to prevail, either against the natural rights of the indigenous population, which it would in effect dispossess, nor against the rights of the Powers as laid down in the Berlin Act.[27]

Leopold replied, beginning laconically, 'Apart from his false conclusions, M. Banning's work is interesting.' He went on: 'He proves what is self-evident, namely that the Powers intended to place the Congo basin under a regime of complete free trade, that is, the right of all foreigners to use the river and to trade on the same footing as that of the native population. He proves nothing more than that.'[28] After working with him for more than thirty years, Leopold terminated his relationship with Banning.

It was possible for Leopold II to dismiss Banning's objections but the commercial bodies had influential supporters. In the Belgian parliament the decrees were attacked and the government asked the king to withdraw the circulars. Leopold refused and looked around for international support. The British government preferred not to be involved. He wrote to the Belgian minister in Berlin, Greindl, asking him to find out what the German government thought.[29] Greindl did as he was asked and consulted Baron Marschall, the minister of foreign affairs. The Germans would not back the king.[30]

The following month the king-sovereign modified the decrees. In a new decree issued on 30 October 1892 the 'vacant' lands were divided into three 'zones'. The first, which became known as the *Domaine Privé*, was to be exploited only by the state. It included the valleys of the Uele and the Aruwimi in the north-east, the Mongala and Itimbiri in the north, and a large region in the west between Lake Tumba and the river Lukenie. The second zone was open to the commercial companies and comprised the Lower Congo region, both sides of the Upper Congo from Stanley Pool to the Falls, and the basins of the Ruki, Lulonga and Kasai. The third zone covered the outlying areas either only recently occupied or where expeditions were planned.

As regards the free zone, it was in reality less than open to all, and important concessions had already been granted in August 1892 in the Lopari and Maringa basins to the Anglo-Belgian India Rubber Company, known as ABIR Co., and in the Mongala basin to the *Société Anversoise du Commerce du Congo*. The ABIR Co. was nominally run by an Englishman, Colonel North. It seems that he had no money in the company and was a front for Leopold. The commercial companies were also given the right to administer on behalf of the state the areas in which they operated.

It was their employees, paid low salaries with commission on the results achieved, whose behaviour was responsible for much criticism later.[31] In addition to the two commercial concessions in October 1892, land around Lakes Leopold II and Tumba was granted to a mysterious Duke of Saxe-Coburg-Gotha. The area of the concession was extended and by a decree of 1896 was constituted as the *Domaine de la Couronne*, although its existence was not officially mentioned until several years later.

At the end of 1892 instructions were sent to officials in the Congo telling them to increase production, especially of rubber. In 1893, 3,500,000 francs' worth of ivory was sold at Antwerp and more than 1,000,000 francs' worth of rubber. Two years later the amount of rubber sold was doubled and the price had risen. From a financial point of view the system worked (see graph on page 235).

16   Emin Pasha

*'It is really their [the Germans'] business if
Emin is a German.'*[1]   Lord Salisbury.

Leopold II had great confidence in his diplomatic ability after his success
at the Conference of Berlin and when the following year he saw an opportunity to extend the EIC towards the Nile valley – the frontiers in the
north-east were extremely vague – he immediately seized it, regardless
of his financial problems.

At the beginning of 1884 when General Gordon had been negotiating
with Leopold with a view to taking over from Stanley in the Congo, the
king, knowing the general's strong feeling about the importance of stamp-
ing out the slave-trade, had asked Gordon how best he thought it could
be done in the Congo. The general had replied that to attack the slave-
trade at its roots it would be necessary to occupy Bahr-el-Ghazal in the
Sudan, as much of the trade in both East and Central Africa was
organized from this region, thus giving Leopold a convincing reason for
aspiring to make the Bahr-el-Ghazal a province of the EIC.

As a result of the Mahdist rising which began in 1881 the British government had decided in 1884 to abandon the Sudan, and General Gordon
was to effect the evacuation of Khartoum. The disastrous end to his mission in 1885, however, was seen in England as a severe blow and was
considered in influential quarters as a failure on the part of the British
government to maintain its obligations to Egypt. Some saw it mainly as
a political defeat but others feared lest the loss of control over the Upper
Nile should lead to attempts to divert its waters away from Egypt, since
nineteenth-century explorers had confirmed the ancient view that this
was possible. The Abyssinian monarch and neighbouring African kings
clearly did not possess either the means or the skills to do this but an unfriendly European Power could be technically capable of achieving it.

In March 1886 Stanley had suggested to Leopold that Belgium should
undertake the reconquest of the Sudan on the grounds that although the

southern Sudan was equidistant either via Egypt or the Congo the natives in the Congo were friendly, in striking contrast to the Mahdists.

> I beg most respectfully to Your Majesty that as these Provinces might be so easily rescued from lapsing into their pristine wildness that some effort should be made to save them ... If we consider the exceeding economy of the pay roll of a Belgian regiment ... their traditional courage – the guaranteed neutrality of the country – the little offense to the *amour propre* of the Great Powers their employment would offer, the conviction grows that a solution of the Egyptian problem lies in this idea.[2]

This highly original idea had all the makings of one to appeal to Leopold. The only drawback, the king knew only too well – for the Mahdists did not intimidate him – was that the Belgian government would never countenance it. Instead he suggested Anglo-Belgian co-operation to the British prime minister, but Gladstone showed no interest: 'We do not ... contemplate any revival of operations in the Sudan.'[3]

The Mahdists, after taking Khartoum, had pushed south deeper into the Sudan and in Europe it was believed that the entire country had been taken over. In fact the governor of the province of Equatoria, Emin Pasha, was holding out at Wadelai, near to Lake Albert. Letters from him describing his desperate situation and asking for help were published in *The Times* in 1886. They made a profound impression on the British public and those who believed that Gordon had been sacrificed through political expediency felt that there was a moral duty to respond to Emin's appeal for help.[4] The British government had washed its hands of the Sudan in 1886 and was not prepared to come to his help but the conviction that the British ought to help the governor of Equatoria was too strong to be checked by a governmental refusal and, as a result of much discussion in the press, the idea of sending a privately-sponsored relief expedition emerged. At first it was seen, as reported in *The Times*, as 'another errand of mercy and of peril – to rescue Emin Pasha (a gallant lieutenant of the lamented General Gordon) who is surrounded by savage and hostile tribes and cut off from the reach and resources of civilisation'.[5] It developed into a scheme to provide Emin Pasha with military supplies as well as 'saving' him.

The romantic Arab-sounding figure in Equatoria was in fact a German. He claimed that he was a Turk who had been educated in Germany but it was convincingly proved that he was born Eduard Carl Schnitzer in Silesia in 1840. Trained as a doctor, he had joined Gordon's service and accompanied him to Equatoria as a medical officer. There he took on administrative duties as well as his medical work and in 1878 he had been appointed governor of the province. He was a talented linguist, reputedly speaking more than twenty languages fluently, an accomplished musician and chess-player, and as a scientist he was held in esteem in scholarly circles in Europe. (At the time he was holding out at Wadelai he was amassing a collection of stuffed birds which he intended giving to the British Museum.) Emin was a small man, always meticulously dressed; he wore a beard and, as he was extremely shortsighted, thick, round spectacles; his basically nondescript appearance was enlivened by the red fez he always wore.

The leading figure in the Emin Pasha lobby in England was William Mackinnon, who had only a short time before suffered a reversal in his hopes to win the contract for building a railway in the Congo, and whose interest was rapidly turning towards East Africa. He was being unofficially supported in this by Foreign Office officials who were viewing with alarm increasing German activity in that area. The Foreign Office had been encouraged by one of Emin's letters in which he wrote: 'Once strengthened in this manner [relief supplies], the organization of a British Protectorate as a *fait accompli* is very easily done.'[6] The 'Mackinnon clan' (as Stanley called it) for its part hoped to use the expedition for 'establishing British commerce and influence in East Africa and for relieving Emin Bey'.[7] In December 1886 the Emin Pasha Relief Committee was set up with Mackinnon as president and principal contributor. The Egyptian government was constrained to support the proposed expedition with £10,000 and the total of £20,000, estimated to be the sum necessary, was soon reached.

There was no doubt who was the obvious leader of such an expedition and Stanley needed no persuasion when Mackinnon mooted the idea to him. Mackinnon did not hide from the explorer that in rescuing Emin, he looked to Stanley 'to open a direct route to Victoria Nyanza and the Sudan and thereby establish stations and commerce in the interior of East Africa',[8] and it seems that the American did not demur.

Despite what has been frequently claimed, Stanley wanted to lead the expedition to Equatoria via the Congo, mainly because this was the route he knew best and, secondly, because he believed (incorrectly as it turned out) it to be shorter in distance than approaching from East Africa. Further reasons he advanced were that desertions by Zanzibari porters would be fewer if they were not on familiar territory and that the antipathy of the Kabaka of Buganda was such that the East African expedition might well be sabotaged by him.[9] Mackinnon and his friends favoured an East African route for obvious reasons but the decisive opinion on how to reach Emin Pasha came from Leopold II.

Stanley was still in the employ of the King of the Belgians and was obliged to ask Leopold's permission before assuming leadership of the expedition. Relations between the two men had become strained over the previous two years as Stanley, much to his chagrin, had not been asked to undertake any work for Leopold in Africa since he returned in June 1884. He had several times asked the king what plans he had in mind for him and had received nothing but ambiguous answers. For Stanley the proposed expedition would be a means of re-establishing his pre-eminence as an explorer.

Leopold had had good reason not to send Stanley to the Congo in 1885–6 – he lacked the money. He was also aware that to send Stanley to Central Africa would endanger his tenuous relations with France, to whom the explorer was a *bête noire*. Stanley wrote to Leopold in December 1886 asking for permission to lead the relief expedition. The king replied by summoning the American to Brussels; Stanley did not relish the encounter with his patron and describes the meeting as 'harrowing'.[10]

> In a few minutes I let him perceive how much he had wounded me by this curious conduct of his and told him frankly that it was inexplicable. 'Well, Mr. Stanley', he said, after I had explained, 'I confess it has been hard upon you but it could not be helped. Circumstances were such that I could not employ you as intended. *Haute politique*, you know ... The King was wonderfully benevolent, almost paternally so, and my hot anger at the 'tricks' I had conceived he had been playing with me cooled, and we proceeded to discuss the Emin Relief Expedition.[11]

Leopold had firmly-held views on everything connected with the proposed expedition. As regards the route to be followed, he was adamant that it should be through the Congo. With gentle blackmail, he told Stanley:

> If the Committee will not agree to this, I do not see how I can lend your services, which are, as you know, pledged to me, for this expedition. I shall want you myself in a few weeks from now on a far more important work than relieving Emin ... But if the Committee will let you go by the Congo, I can postpone the mission for another eighteen months.[12]

The guarded references to other work were in fact real as at the end of 1886 the Stanley Falls station had been attacked and taken by Arabs from the eastern Congo and Leopold was planning to recapture it as soon as possible.

The Sovereign of the Congo Free State was not only interested in the route to be followed by the expedition. His aim was to establish a Congolese foothold in Equatoria and he told Stanley to offer Emin, should the German wish to remain in Equatoria, the post of governor of Equatoria under the Congo Free State. In addition Leopold would contribute

£10,000 to £12,000 a year to the administration of the province, if it could produce a reasonable revenue.

The original humanitarian aim of the proposed expedition had distinctly faded into the background: Mackinnon was looking for territory in East Africa; Leopold II saw the opportunity of moving towards the Nile; Stanley needed his ego boosting and the material for another best-seller. One is not surprised that negotiations took place between the relief committee and various London newspapers as to the publication of reports from the expedition. Large sums of money, for example £1,000 from *The Times*, were paid out long before the expedition had left England.[13]

There was no shortage of recruits for the expedition as a result of the publicity it had received. In early January 1887 Stanley chose his officers, though he was not impressed by those who volunteered, and saw to the necessary supplies. A farewell banquet was held for him and there was a large crowd at Charing Cross station to see him off.

In Cairo Stanley was warned about the pasha by a German who knew him well, and it was pointed out to the explorer that Emin was unlikely to want to leave Equatoria. He also left him in doubt as to Emin's fragile hold on the southern Sudan. Stanley seems to have been in no way deterred by the information and continued his journey to Zanzibar. Recruitment of porters was one part of his mission but more important and more difficult were negotiations with Tippu Tib, an 'Arab' ivory and slave trader who had built up a sphere of influence in the eastern Congo (through which the expedition would have to pass) and established a settlement at Kasonga from where he directed operations.

In return for free passage through areas under Tippu Tib's control, Stanley was empowered by Leopold to offer the Arab the post of governor of the Stanley Falls region with a proposed salary of thirty pounds a month. As Tippu Tib already had *de facto* control over the area it would hardly seem an attractive offer, but he accepted it as he appreciated that Europeans were rapidly assuming mastery over Africa and he hoped that, by co-operating with the EIC in becoming governor of his own territory, he would maintain his own authority by removing from Europeans any excuse to displace him. And while thirty pounds a month seems a derisory offer, it appears that Tippu Tib was short of money in 1887 and the sum was useful to him.[14] In a gesture of goodwill Tippu Tib also promised to provide the expedition with 600 porters.[15] The news of the deal caused a sensation in Europe. Leopold II, champion of the abolition of the slave-trade, was setting up a well-known slave-trader as a state official. The king was soundly castigated in the radical press, particularly over the phrase in the agreement which permitted Tippu Tib to enter into legitimate private trade. This was interpreted as meaning the slave-trade, though in fact he dealt mainly in ivory.

The deal with Tippu Tib sealed and his Zanzibari porters hired, Stanley sailed round the Cape of Good Hope to the port of Banana at the mouth of the Congo where he arrived on 18 March 1887. Unfortunately, the telegraph cable to the Congo had broken and instructions sent by Leopold from Brussels ordering the EIC officials to prepare for the arrival of nearly a thousand men had not been received. Even so Stanley succeeded in chartering several small steamers from the local Dutch and British trading companies and the expedition moved upstream to Matadi, where local porters took over and carried 800 loads of stores and ammunition over-land to Leopoldville and Stanley Pool. Here the expedition encountered a more serious setback. Leopold had offered to lend his Upper Congo flotilla; however, on arrival Stanley found that most of the vessels were either under repair or useless. Even after requisitioning two boats – they were helped in this by Roger Casement, a young Irishman whose job was to build up the state transport-system in that part of the Congo – only four-fifths of the expedition could be carried further upstream and it was at this juncture that Stanley made the decision which has since been fre-quently criticized, namely to divide the expedition into two parts. If he waited until more boats could be procured this would greatly delay his progress towards Equatoria, so he split the expedition into a lightly-equipped advance column led by himself which would move forward as quickly as possible and make contact with Emin, while the rest of the expedition, the rear column, would follow more slowly.

The disasters that befell the Emin Pasha Relief Expedition from the moment the advance column left Leopoldville have been well chronicled. All the Europeans kept diaries, most of which have been published. They have fully recounted the murder by an African of the brutal second-in-command, Edmund Barttelot, the unsavoury habits and later death of another officer, James Jameson, and many lurid stories of beatings and cannibalism. Stanley himself described the march of the advance column through Central Africa in *In Darkest Africa*. He left Yambuya in June 1887 with 389 men, expecting to reach Emin within six months, but he had completely underestimated the difficulties to be encountered in the tropical rain-forest of the Ituri which led to Lake Albert and the headwaters of the Nile. His journey is an appalling saga of privation and suffering: 200 of his men died and of those who survived, many were maimed. In addition seventy Manyema porters died and an unknown number of villagers who fell in the path of the expedition.

Finally, at the end of April 1888, he met up with Emin, who on learning of his approach had set out to meet the explorer at his camp at the south-ern end of Lake Albert. Stanley and the surviving members of the expedition were physically exhausted and their clothes in tatters. Emin, according to Stanley, was wearing 'a clean suit of snowy cotton drilling, well-ironed and of perfect fit'.[16] Most ludicrous of all, the bulk of the relief supplies, the *raison d'être* of the expedition, had been left behind with the rear column and the rescuers were in fact more in need of succour than the rescued, though Stanley had somehow managed to bring five half-bottles of champagne safely with him and he, Emin and the European officers, drank them that evening. One can only hope that it went some way to overcome the anti-climax.

However, even without supplies, Stanley was able to carry out his political mission. As a matter of form, because Emin was employed by the Egyptian government, Stanley had to inform the pasha (something he knew already) that the government wished him to evacuate Equatoria and to return to Egypt.[17] As expected, the German had no desire to comply and the propositions of Mackinnon and Leopold were then put to him. The king's proposal, whereby Emin was to remain in Equatoria as governor of the province in an enlarged Free State, was laid before the pasha though without enthusiasm on Stanley's part. According to Emin, Stanley advised him to turn down the king's proposition.[18] Emin noted Stanley's antagonism towards Leopold and it reinforced his own feelings about the king and the EIC. (He had previously received information telling him that the nascent state was in a perilous position and was unlikely to survive.) Furthermore, Stanley's journey through the Ituri forest had taken much longer than either Leopold or Stanley had anticipated. While Equatoria might be geographically contiguous with the EIC, the state could not hope to link up with Equatoria on a regular basis because of the difficulties presented by the lines of communication.

After the rejection of Leopold's offer, Stanley presented Mackinnon's proposal to Emin, namely that the pasha and his followers should establish themselves on the eastern shore of Lake Victoria where they would work for Mackinnon's East African Association. Stanley also promised to try to persuade Mackinnon to maintain Emin permanently in the East African interior. He had no authority for this but, as he wrote to Mackinnon, 'I have tried everything ...', Emin was 'charmed with his African life where he is king'.[19] Negotiations continued throughout May 1888.[20] During them the explorer came to see the German in a different light; he was, in Stanley's opinion, an irresolute intellectual, not a leader of men, and unsuited to his role as governor of an African province. Even Emin's hold over his men which had appeared so secure when the relief expedition arrived, gradually seemed to be less impressive. The pasha had not taken into account the views of his men when he had embarked on the Lake Victoria scheme with Stanley. This seems somewhat strange as he was aware that for the past four years they had consistently refused to withdraw to the south or north to Egypt. To convince them – they were scattered in various stations throughout Equatoria – that the province was to be abandoned, Emin, with Mounteney Jephson, one of Stanley's officers (Stanley himself had gone in search of the rear column), went on a tour to explain why they should move to Lake Victoria. Their mission was a complete failure.

Stanley, after once more exposing himself to the rigours of the Ituri jungle and discovering the fate of the rear column, met up with Emin and Jephson in February 1889. This time however it was the American who had the upper hand. He could dictate his terms: either Emin returned to Zanzibar with him, or he could stay where he was without any hope of future help from Europe. All idea of attaching Equatoria to the Congo had been abandoned and the idea of establishing Emin on Lake Victoria was tacitly dropped by Stanley, much to the pasha's chagrin. Knowing that he now lacked the support of his men, Emin had virtually no choice but to accompany Stanley.

The march to Zanzibar took four months; of those of Emin's men who had decided to follow their leader to the coast, a sizeable minority deserted on the way. It was a very dispirited and bitter German who arrived at Zanzibar. But all was not yet over for the unfortunate Emin Pasha. The tragi-comedy of the expedition moved into the final act. After a banquet given for Emin and Stanley in Zanzibar, the short-sighted pasha, who was used to living in one-storey buildings, walked out of a first-floor window, believing it to be a veranda, and fell to the street below, fracturing his skull. There is no convincing evidence that it was either attempted suicide or murder, but he was unconscious throughout the following day and developed bronchio-pneumonia. Two months later, however, he was able to walk and write and in 1890 to deliver the *coup de grâce* to those who had set so much store by him, by agreeing to work for the Germans in East Africa.

Leopold himself had already lost interest in the German scholar. But while he had been unable to seduce Emin Pasha into working for the EIC, Emin's withdrawal from Equatoria had created a political vacuum in the province. In this Leopold was most interested. When he met Stanley on the explorer's return to Europe, he greeted him with the words, 'Now, what do you say to the taking of Khartoum?'[21]

17 The Mirage of the Nile

*'Lord Rosebery is sorry for the position in
which King Leopold finds himself, but it is
inherent in the fact that he is attempting to
combine the position of a second-rate Power
in Europe with a first-rate Power in Africa.'*[1]

Lord Rosebery to Queen Victoria, 1894.

Leopold II's Nilotic ambitions were in no way crushed by the failure of
the Emin Pasha Relief Expedition to provide him with a foothold in the
Nile valley, only redirected, and, in the five years that followed, he all
but succeeded in his ambitious plans. The dispute with France over their
frontiers on the Upper Congo – so crucial as a base for expeditions to
the Nile – will be considered in the next chapter. It was but one strand
in the complex diplomacy of this period; the other strand, and the two
become completely tangled later on as Leopold plays one government
off against the other, was the British government's desire to keep the other
Great Powers out of the Nile valley so that Britain could re-establish her
authority in the Sudan when the opportunity presented itself.

Until 1889 Salisbury had intended the British occupation of Egypt to
be temporary and that withdrawal would take place when there was
reasonable assurance of the stability of the Egyptian government. But
the rejection of the proposal that the European Powers should guarantee
the British right of re-entry should it prove necessary, led to a reconsidera-
tion of the British position in Egypt, and Salisbury decided that Britain
would remain in Egypt for the foreseeable future. The corollary of this
was that all others, who could pre-empt British action in the Sudan by
moving in before, were to be excluded.

The particular European Power Salisbury had in mind in formulating
his policy to defend the Nile valley was Italy, which was active in
Ethiopia. The Italians were prepared to do a deal with Salisbury in
which, in return for British recognition of an Italian sphere of influence
in the Abyssinian highlands, the Italians agreed to keep out of the Nile
valley. The Sudan was firmly in the hands of the Mahdists; the remaining
danger as Salisbury saw it lay in Uganda where the Germans were pushing
inland from Witu, accumulating treaties en route. The British government

was at this stage negotiating with the Germans and Salisbury was anxious to create for himself as strong a bargaining position as possible. Bismarck had in March 1890 been dismissed and German foreign policy was to a large extent in the hands of the erratic young kaiser, William II, and it was not impossible that he would choose to become involved in Nilotic affairs.

Salisbury therefore encouraged the Imperial British East Africa Company, the IBEA Co, recently set up by Mackinnon, to strengthen its influence in Uganda. However, there was also pressure of another kind being applied on Mackinnon. In the summer of 1889 he had met Cecil Rhodes who had convinced him of the desirability of a Cape to Cairo railway running entirely through British territory. Mackinnon was much impressed by Rhodes and added to the aims of the IBEA Co. the need to secure a British corridor in those parts of East Africa not in British hands.

The British prime minister's main concern was to preserve the security of the Upper Nile and he had little sympathy for the imperialists. Nevertheless, Rhodes and Mackinnon had powerful friends both in parliament and business and, given the tenuous Conservative position in parliament, Salisbury did not want to alienate them. This placed him in a difficult position in the Anglo-German talks, since the Germans were adamant that if the British acquired Uganda they would as a *quid pro quo* have to concede that German territory to the north of Lake Tanganyika should have a common frontier with the Congo Free State.[2] Karl Peters, the explorer and imperialist, was active in Uganda and Salisbury knew that agreement would have to be reached quickly if he was to keep Uganda. He therefore sacrificed the Cape to Cairo railway.

The imperialists were aware that the government was not committed to the railway scheme and when in March 1890 Leopold was in London he was approached by representatives of Rhodes' British South Africa Company, BSAC. Talks took place and the BSAC presented the king with a draft convention giving the EIC a favourable southern boundary with company territory in the southern Congo, in return for the right of way to construct a railway west of Lake Tanganyika.

Meanwhile, Stanley, en route for Europe after the Emin Pasha Relief Expedition, was staying with Mackinnon at Cannes. Mackinnon was aware of the discussions between Leopold and the BSAC and, realizing that there was little chance of the Germans' providing a corridor, they decided to step in and do what they could for the British empire. Together they boarded the train for Brussels.

Leopold was waiting for them with his price for the all-red route already fixed. He would hand over the requisite strip of territory in return for the renunciation by the IBEA Co. of territory on the left bank of the

Upper Nile in favour of the Congo Free State. By the middle of May a draft treaty had been drawn up and was submitted to Salisbury for approval on the 18th. The king conceded the IBEA Co. a five-mile-wide corridor connecting Lake Albert and Lake Albert Edward, that is the River Semliki. The company for its part agreed to recognize the sovereign rights of the EIC over the left bank of the Nile as far as Lado. The following day Salisbury told Leopold that no objections would be raised on the part of the Foreign Office to the engagements. 'More than this, he expressed his approval and appreciation of the project.'[3]

Salisbury was at this time preoccupied with the Anglo–German negotiations and relieved to feel that he had the imperialists off his back. He had, however, forgotten to take into account France's pre-emption right to the EIC's territory. Sir Percy Anderson, who had been absent from London during the Mackinnon Treaty negotiations, on his return pointed out to the prime minister that it could well lead to trouble with France. He advised Salisbury to have any reference to the IBEA Co.'s acquiring sovereignty over part of the Free State removed from the agreement. Mackinnon, not unnaturally, refused to redraft the treaty. He had an obligation to King Leopold to maintain. He told the prime minister that all he was prepared to concede was the addition of a clause making it clear that no actual cession of territory was involved. Salisbury complained to the queen about this 'unreasonable' man but he was impotent.[4] He soon calmed down and accepted the treaty. After all Leopold had made possible his gaining both Uganda and the Cape to Cairo link. The prime minister felt no unease at having let the King of the Belgians acquire rights on the precious river. The possibility of the Congolese actually advancing to the Nile did not occur to him.

Even before the Mackinnon Treaty had been signed, Leopold had been planning an EIC expedition to the Nile. He wanted to send an all-white force and had dispatched an emissary to Sweden to try and recruit men there.[5] (The following year his gaze fell upon the unlikely countries of Bulgaria and Montenegro.)[6] Neither in Sweden nor in England could men be found to sign up and the king was obliged to content himself with 150 Europeans, mainly Belgians.

Captain Guillaume Van Kerckhoven, a daring and hardy officer who had already seen service in the Congo, volunteered to lead the expedition. In October 1890, shrouded in secrecy, the force left Belgium. In December it arrived at Boma and Van Kerckhoven joined up with the EIC troops who were awaiting him. He was far from satisfied with the number of men at his disposal and after setting out from Leopoldville in January he continued recruiting, but the force never exceeded 600 native soldiers and 14 officers.

The aim of the expedition was to march to Wadelai on the Bahr-el-Jebel, the White Nile, and to occupy as much as possible of the Bahr-el-Ghazal. From Bumba on the Congo, Van Kerckhoven struck north to the Uele, arriving there at the end of 1891. He then followed the river eastwards to Niangara. Here the Uele divides and Van Kerckhoven chose the Kibali, which continues eastwards towards the Nile. Success was in sight when Van Kerckhoven was accidentally killed by his gun bearer. Lieutenant Milz took over and the march continued. Two days later the exhausted column pitched camp on the river Arave, Milz believing it to be a tributary of the Bahr-el-Jebel. He realized his mistake and soon afterwards moved on to Wadelai where he hoisted the Free State's flag. Leopold was on the Nile.

Now he was in Equatoria Milz hoped to enlist the remnants of Emin Pasha's men (those who had refused to accompany Stanley to the coast) in his force to permit him to establish EIC stations along the west bank of the Nile, to say nothing of locating Emin's cache of ivory.[7] The Equatorials under Fadl-al-Mūlā had had no contact with the outside world for several years and were in exceedingly short supply of everything from food to ammunition. They needed no persuading to sign to serve the EIC.[8] Milz accordingly sent Fadl and the majority of his followers downstream to Dufile, where they would be well placed to detect any possible Mahdist advance up the valley of the Bahr-el-Jebel, while the remainder of the Equatorial troops, about 150 men, accompanied Milz westwards to Ganda, where some of the troops were to remain until fresh supplies arrived. Milz, and some of his men, then retraced their steps towards the valley of the Dungu to hand over command to Florimund Delanghe, who had been sent out to replace Van Kerckhoven. While the change-over was taking place, news arrived that the troops at Ganda were marching towards Dungu and, as if this was not enough, that Fadl had left Dufile and was moving towards Ganda.

Milz ought to have known better than to leave the occupation in the hands of troops whose volatile sentiments had been demonstrated towards their previous leader, Emin Pasha but, as second-in-command, it seems he had not been briefed with Van Kerckhoven in Brussels. Delanghe on the other hand appreciated the importance of occupation. However, at Dungu he was told by those officers who knew the region that there were simply too few men to undertake an expedition to the Bahr-el-Jebel and that Fadl's men were totally unreliable. Delanghe was not disheartened and hastened to Ganda to persuade the Equatorials to rejoin the EIC troops and move to the Nile. On 13 July 1893 he led his force from Ganda towards the Nile. After eighteen days of difficult marching they reached the Bahr-el-Jebel at Muggi and moved up to Labore where a new station, named

Fort Leopold, was established on the remains of the former Egyptian post.

However, rumours of a strong Mahdist contingent moving up-river reached Fort Leopold and this, plus continuous trouble with his Equatorials, forced Delanghe in the autumn of 1893 to retire to a less exposed post in the interior. Even this was difficult since the local tribesmen, who earlier on had been terrorized by the expedition's ruthless methods, now attacked the retreating column and inflicted heavy casualties.

Leopold knew better than to rely on one expedition. A second, under Georges Le Marinel, had left the Congo early in 1892 and was moving towards the Nile. Le Marinel established a post north of the Bomu river (the northerly fork of the Ubangi, the Uele being the southerly branch) at Bakuma in March, from where expeditions could be launched north and east into the Bahr-el-Ghazal region. The intention was that, once within the Nile basin, EIC forces would be able to reach Meshra'er-Req and from there strike out for the Bahr-el-Jebel and Fashoda, clearing a route to the river, while at the same time acquiring the vast province of the Bahr-el-Ghazal. To begin with things seemed to go even better than expected. Representatives of local tribes appeared at Zemio on the Bomu river and offered their assistance in expeditions, in return for EIC support against their enemy the Mahdists.

The Free State's commandant at Zemio, Achille Fiévez, naturally encouraged this support, and in March 1893 Lieutenant Nilis led a party towards Hofrat-en-Nahas, in the Bahr-el-Ghazal, the site of ancient copper mines. Leopold had learnt of their existence and was convinced they could be exploited. Nilis drew up a contract in which the mines became the personal property of Leopold II, as a private individual, and not as sovereign of the EIC. Nevertheless it was the EIC which undertook to protect the local tribes in return for the concession.

In March 1894 Fiévez himself led a second expedition to Deim Zubeir, the former capital of the Bahr-el-Ghazal, deserted since the Mahdist withdrawal in 1885. He never reached the Bahr-el-Ghazal as he was recalled to support the deteriorating EIC position on the Uele, though a small party under Sergeant Donckier de Donceel reached Deim Zubeir.

Nilotic diplomacy in Europe tended to be rather out of step with events in Africa, as news was slow to arrive. As regards his own expeditions, Leopold exercised heavy censorship over any news that would weaken his bargaining position. A certain amount of confusion therefore existed in Europe as to what hold on the Nile the Sovereign of the Congo Free State actually possessed. When in February 1892 the first reports reached Europe that the Van Kerckhoven expedition was moving towards the Nile, Leopold wished to demonstrate application of the Mackinnon Treaty and made much of the news. The British viewed things differently.

They had been taken aback on learning of the EIC expedition. Whatever claims Leopold had staked on the Nile they were going to have none of it: the weight of the British empire would be used to evict this obstreperous European monarch who was not prepared to be the compliant accomplice in Great Power politics that the British expected.

The Foreign Office considered that Leopold's deviousness, ambitions and Machiavellian diplomacy were unacceptable. They, on the other hand, could repudiate the Mackinnon Treaty when it became obvious that the king was in fact acting according to what had been agreed to by the British government two years before. Lord Salisbury realized in 1892 that what he had dismissed as a meaningless agreement between a shaky company and a colonial ruler who did not even possess the resources to impose himself on his own colony, was now being used to challenge Britain on the Nile.

On 1 March 1892 Lord Vivian, British minister in Brussels, formally requested that the Congo Free State should remain within the frontiers announced in August 1885 (the fourth parallel and the thirtieth meridian) and that, above all, no attempt should be made to extend the state beyond the western watershed of the Nile.[9] The British were particularly nervous at this time as the IBEA Co. was preparing to evacuate Uganda and they did not possess the resources in Africa to move in physically and fill the void.

Leopold was surprised by this unforeseen demand and immediately produced the Mackinnon Treaty, whereupon the Foreign Office denied that it had ever been anything more than an informal basis for an agreement. Lord Salisbury's approval had been strictly personal and did not represent the official decision of Her Majesty's Government; the treaty had never been formerly communicated and was, therefore, 'unknown' to the government.[10] Furthermore, the IBEA Co. had no powers to cede political rights; and one of the conditions of the treaty, the cession of the corridor, had never been consummated.[11] The king knew that he was being pushed around by the British and there was little he could do to retaliate. He simply asked if he could retain the non-political rights his agents had acquired by their presence on the Nile. His old sparring partner, Anderson, described this as a project 'to keep the carcass and leave us the skin'.[12] A formal note in May 1892 recapitulated the British case and demanded immediate withdrawal.

One might have thought that by 1892 the British would have appreciated Leopold II's diplomatic skill. Apparently they did not. Only a few weeks after the notice to quit, Lambermont let slip to a British diplomat that it seemed that the French were about to make a push to the Nile from their West African possessions. And if there was one subject which made the British nervous, it was this. Suddenly, in the summer of 1892, they were prepared to negotiate with Leopold.

This change of heart coincided with a change of government in Britain. Leopold immediately addressed himself to the new Foreign Secretary, Lord Rosebery, telling him that he had in the past been completely misunderstood by the Foreign Office. His dearest wish was to co-operate with the British. Nevertheless, his friendly letter had a sting in the tail. Unless the British made some concessions to him he would, reluctantly, be forced to come to some agreement with France as regards the Upper Nile. The practical suggestion he put forward for Anglo-Congolese co-operation was that, in view of the British evacuation of Uganda, the EIC should take over the administration of the country subject to British authority. Queen Victoria thought 'it would be a great thing if we could act with the King of the Belgians'.[13] The aged prime minister, Gladstone, thought differently and, replying to the king, told him that Uganda was definitely being evacuated. 'I do not even make any enquiry in order to learn exactly the character of the idea Your Majesty has been graciously pleased to place before me.'[14] Despite the prime minister and the anti-imperialists in the cabinet, Rosebery managed to send a commissioner, Lord Portal, to Uganda, who sometime later declared a protectorate.

Failing over Uganda, Leopold II was obliged to fall back on the threat of Franco-Congolese action.[15] This did not intimidate the British government since they knew that the king was at loggerheads with the French over their common frontier on the Upper Ubangi. It was the news in October 1892 that the Van Kerckhoven expedition had actually reached Wadelai that changed things. The British government demanded immediate withdrawal from the sphere. Leopold defiantly refused to comply and threatened to publish the Mackinnon Treaty and his correspondence with Salisbury in 1890. 'If he is attacked and accused of dishonourable conduct either in parliament or the press, he would not hesitate to invite the judgement of that tribunal upon the four important documents in his possession.'[16] The British recognized defeat and Rosebery then modified his position. The king was merely asked for information, while at the same time warned that his constant taunting of the British government 'must one day lead to most unpleasant consequences'.[17]

Early in February 1893, the French, who for some time had not been active in Nilotic affairs, suddenly re-entered the scene when the new minister for colonies, Théophile Delcassé, announced that he intended to send an expedition to the Nile. There were several reasons for this decision which could not help but aggravate Anglo-French relations yet further: the British refusal to discuss Egypt with the French, Delcassé's own views, pressure from the *Comité d'Afrique Française* and, not least, Leopold

II's suggestion for a Franco-Congolese expedition. His intention was, of course, to put pressure on the British to recognize EIC rights in the Upper Nile; Delcassé though was determined that any mission should be purely French and official.

The Monteil mission was originally conceived as an expedition to the Bahr-el-Ghazal but, as a result of the hydrologist Victor Prompt's paper on how the Nile waters could be dammed on the White Nile, its destination was changed to Fashoda, close to the confluence of the White Nile and the Sobat. By occupying this position the French would be able to forestall the EIC advance from the Upper Nile and at the same time force the British into at least discussing Egypt.

Preparations were begun immediately – Leopold's men in Paris were told to find out all they could – and an advance party left France for Africa in the summer of 1893.[18] However, the leader, Commandant P.-L. Monteil, refused to set off until his government had settled their long-running frontier dispute with the EIC regarding the Ubangi and the Nile. He could more simply have asked for a sufficiently large force to oblige the EIC to let him pass, but he held firm to his diplomatic demands. Delcassé for his part did not wish to be rushed into what would undoubtedly be, from the French point of view, an unsatisfactory arrangement with Leopold. Such an arrangement was precisely what Leopold was aiming at and in September 1893 the king upped his demands. In the face of Leopold's intransigence the negotiations broke down in October 1893 and the French Chamber voted reinforcements to the Monteil mission as an alternative to a diplomatic solution. Even so the leader still refused to set off and maintained his insistence on a settlement. The negotiations dragged on throughout the winter of 1893–4.

With his taste for dangling whales on the ends of flimsy fishing lines, Leopold was still trying to manipulate the British. He had realized early in 1893 that Franco-Congolese co-operation to frighten the British was a non-starter and, on seeing the French organize their own expedition, he again took it upon himself to inform the British government of the dangers of a French challenge. At first the British refused to be alarmed. After the departure of the advance party of the Monteil mission though, Anderson and Rosebery took the threat seriously. But because of the prime minister's and the chancellor of the exchequer's. Sir William Harcourt, strong opposition to a forward policy in the Nile, Rosebery could not send out an expedition to beat Monteil to Fashoda, nor would they permit him to negotiate with Leopold. All he was able to do was to instruct Portal in Uganda that if it was at all possible he should 'send emissaries into ... the Nile Basin, in order to ascertain the state of affairs in ... the British sphere [and] to negotiate any treaties that may be necessary for its protection'.[19] As a result E.R. Owen and a handful of men were dispatched from Uganda to occupy Wadelai. Owen made a treaty with the local chief, planted a Union Jack on either side of the Nile and, most importantly, discovered that there were no EIC forces there. However, this information did not reach Europe until after May 1894.

In fact the Free State's position in the entire Nile valley was tenuous in the extreme. For a start the number of troops involved was small as a substantial proportion of state forces were engaged in the Arab wars taking place in the eastern part of the country. Furthermore, those in service in the Nile campaigns were by 1894 wearied by endless marches, weak and demoralized. The news in September 1893 that the Mahdists were determined to drive them out of the southern Sudan had not improved matters, and desertions increased. Delanghe, and his successor Ernest Baert, lacked the means to pay their men. By November 1893 there was no alternative but to evacuate the Bahr-el-Jebel and retire to Magora; their resources had been stretched beyond what was humanly possible.

Some inkling of these reversals had reached Europe in November 1893, but Lambermont had quickly denied their veracity, with the result that Leopold was able to continue negotiating with France and to maintain his demand for recognition of the Free State's occupation of the Bahr-el-Ghazal. The British similarly believed that EIC forces were on the Nile and were prepared to take the pretensions of the Sovereign of the Congo Free State seriously.

Leopold II's playing on the British fears of France in the Upper Nile may well appear to have been rather an overworked tactic. Yet it continued to work. Even Anderson, who had been dealing with the king for a decade, was susceptible to warnings from Brussels about the French. The internationally respected Lambermont was of great help to the king and his hints early in 1894 about an impending settlement with the French successfully baited the British. To prevent Leopold from coming to terms with France, they proposed an Anglo-Congolese agreement: they would allow Leopold to remain on the Nile to block the infinitely more dangerous French.

In March 1894 Gladstone at last retired and Rosebery was able to get down to business. Harcourt who, with John Morley and Herbert Asquith, was the continuation of the Gladstonian conscience in the cabinet, was only informed after talks had begun 'that we are engaged in secret negotiations with the King of the Belgians with a view to transfer to him under a long lease our "sphere of influence" on the upper Nile'.[20] On Rosebery's instructions, Rennell Rodd, one of the 'Africans' at the Foreign Office was sent to Brussels (via Berlin to conceal his destination from the French) to discuss matters with Leopold. He was to offer the king a lease, terminable on his death, of the left bank of the Nile as far north as Fashoda, including the Bahr-el-Ghazal. In return for this, the king was unreservedly to abandon the Mackinnon Treaty and to recognize the British sphere of influence as defined by the Anglo-German agreement of 1890.

Leopold feigned illness and Edmond van Eetvelde, the EIC secretary of state, informed the British emissary that the king insisted that the lease should be for 'as long as these Congo regions remain as an Independent State or a Belgian Colony under the sovereignty of the King or his direct descendants'.[21] It is some measure of how strong Leopold's position was thought to be that Anderson considered the danger of the king's 'going over to the French' sufficiently serious to make concessions. While he did not like the idea of becoming involved in Belgian dynastic problems, he was prepared to extend the lease beyond the king's lifetime. Nor did he object to the Free State's lease of a port on Lake Albert.

Van Eetvelde arrived in London on 9 April to continue detailed negotiations now that agreement in principle had been reached. He proposed, and it was acceptable to the British, that the left bank of the Nile as far north as Fashoda and as far west as longitude 30° east should be leased to Leopold for his lifetime, while the larger area of the Bahr-el-Ghazal, between 25° and 30° east, should be leased to the king and his heirs. That is to say, Leopold gained what he considered the most important part in perpetuity: the British were pleased to have a buffer against the French for the next few years, in the knowledge that before too long it would revert to them. In addition, in exchange for the permanent lease from the British of a corridor from the Congo to the Nile, Leopold was to lease a similar corridor to the British from Lake Albert Edward to Lake Tanganyika.

Surprisingly, in view of van Eetvelde's protracted presence in London, the French had not got wind of the Anglo-Congolese agreement and were still anxious to reach a settlement with Leopold themselves. However, finding himself able to play off the two great colonial Powers in this way rather went to the king's head and at this point he overreached himself.

Not content with the agreement signed on 12 April with the British, on 16 April Leopold welcomed a French delegation led by Gabriel Hanotaux, the African expert at the Ministry of Foreign Affairs, in Brussels. The French offered a settlement of the Ubangi frontier dispute on terms favourable to the EIC on condition that France was assured of free access to the Nile. Hanotaux himself took a much harder line than Jean Casimir-Périer, the minister of foreign affairs, who had, in theory, instructed him. Leopold for his part was as uncompromising as Hanotaux on the subject of 'Zemio's country', that is territory north of the Bomu, leading to the Bahr-el-Ghazal. After a few days of discussion the talks broke down and Hanotaux, who by now suspected that the king had done a deal with the British, left Brussels uttering threats that Leopold's colonial policy would not only have grave repercussions in Africa. He intended to launch a press campaign in France that might well lead to the overthrow of the monarchy in Belgium.

For once even Leopold II was apprehensive. He rather nervously asked the Foreign Office if the Anglo-Congolese agreement could be post-dated, knowing full well that the French would be furious if they discovered that he already had come to terms with the British before the Hanotaux mission. The foreign secretary, Lord Kimberley, refused and said that he intended to publish the agreement at once. The king begged for a delay; the British, knowing that he wanted time to try and explain himself to the French, were unrelenting.

Leopold informed Casimir-Périer privately that he did hold certain leases from the British in the Nile basin and the minister seemed to accept this without protest. He did not, though, tell Hanotaux. The king's fears were assuaged and he told the British government that he was perfectly happy with the agreement. In fact, he was prepared to make an amendment which protected England even more completely from any EIC claim arising out of the Mackinnon Treaty, or through prior occupation. Then, on 9 May, van Eetvelde suddenly informed the Foreign Office that the king wished to sign the amended agreement immediately. He had changed his mind because the previous day it had become clear that the French government was about to fall.

Fortunately for Leopold, France was in the throes of one of its frequent and long drawn-out ministerial crises when the agreement was made public and Casimir-Périer, now *ministre démissionaire*, would only issue a rather half-hearted official protest. For a week or so it looked as though Leopold had succeeded. There is unfortunately no first-hand evidence as to how the king reacted when at the beginning of June the new French minister for foreign affairs was announced, but one can well imagine. It was to be Hanotaux.

In the Chamber on 7 June the new minister set to attacking the Anglo-Congolese agreement. He disputed its legal validity on the grounds that it was irreconcilable with the 1885 Berlin Act and that it violated the territorial integrity of the Ottoman Empire.[22] Furthermore, 'In order to prevent a *de facto* occupation of these territories by the Congo Free State from taking place, the French government had taken the necessary steps to strengthen French posts on the Upper Ubangi.'[23]

Leopold was greatly alarmed at the intensity of the French reaction, which he described to Victoria as 'a fit of rage', and he was said to be in a most gloomy mood.[24] Then to add to his troubles Germany, not unnaturally, joined the French in strenuously opposing the agreement. Part of the reason for the belated German reaction was that it did not stem from the government but from Pan-German circles. Karl Peters and his friends (with the kaiser's tacit support) denounced the agreement in the press, on the grounds that the partition of Africa was gathering momentum. Here was an example, and as a result Germany was being left behind. The German government was obliged to take account of the violent agitation in the press. At first Germany had only asked that the corridor leased to England by Article III should run at a distance of at least twenty kilometres from the German frontier. Now they demanded complete abandonment of the corridor. In menacing language Leopold was told that if the EIC chose to promote England's aggressive colonial designs, then Germany would cease to protect the Free State and would prefer France as her African neighbour.[25]

Leopold had overplayed his hand and the Great Powers were turning on him. Not only this, he found himself under considerable pressure at home from his entire cabinet. His ministers were greatly alarmed at seeing the king quarrelling with both Belgium's powerful neighbours at the same time. A general election was impending and such reckless behaviour would strengthen the socialists. And France was insisting that the Belgian officers in the service of the Congo State should be withdrawn as this represented a breach in her obligations of neutrality.[26]

Leopold was prepared to withdraw the offending corridor lease to appease the Germans and thus to isolate the French. But by now this was not enough to satisfy Berlin and cancellation of the entire agreement was demanded. The king turned to England for support. In vain, for Germany had already hinted that her support for England in Egypt would be withdrawn if the British did not comply. Rosebery agreed to remove the offending Article III.

German success spurred on the French to press their objections. At the same time it had the effect of making the British determined not to lose yet more face by giving in a second time. The French seeing this therefore applied the pressure on Brussels. Leopold was isolated. He played for time and offered to send a delegation to Paris to discuss matters; Rosebery, learning of this, was insistent that the king should not capitulate.

However, the majority of the cabinet disagreed with the militant prime minister, and were prepared to climb down and leave Leopold to the tender mercies of Gabriel Hanotaux, or, in more diplomatic language, to authorize him to come to an agreement with France. As a result a convention was drawn up a few days later. The king relinquished to France his claims to the Bahr-el-Ghazal. All the French left him with was the south-east corner bounded by 5° 30' north and 30° east, the Lado Enclave. He had been a useful tool in the hands of the Great Powers; his usefulness over, he was rapidly discarded.

18 The New Frontiers

'For Geographers in Africa-Maps
    With Savage-Pictures fill their Gaps;
And o'er uninhabitable Downs
    Place Elephants for want of Towns.'[1]

Jonathan Swift.

The exact frontiers of the Congo Free State had been left understandably rather vague at the end of the Berlin Conference: many areas of Central Africa had yet to be explored and without a better knowledge of the terrain, especially the river system, decisive borders could not be drawn. In the north-west, south-west and south-east, where the topography was known, realistic frontiers were agreed and adhered to, but in the north-east, south and east, where the geography was still uncertain, the final borders with the French, Portuguese and Germans respectively could not be fixed without further exploration and negotiation. In addition the state had yet to establish its authority in the vast area it now governed, especially in its Arab-dominated eastern region and in the area, so cunningly acquired by Leopold, around Katanga.

The EIC's border with the French on the Upper Congo, because of its strategic position as a gateway to the Nile, proved the most difficult to settle and, as described in the last chapter, ended unsatisfactorily for Leopold. In the 1885 agreement with France the border was to be:

> A median dividing Stanley Pool; the river Congo up to a point to be determined on the river Likona–N'Kundja; a line to be determined from this point to the 17th parallel east, following as much as possible the watershed of the Likona–N'Kundja basin, which is a French possession, and 17° longitude east.[2]

The problem was to identify the Likona–N'Kundja. De Brazza, basing himself on an 1885 map accepted by the EIC, disingenuously it would seem, claimed that the mouth of the Likona was shown at 0° 30′ south, that is the same latitude as the confluence of the Ubangi and the Congo. The Likona, *quod erat demonstrandum*, was one and the same river as the Ubangi. If this was so, then the EIC–French Congo frontier was pushed eastwards to the detriment of the EIC.[3]

To resolve the issue it was decided to send out a group of experts from both sides to examine the problem *in situ*. Fairly incredibly, they reported in favour of the French thesis and recommended that the frontier should follow the Ubangi northwards from its confluence with the Congo. The EIC refused to accept the findings of the experts and in April 1886 insisted that the dispute should be resolved by the respective governments. While the EIC was not willing to abandon the entire Ubangi valley, it was prepared to let France have part of it, for in the spring of 1886 Leopold was at the mercy of the French government as regards raising money in France and in the bargaining over the Ubangi the French held the upper hand. The king was strangely unassertive throughout the negotiations although there was a Leopoldian touch in his attempt to be awarded territorial compensation elsewhere if the French were intransigent as to the Ubangi: 'A concession in Indo-China close to Siam and the size of Goa ... would provide me with a source of recruitment,' ie for the Congo.[4]

The French dismissed the suggestion of sharing the Ubangi; the EIC replied by demanding that the subject should be referred to arbitration. In the face of the Free State's insistence and the unfavourable impression created internationally that its refusal produced, the French in September 1886 gave in. However, the simultaneous appointment of a new, optimistic and conciliatory French minister to Brussels, resulted in a change of plan, for the minister was convinced that agreement could be reached without recourse to arbitration. Leopold was prepared to try this.

But it was the results of an expedition in the Ubangi in 1886 led by a Belgian, Alphonse Van Gèle, and a German, Wilhelm Junker, that made serious negotiations possible. They showed that the Ubangi was not the same as the Likona. Leopold had attached great importance to Van Gèle's exploration and his belief was vindicated. In April 1887 the French were prepared to sign an agreement which fixed the EIC–French Congo frontier along the Ubangi as far north as 4° and, beyond this, the Ubangi for as long as it remained above the fourth parallel (it does in fact all the way until it divides to become the Bomu and Uele, but this was not known in 1887).

Leopold felt satisfied with the settlement. The substitution of the Ubangi, which runs between 18°–18° 50', for the seventeenth parallel entailed a considerable territorial loss on the right bank of the Ubangi but the king was compensated with additional territory in the north and the right to raise a loan in France.[5] The French had reason to believe that they had done a good deal for they had acquired the entire right bank of the Ubangi: in practical terms this meant that they controlled a wedge of territory extending towards the Nile.

The scene of action then moved from Europe back to Africa as both parties hastened to occupy what had been attributed to them. In particular, both sides were interested in the Upper Ubangi, that is above 4° north where it flows roughly east–west. Otherwise stated, both were anxious not to allow the other to block the way to the Nile. In 1887 it was not known whether the Ubangi and the Uele were one and the same river and there were thus valid geographical reasons as well as the desire to occupy territories granted by the April 1887 settlement – to say nothing of eventual Nilotic ambitions – behind the 1887 Van Gèle expedition.

In his 1886 expedition Van Gèle, like others before him, had only been able to follow the Ubangi up as far as Zongo so that the following year he approached by the Itimbiri, a northern tributary of the Congo which flows towards the Uele. In January 1888 he descended the Uele to its confluence with the Ubangi and resolved the question.

In 1891 another expedition led by Lieutenant Charles de la Kethulle, starting from Yakoma at the confluence, followed the northern branch of the Bomu upstream as far as the Congo–Nile divide. On the way he set up EIC stations. A certain number could not be maintained after he returned but nevertheless the EIC had made its presence felt in the region. The French were similarly active in occupying the right bank of the Ubangi and up until 1889 they had roughly kept abreast of the EIC on the other bank. By 1891 though the Free State was ahead. The French founded a port at Les Abiras on the right bank of the Ubangi–Uele confluence but EIC expeditions were already further to the east and pushing north of the Bomu towards the Bahr-el-Ghazal.

This situation arose mainly because French colonial policy was directed towards reaching Lake Chad and de Brazza, now governor of the French Congo, was charged with implementing it. In 1891 he sent an expedition under Victor Liotard northwards from the French Congo to an area which was intended to become the Algerian Sudan. Nevertheless, at the same time, de Brazza hoped that Liotard would found a post on the Upper Ubangi which would serve as a base for future operations towards the Nile. Liotard's mission was a failure. At Les Abiras he found the French post virtually surrounded by EIC forces. Then in May the commandant and most of the garrison were ambushed when out foraging. Throughout the Upper Ubangi the story was much the same.[6]

By a highly contentious interpretation of the 1887 settlement the EIC was trying to block the French on the Upper Ubangi. The EIC claimed that the agreement only concerned the Ubangi; the Ubangi ended at the confluence of the Bomu and Uele, therefore it did not apply further east. On the other hand, the agreement stipulated that the EIC frontier was not to be above 4° latitude, and they were active well beyond this parallel: the state's answer to this was that the 4° north limit only applied on the Ubangi itself. A further source of dissension was that from the end of 1891 onwards, following the decrees, the EIC was mounting large-scale ivory hunts; it was also claimed that their officials armed the natives and incited them against the French. There was an obvious danger of open hostilities between the French and the EIC breaking out.

Talks about the Upper Ubangi had taken place between the EIC and France in the latter part of 1891, but the situation in Africa was too fluid for there to be any incentive to reach an agreement, since both sides believed that their respective positions were about to improve. By April 1892 the French knew that their position had deteriorated. When therefore Leopold informed them that the EIC laid claim to the Lower Bomu and he proposed that a mixed commission should settle the exact frontier they were prepared to negotiate.[7] Two months later he came forward with more specific ideas. The frontier should be a line running from a little above the Uele–Bomu confluence to the Congo–Shari watershed. This would have allowed the EIC to expand northwards virtually as much as it liked and would at the same time cut the French off from access to the Nile.

Publicly Leopold adopted the stance of the little man being pushed around by the big: France should not be allowed to dictate to those not as strong, he claimed.[8] An example which shows who in reality was doing the running is Leopold's suggestion in June 1892. 'If they take the Bomu from us, I was thinking in terms of an enclave in Tunisia, a small area on the sea surrounded by French territory; an enclave that would not pose any problems for the French'.[9]

The French government wanted the irritating dispute settled as quickly as possible and in June 1892 agreed to a frontier generous to the EIC. There was an immediate outcry in colonial circles and they changed their minds a few days later.[10] Leopold was furious at the French tergiversation. 'France', he wrote, 'treats the EIC like an artichoke from which she removes the leaves one by one.'[11] To convince the British government that the French ought to agree to arbitration – and also to strengthen their own Nilotic negotiations with England – alarming stories of French designs on the Nile were successfully produced. Leopold also tried to enlist German support but the German government saw no reason to become involved in the dispute.[12]

The French refused to go to arbitration on the grounds that it was only necessary in a situation that could lead to war and there was long drawn-out diplomatic squabbling about the difference between mediation and arbitration.[13] Finally, by the time negotiations were reopened, the Van Kerckhoven expedition had reached the Nile and Leopold demanded that the French should recognize EIC territorial acquisitions both inside and outside the Nile valley.[14] In addition, France should cede a corridor to the Nile to the east of the French Congo. France, on the other hand, would have access to the Nile through the Bahr-el-Ghazal. Even with modifications the French were not prepared to accept the deal and the negotiations were broken off in January 1893.

They began again the following April and continued spasmodically throughout the year. Neither side had much that was new to suggest. Nevertheless the situation was evolving. The EIC was trying to establish itself on the Nile; the French were about to launch the Monteil expedition in the same direction.[15] Clashes between French and EIC troops in the Bomu area were increasing and Liotard, who had by now received reinforcements, decided to move upstream to recapture Bangasso, which had been taken by the EIC in 1890. The EIC force on the other side of the river saw Liotard leave Les Abiras and troops were moved rapidly to Bangasso (intelligence reports probably revealed his destination) to wait in battle formation. Liotard wisely did not fight, as the Free State force was larger and better armed and he was interned at Bangasso.

Leopold had the French government as well as Liotard at his mercy, and they knew it. Talks were resumed in April 1894, though despite their weak position the French were not very conciliatory – probably because they had heard rumours that Leopold was also negotiating with the British against them for territory on the Nile. Their behaviour certainly suggests it, for on 25 April, without warning, they broke off negotiations and left Brussels. After opposing the idea for years, they announced that they were prepared to have the matter settled by arbitration. Their angry reaction to the EIC's agreement with the British when it was published the following month and its effect on the negotiations has already been described.[16] Faced with German as well as French displeasure Britain recanted its promises to Leopold and the king was forced to come to an agreement with the French and on their terms. But as the French were most concerned to make him renounce the Bahr-el-Ghazal, once he had given in on this (i.e. not blocking them towards the Nile), they were prepared to allow the EIC to keep the Lado Enclave and to have the Bomu (as far as its source) as its northern frontier. The French nevertheless insisted on having the right to police both sides of the river and the EIC had to hand over to France the stations it had set up north of the Bomu.[17] It was in many ways a humiliating agreement even though the EIC had considerably extended its north and north-eastern frontiers and rich lands had been incorporated into the state.

The EIC's frontier with its southern neighbour, Portugal, had also been fixed by the agreement of February 1885, namely, the Nokki parallel as far as its intersection with the river Kwango; from there southwards along the Kwango. The Lunda was therefore included in the EIC limits and was marked as such on internationally accepted maps of that time.

The southern part of the new state was largely unknown territory and a German, Ludwig Wolf, was charged with continuing the work of a fellow countryman, Hermann Wissmann, who had explored the Kasai river valley for the state in 1885. Wolf went further up the Kasai and founded a station at Luebo on the Lulua before moving on eastwards to the Sankuru. Wissmann was continuing his explorations in the Lulua and Loubi valleys and two Belgian explorers were also active in the region. All these expeditions were directing their attention to the eastern tributaries of the Kasai.

In 1889, to open up territory to the west, Frederik Vandevelde was sent up the Kwango and explored as far as Kasongo–Lunda before turning eastwards. Throughout the area he concluded treaties with local chiefs and as a result he ran out of supplies and could not advance further up-river. The following year, a young man called Lieutenant Francis Dhanis was chosen to push further south, and reached Capenda–Camulemba.

To begin with the Portuguese had tacitly acquiesced in the EIC's claim to Lunda – no protest was made about the maps including it in the EIC, but in 1888 the Portuguese minister of foreign affairs informed van Eetvelde that there were certain territorial questions which remained to be settled. Without specifying it, there was a *sous-entendu* that the Portuguese were claiming Lunda. The EIC sent a very Leopoldian reply. Portuguese claims would only be recognized if in return the state received some Portuguese territory in East Africa.

Van Eetvelde held that the Portuguese had only claimed Lunda for internal political reasons as England was at the time demanding Portuguese territory elsewhere in Africa. The idea of stripping the EIC originated, he claimed, with perfidious Albion. Be that as it may, Portuguese diplomatic ineptitude proved to be the EIC's strongest weapon. At the Anti-Slavery Conference then taking place in Brussels, the Portuguese asserted that they had set up anti-slavery posts in the African hinterland. When they showed the map the posts were seen by Britain and the EIC to be in areas they were claiming. The weight of the British empire descended on the unfortunate Portuguese and Leopold took advantage of the cover it provided.[18]

He immediately issued a decree announcing the creation of a new district of East Kwango and dispatched an EIC officer, Colonel Liebrechts, to England. Liebrechts let everyone know 'in confidence' that he was there to buy two second-hand gunboats to use against the Portuguese in Africa. Whether this dramatic gesture – no gunboats were purchased – had any effect is doubtful. In any case, the Portuguese were preoccupied by a long drawn-out internal political crisis. When this was resolved the new minister of foreign affairs, the Marquis du Bocage, proposed reopening discussion of Lunda and talks began again early in 1891. The Portuguese proposed the Kasai as the frontier; the EIC from its position of strength as the occupying power in Lunda would not consider it. The Portuguese then conceded that the Kwango should be the frontier as far south as the eighth parallel and from there roughly in an easterly direction to the Kasai.

Talk of mediation by the pope, who was believed to favour Portugal, persuaded Leopold to accept the Portuguese compromise and an agreement was signed in May 1891. Even so, the agreement was a singular triumph for the EIC, which now possessed *de jure* the fruits of its explorations in the Kasai–Kwango region.

As a result of the Brussels Anti-Slavery Conference, Leopold II had an international commitment to stamp out the slave-trade in the Congo. His penury had long prevented him from doing anything about the Arab hegemony in the eastern Congo and he had been forced to come to a *modus vivendi* with the Arabs. (The most striking example of it was the appointment of Tippu Tib as governor of the Stanley Falls area.) However, with the conference's authorization of import duties and the 25,000,000 franc loan from Belgium, Leopold could, at last, contemplate trying to assert state authority in the east.

The first step consisted of establishing two armed camps, one at Basoko in the north and the other at Lusambo on the Sankuru. The Arabs interpreted these excursions into their territory as hostile actions.[19] However, the most important cause of worsening relations with the Arabs was the EIC's interference in the ivory trade. From the outset, Leopold had been trying to divert the trade from the east to the west coast, which clearly ran contrary to the Arab trading pattern, though as long as the price was right they were prepared to do business with traders from the Congo. Following the decrees in 1891 the EIC intervened in the trade and forced the price down. Van Kerckhoven, the EIC administrator in charge of the region, went as far as confiscating Arab ivory worth 1,500,000 francs.[20]

Leopold, who was preoccupied with expansion in the north and northeast, felt no urgency in dealing with the simmering Arab problem; events forced his hand. In April 1892 a Belgian, Arthur Hodister, and about twenty other men trying to buy ivory in the Kasonga area, were told that they were not welcome. They refused to leave. In the middle of May Europeans of the party were murdered at Riba-Riba. The Arabs threatened the same fate for any Europeans who remained. The Europeans were not intimidated; a week later Hodister and three more men were killed. Two days later a further two met the same fate at

Lomo. The Arab leader at Nyangwe, Mohara, who did not try to hide his hatred of Europeans, made no secret of his responsibility for the killings.[21]

General hostilities did not follow and the Arab leader at Stanley Falls, Raschid, a nephew of Tippu Tib, and Sefu, Tippu Tib's son, who ruled at Kasongo, proclaimed their fidelity to the state and the EIC authorities, for their part, saw no reason to change their policy.[22] However, Ngongo Lutete, who had begun as one of Tippu Tib's African slaves and now ruled the area around Ngandu on the Lomani, was defeated in several clashes with state troops under Captain Dhanis. In September 1892 he asked the state for protection and in return handed over his rights.[23]

Dhanis's action against Ngongo was interpreted – wrongly in fact – as a declaration of war by the state and Sefu joined up with Mohara in open hostility to the EIC. At Kasongo the Arabs took two of the European officials, Henri de Bruyne and Joseph Lippens, hostage.

A state expedition sent to relieve them did not dare to cross the Lomani river into Arab territory and de Bruyne persuaded Sefu to let him out, accompanied, to put forward the Arab case. Sefu set out his terms which de Bruyne communicated to Jean Scheerlinck, the leader of the state expedition. Scheerlinck suggested to de Bruyne that he should make a dash for freedom by swimming the river but de Bruyne refused on the grounds that it would condemn Lippens to certain death. As regards Sefu's propositions, Scheerlinck promised a reply within a few days since the area commander, Dhanis, was expected. Dhanis was a man of action and not conciliation; on arrival he refused to treat with Sefu and led his men across the Lomani – in defiance of orders from Brussels – into the Arab zone. He announced to his troops: 'I have no intention of coming back alive from this campaign if it turns out badly. If any of you have the misfortune to be taken prisoner by the enemy, I shall regard him as dead and shall not risk a man to save him.'[24] In the battle that inevitably followed Dhanis's provocative stand, the Europeans, with their superior armaments, triumphed. About three thousand men died in the encounter and one European officer reported: 'I doubt whether any demon sabbath could be compared with this Christian vengeance. The Arab losses were terrifying.'[25] It need hardly be said that the captive de Bruyne and Lippens were murdered.

The unscrupulous Ngongo Lutete then joined up with Dhanis, bringing 1,500 armed men with him. The 'latter were a considerable help in fighting, but were somewhat embarrassing allies since after each combat they rushed to eat the slain.'[26] In December 1892 Dhanis plus Ngongo defeated Mohara's son in battle and early in 1893 repeated the feat on Mohara himself. A few weeks later Dhanis reached Nyangwe, the Arab 'capital', but by the time reinforcements had reached him to enable him to attack the town, the Arabs had evacuated it, leaving only Africans, and it was taken without difficulty.

Next in line was Kasongo which Dhanis took in April 1893, but he lacked the men necessary to pursue the Arabs further and concentrated his energies on establishing state authority over Nyangwe and Kasongo. However, state forces under Commandant Chatlin were moving up the Lualaba and had been victorious at Chari and Riba-Riba. From there they had relieved Stanley Falls before moving south to join up with Dhanis. Another expedition under Lieutenant Lothaire recruited men in Angola and brought them over to Kasongo also. All these forces joined together to confront the Arabs under Rumaliza, the Arab overlord from Udjiji up the eastern side of Lake Tanganyika who had come to the help of his fellow Arabs. Despite his support the Arabs were defeated at the battle of Lublakole in September 1893. It took a few more months before the Arabs were pushed further east and Kabambare was taken. But the war was to all intents and purposes over. Rumaliza disappeared back into German East Africa; the Arabs lost hope and the Congo Free State forces began what today are known as mopping-up operations. (Lake Tanganyika formed a natural frontier between the EIC and German East Africa but towards the end of Leopold's reign the Germans claimed the area around Lake Kivu. The dispute was unsettled at the time of his death.)

Leopold II had fulfilled his promise to exterminate the slave-trade in the Congo, and a further valuable area had been brought under the effective jurisdiction of the state.

19 Katanga

'The rocks are green in the land called
Catanga.' Portuguese Travellers, 1806.

It is rather surprising that Leopold II had in 1885 considered Katanga poor compensation for the loss of the Niari–Kouilou, as its copper mines were known, and there were some who were convinced that Katanga was an African Eldorado. From the fifteenth century when Europeans first began trading in Africa it was known that somewhere in the interior copper was produced, though the first expedition with the specific objective of exploring Katanga was that organized in 1883 by the German branch of the AIA and partly financed by Leopold. Led by a twenty-four-year-old German, Doctor Paul Reichard, it arrived in Bunkeya, the capital of the tyrannical ruling chief of Katanga, M'siri, in January 1884.[2] M'siri was not a native of Katanga but an African trader from East Africa who had carved himself an empire and made himself rich by raiding his neighbours and selling them as slaves to the Arabs.

'A man of subtle cruelty,' Reichard wrote to M'siri, 'this African ruler is most at home playing the role of executioner and he very much enjoys burying his victims up to the waist and then letting them die of hunger.'[3] The German and his party could make little headway with the task on hand and many were killed by M'siri's men. In the end only Reichard survived the expedition. Two Portuguese explorers from Angola had much the same experience. Yet a Scottish missionary, Frederick Arnot, who arrived in 1886, was allowed to establish a mission station close to Bunkeya. It was his book,[4] published in 1889, in which he painted a glowing picture of the countryside, the climate and, not least, of the extensive copper mines he had seen which spurred the prime minister of Cape Colony, Cecil Rhodes, to find out more about Katanga. Rhodes was at that time setting up the British South Africa Company, the BSAC, a chartered company which was to develop the region between Bechuanaland and the Zambezi (it later became Northern and Southern Rhodesia).

Katanga sounded interesting to Rhodes and he lost little time in sending a BSAC representative there. The man fell ill and died; a second arrived soon afterwards but he fell foul of M'siri and was lucky to escape with his life.

Leopold was greatly disturbed by the mounting signs of English interest and activity in Katanga. Unfortunately in 1889 his resources were more than fully stretched in other parts of the state. Katanga was included within the EIC boundaries on the map accepted by the Powers in August 1885 but the state had not done anything to occupy the territory. British maps were now showing Katanga as a no-man's land and there was talk in the press of indefinite British penetration in Central Africa.

To prevent any future 'misunderstanding', in April 1890 Leopold proposed to the BSAC that they should fix their common frontier at 14° south.⁵ His fears were not assuaged when he received a reply saying that as Rhodes was absent, and because of the negotiations taking place with Germany, the company could not give an answer for the moment. The king immediately wrote to Lord Salisbury. The prime minister only acknowledged the letter, which was disquieting enough; worse, a semi-official map of Africa was published in England in which Katanga was not included within the EIC frontiers. Leopold let the British government know that he was aware what was going on:

> Sir John Kirk will no doubt have submitted to Your Lordship, [Salisbury] on my behalf a map taken from *The Graphic* which shows a major part of Katanga as not forming part of the Congo State. It is said that this is the work of Mr. H.H. Johnston, British Consul at Mozambique. I have requested Lord Vivian to bring to Your Lordship's notice that Mr. Johnston is said to have admitted recently to someone in London, who repeated it to me, that at the end of 1889 he had concluded political treaties with several chiefs of the Itawa [south-western coast of Lake Tanganyika] aimed at removing certain areas from the Congo Free State, judging, he added, that the time had come to take as much as possible away from the Free State. To prevent complications arising at a later date, I am obliged to take certain steps to protect our interests.⁶

Sir Percy Anderson needed all his skill to draft a suitable reply for Salisbury to send to the king. It was a friendly letter but there was no indication as to what the British considered the EIC–BSAC frontier to be and Lambermont agreed with Leopold that the British were being less than straightforward. The baron therefore called Vivian in and showed him the August 1885 map which had accompanied the declaration of neutrality; in a later letter though, Salisbury spoke of the February 1885 declaration of neutrality, that is at the end of the Conference of Berlin when no map was used. Leopold knew who he was fighting and it was not Salisbury but Rhodes and Harry Johnston, and he directed his energies to protesting to the British about Johnston. He saw Salisbury in spring 1891 and, according to the prime minister, 'He spoke to me at length about Johnston, to whom he ascribes infinite enormities in the way of map-making and article-writing.'[7]

The king had good reason to believe that Johnston was advocating the annexation of Katanga by the British, though he could not have known of a document Johnston had sent to Salisbury in August 1890.

> I have reason to believe that the King of the Belgians wants to chase us out of an important piece of territory which we need to complete the new province of British Central Africa. This territory is Garanganze ... Garanganze, called by the Swahili Arabs Katanga, is the richest country in minerals (gold and copper) in all Central Africa. It is fairly healthy and has a fertile soil. Its people are peaceful and industrious. The King of the Belgians has no right to it. On the official maps of the C.F.S. territory issued by him after the Berlin Congress he does not even include it in his dominions. Of late through the indulgent carelessness of British mapmakers it has been allotted to the C.F.S. on the map ... From a Belgian point of view he is an admirable patriot, who has by many a hook and crook, by many a wile and intrigue, by much expenditure of his own and not a little of that subscribed by the rich English people whom he bamboozled, created a fine African Empire for little Belgium. But why his enterprise should be viewed by *us* ... with indulgence ... I cannot conceive.[8]

Leopold used all the tools at his disposal to combat Rhodes and the BSAC lobby. He wrote to Victoria and to the Prince of Wales; he asked Greindl to find out if the German government would support him. On this occasion their interests coincided with those of the EIC, as British expansion from the south of the continent would jeopardize German territories in East Africa.

The obvious course of action for Leopold was to occupy Katanga. But – and one is forced to repeat it once again – in 1890 he did not possess the means. Clearly if it had been possible in previous years he would have already done it. He had sent expeditions to the Ubangi, the Bomu, the Kasai, to Lunda, to say nothing of trying to administer vast uncontested areas of the country. And it should also be borne in mind that the king was committed to taking action against the Arab slave-traders as soon as he could get together enough money and men.

However, in view of the mineral resources known to exist in Katanga, it was possible for Leopold to propose that the Congolese commercial companies should to some degree finance the expeditions necessary to occupy Katanga. He suggested to Thys that a joint EIC–commercial expedition should be sent, but the commercial companies preferred a free hand, and the king decided to send a separate EIC one.

Thys set to organizing a CCCI expedition in September 1889 and Alexandre Delcommune, who had many years' experience in the Congo, was chosen to lead it. Delcommune left Europe in the summer of 1890 and Leopold himself managed to send an expedition into Katanga at the end of 1890 by ordering the commander of the Free State post at Lusambo on the Sankuru – not far outside Katanga – Paul Le Marinel, to get together a force and to march to Bunkeya, about eight hundred miles away, as quickly as possible. Le Marinel and his party of about 300 Africans and two other Europeans reached Bunkeya in record time (and ahead of Delcommune's expedition) on 18 April 1891. M'siri's reception was not hostile but he refused Le Marinel's invitation to submit to the EIC. On the other hand, he was prepared for the state to set up a post not far from Bunkeya. (M'siri probably considered the arms and ammunition held in the post as virtually his own.) The two Europeans other than Le Marinel were left at the new station of Lofoi and Le Marinel himself left Bunkeya in June 1891 and returned to Lusambo.[9] Delcommune arrived at Bunkeya on 6 October 1891, but he had no more success than Le Marinel in persuading M'siri to submit to the EIC and he set out to explore southern Katanga.

During his absence from Europe, Delcommune's employer had changed from being the CCCI to the *Compagnie du Katanga*. The new company was set up essentially as EIC retaliation to the BSAC, though there were other reasons for its creation. It was not enough for the CCCI to have an interest in Katanga; it was already occupied with a wide range of projects in the Free State and Katanga, which held out such commercial promise, justified a separate organization. Moreover, in creating a new company with good prospects, new money could be attracted, and it was hoped to include some English capital to allay pressure for British annexation of Katanga. The new company constituted in April 1891 was granted a third of the lands in the region with a ninety-nine-year concession for the exploitation of mineral wealth, plus a twenty-year preference right for the exploitation of all mineral resources discovered in the lands belonging to the state.

As well as taking charge of the Delcommune expedition, already in Africa, the *Compagnie du Katanga* sent out two more politico-commercial expeditions and one purely commercial. And, while Leopold had no official say in the *Compagnie du Katanga*, he told it to order its agents to make treaties with African chiefs in unoccupied lands within the British sphere of influence, if they found that the British had already elicited treaties from M'siri. Such treaties could be used for future bargaining if it proved necessary.

The first expedition was led by William Stairs, a Canadian-born Englishman and professional adventurer who had taken part in the Emin Pasha Relief Expedition. Under him was an Irishman, Doctor Moloney, Moloney's manservant, Robinson, a Frenchman, the Marquis de Bonchamps, and a Belgian officer, Captain Omer Bodson. Arriving at Bunkeya on 20 December 1891, Stairs found a different state of affairs from the one Le Marinel had encountered only months before. 'The famine is such', wrote Stairs, 'that if one offered a treasure one could not buy provisions; there are none. No more firewood either and the water is execrable. The English missionaries are terrorized by M'siri.'[10]

Stairs rapidly came to the conclusion that it was necessary to depose M'siri, although it was Bodson who during a heated discussion, either with premeditation or having lost his head, drew his revolver and shot M'siri several times, killing him outright. Bodson himself was severely wounded and died the following day. According to Stairs, just before losing consciousness, Bodson said, 'Doctor, I don't mind dying, now that I have killed M'siri; my death will not be in vain. I have delivered Africa from one of her most detestable tyrants. Long live the King.'[11]

The *coup d'état* was successful because of widespread disaffection among the native population with M'siri's rule, and Stairs had little difficulty in establishing the political authority of the EIC. However, he faced a problem of a different kind. Food supplies in the region, which had been scant enough before, were rapidly running out. Men were dying daily and Stairs himself was ill. On 30 January 1892 news was brought that a caravan was approaching from the west: it was the *Compagnie du Katanga*'s expedition led by Lucien Bia. It was decided that Bia should take over from Stairs who with the other Europeans would return to Zanzibar. Only one of them, Moloney, could walk. Three months later they reached the coast. Bonchamps and Robinson had recovered but Stairs died on the day that the ship to take them to Europe entered port.

Bia had under him a geologist, Jules Cornet, a doctor, Jules Amerlinck, and two officers, Lieutenants Emile Francqui and Eugène Derscheid. They faced a rude beginning to their task. Bunkeya and the neighbouring countryside were famine-stricken. Francqui described the situation:

> What frightful scenes were witnessed during those two months ... Every morning we found corpses in the native huts and heaven only knows how many more of the poor devils went away to die. Dysentery, the inevitable consequence of these appalling conditions, also took its toll and the number of dead to be buried grew each day.[12]

The political side of the mission, namely, to make treaties with local chiefs and to proclaim the sovereignty of the Free State, had been accomplished without any difficulty, and Bia could now concentrate on the geological side. Francqui was left in charge at Bunkeya while Bia and Cornet went off in search of the much spoken-of copper mine at Kambove. Kambove lived up to expectations. On their return, Bia decided that the next step was to set up camp away from Bunkeya, in hopefully less rigorous conditions. From the new post at Kipuna, twenty-five miles east of Bunkeya, the expedition split into two groups. Cornet was ill and had to remain at Kipuna until August 1892 when he was well enough to be able to continue his prospecting in the southern part of the region, that is around what later became Elisabethville.

Bia and Francqui meanwhile had left Kipuna in February 1892 to explore the unknown regions of Katanga. They headed first north-eastwards towards Lake Moero and then southwards before turning eastwards again and heading for the village of Chitambo in British territory. There was nothing to be gained by the long detour through BSAC country but Bia had promised the English that he would place a plaque at Chitambo, where Livingstone, the most revered of all the African explorers, had died nearly twenty years before. Bia, already a very sick man, would not be deflected from his mission.[13] He accomplished his task but he was able to do little more. The terrain in that part of Africa had done much to hasten Livingstone's death, and Bia's health inevitably deteriorated yet more when he was forced to march for long periods with water up to his knees. He reached Tenké, south-west of Bunkeya where Cornet was to rejoin the expedition, but died soon afterwards. Francqui took over command of the expedition and from there they made their way northwards to Lusambo. Four-fifths of the Africans on the expedition had died during its course.

The third expedition to Katanga was that under the auspices of the *Syndicat Commercial du Katanga*, a company formed in October 1891 to exploit the concessions granted to the *Compagnie du Katanga*. The *Syndicat*'s interests were purely commercial and it did not organize an expedition as such but charged Arthur Hodister, who was already in Africa, to act on its behalf. Hodister and his party, as has already been described, were murdered by Arabs in the eastern Congo in May 1892.

The cumulative result of the Le Marinel, Delcommune, Stairs, Bia-Francqui expeditions was that within three years the greater part of Katanga was explored, its mineral wealth established and the most important copper deposits located. Moreover, the EIC had asserted its claim to the territory which henceforth was not disputed, and in 1894 the British government recognized the southern frontier claimed by the state. But neither the EIC nor the *Compagnie du Katanga* was in a position to undertake commercial exploitation of the copper mines.

Other natural resources of the Congo, above all ivory and rubber, were more easily available, and the rubber boom of the 1890s was such that other products were not sought after. Copper was worth only four francs a kilo, and this presupposed that the ore could be smelted on the spot.[14] Nevertheless, Leopold II wanted to open up Katanga as soon as he had the means to build the necessary transport outlets, for this was central to the problem. Most parts of Katanga were at least twelve hundred miles from the coast; the Lualaba penetrated into the region but its frequent rapids made it unusable as a trade route; to the east high mountains formed a barrier. The route Leopold envisaged was by building a railway from Katanga northwards which would join up with a prolongation of the Matadi–Stanley Pool line. Another possibility, much shorter in distance, was for a line to run from the Angolan coast to Katanga, but Leopold did not want to have recourse to involvement with other countries. However, the obvious route was to link up with the Cape-to-Cairo railway. But Leopold had by now very little faith in the British and he loathed Rhodes personally. 'It is by the North, not the South', he held, 'that Katanga must be attached to our national activity.'[15] If Leopold's own scheme was to be the means of opening up Katanga it would not take place for a long time.

For the second time, it was British activity south of the frontier that forced Leopold's hand. Rhodes's associate, a Scottish engineer, Robert Williams, had discovered rich copper and gold seams in Rhodesia in the last two years of the nineteenth century, and the BSAC granted him the concession to exploit them. In 1899 Williams set up his own company, Tanganyika Concessions, Tanks as it came to be called.

Williams believed that the Rhodesian seams extended into Katanga and approached Leopold for permission to extend his exploratory work within the EIC frontier. The king would have much preferred to use his own resources for the work but even in 1900, when the Congo had become a viable concern, the number of qualified men he could call upon was limited, and in any case Williams had a technical head start. Leopold recognized that he would have to do a deal with Williams.

Before doing this, the relative claims of the EIC and the *Compagnie du Katanga* had to be resolved, as virtually nothing had been done since 1891 to work out which areas belonged to the state and which to the company. To avoid a long drawn-out haggle it was decided to combine and to form a joint enterprise, the *Comité Spécial du Katanga*, the CSK. The convention drawn up in June 1900 stipulated that the *Comité* would consist of six directors, four to be named by the state and two by the *Compagnie du Katanga*. The president was to be Hubert Droogmans, secretary of state of the EIC. Later in the year the CSK came to agreement with Tanks, granting the latter a monopoly of mineral prospecting rights in Katanga. The csk and Tanks would provide the capital 50–50 but the profits would be divided 60–40 in favour of the csk. The working arrangement was to last for thirty years.[16]

Prospecting in Katanga began in 1901. The engineers confirmed Cornet's discoveries of a decade before: all that was lacking was a railway line. Leopold was still attached to the construction of a northern line from Katanga but, *force majeure*, he was prepared to make an arrangement with Williams in 1902 for the British line from the south to enter Katanga. To this end the *Compagnie du Chemin de Fer du Katanga* was created in March 1902. At the same time the west coast outlet had not been forgotten and the Benguela Railway Company was set up in 1903 (in which Tanks had a considerable interest) and work began on the line from Angola at the end of 1904. The British had meanwhile been pushing ahead fast with the Cape-to-Cairo railway to open up Rhodesia. It reached Broken Hill in January 1906 and was to be extended into the copper belt that ran alongside the eic–Rhodesian frontier and from there into Katanga.

So far Tanks and the csk had remained separate companies, but now that closer and prolonged co-operation was imminent, it was decided to create a new company to take charge of the large-scale industrial exploitation of Katanga and the allied transport and distribution of the copper produced. Leopold II, however, had in 1906 personal reasons, brought about by the projected annexation of the Congo by Belgium, for wanting a new arrangement. The eic had a controlling interest in the csk which Leopold wanted to thin down to prevent the Belgian state from laying claim to it. The csk therefore handed over large areas of land in Katanga to the new body and transferred its share of csk capital to the *Société Générale de Belgique*, in the knowledge that the Belgian government would not be able to wrest it back once it was in the hands of the *Société Générale*. Thus in October 1906 the *Union Minière du Haut-Katanga* was founded.

The railway from Rhodesia crossed into Katanga on 11 December 1909, six days before Leopold II's death.

20   Fashoda Revisited

*'I am sure that the English people after such
a struggle with the French are not going to
have it [the Bahr-el-Ghazal] handed over to
the Belgians.'*[1]   Cecil Rhodes.

One might well have imagined that Leopold II had had his fingers sufficiently burnt in 1894. Far from it. As soon as he had dealt with the threat
of Belgian annexation of the Congo,[2] seemingly unperturbed at the prospect of becoming embroiled in increasingly acrimonious Anglo-French
colonial rivalry, he again plunged into Nile affairs.

By February 1895 all the Free State's forces previously within the Nile
basin had returned to Zemio in accordance with the Franco-Congolese
convention of August 1894. However, to the consternation of all his
advisers, in the summer of 1895 Leopold was planning another push to
the Nile. Van Eetvelde, who was aware of his master's thinking, was
greatly alarmed at the idea and suggested to the British that they should
move in and occupy the Upper Nile to put an end, once and for all, to
the king's ambitions.

Leopold on the other hand was advising Lord Salisbury to evacuate
Egypt. The prime minister was incredulous. He reported Leopold as
arguing:

> 'If the British left Egypt', they could 'annex China to the Indian
> Empire; and then, if the Ottoman Empire fell in pieces', they could
> 'have Egypt back again'. But in dealing with Egypt, we were first to
> persuade the Khedive to give a concession of the Valley of the Nile
> from Khartoum upwards to some person who was *'au courant* of the
> affairs of Africa'; he was too modest to mention who that person was.[3]

There were several variations to the theme. One was that, if the Upper
Nile were in the hands of the Free State, a Sudanese army trained by
EIC forces might be placed at British disposal. Such an army, Leopold
assured Salisbury, could be used:

> 'For the purpose of invading and occupying Armenia and so putting

a stop to the massacres which were moving Europe so deeply ...' The idea of an English general at the head of an army of dervishes, marching from Khartoum to Lake Van, in order to prevent Mohammedans from maltreating Christians, struck me as so quaint, that I hastened to give the conversation another turn, lest I should be betrayed into some disrespectful commentary.[4]

Even if the king's ideas had been less fantastical, Salisbury had not the slightest intention of allowing Leopold to expand from the Lado enclave. He knew that the king was unable to occupy Lado and by the time that Leopold could muster the necessary resources, the British meanwhile would have established a preponderant position on the Upper Nile. This was to be done by constructing a railway from Mombasa, through the Kikuyu country to Lake Victoria, a distance of about 600 miles. Ultimately the British hoped to reconquer the Sudan. 'Our only chance', he told Victoria, 'is to keep the thing quiet until our railway to Uganda is sufficiently far advanced to enable us to send troops by it.'[5] Despite estimates that the railway would cost the then enormous sum of £3,000,000, the British parliament voted the money.

Events outside his control obliged Salisbury to alter course in 1896 when the Italians were resoundingly defeated by Abyssinians under Menelik at Adowa. 'I could have wished', Salisbury remarked, 'that our friends the Italians had less capacity for being beaten.'[6] Adowa was one of the few African victories over the technically superior European armies and led to the collapse of the Italian hold in Ethiopia. However, an important Italian garrison was holding out at Kassala, a town dominating one of the affluents of the Nile. Salisbury, who until then had been unsympathetic to the mess in which the Italians found themselves in Ethiopia, spotted the opportunity that Adowa offered. Under the guise of helping the Italians, the reconquest of the Nile would begin. It remained only to persuade Lord Cromer, the British agent in Egypt, of the necessity of the plan since it was known that, after years of hard work to re-establish Egyptian finances on a sound footing, Cromer would not want to see his efforts frittered away on wild expeditions upstream.

The Triple Alliance, of which Italy was the junior partner, and the House of Commons, accepted the need for the British to invade the Sudan in 'the cause of civilization in Africa' and on 13 March 1896 Colonel Herbert Kitchener was ordered to advance with an Egyptian force from Wadi Halfa, on the Nile in Egypt, upstream to Dongola – the Nile rather than the Eastern Sudan being chosen as the theatre of operations to avoid any clashes with the Ethiopians. The relief of the Italians at Kassala was to revive French and EIC interest in the Nile valley.

The French, like the British, had been preoccupied with non-African affairs in 1895 and did not attach great importance to Leopold II's visit to Paris in September 1895. The king was on good terms with Félix Faure, president of the republic, and did his best to ingratiate himself with ministers and the French public. Leopold was at this time trying to court favour with the British but, never one to put all his diplomatic eggs in one basket, he tried out on the French his ideas for a neutral solution to Anglo-French rivalry by handing over the Bahr-el-Ghazal to him. The French treated this proposal no more seriously than the British had done but it was agreed to work together on Nilotic affairs and the EIC gave active support to Jean-Baptiste Marchand's expedition in 1897.

All this was secondary, as the French had plans of their own for dealing with the British. The Monteil expedition as a political force had fizzled out in the Ivory Coast in 1895; only one young officer in it had not accepted defeat. Jean-Baptiste Marchand returned to France disappointed that France had seemingly given up establishing herself on the Nile. He canvassed his idea for a new expedition to the Nile valley with Hanotaux and senior officials at the Ministries of Foreign Affairs and the Colonies, and found sympathetic listeners. Yet another political crisis took place at this stage and resulted in a new man at the Quai d'Orsay, Marcelin Berthelot, a distinguished chemist inexperienced in foreign affairs. Berthelot, pushed by the colonial hawks in the ministries, let himself be persuaded by the plausible Marchand – Hanotaux had treated Marchand with scepticism and appreciated the wider implications of the sort of action the young man was advocating – to authorize a mission to the Bahr-el-Ghazal. It would be completely non-military and almost unofficial. Hanotaux returned to the Quai d'Orsay in June 1896 by which time the Marchand expedition was a *fait accompli*. He could only hope it would be successful. 'Go to Fashoda,' he told Marchand. 'France is going to fire her pistol.'[7]

To back up Marchand, Hanotaux sent a deputation to Ethiopia to woo Menelik with arms and ammunition and the promise to recognize his claims to the eastern bank of the Nile. In return he agreed to allow French expeditions to move towards the Nile from Ethiopia. The British would be caught in a pincer movement.

It would have been out of character if Leopold II had sat back and let the British and French settle things between themselves in the Nile, and he was indeed as active as he had ever been. The French suspected that he was in league with the British advance from Wadi Halfa and in September 1896 Hanotaux repeated his threat to Belgium that her nationals would have to be withdrawn from EIC forces. Salisbury refused to have anything to do with the king's schemes. Leopold decided to act alone.

Two Belgian officers who had distinguished themselves in the Arab wars, Captain, now also Baron, Dhanis, and Commandant Chatlin, were chosen to lead the new expeditions. They would, by different routes, move into the Nile valley to join up at Rejaf, close to the Lado Enclave. No-one could take exception to such a legitimate aim. But Lado was only a halt; they had secret orders to advance towards Khartoum.

Dhanis's expedition, the largest of all nineteenth-century African expeditions – 3,000 men – left Stanleyville in October 1896. The leader was under instructions to follow the Aruwimi valley, the tropical inferno which had wreaked such havoc with the Emin Pasha expedition a few years before. This notoriously difficult route was chosen to conceal the size of the expedition, as the Uele route was under French observation. Leopold would have done better to have taken heed of Stanley's experiences in the late 1880s: Dhanis's expedition suffered similarly in the tropical rain-forest and in February 1897 his Batela troops, natives of the southern Congo, mutinied and fled. Leopold's grandiose plans were similarly dissipated.

Chatlin's smaller force, about 700 men, fared better. He had consolidated the EIC position during the previous year and had no difficulty moving up the Uele in October 1896. By December he was at Dungu and in January 1897 at Faradje. A few days after arriving at Faradje, he received a message from Dhanis asking him to wait for the main force. For whatever reason, he chose to disregard his superior's orders and pushed on to Bedden where he arrived in mid-February. Here the local chief, Arabi-Dafa'allah, brought out his troops; despite their small number Chatlin's men routed Arabi and entered Rejaf.[8]

The two EIC expeditions into the Nile valley in 1896 were ambitious enough, but Leopold was too much of an opportunist not to try to profit by the simultaneous Italian collapse in Ethiopia. He immediately brought out his favourite neutral-presence plan and volunteered to take over the country. In fact, even before the Italian defeat at Adowa Leopold had been interested in Ethiopia. During the Arab wars he had tried to recruit Ethiopians into the Free State's forces and, seeing how precarious the Italian hold was, he had contemplated a move from the Nile into Ethiopia.[9] After Adowa, however, his chances of gaining at least part of Ethiopia increased considerably.

An influential, pro-colonial Italian deputy, General dal Verme, had already proposed that Italy should only abandon Abyssinia itself; Eritrea should be temporarily leased to a custodian, at a good price, until such time as Italy was in a position to take over again. It was an extraordinary idea and, as was so often the case, exotic diplomatic schemes sooner or later involved Leopold II.

During the early months of 1897 dal Verme visited Brussels several times and was much impressed by the king. Leopold, for the first time for many years, visited Italy. To dissimulate the reason for his being there, as the scheme was a secret even from van Eetvelde, he took with him his daughter Clementine, with whom he played at being a tourist. From Milan they went to Turin, Pavia and Como. Leopold even went to an art exhibition, not something he was normally in the habit of doing.

A draft document was produced by the summer in which it was proposed to create a *Société Congolaise de Colonisation et d'Exploitation* – language reminiscent of that dear to the heart of the Duke of Brabant in the 1860s. The company would lease Eritrea, except for Massawa. Half the officers of the company would be Italian and the Italian government would receive half the revenues. As in the Anglo-Congolese agreement of 1894 the lease was to last for as long as Leopold ruled the Congo or it remained independent.

Leopold had suffered enough at the hands of the Great Powers in recent years not to be wary of going too far in a plan without securing their approval. His relations with France were good at this stage, as he was supporting the Marchand expedition; Germany and England needed to be squared. He knew only too well that his personal reputation in Berlin and London was none too good so he asked the Italians to make the approaches. 'If I myself – ruler of a small country – were to make the request, it would be said that I have ambitions to everywhere and I would probably not be listened to.'[10]

Dal Verme took it upon himself to approach Lord Cromer, who was passing through Italy in September 1897, to test out the British reaction. He joined the agent on the train between Turin and Alessandria and began talking about Italian colonial problems. As a result of the Italian's persuasion, Cromer promised that the British would take over at Kassala, as the Italians were anxious to leave the garrison there. Then, moving on to the subject of Eritrea, dal Verme began a new *exposé*. He was not allowed to finish it. Cromer stood up and laughingly said, 'The King of the Belgians is very cunning'.[11] He then left the compartment. Dal Verme realized that the British would never consent to King Leopold's presence in Ethiopia.[12]

For the Italians this brush-off marked the end of the project: Leopold, more tenacious, tried modifying the plan to merely the lease of a corridor through Ethiopia giving the Congo Free State access to the Red Sea. The British would not hear of it. By now their position in the Nile valley was sufficiently strengthened for them not to have to explain themselves.

In spite of help from the EIC authorities in the early stages of his march, Marchand was four months behind schedule. It was not until July 1898 that he reached Fashoda, hoisted the Tricolour, and took possession in the name of France. Knowledge of Marchand's march had, hardly surprisingly, altered British plans and Kitchener had been ordered to advance up the Nile. By the beginning of September he was before Omdurman. He had with him about 17,000 Egyptian and Sudanese troops plus 8,000 British ones who had been sent out when the aim had changed to total reconquest of the Sudan. His famous defeat of the Mahdists at Omdurman in September made the retaking of Khartoum a few days later easy; from there the triumphant army – Winston Churchill, who took part in the campaign, has described it in *The River War* – went on to face Marchand and his handful of men at Fashoda.

For both France and England the reaction to the meeting was spontaneously hysterical and aggressive. The English public was virtually unanimous in calling on the government to hold firm. In France opinion was more divided, though the war cries were strident enough. Salisbury told the French to withdraw Marchand or England would declare war: the French refused and began mobilizing. They soon realized, however, that it was an inopportune moment, their nerve cracked and they gave in.

On 21 March 1899 an Anglo-French agreement was signed delimiting British and French spheres in the Sudan. The French were excluded from the Nile valley. Britain then went on to make another agreement with Egypt according to which the two countries undertook to rule the Sudan together.

After the dénouement of Fashoda British supremacy on the Nile was acknowledged by all the Powers. The British government was, therefore, extremely irritated when Leopold II began pressing his claims. The British minister to Belgium, Sir Francis Plunkett, warned the Foreign Office that trouble was in store. 'We are fighting on the Upper Nile a first-class intellect which, in addition to the advantages arising from the sanctity of a king, has the further enormous advantage of thoroughly knowing its own mind and has neither Parliament nor Conseil to hamper it.'[13]

Although the Anglo-French agreement appeared to have put an end to Leopold's ambitions on the Upper Nile, the king saw things differently. Delcassé was amazed when a Belgian diplomat approached him with a view to annulling the Franco-Congolese convention of August 1894 which restricted Leopold to the Lado Enclave: in Belgium articles began to appear in *Le Mouvement Géographique* and *La Belgique Coloniale* arguing that the Anglo-French agreement had given full force to the Anglo-Congolese agreement of May 1894.[14] Plunkett immediately informed Adolphe de Cuvelier, who was nominally in charge of the Free State's foreign affairs, that the British government not only rejected the EIC claim, but added that serious consequences would follow if Leopold tried to advance beyond the Lado Enclave. If 'His Majesty was seeking to steal a march on us, and bring us up short by some secret *fait accompli*, he should think of Fashoda, and see how little that had profited the French'.[15]

This did not intimidate Leopold II. The *Société Générale Africaine* announced preparations for a commercial expedition to the Bahr-el-Ghazal to look into trading possibilities. A second expedition led by Chatlin was to march, as he had done in 1897, to Rejaf and from there to descend the Nile towards Fashoda, occupying as much as possible of the Bahr-el-Ghazal. Strangely enough a third expedition, and the only one to have a favourable outcome, was completely unauthorized. A Belgian, Commandant Henry, and a handful of EIC officers based on Kiro in the Lado Enclave, fed up with the equatorial climate and distinctly bored, decided to reconnoitre the Nile swamps. En route they joined up with some similarly inclined British officers based in Uganda and at Shambe a French officer and some Senegalese joined the group. The going became increasingly difficult. After four months of struggling through the vast Nile swamps, despairing of ever getting out alive, they came upon an official British sudd-cutting party on 19 January 1900. The officer in charge, Major Peake, informed Cromer and Kitchener, his superiors in Egypt, who interpreted the news as an EIC incursion into the Bahr-el-Ghazal; Salisbury even contemplated sending an expedition from Uganda into the area but Kitchener dismissed the idea on the grounds that an expedition 'merely to report on what is going on in . . . the province would not repay the outlay'.[16]

Under orders from Cairo, Peake informed Henry that Britain 'did not recognize that the King of the Belgians had any right of permanent possession to any part of the Nile valley'.[17] Henry's amazement at such language forced Peake to realize that the expedition was not the vanguard of a new Leopoldian move into the Nile valley and he entertained the Belgian and his men in the British camp. When Leopold came to hear of the incident, he was not amused. By leaving the Lado Enclave without orders Henry had aroused British suspicions at precisely the time when the king was trying to assuage them.

In fact Anglo-Congolese relations improved after the fiasco of the Henry expedition which had acted as something of a warning to the British not to read too much into every movement in the Nile valley. When Leopold asked to be able to use the Nile for transporting goods to Lado his request was granted, and without any reciprocal concession. The British were more concerned with mopping-up what remained of Mahdist armies and consolidating their hold in the northern Sudan. Occupation of the southern part of the country could, in any case, only be contemplated when the river and its tributaries had been cleared of the sudd and that would take some time. Furthermore, events at the other end of the continent, namely the Boer War, preoccupied the British government in 1899 and it relaxed its diplomatic surveillance of the southern Sudan.

The Boer War, and the unpopularity that it brought the British government on the Continent, was too great an opportunity for Leopold II to forgo. He therefore chose the moment to assert the validity of a commercial concession granted him in the 1894 Anglo-Congolese agreement. This concession applied to all the leased territories and had been granted to the *Société Générale Africaine*, which in turn had sublet its rights to two British-run firms, the British Tropical Africa Company and the Anglo-Belgian-Africa Company.

A little later Leopold came out with a project for a Congo-Nile railway, from Stanleyville to Rejaf, which would open up the Congo to more markets and at the same time provide a strategic link between the Congo and its Nilotic possessions. A representative of the Anglo-Belgian-Africa Company, P.G. Boyle, was at that time on a mission to the Bahr-el-Ghazal to report upon the commercial opportunities of the region. The king privately asked him to collect information relevant to the railway project. The British reaction when they came to hear of Boyle's activities was predictably wrath at yet another example of Leopoldian deviousness.

Lord Salisbury had had by now a surfeit of wrangling with Leopold II over the Bahr-el-Ghazal. He was by 1900 a tired old man – though Leopold, only five years younger, maintained his full vigour. All he could cope with was the South African war; as regards the southern Sudan, he did not want to become involved in negotiations. His only positive action was to request the establishment of a British post on the north side of the Lado Enclave to keep Leopold within bounds. Work began immediately some four miles north of the EIC post of Kiro. The EIC force watched with amusement. Once the post was finished they pointed out to the British officer in charge that it was south of 5° 30' and hence four miles inside Lado instead of outside. Naturally, the post had to be handed over to the EIC and another built further north. However, because of swampy conditions, no suitable place could be found and the British had to move to the east bank of the river and nine miles north of Lado.

Such farce, the stream of suspicious travellers from the Congo who kept turning up and the barrage of claims from Brussels, irritated Foreign Office officials. They pressed hard for effective British occupation of the Bahr-el-Ghazal and this was begun at the end of 1900. However, it was a vast area and the natives were hostile. They could not make rapid progress so that there was no *de facto* British presence that could be used against Leopold. He, of course, appreciated this and, in no way put off by British military operations, encouraged the Anglo-Belgian commercial companies to go ahead with their plans for the exploitation of the region.

Not only could the British not occupy the Bahr-el-Ghazal, they were forced to recognize that the king had a good legal case. Leopold himself was aware of this as he had called upon a number of leading international lawyers to give their opinions as to the validity of his claims in the Bahr-el-Ghazal. They all agreed that not only were Leopold's political rights legally unassailable, but that the commercial concessions were similarly valid. The Foreign Office made show of dismissing these legal opinions but there is no doubt, and it is crucial to their policy during the next few years, that the British feared that a court of arbitration would decide in favour of Leopold.

The king had formally submitted his demands in November 1900, their main point being that Britain had never repudiated the Anglo-Congolese agreement of May 1894. The Franco-Congolese agreement of August 1894, to which the British government had expressly declined to be a party, could not, *inter alios acta*, affect the reciprocal rights and duties assumed by Britain and the Congo Free State in their earlier agreement. The British were determined first and foremost to prevent the EIC from becoming a permanent riparian power. They were however prepared to allow Leopold to keep the Lado Enclave for his lifetime and would give him extensive permanent possessions inland.

Negotiations continued throughout the winter of 1901 and the British made a considerably more generous territorial offer early in 1902. But Leopold would not be tempted by large tracts of hinterland to keep him off the Nile. He was obsessed by the river. 'It is', he told van Eetvelde, 'my glory: its occupation has been my objective for years: I have dedicated my energies to it; rather than renounce I will resort to violence.'[18] Strong words, but clearly putting over the intensity of the king's feelings. He wanted possessions on the Congo *and* the Nile; he, Leopold, was to be the man to join up the two great waterways of Africa. It was not even pure power he was after, it was a vision. Certainly, his goal was not money, for if he had been concerned with the latter he would have accepted the British offer of 1901 with its trading opportunities. It was not a question of economic imperialism, though the issues quite often involve commercial concessions, but of an old man whose passion for colonies had turned in old age into fanaticism; even megalomania.

If Leopold's judgement was impaired, his physical energy certainly was not. At the beginning of 1902, under his impulse, a railway company was set up, the *Compagnie des Chemins de Fer du Congo Supérieur aux Grands Lacs Africains* with a capital of 25,000,000 francs, raised mainly from French sources. Two railway lines were to be built, one from Stanley Falls to Lake Tanganyika, the other to Mahagi on Lake Albert, that is, to the Nile. Twenty-five million francs was far from enough for the project but Baron Empain, leader of the group of financiers who under-wrote the issues, was confident that the stock issue would be subscribed.

At the same time the king was planning yet another expedition into the Bahr-el-Ghazal from Lado. In the latter months of 1901 three large consignments of munitions, guns and equipment were sent to Lado and British intelligence reported that the Congolese were constructing per-manent brick buildings with well-laid-out gardens, making entrench-ments and positioning field guns to command the river. By 1902 there were nearly 2,400 native troops there, and 60 European officers. Except for South Africa, it was the largest concentration of troops any-where in Africa.

Such were the back-up activities. In February 1903 the first of several 'scientific' missions arrived at Tambura with the intention of penetrating deep into the Bahr-el-Ghazal. It was led by Captain Royaux, the destina-tion being the copper mines at Hofrat-en-Nahas which Leopold not only claimed under the 1894 agreement but by a treaty made with a local ruler in the same year by Nilis. An advance guard reached Deim Zubeir but there they were confronted by British officials who were not con-vinced that such a well-armed expedition could be purely scientific and firmly told Royaux to withdraw. The British were wary of the EIC force as they feared it might try to provoke an incident to force the British into arbitration.

There had been some respite for the British government in its intermin-able dealings with Leopold in the second half of 1902, as the death of Marie-Henriette in July diverted the king's attention to family squabbles. This lull proved to be highly detrimental to Leopold, for by the beginning of 1903 the Foreign Office had come to be convinced of the case against the king's administration in the Congo and were thus less sympathetic to his aims at aggrandizement in the Nile. In addition, Lord Lansdowne, the Foreign Secretary, had come to see the Bahr-el-Ghazal less as the 'wretched stuff' Salisbury had considered it. Information describing the resources of the region – iron, ostrich feathers, ebony, timber, gum, wax and rubber, and the potential trade in them – caused Lansdowne to wonder whether it really was a good idea to hand it over to Leopold. They were, furthermore, determined to put an end to the railway project Leopold had been pursuing. By planning to construct a railway to Lado the king was presuming that he would hold on to the enclave, exactly what the British intended he should not do. And even if he gave up the enclave, a railway company with a terminus there would need to maintain a concession. It did not take much imagination to see that Leopold would try to control, directly or indirectly, the concessionaire.

In the light of the cooler views about the king, the failure of the Royaux mission and the supposed economic potential of the Bahr-el-Ghazal, Cromer's view prevailed with Lansdowne. That is, a deadline ought to be set for negotiations and, if a settlement was not reached, then they would simply have to wait until Leopold died. In line with this new policy, Lansdowne informed the British minister in Brussels, now Sir Constantine Phipps, that if the British proposals were not accepted by 1 November 1903, then the British government would withdraw its offer.[19]

Leopold was furious at the ultimatum and what he described as the 'offensive and humiliating' terms being offered him.[20] But worse was to come, for in May 1903 a debate on the Congo took place in the House of Commons. A motion was passed unanimously condemning the maladministration of the Congo. Then, in the following August, when the Foreign Office appropriations came before parliament, the reformers spotted the opportunity to object to any concessions in the Upper Nile by voting against the government. 'Every speaker agreed', wrote Sir Charles Dilke, 'that we could not hand over the Sudanese natives to the tender mercies of Leopold II'.[21]

By now Lansdowne's chief fear was that Leopold might suddenly accept the British offer of 1901 which would bring the wrath of the reformers on to his government – the Conservative majority being slight at this time. To keep on the right side of the angels they therefore sent off a note to the signatories of the Berlin Act accusing the EIC of violating the act and calling for a conference on the subject. The tactic worked as planned. The reformers gave Lansdowne a breathing space and Leopold went into a huff, swearing that he would not accept the unsatisfactory British offer of 1901. If the king had still been the diplomat he was in previous years, he would have seized the British offer in 1903 before the current in England and Belgium ran too strongly against him. But now isolated – for van Eetvelde who had from the outset advocated a settlement with England was no longer in his confidence – and in an even more truculent mood, he resorted once more to action. Additional large quantities of arms and ammunition were poured into Lado and a contingent of native Congolese troops under Italian officers arrived there from the Congo.

Seeing the deterioration in his relations with England, Leopold looked to France, as he had done so many times in the past, for support against England. In September 1903 he visited Paris where he talked to the president, Emile Loubet, and minister of foreign affairs, Théophile Delcassé. Times had changed though, and the two colonial rivals were feeling their way towards the *Entente Cordiale*. Leopold returned empty-handed to Brussels.

Beernaert, Baron Smet de Naeyer, the prime minister, and practically every man of standing in the Belgian government, witnessing the king's position crumbling fast, advised him to take up the British offer before it was too late. Leopold instead submitted yet another set of proposals to the British government; they were of course unacceptable and with due public indignation and private relief, Lansdowne terminated the negotiations.

The collapse of the Anglo–Congolese talks led both Leopold and the British government to yet further attempts to gain by actual occupation what they had failed to secure by diplomacy in Europe. The Free State was the first to be active in the Bahr-el-Ghazal, simply because a mission sent out in 1902 arrived there on 27 November 1903, just after the breakdown in negotiations, and thus at a time when the British were extremely sensitive. The leader of the expedition, Captain Charles Lemaire, had a considerable reputation as a scientific explorer (which was why Leopold had chosen him) but, on confronting him in the Bahr-el-Ghazal, the British refused to believe that he was not leading a political expedition and interpreted his mission as a Leopoldian means of forcing England to reopen negotiations, or of accepting arbitration as a result of an unpleasant collision.

Without mincing their words, the British government demanded that Lemaire should withdraw. The EIC authorities in Brussels refused, saying that if they concurred, this would be tacit admission that the EIC had no right to occupy the territory involved in the 1894 agreement. At the same time reports reached Europe that the Lemaire expedition had been reinforced and that it was erecting permanent buildings. In Europe, on the other hand, it was repeated many times that Lemaire would be retiring when his scientific work was completed. Leopold was not afraid of a collision and Cromer was all for military action to evict Lemaire. Lansdowne, on the other hand, was well aware that a military campaign to drive Leopold from the enclave would be exceedingly expensive and would, more importantly, be unfavourably viewed in Europe.

So to prevent any further EIC expeditions moving into the Bahr-el-Ghazal, effective British occupation of the southern Sudan was begun towards the end of 1904. About 1,000 men, divided into two columns, under Colonel 'Bully' Boulnois, marched into the southern part of the region to confront the Azande ruler, Yambio. Unbeknown to Boulnois, an EIC force was heading up from the south with the same intention. It inflicted heavy losses on the Azande but two months later one of the British columns killed Yambio and established control without a pitched battle.

The second column had, meanwhile, discovered two EIC posts deep in the Bahr-el-Ghazal and had also tracked down the elusive Lemaire. When Boulnois and Lemaire finally met, the latter held that he was merely

acting in accordance with the 1894 Anglo-Congolese agreement and that
any alteration in this position would have to be settled by the respective
governments. Boulnois, who was under orders to avoid any clashes with
the EIC forces, was impotent. Although Leopold had not told Lemaire
to create the incident the presence of the well-armed troops provided him
with a powerful diplomatic and military tool.

What followed in Europe was the oft-repeated saga of British protest
and the EIC's demand for arbitration. Little had changed since 1901 and
there did not seem to be any obvious way out of the impasse. 'There
is no concealing the fact', even Cromer admitted, 'that the Belgians have
a strong case.'[22] There was only one way of dealing with the situation,
and a far from satisfactory one at that, namely to stall by reopening
negotiations.

But Leopold, even in his declining years, was not so easily fobbed off
and in May 1905 he issued a decree from Ems, where he was taking the
waters, a unilateral declaration according to which the disputed territory
was incorporated into the EIC. This was done to strengthen the EIC position in arbitration and in the hope that France would come to the king's
help in view of the pre-emption right. The British government was
stunned. The decree was so impertinent and provocative that at first they
did not believe it. After digesting it, however, they sent a thinly-veiled
threatening reply warning the king that if these posts 'are not withdrawn
and if the terms of the recent decree are not so altered as to exclude them
from Congolese territory, His Majesty's Government will be compelled
to hold the Government of the Congo State responsible for any consequences which may result from such an infringement of the rights of
Egypt which were expressly reserved at the time of the signature of the
Agreement'.[23] In Egypt the opinion was that 'the King must be made to
feel the prick of the bayonet or he won't budge – it is all a game of bluff',[24]
and one suggestion was to withdraw the commitment to Belgian neutrality.

Opinion throughout Britain was by now so hostile to Leopold II that
it was politically unthinkable to hand over any territory in Africa to him:
the Cabinet was prepared to resist by force any further EIC advance in
the Sudan. Unfortunately from the British point of view their position
in the southern Sudan was still weak. The Congo Free State had 500 men
in five posts scattered throughout the disputed territory and 2,500 more
men at Lado, not to mention the considerably larger forces which were
garrisoned in the Uele and Bomu valleys to the south and west. The British
had one Sudanese battalion distributed over the whole province. Lansdowne tried to reassure himself: 'We are not losing anything by the presence of this small Belgian post [Lado] within our limits. The country
is of no value and if we are to judge from a recent telegram (which I

quote from memory) the invading force is dwindling owing to disease and desertion. We can afford a waiting game.'[25]

Leopold could not. There was no assured succession to the Sovereign of the Congo Free State and the pressure for annexation of his colony by Belgium was mounting. He wanted to hand over the Congo on his own terms and his position would be weakened if the colony were saddled with a dispute with England. The king had to resolve the issue, and quickly. Fortunately van Eetvelde was once more in charge of EIC affairs and he argued strongly for a settlement with England. He was successful and the king agreed to reopen negotiations. Van Eetvelde saw the British minister to Belgium in February 1906 and told him of the king's desire to reach agreement. He intimated that any proposal of the Congo government would recognize that the primary objective of the British government 'was to secure that the entire course of the Nile should be under Anglo-Egyptian control and free from the jurisdiction of any Foreign State'.[26]

Foreign Office officials, by now old hands at dealing with Leopold II, took the new overtures with a pinch of salt. What was the king doing in the Sudan they wondered, knowing that so often in the past his European diplomacy could be quite different from his actions in Africa. This time though, intelligence reports showed that the EIC forces were being told to co-operate with the British and were no longer indulging in what had almost become the sport of erecting boundary pillars (promptly pulled up by the Anglo–Sudanese) along what they considered to be their frontiers. Moreover it later transpired that what had been thought to be boundary pillars were in fact geodetic points, no more.

After so many years of diplomatic chess of a higher order – though Cromer considered it more like poker – Leopold, for no obvious reason, crumbled in the early months of 1906. Suddenly he drew back from sparring with the British. Was it because he realized that in a showdown he would be no match for the forces of the British empire? Maybe it was because he came to terms with being an old man and that prolonging the dispute could only work against his interests.

For whatever reasons, and a combination is most probable, van Eetvelde found himself freed from royal shackles and able to begin genuine negotiations with the British government. Even so, he went to London to conduct them to avoid any possible interference by the king. The British also wanted a quick settlement so as to prevent the Congo reformers stepping in and causing a rumpus about even dealing with the King of the Belgians. It would have been only too easy to have found reasons for disagreement but both sides were eager for a solution and van Eetvelde telegraphed to Brussels only a general outline of the agreement reached on 9 May 1906.

The agreement annulled the Anglo-Congolese agreement of 1894 and both parties agreed not to put forward any claims in the future arising out of leases granted under that treaty. The king was given the right to occupy the Lado Enclave for the duration of his reign, after which it was to be handed over to the Sudanese government. The Congo–Nile watershed was to form the frontier between the Sudan and the EIC. Leopold received a concession to build a railway from the Congo frontier to the navigable Nile. Furthermore, the Sudanese government was to open a port on the Nile at the terminus of the railway and acceded to van Eetvelde's demand that all goods and persons passing to and from the Congo Free State would receive equal treatment with Egyptian or British individuals and merchandise. Finally, it was agreed to refer all boundary disputes between the two contracting parties to The Hague Tribunal.[27]

The agreement was a definite diplomatic triumph for England, since Leopold had renounced all his territorial claims in return for a railway concession subject to Sudanese regulations. He received much less than Lansdowne was prepared to give in 1902; his only further gain was the long sought-after provision to submit boundary disputes to arbitration.

Of course Leopold himself had not been present at the talks and when he saw the text of the agreement he was furious, 'a simple act of spleen' was how the British minister described it.[28] He vented his feelings on van Eetvelde, a man who had served him loyally and ably for twenty-five years, demoted him and treated him to public vilification. The king's behaviour was that of a man on the run. He identified withdrawal from the Bahr-el-Ghazal as part of the campaign to take over the Congo and, despite strong language from the British government, flatly refused to carry out the provisions of the 1906 agreement.[29] Leopold was still hanging on at the end of the year and the Belgian minister of foreign affairs felt compelled to remind him of his obligation to quit.[30]

As regards the railway clauses on the other hand, Leopold was prepared to act in accordance with the new agreement and a survey party was sent out. Winston Churchill, who travelled extensively in Uganda and the Sudan in 1907, considered the project a 'perverted development of Central African railways'. If such a scheme went through it would be a 'shocking waste of money and a fantastic and even vicious result'.[31] The Nile route was too long and could not compete with a line to Mombasa. The Uganda railway, properly extended to Lake Albert, could receive, Churchill thought, Congo traffic which would in that way reach the sea more quickly and more cheaply. In Belgium the Nile railway project was dismissed as unfeasible. The opposition to it was not, however, too vociferous, since there was general agreement with the view expressed by the British minister that when the Belgian government took

over the Congo – for annexation was imminent by then – the Congo–
Nile railway scheme would be dropped.[32] 'Astute as he is,' wrote the
minister, 'we have sold him an unsound horse; but he and Belgium are
bound to discover the truth sooner or later, and meanwhile we can, I
think, afford to humour him with the details of a scheme which will probably be found to be impracticable.'[33] But Leopold had not been taken
in; his advocacy of the railway project in 1907 was no more than a desperate gesture of defiance. He knew that the end of his Nilotic dreams had
come in May 1906. When news of the Anglo-Congolese agreement
reached him his secretary heard the king say to himself, 'this is our
Fashoda.'[34]

21 Morocco and other Enterprises

*'There are no such things as small states;
there are only small minds.'*[1] Leopold II.

Less than a month after the Conference of Berlin, Leopold was looking
at another part of Africa – Morocco. He called in Baron Whetnall, the
newly-appointed Belgian minister to the Cherifian court, and informed
him that he was looking for a small port on the west coast of Africa which
would provide, in the first instance, bunkering facilities for ships en route
from Antwerp to the Congo.[2] Once in Morocco, Whetnall set about making enquiries and was encouraged when he learnt that the King of Spain
had recently acquired 300 miles of coast in the south of the country, the
territory having been bought on his behalf by a private company – the
formula Leopold had so often advocated. When Whetnall proposed that
a Belgian company should similarly buy territory in Morocco which it
would later sell to the EIC, it naturally found favour in Brussels. Under
the guise of seeking new outlets for Belgian trade, the minister therefore
set out from Tangier on a tour of the Atlantic coastline.

A standard means of European penetration overseas in these years was,
of course, railway building. Morocco was in 1885 virgin territory in this
respect and to try and persuade the sultan of the advantages of modern
transport, Whetnall came up with the crude idea – which Leopold
approved – of giving the sultan a small-gauge train and rolling stock.
It was duly installed in the park at Meknès and was followed up by a
request to construct a line from Tangier to Fez. The sultan replied, as
he had done before, for Belgium was not the first to propose building
railways, that Morocco was not at a stage of development that called
for such modern means of transport.

As the direct approach had failed, in 1887 Whetnall, again with the
king's backing, turned to more subtle methods of penetration. A Jewish
trader, Levi Cohen, with good contacts in Morocco, was employed to
seek out locations which were for sale and where Belgian factories could

be built.[3] Leopold followed with great interest what he called 'the Cohen affair' and paid out considerable expenses to the businessman. After a few months without anything substantial emerging, the king became impatient with Cohen and suggested to Whetnall that they should deal directly with one Donald Mackenzie, with whom Cohen had been negotiating for the sale of land at Cap Juby at the extreme south of the Moroccan Atlantic coastline.

Mackenzie was the founder of the North-West Africa Company and had bought large tracts of land at Cap Juby from a local potentate – territory nominally under the sultan but in reality outside his effective control. After a visit to England in 1888 – the company was not doing well – Mackenzie was joined at Gibraltar by two Belgians, Major Auguste Lahure, a young diplomat in the confidence of Leopold II, and Lieutenant Adolphe Fourcault, a naval officer. They told Mackenzie that they had been sent to see whether it would be possible to buy land so that the Belgian Red Cross could build a sanatorium.[4] In his report, however, Lahure adds other aims. 'To get to know the interior of the country, its resources, which are the fertile parts where emigrants could found settlements, and to make contact with the local ruler.'[5] Mackenzie approved of the Belgians' ostensible intentions and took them on a tour of the Cap Juby region. He does not seem to have suspected any ulterior colonial motives, although when Lahure suggested buying land for the sanatorium, he refused: he would offer a lease, no more. However, any further progress depended on 'the philanthropic body' or Red Cross in Belgium building the sanatorium. As neither existed, Leopold set to creating (by royal decree) an African branch of the Red Cross. At the inaugural ceremony he made an appropriate speech:

> The great cause of African emancipation has, as you know, already claimed its martyrs ... It is time to think of those wounded in the course of the civilizing work and to extend the benefits of the Red Cross to those to whose devotion we owe so much ... It is up to us to provide them with the facilities for recovering their health.[6]

Beernaert, who was present at the ceremony, was alarmed that the king was taking on too much, as it was the height of his Congolese financial difficulties. Leopold tried to soothe him. 'The estimate for building a sanatorium is about 90,000 francs ... So as not to increase my expenses, I have just cancelled my subscription to the International African Association.'[7] (It was still officially in existence.) On the other hand, in the same letter Leopold spoke of a Red Cross establishment – somewhat vaguer than a sanatorium – and added 'perhaps a centre for Belgian emigration'.[8]

The project developed in a strikingly Leopoldian manner. Mackenzie was told that the African branch of the Red Cross did not feel able to undertake the financing of the sanatorium; a new company would be set up to deal with this side of the project. Furthermore, it was necessary, so as not to frighten the English shareholders in the North-West Africa Company and to increase the possible sources of finance, for the new company to be Anglo-Belgian. All was in vain. The money could not be raised and such was the penury of Leopold II in 1889 that he could not find it himself.

The North-West Africa Company also faced difficulties. The local population was hostile to their installations and the company was not doing well financially. Mackenzie again made contact with the Belgians. By then though the position had been reversed and Leopold had the upper hand. He told Lahure to tell Mackenzie: 'that if he really wants to come to an arrangement with the Red Cross, he will have to come to Brussels. It is a propitious moment, but it will not last long.' Anticipating things rather, the king went on, 'Belgium is going to take over the Congo and has voted £1,000,000 on account.'⁹

Mackenzie did not hurry to Belgium, much to Leopold's annoyance, but went instead to London. Lahure was sent to meet him there. Nevertheless, the money Leopold had to offer was not enough to tempt the English to sell. There was, however, a reason behind the hardening of the British position in 1890. The Foreign Office had come to hear of the negotiations with the Belgians and had told the North-West Africa Company not to cede anything. Salisbury ordered that 'some means should be devised for preventing Belgium getting this [territory]'.¹⁰ When Leopold learnt of the British government's opposition he decided to forgo the project.

Seven years elapsed before Leopold II was again active in Moroccan affairs and this time it was in person. In September 1897 he left Antwerp on board a rented yacht, flying the ensign of the British Royal Yacht Squadron and manned by a British crew. It was not in itself unusual for a man of sixty-two to go on an autumn cruise in a warm climate, and the yacht (temporarily renamed the *Clementine*) headed for Madeira and then the Canaries. Leopold was travelling under the name the Count de Ravenstein, one of his favourite 'incognitos' that deceived no-one but seemed to give him pleasure, and the Belgian press announced his arrival in Mogador on 23 September. On stepping ashore the king announced that Mogador reminded him of Ostend and observed that it was an ideal site for a large hotel, or maybe even a winter residence for himself. The less touristic ports of Mazagan and Larache were next on the king's itinerary. Here he took great interest in the port installations. He also visited the interior of the country, mounted on horseback with a caravan of mules carrying the tents and equipment. His remark that the country would benefit from railways is in the circumstances understandable.¹¹

The press, who suspected ulterior motives for the king's visit, were assured that, 'He has come to Morocco for the same reason as he recently visited Tunisia, namely to relax and enjoy himself.'[12] However, a few days later Leopold announced that he was looking for a suitable site for a colonial villa where Europeans returning in ill health from the Congo could recuperate. This sparked off a debate in the press on the subject and good reasons were advanced against the plan on the grounds that sick men should either be treated closer to the Congo or in the modern facilities of northern Europe. These arguments, of course, had no effect on Leopold.

More ambitious aims than merely founding a convalescent home were attributed to the king by some of the French newspapers, which also pointed out that Leopold had not feared falling foul of France and England in the Upper Nile and that it was not impossible that he had broad colonial aims in Morocco.[13] Through its own services as well as by newspaper articles, the Quai d'Orsay was alerted to Leopold's activities and Hanotaux took note. The king was careful not to give Hanotaux cause for complaint during his visit to Morocco, although the press claimed that he had bought land close to Cap Spartel near Tangier.[14] Even if it were true, Leopold could do nothing to activate his colonial villa project because of French surveillance. The king was accused by some French newspapers of being the front for British designs on Morocco. But whether it was he himself or others who wished to gain a foothold in Morocco, the French would not permit it and because of the delicate state of his relations with France in the Nile and China, Leopold did not dare to act in a provocative way. Whether Leopold formally abandoned the sanatorium and colonial villa project is not known.

From 1898 onwards Leopold was looking to south Morocco for a territorial concession. The Rio de Oro region was being explored by Martin-Joseph de Kinet, a Belgian, on behalf of the *Société d'Etudes Hispano-Belge* in 1899. De Kinet reported that the area did not lend itself to potential colonial enterprises because of the infertile soil and the paucity of population. On the other hand, he considered that profitable fisheries could be set up along the coast.[15] As a follow-up, Doctor Arthur Tacquin, an oceanographer and marine biologist, was sent on holiday on horseback from Tangier to the mouth of the Dra. He reported back that there were ideal fish-breeding grounds off Agadir.

At this stage Leopold decided that he would need help to develop the project further and he called in Empain, who had already been active in furthering the fishing industry on the Belgian coast. Empain was interested in the Moroccan idea but said that he thought it would be 'indispensable to obtain from the Sultan of Morocco a territorial concession ... so as to set up in Agadir establishments to treat the fish and provide houses and allied services for the personnel'.[16] To see if this was possible, Empain decided to go to Morocco himself.[17]

Leopold was trying to keep things as quiet as possible but as soon as the well-known financier and his lawyer, Georges Grimard, arrived in Morocco, rumours began to circulate. Grimard was trying to raise 50,000,000 francs to finance the enterprise when the French came to hear of it. The year was 1904: the Anglo-French *entente* had just been signed. The British had agreed that Morocco was a French sphere and Delcassé was none too pleased to hear reports about Belgian activity there. The Belgian government insisted that all they were seeking was a small fishing concession. But even that, assuming it to be all, was too much for Delcassé.

For a while all seemed lost. Then at the end of March 1905, the kaiser made his notorious visit to Tangier when he declared that Morocco ought to be open to all nations on an equal footing. Belgium hoped to latch on to the German bandwagon and friendly gestures were made towards Spain, whose influence in Morocco had been usurped by the French. All hope for Belgian interests was, however, lost when the Conference of Algeciras, convened in 1906, demonstrated the solidarity of the Anglo-French *entente*. In the face of British support for French control in Morocco, Leopold was forced to withdraw from the field.

Thirty years had passed since Leopold II attempted to buy the Philippines from Spain. But if Spain had been in a weak position in 1868, her military defeat by the United States in 1898 emasculated her power further and Leopold put forward the idea of a private, neutral (Congolese-registered) company to lease some of Spain's overseas possessions.[18] The Spanish government was, according to the Belgian minister, Léon Verhaeghe de Naeyer, favourably disposed and discussions were begun, which after a while came to focus on the Caroline and Canary Islands.[19] On 12 December 1898 Lambermont was greatly surprised by a visit from an extremely angry German minister to Belgium: the German government had themselves been negotiating with the Spanish government for several months with a view to acquiring the Carolines, a scheme very dear to the kaiser himself, and they considered it a distinctly unfriendly action on the part of the Belgians to step in subsequently and jeopardize their bargaining position. The complaint was repeated to the minister of foreign affairs, Baron de Favereau, who, like Lambermont, was totally unaware of any Belgian interest in the Carolines. De Favereau was furious at what was obviously a private scheme of the king's. He asked for an audience and pointed out to his sovereign that such personal action made the maintenance of amicable relations with the Great Powers extremely difficult.[20] The vehement German protest put an end to

Leopold's idea of leasing the Carolines and they were eventually acquired by the kaiser.

Not all Leopold II's expansionary ideas involved territorial concessions. The acquisition of purely commercial and industrial privileges was in some cases, Leopold himself recognized, all that could be hoped for. Russia was a case in point.

In 1859 his attention had been attracted to the possibilities of the Russian market and he had written to the Belgian minister in St Petersburg urging him to do all that he could to encourage the Russians to trade with Belgium.[21] Cockerills had already entered the field and had been selling arms – which the Russians had used against the French and British in the Crimean War. Ten years later Cockerills built a small shipyard near St Petersburg to assemble small cannon boats for the Russian navy from material produced in Belgium. However, the market was destroyed by the protectionist policy adopted by Russia after 1877 and the Belgians turned to direct investment. Iron-ore mining concessions were obtained without too much difficulty and Cockerills decided to construct large steel mills. A Russian subsidiary was set up, the South Russian Dnieper Metallurgical Company, to implement the concessions, and a few years later they moved into coal-mining. The South Dnieper was paying 10% on its capital in 1891 and 40% in 1895. A spate of other Belgian investment followed, including Empain's tram company. By 1900, Belgian capital investment in Russia was greater than that of any other foreign country, 220,000,000 roubles, compared with France's 210,000,000, Germany's 197,000,000 and Britain's 103,000,000.[22]

An attempt was made to break into the neighbouring Persian market and a *Société Anonyme des Chemins de Fer et Tramways en Perse* was created in 1886. Some Belgian businessmen tried to establish commercial relations but complained of their difficulty in making suitable contacts. The English and Russians were dominant in Persia and they did not take kindly to the entry of a competitor but, undiscouraged by Anglo-Russian hostility, a Belgian consul in Teheran was appointed. The king took a personal interest in the appointment but within a couple of years, mainly because of his strained relations with the businessmen of the rue de Bréderode, his interest in Persia, which had never been more than a fringe involvement, ceased.[23] The ancient Iranian civilization never fired Leopold's imagination like those of the Nile and China.

22 The Celestial Empire

'It is in the national interest that Belgians
should take full advantage of the business
opportunities available in China and it is my
job to further the national interest.'[1]

Leopold II.

Leopold II's obsession with China, like that with Egypt, originated when
he was a young man. The Chinese empire, with a population of
400,000,000, had been decaying throughout the nineteenth century, and
the Manchu dynasty which had been ruling the country for three centuries
had lost control of much of the country, despite its enormous bureau-
cracy. It tried hard to centralize power but the provincial viceroys and
governors did virtually as they liked.

To maintain their hold over the population the mandarins tried to
exclude all foreign influence, fearing that it would weaken their own position. However, the Chinese market was too tempting for the Great
Powers and the Chinese had been forced, in the Anglo-French operation
of 1860, in which both Leopold I and his son had tried to participate,
to open about twenty ports to European ships. The Western Powers had
also tried to impose railways on the Chinese but the mandarins energetic-
ally repulsed an innovation that would open up the hinterland. It was
not until 1895 that a combination of events provided Leopold with the
opportunity for which he had been waiting. In the war which broke out
between China and Japan over Korea, China was overwhelmingly
defeated and forced to accept peace on terms dictated by the Japanese.
Apart from territorial losses, the Treaty of Shimonoseki imposed extremely onerous reparations, and as the Chinese could not raise the
money themselves, they were reluctantly obliged to look to Europe for
financial assistance. It was a propitious moment for Leopold, as in 1895
the Congo became profitable and, moreover, the Belgian economy had
recovered from the depression; production had increased and it was seeking new markets for its products and surplus capital.

As he was considered to have been to a large extent responsible for
the defeat at the hands of the Japanese, the mandarin Li-Hung-Chang

was sent on a punitive voyage to Europe with orders to cultivate good relations with the occidental Powers. The Chinese were only too well aware that these countries were poised ready to dismember the Celestial Empire.

Belgium was not on Li-Hung-Chang's itinerary but Leopold II was determined to make contact with the mandarin who, in spite of his disgrace, was recognized as a key figure in China. For reasons which remain obscure an aide-de-camp of Prince Albert, Leopold's nephew, was charged with the invitation. He met Li at a ball in Moscow and successfully persuaded him to visit Belgium. Leopold was extremely anxious to demonstrate the advanced level of industrial development in Belgium and at the same time to emphasize the country's neutrality. No expense was spared in entertaining the mandarin in Brussels, though Li kept his own staff with him and, for example, after an enormous European meal, sharks' fins, swallows' nests and other Chinese delicacies were placed before him.[2] After two days of exhausting social life, the aged Li was taken to Seraing where the managing director of Cockerills showed him the steel works. It was all very impressive. Nevertheless, Li successfully extricated himself from watching military manœuvres at Brasschaat. 'Why is it,' he asked a Belgian diplomat with studied innocence, 'that Europeans, when they invite foreigners to come and talk of peace and friendly relations, find it necessary to display so many soldiers and guns?'[3] He sent his son to Brasschaat and went himself to Antwerp zoo instead.

It is extremely doubtful whether the various demonstrations had any influence on Li. His private discussions with Leopold II were another matter. The king, as usual, demanded to be well briefed. The main subjects he wished to discuss were Chinese diplomatic representation in Brussels; a maritime cargo service between Antwerp and China; the construction of a steel complex in northern China; a concession to build part of the proposed Peking–Canton railway line; and the award of the Tientsin–Chinkiang railway concession to Cockerills. Li showed little interest in the first three. However, the suggestion of Belgian participation in the construction of a railway from Peking to Hankow found favour with him – since by 1896 the Chinese had accepted the inevitability of railways.

An imperial railway company was created in October 1896 and given the Peking–Hankow concession. It was permitted to seek its capital abroad and the director, Sheng Husan-Huai, had by the end of 1896 obtained the promise of a loan from the American China Development Company, the ACDC. Neutral though the United States was considered, the Chinese government advised Sheng that it was preferable to look to the Belgians for finances. A new Belgian minister, Baron de Vinck des Deux Orp, arrived in Peking at this juncture. De Vinck had been briefed as to Leopold's aims in China and once in China he set to making contact with Sheng. The mandarin told him that if the Belgians could raise a loan of £4,000,000 over thirty years, they would receive the order for all the materials and could provide the personnel.[4]

The Belgian minister of foreign affairs was delighted when he received de Vinck's telegram and passed the information to the *Société Générale* and Cockerills. The *Société Générale* was unenthusiastic about the idea, saying that such a project would entail detailed studies before a loan could even be considered. Cockerills replied that they would be willing to furnish the materials but they could not raise the money. The French minister to Peking was aware of the Chinese offer to the Belgians and he informed the Quai d'Orsay, which in turn broached the subject to French financiers and industrialists. The reply was that they were interested in the concession. The French appreciated though that the Chinese were anxious not to have the concession exploited by one of the major European Powers. They would have to hide behind a Belgian front and then, once things were in hand, 'throw away the mask'.[5]

Under pressure from Baron de Favereau, at the Ministry of Foreign Affairs, the *Société Générale* was persuaded to take the projected scheme seriously. If it was clear that the money could not be raised on the Belgian market then it would be necessary to look to France. The governor was dispatched to Paris to consult with the *Banque de Paris et des Pays-Bas*. Both sides agreed that the first thing was to send a mission to China to make a project evaluation.

The following March, 1897, a *Société d'Etudes de Chemins de Fer en Chine* was created and as sufficient capital was not forthcoming, Leopold II contributed 60,000 francs of EIC money. The total capital was 330,000 francs. This money was to be used in the first instance on a technical mission to China.

The Chinese proposed that a loan of 100,000,000 francs should be made in four parts over two years, though the Chinese would provide 50,000,000, guaranteed by the government, at the beginning of the operation. Belgium would provide all the personnel and part of the materials. The reaction in financial circles was cool. They wanted the engineers' report first and they also considered that a Chinese government guarantee was not enough – the loan should be contracted with the government itself.

The Belgian consul in Hankow, Emile Francqui of Katanga fame and a man in the Leopoldian mould, feared that the Chinese would in exasperation turn again to the Americans, and he took it upon himself to sign a preliminary contract, despite the fact that the bankers had not given their consent. Leopold approved of Francqui's action, although it was, to say the least, unorthodox. The bankers were distinctly put out and members of the mission to China told de Vinck that they had made the journey 'not to conclude the affair but to prevent its taking place'.[6] The diplomats tried to persuade the Belgian bankers that the proposed deal was not financially irresponsible and, to placate them further, Sheng was asked if some modifications could be made to the contract. Pressed by de Vinck and Francqui, the engineers gave in and sent a telegram to Brussels: 'Mission to China successfully terminated. Long live the King!'[7]

In all this the French financiers who were to raise most of the money had been overlooked. They demonstrated their pique in August 1897 and refused to raise the money asked for. Leopold on a visit to England turned to his favourite tactic in such circumstances and told Salisbury that, 'the Belgians ask for nothing better than to be associated with British capitalists'.[8] The Quai d'Orsay, well used to such methods, ignored the king's threats, knowing full well that another country would be likely to be much more demanding than France over having a share in providing the material. As France refused to react as hoped, Leopold looked to Germany for the money to save the contract. For much the same reasons as had been advanced by the French, the Germans refused to help.[9]

It was by now the middle of December 1897. In a fortnight the *Société d'Etudes* either had to find £350,000 or the contract would lapse. Leopold was pessimistic and told the Ministry of Foreign Affairs to inform de Vinck that it would not be possible to raise the money by the end of the year. However, he added rather wistfully that it was a pity that the Chinese government was not prepared to accept staggered payments of the loan. Such an arrangement, the king was keen to emphasize, should not be asked for outright but rather Sheng should be persuaded of its necessity *motu proprio*. In the event the Chinese were prepared to go along with this.

Unbeknown to Leopold the French government was telling financiers that it would be a great pity to let the opportunity pass and in January 1898 a group of French banks agreed to raise the money.[10] They submitted their proposals to the French and Belgian governments who gave their approval.

So far the Peking–Hankow affair had been conducted away from the political spotlight, but when in 1898 the Great Powers began dismembering the Chinese empire in earnest, the railway project was inevitably affected. Two German missionaries had been murdered in 1897 and the German government insisted on sending troops to Kiachow. A few months later they had successfully extorted a lease on the port. Russia followed suit and took Port Arthur and Talienwan. Her ally France obtained a coastal strip in the south and the Tongking–Yunnanfu railway concession. England, not to be left out, secured a lease on Wei hai wei and established a sphere of influence in the Yangtze valley.

Hankow was, however, on the Yangtze river. Sheng realized that the

British would not tolerate anything that could be construed as an incursion into their sphere. Belgium was sufficiently small and neutral to be acceptable; French participation in the Peking–Hankow railway project on the other hand – for this was early 1898, a few months before Fashoda – would clearly be unacceptable to the British. The Chinese therefore told the Belgians that any mention of French participation must be removed from the contract. Not unnaturally the French financiers insisted that if they were to provide the money for the railway then this had to be stated in the contract. In the end a compromise was arrived at by drawing up a separate agreement, in addition to the contract which acknowledged the French investment.

Nevertheless, the affair strengthened the Belgian position as the French were obliged to keep a low profile in the construction of the line. Belgium provided double the amount of equipment in value terms and the Belgian engineer in charge of the project, Jean Jadot – rightly because he was a man of first-class ability – dominated the enterprise. The Belgian success in playing such a major role in the construction of China's first important railway line marked the high-water mark of Leopold's Chinese policy.

While Leopold II's energies in the early months of 1898 were directed towards saving the Peking–Hankow project, the Great Powers were despoiling China. The king, as mentally agile as ever, took little time in coming up with an idea to acquire a territorial concession himself. The efficient functioning of the railway would entail having suitable facilities for landing supplies, assembling material and suitably housing Europeans; Hankow seemed the obvious place.[11]

The Chinese government would certainly offer to provide the facilities themselves. The question was, what could be done to persuade them to cede territory: de Vinck cynically advised de Favereau that there were only two means, 'money and the fear of force'.[12] Unfortunately the Belgians were financially over-stretched and without substantial military resources, and the Chinese duly rejected their demand. De Vinck then came up with a new tactic. He warned the British ambassador to Peking that if Belgium did not obtain a concession at Hankow, then France would insist on the administration of the line being carried out on French territory. Salisbury was informed of the French 'danger' and agreed to support the Belgians.[13] The British ambassador then made the request to the Chinese on behalf of the Belgians. A modified concession was granted at Hankow, that is, permission to build houses, a church and hospital but no more.

There was a considerable outcry in the Belgian press about the projected concession which, it was feared, was the beginning of a colonial venture, and the German government was hostile. As relations between the EIC and Germany were at that time strained in connection with their common frontier in the eastern Congo, Leopold did not want to exacerbate matters. The new Belgian minister to Peking, Daniel Siffert, then came up with the solution. He knew of 115 acres that could be bought for 700,000 francs from Sheng's railway company, as opposed to the Chinese government. By buying land outright the Belgians would have a freer hand. The Belgian government, however, did not have the money to spare. Rather than let the opportunity slip through his fingers, Leopold himself produced the necessary sum. There are no documents showing the source of the money. It would seem that it came from the king's personal fortune and that he hoped to recoup it when the land was exploited.

For the best part of a decade Leopold, already in his sixties, maintained several consecutive schemes in China, and as fast as any one of them was resolved he turned to a new one. An excellent example of his continued mental and physical vigour is provided by his visit to Paris in 1898. Over lunch on 12 April, Hanotaux politely mentioned that he would be pleased to see Franco-Belgian co-operation in seeking mining concessions in China. The following day Leopold returned to Brussels and immediately sent for the governor of the *Société Générale*, Frédéric Baeyens. He told Baeyens to set to finding the money that would be needed for a joint mining-venture. On 16 April Baeyens had 500,000 francs available, of which three-fifths came from Belgian sources.[14]

The *Société de Recherches Minières* was duly created and Leopold tried to come to an understanding with the Anglo-Italian Peking Syndicate which was already active in the field. However, the syndicate was in financial trouble and a new Anglo-Belgian grouping, the China Exploration Company, was formed, dominated, in compliance with the king's wishes, by Belgian interests. As if this was not enough, Leopold was thinking of investing in its rival, the Eastern Pioneer Company, which had recently been set up by an Englishman, Pritchard Morgan, who had acquired some mining concessions in China.[15]

Also in the spring of 1898, Leopold was planning to supplement the financial and industrial bonds that were developing between Belgium and China with closer political ties. The official Belgian representation gave the king little scope for intervention. However, the Congo Free State was not represented at Peking and this provided Leopold with sufficient reason to send an EIC delegation to China. It was headed by Count Charles d'Ursel, a Belgian diplomat seconded from the Ministry of Foreign Affairs, but it contained, surprisingly in view of its supposed intentions, an engineer, Major Gaspard Fivé. D'Ursel had instructions in addition to securing the exequatur of the EIC. He was to negotiate a trading treaty between China and the EIC, or at least to obtain a declaration assuring the EIC of most favoured nation status. In addition he was to propose that the EIC should employ coolies in the Congo and that native Congolese soldiers should serve in the Chinese army. Today it seems incredible that so intelligent a man as Leopold took the latter idea seriously, but clearly he did.

Shrouded in secrecy – which inevitably led to suspicions being aroused – the d'Ursel mission left Belgium in April 1898 and arrived in China a month later. The German ambassador to Peking was extremely hostile to it, although the Wilhelmstrasse was neutral, and he put it about that d'Ursel was seeking new railway concessions for the King of the Belgians. The rumours had their desired effect, the British ambassador refused to co-operate with the mission and the Peking diplomatic corps in general behaved in an unfriendly way towards what they considered a bogus representation. D'Ursel's behaviour did not help matters. He had a rather inflated view of his own importance and even annoyed the Belgian ambassador. The Chinese for their part treated the EIC deputation with scepticism. Li-Hung-Chang, smiling, asked d'Ursel, 'Where is the Congo?' 'In Africa,' the diplomat replied, visibly embarrassed. 'Am I right in thinking that Africans are black?' 'Yes.' 'But you are not black.'[16]

Fivé for his part had been given personal instructions from Leopold to look for mining concessions and he discreetly left d'Ursel in Peking in June 1898 and moved into the Chihli province, south of the capital. There he purchased two parcels of land for the EIC at Peitaiho and was about to buy more at Chingwantao when the Chinese government stepped in and prevented him. They felt that they had by now given quite enough to satisfy the appetites of the European Powers and a decree was issued in November 1898 stipulating that any contract signed between foreigners and Chinese individuals would need governmental approval, and in any new companies the administration and management must remain in Chinese hands.[17]

As a result Fivé was only able to acquire one coal-mining concession. Leopold, in the face of the new restrictions, remained confident that it would even so be possible to obtain concessions in north-west China, away from the watchful eyes of the Peking mandarins, but the results of Fivé's prospecting were disappointing. However, it was not for this reason that Leopold was obliged to tell his agent to stop work: such was the hostility of diplomats in Peking that the king dared not allow an agent of the EIC to incur their mounting displeasure.

Spring 1898 was a highly fecund period for Leopold II's Chinese ideas, for yet another scheme emerged at this time. Logically it was a corollary of the Peking–Hankow railway project; indeed it is hardly surprising that

Leopold sooner or later turned his attention to the prolongation of the Peking–Hankow railway to Canton on the southern coast.

No sooner had he begun making enquiries as to a possible concession than he was told that it had already been granted to the ACDC and the Americans, who, having seen the Peking–Hankow line snatched from them by the Belgians, were determined not to let the same thing happen again. Flexible as ever, Leopold ruled out direct competition with the Americans: instead he would volunteer Belgian co-operation in the project.

A Belgian banker was dispatched to the United States to propose a 50–50 association, or, better still, to buy out the Americans. The directors of the ACDC were not interested in either proposition. Leopold informed de Vinck of the approach to the Americans and told him to put it about that the Chinese had had enough of international rivalries and were thinking of buying back the Hankow–Canton concession. The Americans would, it was hoped, be put off the scheme and would sell out cheaply to a Belgian group, which would in turn hand over to the Franco-Belgian *Société d'Etudes*. The scheme did not have the desired effect.

In previous dealings the Americans had been suspicious of the Belgians and the king thought that he saw a way out of this problem.

> What we need to further Belgian business interests is a very active and intelligent American ... [someone who could act] as correspondent and, if need be, as an associate, not to provide funds but to give a certain American cover to projects and to enable them to enjoy the backing of American legations and consuls.[18]

A man fulfilling the king's requirements was not difficult to find. General Charles Whittier was a retired soldier with wide business contacts and a taste for the Far East; he liked the idea of working with the Belgians and the proposed salary, and came to Brussels to discuss matters. Leopold had been thinking in terms of raising money to make an offer for the company, but Whittier suggested that a better way of proceeding was to buy up shares as they came on to the market. The king was persuaded and it was decided that a syndicate made up of the *Compagnie Internationale pour le Commerce et l'Industrie* (set up the previous year on Leopold's initiative), the *Société Générale Africaine*, the *Banque d'Outre-Mer* (in which Leopold had an interest) and Sam Wiener (the king's lawyer) should be the purchasers. After a while the favourable market pushed the share price up to 60% to 80% above face value and the financial bodies – created by Leopold to further his political aims – refused to pay the higher prices demanded. There were fifty-one shares in all, of which the Belgians held seven. The financiers declared themselves content with a minority participation in the ACDC. Leopold saw things differently. 'To hold less than a half plus one share in the syndicate,' he said, 'is to throw one's money away.'[19]

The opportunity the king sought was not long in coming. Whittier telegraphed on 19 December 1899 that a sizeable majority of the shares could be bought for $500,000. Leopold was keen to buy but the hard-headed bankers held out. They were not convinced that the ACDC was worth buying for $500,000. They made a gesture and bought one extra share for $6,700.

By now it had become clear that the cost of building the Hankow–Canton line would be much greater than had previously been thought. The ACDC therefore decided to increase its capital by going public. The old shares were doubled in value (to $10,000 each) and a hundred new shares with a nominal value of $10,000 each were issued. Leopold told Wiener to urge the Belgian syndicate to buy up as many as possible of both old and new shares (with a capital gain of 100% the old shareholders might be in a mood to sell). But the king had overlooked the importance of official support in the enterprise and Whittier warned Leopold that the United States government would only support a company in which Americans had a controlling interest. The king very reluctantly demurred to pressure that the Belgian share should not exceed a third. With such a share the Belgians were assured of a major say in decisions and likely to receive substantial contracts for equipment.

Although the Hankow–Canton railway project was the major one, Leopold had, as usual, not placed all his hopes on this one concession. In September 1898 he had conceived – it would seem from a study of maps – that there ought to be a line from Hankow to Foochow, and maybe as far as Amoy. If he had a second string to his bow, Leopold calculated, it would enable him to exert pressure on the Americans in negotiations over the Hankow–Canton line.

De Vinck was not optimistic about the chances of obtaining the Hankow–Foochow concession, as the Chinese government had not even decided that it wanted such a line. Yet when the minister posed the question the Chinese authorities did not dismiss it out of hand. They simply demanded 1,000,000 francs in bribes for a favourable consideration. Leopold immediately raised this large sum of money.[20] But the project never developed much further. It was one of the many victims of events in China in 1900.

So far Leopold II's Chinese policy had been based on economic penetration. Suddenly, in the summer of 1900, the opportunity for political action arose as a result of the Boxer Rising.

The Boxer movement was essentially xenophobic: it objected to foreign encroachments in China and attempted to make 'foreign devils', with their greed for territory and distasteful modern inventions, leave the country. The reaction of the foreign diplomats was simply to tell the Chinese authorities to put the Boxers down. Only half-hearted measures were taken and the situation deteriorated, culminating in the Boxers laying siege to the foreign legation in Peking in May 1900, and attacking missionaries and other foreigners elsewhere in the country.

For a while, when the lives of their nationals were in jeopardy, the Europeans worked in unison, but as soon as the danger was over their individual rivalries again came to the fore and they all used the 'rebellion' as an excuse for extorting yet more from the Chinese. During the rising the Boxers had attacked the Peking–Hankow railway and had destroyed part of the line, the telegraphic cable and had attacked foreign workers, killing six Belgians. And while there had been no fatalities in the Belgian legation in Peking, several Belgian missionaries had been murdered in northern China.

The Great Powers were dispatching troops to China to exact reparations. Leopold saw the opportunity for sending a Belgian contingent. Public opinion in Belgium was outraged – as throughout Europe – at the treatment of its nationals in China and it provided Leopold with the necessary impetus.

On 21 July, National Day, the mayors of the four most important Belgian cities, in the name of all the other mayors, issued a proclamation deploring the situation in China and calling for 'the immediate constitution of a committee to take charge of forming a battalion of Belgian volunteers to assist the Allies in China'.[21]

Normally such an initiative would have come from parliament or the government, and in some quarters it was asserted that it was the king who had instigated the proclamation. Two days later a retired general, Georges Verstraete, volunteered to lead a Belgian force and the following day an anonymous donor placed 3,000,000 francs at the disposal of the Belgian contingent to China. It was an enormous sum in 1900, worth about 225,000,000 Belgian francs in today's terms, and could, it was clear at the time, come from only one source, namely the king. (When later on the greater part of the sum was repaid it was credited to the account of Baron Auguste Goffinet, who dealt with Leopold II's personal financial affairs.)[22] A few weeks later 633 volunteers, equipped with arms, new uniforms and the necessary supplies, were ready to set sail from Antwerp.[23]

There had been good reason for Leopold to act through the mayors to create an 'independent' contingent, rather than by pressing the Belgian government to step in. The king remembered the objections raised in the past by the Great Powers to Belgian participation in military action and, while the Boxer expeditionary force was not an official one, the Belgian government nevertheless had to inform the other Powers who had guaranteed Belgian neutrality in 1839 of the action being taken to defend Belgian interests in China.

The British government refused to comment for the moment (it was too embroiled in the Boer War at that stage) but it was clearly unenthusiastic; the French government supported the enterprise, as did the Americans. It was the reaction of the German government that was, rightly, feared, for by 1900 the Germans were continually on their guard as to any initiative of Leopold II. The kaiser loathed the King of the Belgians and insisted that all projects involving him should be placed before him personally so that he could, if possible, sabotage them.[24] When notification of the proposed Belgian contingent reached Berlin – and it was an open secret that Leopold II was behind it – the German government objected on the grounds that it constituted a violation of the 1839 guarantees. It was appreciated that the veto was a personal gesture of the kaiser against Leopold II.[25]

The failure of the expedition caused considerable loss of political face for Leopold. He ignored it, and the half-million francs wasted as a result of organizing the force – the money probably came from the EIC treasury.[26] As undeterred as ever, he pushed on with his Chinese policy.

Belgium had failed to gain any political advantages from the Boxer Rising, but there remained the question of financial compensation. Leopold was pleased when an international commission set up to decide upon the damages that China would have to pay, chose the Belgian minister to Peking as chairman, although the indemnity of 31,000,000 francs which Belgium received owed more to the exertions of the engineer Jean Jadot who was in charge of the Peking–Hankow line.[27]

The next question was what to do with the money. Other countries were using their indemnities to set up banks in China, and de Favereau and Baeyens both favoured this policy for Belgium, although there were others, notably van Eetvelde, who considered that the money would be better placed in one of the big banks, either American or British. The former prevailed and so came to be formed the *Banque Sino-Belge* in March 1902. Leopold himself invested 120,000 francs in the new bank.

Even so, the bank did not play a major role in Leopold's Chinese policy during the next few years. The king left investment, other than in the Peking–Hankow railway line, to groups such as Empain's *Compagnie Générale de Chemins de Fer et de Tramways en Chine*. He had been frustrated in his attempts to buy out the Americans and to control the 'spinal column' of China and, obstinate in the extreme, he was determined to devote his energies to try once more to gain the upper hand. This time Leopold turned to the supremely able Thys to pursue his policy, and in the second half of 1900, Thys's *Compagnie Internationale de l'Orient* was told to buy up the ACDC and to transform it into a new company with a Belgian majority but one-third owned by a blue chip American group. In this way the company would be able to call upon American diplomatic support.

Leopold was optimistic as to the outcome, although Thys had reservations about the financial wisdom of involving the *Banque d'Outre-Mer* and the *Compagnie Internationale de l'Orient* in the Hankow–Canton project. After a while the king became dissatisfied with Thys's lukewarm attitude and decided that the only way to guarantee that the scheme would develop in the way he wanted was to acquire a controlling interest himself. Naturally the King of the Belgians could not be seen to be running a commercial concern and Leopold had to create a front organization behind which he could act. It was called the *Société Asiatique*.[28] Alexandre de Browne de Tiège, an Antwerp banker, allowed the king to use his name for shareholding purposes and the other shareholders – Belgian law required at least seven – were friends of Leopold's such as Empain, who was becoming increasingly interested in railway concessions in China.

Meanwhile, the Chinese had become restive about the procrastination in Europe and threatened to annul the concession if matters did not advance faster towards implementation of the scheme. There were also rivals who would be only too pleased to take over the concession themselves. For these reasons Leopold was anxious to push ahead with the construction of the line, but unfortunately the money raised had been sufficient to finance no more than the technical studies. About 200,000,000 francs would be needed, not a sum easily raised on the open market, and certainly way beyond the capacity of the Belgian market alone. However, if the concession was not to be lost, Leopold had to find enough money to get things going. He turned first to Empain, but when even the successful banker could not raise such a sum in the unfavourable market conditions of 1901, he set to work on John Pierpoint Morgan, the American banker and financier, who was the largest single shareholder in the ACDC. Leopold met him twice and in October Morgan agreed to advance the 15,000,000 francs needed for work to begin. This was only a short-term loan, and on onerous terms. There still remained the problem of finding the money on a longer-term basis.

In August 1901, Empain was again sent to Paris to persuade the French to participate in return for two places on the board of directors of the ACDC. It was not an attractive enough offer for the French. Two months later Leopold himself made the journey to Paris and made much the same offer, adding only that France would receive a third of the orders for the first part of the work. The French asked for a larger share; Leopold refused. Finally, and it says much for the king's personal powers of persuasion, Joseph Caillaux, the minister of finance, agreed to 'invite' French financial participation.[29] When Delcassé learnt of Caillaux's capitulation he protested. 'The Belgians have retained a predominant position and have consistently endeavoured to limit our role to that of simply providing the funds.'[30] The Council of Ministers had to resolve the dispute and came down in favour of Delcassé. Leopold would have to look elsewhere.

The British did not rise to the bait when the subject was broached to them. Leopold then went to Paris to see Morgan. He came away empty-handed. There was now only one other source of such sums available: the Congo.

By the turn of the century the EIC had become a highly profitable concern and van Eetvelde believed that it would be relatively easy to convert the 1888 bonds (of which 690,000 had been sold) into a new issue. The old non-interest-bearing shares would be exchanged for bonds with 3% per annum interest and they would retain the lottery facilities.[31] This would surely be attractive to the bond holders, and it would enable the EIC to take over the reserve fund (now worth 50,000,000 francs), which in view of the obvious financial viability of the state could be considered as no longer necessary.

As expected, the *Société Générale*, where the reserve fund was deposited, objected to the proposed conversion and the two other members of the committee controlling it followed suit. Leopold therefore decided to increase the members of the committee with men who would do his bidding. To be able to do this he had to sell more shares; there remained 800,000 of the original issue of 1,500,000 unsold, and it was a matter of disposing of these and consequently acquiring the right to nominate a further four members of the committee supervising the reserve fund. The king ought to have sought the permission of the Belgian parliament before making the new issue. He dismissed such considerations. 'It is bad policy to consult people beforehand, for they always say no. It is better to explain and justify the *fait accompli*.'[32] The transaction was, to put it mildly, of dubious financial probity.

There was no outcry either from the Belgian government or parliament when the new shares went on the market, and van Eetvelde and Empain began placing the shares with suitable banks. The latter, who had the dominating role, insisted that the issue would only be a success if it was open to foreign participation. Leopold, convinced by Empain's argument, allowed the financier to go to Paris where he successfully sold half the shares, although he was forced to provide guarantees himself that could cost him more than 3,000,000 francs.

Nevertheless, many more shares would have to be sold before the railway was completed, and at this stage Leopold distinctly overreached himself by insisting that the semi-official Belgian *Caisse Générale d'Epargne et de Retraite* should buy some shares. The Socialist leader, Emile Vandervelde, got to hear of the proposed transaction and denounced it. The idea of using the *Caisse Générale* was dropped.

The search for capital continued and after a further unsuccessful approach to Pierpoint Morgan, Empain advised the king to change tack. American participation in the ACDC could be reduced by doubling the share capital and ensuring that all new subscribers were Belgian.[33] Leopold immediately told Thys and his associate, Joseph Devolder, to double the capital of the ACDC and to reserve exclusive rights on the new shares for the Belgian group.[34] The businessmen naturally protested and Thys and Devolder pointed out that such action was against American law. Leopold refused to desist. The bankers held firm; they would not go along with the king and both resigned from the syndicate. Thys also resigned as equerry to the king, ending his twenty-year-old collaboration with Leopold. Despite the ruptures, and with no sign of regret, Leopold continued as before.

Empain, however, had reservations about increasing the capital and Leopold let the matter drop for the moment as he had other, more urgent problems to deal with. The Chinese had protested to the Americans about the Belgian participation in the ACDC and when the American engineer in charge in China was replaced by a Belgian in 1904, anti-Belgian feeling was aggravated. Furthermore, the work was not progressing as planned because of lack of available funds and because of obstruction by the local population. In October 1904 the money ran out and work stopped.

The dirt now started to fly and William Parsons, one of the leading Americans in the ACDC, wrote to John Hay, the United States secretary of state for foreign affairs:

> The internal affairs of this Company have reached a point where it is impossible to continue. As you are aware, the Belgian shares are owned entirely by the King. He has now become dictatorial to such an extent, that his own representatives have been obliged to leave the Board.... We cannot, however, continue to place our interests and our money under the dictatorial whim of a man, who unfortunately for us, is not a business man and who at times fails to differentiate between Royal prerogative and commercial custom.[35]

Hay was impressed by Parsons' letter, but more important opposition came from Pierpoint Morgan, backed by Thys and Devolder. The State Department informed the Belgian Ministry of Foreign Affairs that it could not accept Belgian control of an American company. Leopold accepted that he would have to sell some of his shares, as the Americans were threatening to offload all theirs if he did not.

At least to all appearances the king complied. In fact he was trying to sell some of his shares to Americans who would be prepared to act on his instructions, but the Americans by now distrusted the king and were watching closely. Pierpoint Morgan insisted that Leopold should sell to him. He offered a good price and bought 1,200 shares. However, the Chinese felt that they had suffered a surfeit of Western financial manipulation and duplicity and threatened to revoke the contract on the basis of Article 17, 'bad management'.[36]

The American government promised the Chinese that the ACDC would rapidly put its house in order, although the company itself was contemplating selling its contract back to the Chinese. Quite a few shareholders had had more than enough of the company and simply wanted to rid themselves of their share. Edmond Carton de Wiart, Leopold's secretary, who happened to be in the United States in April 1905 (defending the Congo), learnt of this. He immediately telegraphed the king: 'I believe I can buy all the American shares at 625. Top Secret. It is imperative that your name is not mentioned.'[37]

When he received the telegram Leopold immediately spotted a new way to take over control of the Hankow–Canton project. The Franco-Belgian *Société d'Etudes de Chemins de Fer en Chine* would buy the shares with the backing of the French government – which was popular in China – and would continue the project. The Quai d'Orsay, knowing the Chinese would not be taken in, declined the offer.

Leopold was alone in trying to stop the Americans from selling out, but he refused to accept defeat. He wrote to Theodore Roosevelt, the American president, and when he heard that one of Roosevelt's personal friends, Senator Henry Cabot Lodge, was in Europe, Leopold seized the opportunity to invite him to lunch. The king used all his charm and persuasiveness. It worked and Cabot Lodge cabled Roosevelt: 'I think it would be a real misfortune to let go this great line of railway, [it would be] a blow to our prestige and to our commerce in China.'[38] The president was prepared to support the ACDC as long as it showed its determination to stand by the railway contract but Morgan, who saw Roosevelt several times, wanted to sell. In view of this, it only remained to work out the price to be paid by the Chinese for the company.

In addition to the expenses of the railway company, the Chinese paid out five times the nominal value of ACDC shares, and most American shareholders made about a 400% profit. Leopold's capital gain on his shares was lower, as he had bought when the shares were high. Nevertheless, he made a profit of 4,700,000 francs.[39]

To the king, though, it was slight compensation; he had set his sights on controlling the entire north–south railway line in China and then using it as a basis for Belgian commercial, and maybe territorial, expansion in the Celestial Empire. Leopold was, according to his secretary, extremely dejected after the sale.[40] 'It is a national defeat,' he repeated bitterly.[41]

While engaged in the Hankow–Canton railway project, Leopold had also had an interest in Thys's *Compagnie Internationale de l'Orient*, and he was in addition following closely the development of Anglo-Belgian mining co-operation in Kaiping. Thys was convinced that it was necessary to work with the British–Chinese Engineering and Mining Company, but the king did not like the English participation and when Thys found himself approached by a potential buyer whom he discovered had been sent by Empain, he dispatched a strong letter to the Palais Royal. It demonstrates Thys's strength of personality, for few men would have dared to have written in such terms to Leopold II in 1903:

> It is clear to me that Monsieur Empain is trying to buy shares for the Asiatic, presumably under instructions from the King. This is not only wrecking the market but it makes nonsense of the work of the syndicate ... Empain must stop buying ... I don't like getting involved in other people's business ... However, in this instance, if we're not careful we'll get our fingers burnt.[42]

The Thys group of companies was in the long run financially successful in China. On the other hand, the king's business enterprises met with singular failure. The *Société Générale Africaine* for example was undercapitalized and it was forced to merge with the *Banque Sino-Belge*. As regards the mining concessions in Kansu, Leopold was unable to develop them and lost interest. In his real estate dealings, however, Leopold made a profit. For several years he had hoped to exploit the land he had bought at Hankow but after the failure of the Hankow–Canton railway project he gave orders to sell. The plots were sold for 3,100,000 francs. Allowing for expenses incurred while he had held it, Leopold made 1,900,000 francs on the deal, that is, 180%.

It has been calculated that Leopold had invested almost 12,000,000 francs in his various commercial and financial enterprises in China during the decade ending in 1906 and that his total income over the same period – including capital realizations – was about 11,000,000 francs. In addition he lost 500,000 francs on the Boxer expeditionary force; that is in all he lost 1,500,000 francs.[43]

Although practically all Leopold's dealings with China were of a financial or commercial nature, his interest in China was not simply that of a businessman trying to break into the Celestial Empire and make money in the virgin market. As in his Nilotic policy, if his aims had been pecuniary, Leopold would certainly have behaved differently on several occasions, for example, when he bought shares at the top of the market. Imperialism was the driving force behind all that Leopold embarked on. He wanted territory overseas, even if it was economically worthless, though if it produced income so much the better. In China he found himself unable to compete with the Great Powers in the land grabbing that took place at the end of the nineteenth century; instead he used his financial and diplomatic resources to acquire the next best thing for making the Belgian presence felt: control of an important railway line. But Leopold was not satisfied with his successful role in the construction of the Peking–Hankow line and when the Americans chose to challenge him he was outmatched and his Chinese policy came to an abrupt end.

23 The Age of Autocracy

*'Power tends to corrupt, and absolute power
corrupts absolutely.'*[1]   Lord Acton.

The 1890 loan from the Belgian government to the EIC had saved the
Congo from insolvency but it had not resolved its endemic financial weakness. For despite the decrees and the increased revenue that resulted from
the domainal system, plus the revenue from import duties, the EIC's expenditure – hardly surprisingly in view of the expeditions – remained
greater than its income.

In the autumn of 1894 Leopold II admitted to a small group of confid-
ants (van Eetvelde, Thys, Empain and Colonel North of the ABIR Co.)
that in November 1892 he had borrowed 5,000,000 francs from an
Antwerp banker, Alexandre de Browne de Tiège, on the security of
40,000,000 acres of land in the Congo. This land would be forfeited if
the loan were not repaid by the end of June 1895. The EIC's treasury,
the king said, was empty. (Leopold's admission was a clear breach of
the undertaking he had made in 1890 not to contract any further loans
without parliamentary approval.)

To avoid ceding the land to Browne de Tiège the king proposed creating a *Société Générale pour la création de cultures et l'acquisition et la
mise en exploitation de terrains au Congo.*[2] The company, which was
a secret from the government, would buy lands around Lake Leopold
II and Lake Tumba from the EIC, while the state would reserve the right
to collect the natural products of these lands for fifty years, and to keep
two-thirds of the profits from their sale. Most of the 8,000,000 francs
capital, it was said, would be raised in England but in reality Leopold
intended to provide it himself.

The *Société de Cultures* was formally constituted on 30 November
1894; on 4 December the *chef du cabinet*, Jules de Burlet, came to hear
of the project – Beernaert may well have been the source of the leak –
and he immediately asked for an audience with the king. Leopold, realiz-

ing that the government would not allow him to extricate himself from his financial difficulties by means of the *Société de Cultures*, decided to adopt an air of frankness with de Burlet. The EIC would run up yet another budgetary deficit in 1895; he needed to be able to raise a further loan and he asked therefore to be released from the obligation to inform the Belgian government of any EIC loans. He also told the chief minister of the proposed land sale to the *Société de Cultures*. On the other hand, Leopold did not mention the Browne de Tiège loan.

De Burlet was greatly disturbed to learn of these transactions and the demand for financial freedom, and he summoned a cabinet meeting for later that same evening. The other ministers were equally shocked and they unanimously called upon the king to rescind the EIC decree creating the *Société de Cultures*. They also refused to allow him to modify his 1890 commitment. But, what was far more important, the cabinet announced that it had decided to annex the Congo.

Although he did not like being dictated to by his ministers, Leopold had little choice in the matter and he was in fact in favour of annexation. Two years before he had told the British minister that he 'would hail with joy the arrival of the day when the Congo became a province of Belgium'.[3] In 1895 he told various people that he could not go on any longer; the Belgian government would be obliged to take over the state.[4]

Van Eetvelde was a partisan of annexation – as were Lambermont and Banning – and he provided the Belgian government with the financial information they asked for in such a way as to convince them that it would not be too difficult to make the state pay its way. In the meantime, Leopold had for his part made his *mea culpa* about the Browne de Tiège loan. A treaty of cession was drawn up in the second half of December 1894 and was approved by the cabinet and the EIC on 9 January 1895. This was, of course, the first and easiest stage in the operation. The treaty would then have to be passed by both houses of parliament.

As soon as the proposed treaty was made public there was an immediate outcry from the Liberals, the Socialists and the 'old' Catholics who opposed annexation. To the left the proposition was repellent as it would, they believed, divert Belgium's limited resources from their proper use at home. The right feared the country's taking on additional international responsibilities. It was the personal supporters of Leopold II and his colonial policy who advocated annexation. The commercial companies in particular saw Belgian control as providing a more stable framework in which they could operate and the 'young' Catholics gave their backing to the business interests. Some middle-of-the-road Catholics adopted, if the word may be used, an agnostic attitude. If the Congo was a 'good buy' then it should be taken over. If it was not, then the project should be dropped.

The subject was hotly discussed in the Press as well as in parliamentary circles, and de Burlet in February 1895 warned Leopold that he did not rate the bill's chances of success highly. Even deputies who did not hold strong views on the subject itself, did not like the projected annexation as they knew that it was unpopular with the electorate, an important factor now that there was universal male suffrage. A further problem arose when Hanotaux learnt of the Belgian government's intentions because of the French pre-emption right.[5] De Burlet held firm as to Belgium's right to take over the EIC because of the financial liabilities of the latter to the former, and in the face of Belgian firmness, Hanotaux gave way.

The minister of foreign affairs, the Count de Mérode, was unyielding in his commitment to annex the Congo Free State, while de Burlet was not sure that he wanted to go on. By the middle of March 1895 the moderate Catholics had swung towards dropping the annexation proposal – leaving the difficult decision for another day – and the *chef du cabinet* was of the same opinion.

But what effectively ended the project was Leopold's own *volte face* in March 1895. It seems that he received information showing that as a result of increased rubber production the Congo would rapidly become self-sufficient, if not profit-making. Dunlop had invented the pneumatic tyre in 1888, bicycles were increasingly popular and the era of the motor car was beginning. Leopold from then onwards simply asked for 6,500,000 francs to pay off his debt and to be left alone to pursue his own course of action. De Burlet and most of the cabinet were relieved and only de Mérode resigned when it was decided to drop the annexation bill and to lend the king the money for which he was asking. What the Belgian government did not know, however, was that Browne de Tiège had never lent Leopold 5,000,000 francs. It was a device to extract a further loan.,

Six years later when the Belgian government had a clear right to annex the Congo, as the 1890 ten-year loan had not been paid off, the situation was very different. That the loan had not been repaid was neither here nor there: the Congo Free State was making an enormous profit, largely from rubber sales,[6] and Leopold had no intention of handing over what he now called 'my property' to the Belgian government (see graph).

In late 1900, several months before the subject was due to be raised, the king wrote arrogantly to the *chef du cabinet*, now Count Smet de Naeyer: 'I do not wish to fix a new date for when Belgium could take over the Congo. Let us leave the door open; that will suffice. The country must have confidence in me.'[7] Smet de Naeyer was not prepared to go against the king's wishes and proposed a bill adjourning annexation *sine die*. But not all Belgian politicians were so pliant. The aged Beernaert,

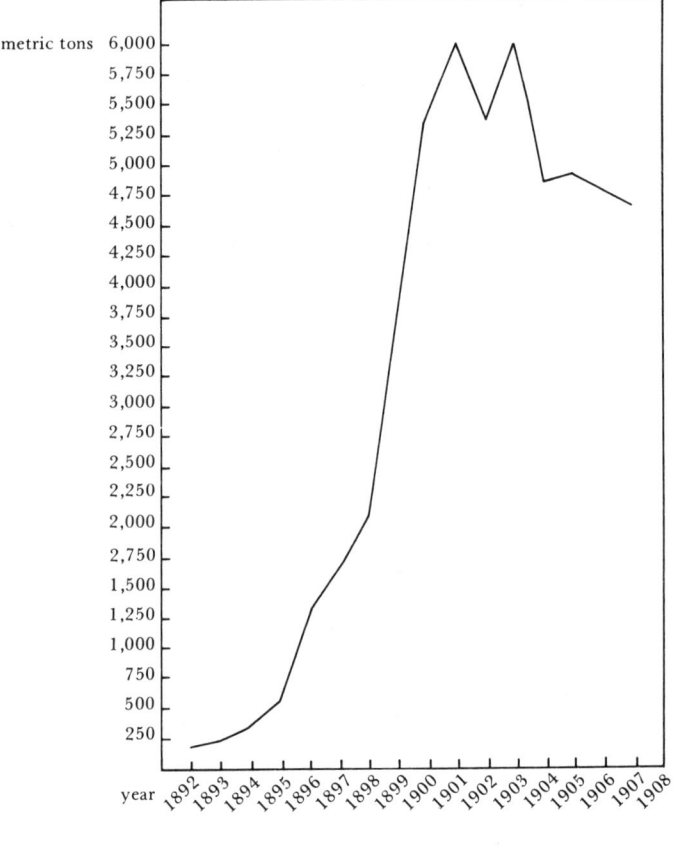

Exports of Rubber from the
Congo Free State

metric tons 6,000 —
5,750 —
5,500 —
5,250 —
5,000 —
4,750 —
4,500 —
4,250 —
4,000 —
3,750 —
3,500 —
3,250 —
3,000 —
2,750 —
2,500 —
2,250 —
2,000 —
2,750 —
1,500 —
1,250 —
1,000 —
750 —
500 —
250 —

year 1892 1893 1894 1895 1896 1897 1898 1899 1900 1901 1902 1903 1904 1905 1906 1907 1908

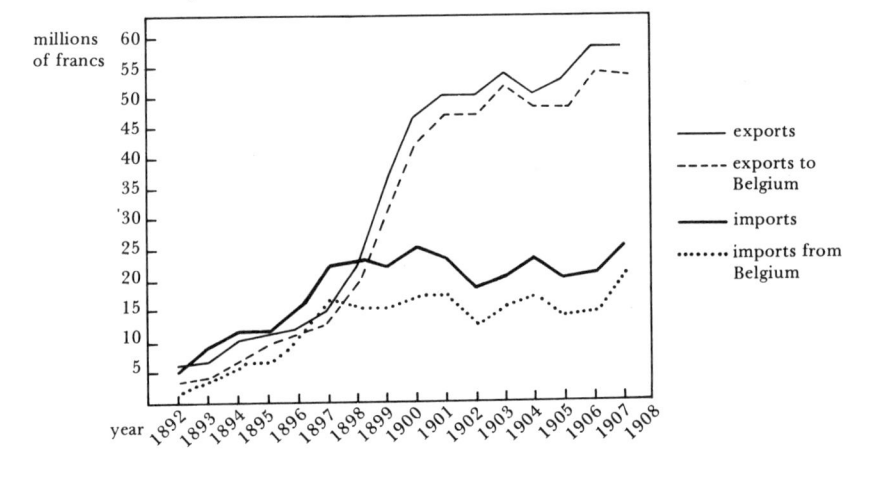

Total Exports and Imports from the
Congo Free State

millions 60 —
of francs 55 —
50 —
45 —
40 —
35 —
'30 —
25 —
20 —
15 —
10 —
5 —

year 1892 1893 1894 1895 1896 1897 1898 1899 1900 1901 1902 1903 1904 1905 1906 1907 1908

———— exports

– – – exports to
Belgium

——— imports

········· imports from
Belgium

a man who had dominated the able men of the 1880s and 1890s and who now in calibre towered above the epigones of the twentieth century, was not prepared to let things go by default. Beernaert feared Leopold's absolutism in the Congo both in itself and because of the dangers to which it exposed Belgium. He brought up the subject of annexation before parliament in June 1901 but in the face of the king's seemingly invincible position, parliament could not but let Leopold continue as he liked.

While there was general support for and approval of Leopold II in Belgium in 1901, elsewhere the king and the Congo Free State were coming to be viewed rather differently. There had been criticism of the administration of the state as early as 1890 when an American negro historian, George Washington Williams, visited the Congo on a fact-finding mission. Williams hoped to find an African country to which Americans could be urged to emigrate. He was bitterly disappointed by what he found, and on his return to the United States he published a denunciation of the EIC government, 'A Report on the Congo State and Country to the President of the Republic of the United States'.[8] Williams died the following year but there was no shortage of persons coming forward with evidence that all was not well in the new state. From 1891 onwards several notes of protest were received by the British Colonial Office about African workers recruited in British territories to work in the Congo. The West Africans claimed that they had been flogged (and that some of them died as a result), imprisoned and kept in chains without trial, treated like beasts of burden and forced to remain in the Congo after their contracts had expired.[9]

The British consul in Portuguese West Africa, William Pickersgill, was in 1892 told to extend his area of jurisdiction to cover the Congo and to provide the necessary protection and assistance for Africans from British colonies. He was not to concern himself with the indigenous population. However, rather than decreasing, the complaints against the EIC were multiplying and the British governors of the Gold Coast and Sierra Leone banned recruitment by the Free State authorities in their territories in 1895, on the grounds of the inhuman treatment of Africans in EIC employment.

The Foreign Office was disturbed by the stories emanating from Africa and Pickersgill was asked in 1896 to investigate the accusations against the Free State. The consul came to the conclusion that the charges were well founded and the colonial secretary, Joseph Chamberlain, banned further recruitment from all British colonies. Van Eetvelde protested against the imputation in the ban and, with support from British business interests, it was modified.

It was, however, an individual case that most strained Anglo-Congolese relations at this time. In 1895 a British trader of some standing in East Africa, Charles Stokes, had been summarily executed in the eastern Congo by a state official, Captain Lothaire, on the charge of supplying arms and ammunition to the Arabs. However, although the EIC admitted liability and paid compensation to Stokes's family and to Germany, for whom Stokes had been working, the blatantly biased trial and acquittal of Lothaire contributed to the disenchantment with the Free State felt in England and Germany.

Just as agitation over the Stokes affair was dying down, fresh complaints against the EIC were made public. The missionaries in the Congo had over the years become increasingly unhappy about the state's administration. The British Missionary Society was receiving a stream of allegations of cruelty to natives, looting by state soldiers and the missionaries' reports were given wide coverage in the British press. Leopold was alarmed by the attacks, particularly in *The Times*. He had maintained amicable relations with Stanley and he wrote to his old colleague asking for his help in rebutting the attacks. Stanley complied but he wrote to the king advising him that something ought to be done to prevent the repetition of malpractices in the Congo. 'The English people are such believers in what they see in print.' Nevertheless, Leopold should avoid giving 'the appearance of defying public opinion ... England is already exasperated on account of Lothaire and it only requires a few more incidents from the Congo to confirm her in the opinion that everything must be radically wrong in the State.'[10]

Stanley's warning did not go unheeded, as the king seemed greatly upset by the attacks. 'If there are abuses in the Congo, we must stop them. If they are perpetuated, they will bring about the collapse of the State,' he wrote to van Eetvelde in the same month.[11] Leopold immediately set up a commission for the Protection of Natives made up of three Catholic and three Protestant missionaries who were to inform the governor-general of any maladministration that came to their notice. It was a gesture, but not an effective one; it is an open question as to whether it was made in good faith. The members of the commission were separated in some cases by six hundred miles, the concessionary areas in question were not infrequently three hundred miles away and the commission members did not have the right to demand information.

The creation of large concessions in 1890–1 had led to the exploitation of vast areas of land by the state and a few large concessionaires, notably the ABIR Co. and the *Société Anversoise du Commerce du Congo*. Certain quotas of rubber – for rubber production was central to the system – had to be produced by a state or concessionaire employee. If it was felt that the natives were not producing as they ought the agents (some of whom worked on a commission basis) were able to use whatever methods they liked to induce the Congolese to meet targets. The worst abuses took place in the company areas, though it should be pointed out – as the state tried to lay the blame on the concessionaires – that the state held 50% of the shares in both major companies.

There were undoubtedly some able and honest employees of the Free State and van Eetvelde expressed the feelings of those Belgians who felt that the English were making unjustified attacks on all officials and who 'appeared to believe that Belgians were essentially a cruel race'.[12] His indignation is understandable; nevertheless, the international reputation of Belgians employed by the EIC was poor. The British minister gave a reason for the low quality of the men employed.

> In Belgium the Congo service has not hitherto been regarded as quite the thing for a man who can make his way otherwise. 'Ses affaires marchaient mal; il est parti pour le Congo,' is a remark often heard. The failure to attract suitable candidates is not difficult to understand and when it is realized that the whole service is run on commercial lines, that promotion depends not on administrative capacity, but on ability to collect taxes.[13]

One returns each time to the system.

In state-run areas the severity of the system varied but even where officials were not cruel, the remuneration of the native population was nevertheless nugatory: fifty centimes a kilo for rubber which sold for ten francs a kilo at Antwerp, though many never received any cash. And as the state was not a cash economy taxation was in kind – forced labour – the level being set arbitrarily at high levels by officials for a number of years. In 1903 it was fixed uniformly at forty hours a month but what an official considered the amount of rubber that ought to be brought in in that period all too often did not correspond with the time it took a native to collect it, for by that time all the easily available wild rubber plants had been tapped. The Revd John Harris reported:

> The people from Esanga told how, on one occasion, because forty-nine instead of fifty baskets of rubber were brought in, some were imprisoned, and sentries were sent to punish the people ... All had harrowing stories to tell of the brutal murder of near relatives. Some they had seen shot before their eyes; in other cases they had fled to the bush to save themselves, and when they returned had found the dead bodies of their relatives lying about ... Whilst the men were in the forest trying to get rubber their wives were outraged, ill-treated, and stolen from them by the sentries. In the light of all they have suffered at the hands of their oppressors, one wonders that they do not hate the very sight

of white men. We missionaries sometimes feel that our message of salvation must seem like a mockery to them.[14]

In theory the natives could complain to their own chief or to the European courts, but the state systematically broke down the tribal structure and replaced the chiefs with its own nominees. Quite often the replacements were native soldiers, askaris, who, once in a position of power over their fellow Africans, became petty tyrants. Summary arrest by the askaris was widespread. No defence lawyers were available, 'the only men with legal training being the Law Officers of the Administration. Men in trouble are therefore in the great majority of cases forced to plead their own causes and through a faulty interpreter, or no interpreter.'[15]

The Congo question – as it came to be called – had so far been discussed only in the British press. In 1897 it took an official turn when Sir Charles Dilke brought the subject up in the House of Commons. Basing himself on the recently published book by Doctor Sydney Hinde, *The Fall of the Congo Arabs*, which held among other things that the state condoned cannibalism, Dilke called upon the British government to convene the signatories of the 1885 Berlin Treaty. 'We should take action,' he said, 'to remove from ourselves the disgrace which had fallen upon our declarations.'[16] The British government, however, did not feel able to take any action against the Free State. One reason was that the situation on the Nile was most delicate and if Leopold was attacked by the British, it might well drive him into the arms of the French, perhaps even to the extent of his handing over the Congo to France.[17] A second reason was that there was no provision under the Berlin Act for international intervention. 'Beyond strong remonstrance we have no further remedy, short of the employment of actual force.'[18]

Agitation against the EIC was greatest in England, but in Germany similar accusations were being made. The *Kölnische Zeitung*, probably with official backing, in 1899 published a report entitled 'Congolese Atrocities' in which Achille Fiévez was accused of 1,308 mutilations.[19] Further articles on the same line followed and the paper concluded that the Free State was no more than an extensive commercial operation.

The evidence of maladministration built up into a torrent by the turn of the century. Some of it was untrue, some exaggerated and part based on no more than hearsay. The reporting was biased and personal axes were ground, inaccuracies occurred, photographs were specially posed and touched up. One cannot believe all that the reports contained. Nevertheless, the overall picture of the state would seem to have been well founded and appalling.

So far little notice had been paid in Belgium to complaints against the EIC. As long as the king did not ask Belgium for money he was left alone.

But by 1900 it was impossible not to be aware of the accusations made in England and Germany, and socialists were beginning to ask questions in parliament. The state administrators were anxious above all to exculpate themselves and they tried to show that those individuals who attacked the state did so out of personal vindictiveness, for example that they had been sacked from its employment. Dilke among politicians was reviled. He bore a grudge, it was claimed, against Leopold for jettisoning the 1884 Anglo-Portuguese Treaty for which he was responsible, and was trying to revenge himself. There is no reason to believe that Dilke had taken the demise of the treaty personally and this charge, which has been repeated by modern historians, was blatantly unjust.

In England many businessmen with interests in West Africa supported the reformers and the EIC authorities decried the campaign as being instigated by those with vested interests. However, the movement spread well beyond such circles. The Aborigines Protection Society led by Herbert Fox Bourne, which had done most to keep the Congo in the public eye in the 1890s, redoubled its efforts at the turn of the century and organized a public meeting at the Mansion House in May 1902. The meeting was well attended and the assembly decided to call upon the signatory Powers of the Berlin Act to co-operate in forcing reform of the Congo administration. In July 1901 *The Times* had come down in favour of the reformers and reputable and influential newspapers, such as the *Morning Post* and the *Manchester Guardian*, gave their support; religious bodies such as the Free Church Council and the Baptist Union passed resolutions calling for reform in the Congo.

Most officials in the Foreign Office, though wary of humanitarians, came to be convinced of the iniquities of the Congo regime and a damning report by Lord Cromer, the doyen of colonial administrators, confirmed them in their opinion. In January 1903 Cromer visited those parts of the southern Sudan occupied by the EIC. He was unfavourably impressed by the state officers:

> ... as the Congo Administration does not aim at civilization, but, under the impulse given by King Leopold, is conducted in the most extreme and objectionable form of mercantile enterprise, this consideration is obviously of no importance from a Belgian point of view ...I had heard so many and such contradictory accounts of the Belgian Administration – if, indeed, Administration it can be called – that I was very desirous of ascertaining some precise and definite evidence on this subject. During a hurried visit, and with opportunities of observation confined to the banks of the river, I scarcely anticipated that I should be able to arrive at any independent opinion on the point at issue. I saw and heard, however, quite enough to gain an insight

into the spirit which pervades the Administration ... The Belgians are detested. The people fly from them, and it is no wonder that they should do so, for I am informed that the soldiers are allowed full liberty to plunder, and that no payments are ever made for supplies ...[20]

When the first charges against the Congo Free State had been made in the last years of the nineteenth century, Leopold had been wounded by the attacks. 'These horrors must end or I will retire from the Congo. I will not be spattered with blood and mud; it is essential that any abuses cease.'[21] But as the campaign developed he came to see it as a selfish British plot to wreck his life's work. Interpreting the allegations of maladministration as spiteful jealousy, Leopold retreated into an entrenched, purely defensive position from which no-one could save him. Nevertheless, to claim that Leopold deliberately instituted a system he knew to be cruel is a distortion.[22] He could not have predicted the windfall of the rubber boom of the last five years of the nineteenth century which was at the root of the abuses. Leopold had pursued the Congo for political reasons but as soon as he realized that his personal investments of the previous twenty years were suddenly paying off, he was seduced by the additional power that wealth conferred. His greed could not be contained. He demonstrated a frightening case of moral decadence, for he did not see that he had created a political hydra.

Leopold became immune to the torrent of abuse and insults in the British press and parliament, but when it became clear to him that his cousin the King of England was cold-shouldering him, he was greatly offended. The British minister to Belgium, Sir Constantine Phipps, wrote numerous dispatches calling for greater understanding of the EIC's problems in England. They were read by Edward VII but the king also read the press and Foreign Office documents which convinced him that atrocities were taking place in the Congo. His private secretary wrote to Phipps telling him in plain language that on the Congo question,

HM entirely agrees with his subjects, and certainly [his opinion] is not one which is favourable either to the King of the Belgians or to his Ministers. No doubt exists in the minds of the British Public, and I believe also of the British Govt., that great cruelties have been committed in the Belgian Congo territory, and ... the King of the Belgians is held to be in a great measure responsible for them, at all events to the extent that, if he had really wished it, he could have taken steps to mitigate these cruelties ... The King cannot, therefore, feel attracted towards a Sovereign, whether he is a Relative or not, who, he considers, had neglected his duty towards humanity.[23]

Despite their being convinced of the correctness of the charges against the Congo Free State, because of the negotiations still taking place over the Bahr-el-Ghazal, the foreign secretary and his officials were still not prepared to take action against the EIC. The reformers therefore decided to force the government to declare its position by initiating a debate in the House of Commons. Herbert Samuel placed before the House a motion that the British government should confer with the signatories of the Berlin Act to end abuses in the Congo. In the debate on 20 May 1903 Dilke discussed the injuries to British trade, John Gorst spoke of the British legal right to intervene, Alfred Emmott raised the humanitarian aspects. The government was obliged to react to the unanimous vote in favour of Samuel's motion and pledged itself to consult with the other Powers. Lansdowne wrote to Phipps:

> The feeling in the House was so strong and widespread in support of the resolution and in condemnation of acts complained of that Lord Cranbourne [the Foreign Office spokesman] found it difficult to obtain any consideration for what he had to say in mitigation of the attack on the Congo administration. Any attempt to obtain withdrawal or rejection of the resolution would undoubtedly have resulted in the defeat of the Government.[24]

British action took the form of a circular from the Foreign Office in August 1903 asking the Powers for their opinions as to how to resolve the Congo question. The British consul in Boma, Roger Casement, was instructed to tour the interior and to report on conditions.

The note to the Powers was a failure, although the British government might not have expected it to produce anything positive. It was above all a gesture to satisfy the reformers. The dispatch of Roger Casement into the Upper Congo had very different results.

24 The English Attack

'England thou sheltering friend of woe,
The despot's fear, the tyrant's foe,
The Congolese have heard thy name,
When shall they verify thy fame?'[1]

Hymn composed by the Revd A.T. Brainsby
for CRA meetings.

Leopold II had met Roger Casement in Brussels in October 1900. Casement had just been appointed British consul in the Congo and the king expressed the desire to meet him before he left Europe to take up his duties. Leopold invited Casement to lunch and used all his charm and powers of persuasion to impress upon the young Irishman that his primary aim was still the well-being of the native population. They continued their discussion the following day and Leopold, according to Casement, 'in bidding me farewell, asked me to write to him privately at any time, and to write frankly, should there be anything of interest I could, unofficially, advise him of for the advancement of the general situation on the Congo'.[2] The British minister, Sir Constantine Phipps, believed that Casement had been favourably impressed by the king but there is no direct record of the consul's opinion.[3] On the other hand, Casement did not seem to doubt the king's good faith.

The new consul already had sixteen years' African experience. In 1884, bored with his job in the office of a Liverpool shipping line, he had gone to the Congo to work for the EIC. For a few years he was employed by the new state in various junior capacities, and then in 1890 he took part in the survey for the Stanley Pool–Matadi railway line. The following year he was again looking for a job as all his previous work was done on short-term contracts. The British government gave him employment in the Niger Coast Protectorate, and in 1895 he was promoted to British consul in Lourenço Marques, the capital of Portuguese East Africa. Until 1900 there had been no British consul in the Congo but, as a result of the increasing number of complaints being received, the Foreign Office decided that it was necessary to have someone on the spot to look after the interests of British subjects and to provide first-hand information as to the general situation.

Casement arrived in the Congo early in 1901. The consulate was situated at Boma on the Lower Congo, but he took it upon himself to go
up-river to Leopoldville and he visited some of the villages around Stanley
Pool. He was shocked by what he saw and sent dispatches to the Foreign
Office graphically describing the 'rotten system'.[4] Roger Casement was
a man of high intelligence and a talented writer; he was also an emotional
idealist and his dispatches to the foreign secretary are much more passion-
ate in language than was usual in diplomatic documents. Casement
wanted to visit the interior of the country from where most of the stories
about atrocities emanated. Illness prevented him and in 1902 he returned
to England to recuperate. As soon as his health would allow, he intended
to make the trip. By the beginning of May 1903 he was once more at
Boma. A few weeks later the debate on the Congo took place in the House
of Commons, as a result of which the British government promised to
investigate the state of affairs in the Free State. Casement was raring to
go.

After chartering a steamer, the consul set off in July 1903 and made
first for Bolobo, where there was a large mission station. He had known
this part of the Congo in 1887: it had been an important native trading-
centre; in 1903 he found the native settlements overgrown, trade non-
existent. There could be no doubt that the indigenous population had
declined in number over the previous twenty years. State officials claimed
that it was due to sleeping sickness; the missionaries thought otherwise.
They told Casement of the state's exactions, the harshness of the system
of forced labour, the beatings, mutilations and imprisonments which had
weakened the natives' resistance to illness. It was the minor officials of
the concessionaires and the African soldiers who were at the root of the
trouble. It was they who forced the natives deeper and deeper into the
forests in search of rubber, where they died of starvation or exposure,
and who brutally punished those who refused to leave their villages to
work. To begin with, Casement was prepared to believe that many of
the stories were exaggerated but as he penetrated further into the hinterland he saw for himself the reasons for the diminution and demoralization
of the native population.

The consul had intended to continue further into the interior, but by
November 1903 he had seen enough. Distraught and physically
exhausted, he returned to Boma. As a parting sally he wrote a letter to
the Governor-General letting him know in blunt terms what he thought
of the state, and took ship for England.

Leopold had realized as soon as the Casement mission was announced
that the consul would report unfavourably. He therefore set to establishing the machinery necessary to combat the expected adverse publicity

the EIC would receive. His first step was to create the 'Federation of industrial, commercial, scientific and patriotic groups for the defence of our interests abroad', the latter part of the unwieldy name being modified soon afterwards to 'Belgian interests'.[5] The federation undertook regular publication of a leaflet called *La Vérité sur le Congo* and issued various other eulogies of the king-sovereign and the EIC. *La Vérité* was widely distributed and was to be found, for example, on bedside tables in European wagons-lits. Leopold was a major shareholder in the company.

Leopold II was a past master at making use of business contacts and exploiting people's self-interest. The Liverpool shipping line of Elder Dempster held the monopoly of the Antwerp–Congo line and its chairman, Sir Alfred Jones, was *inter alia* consul of the Free State in Liverpool. However, Elder Dempster's contract was due to expire at the end of 1904. *L'Etoile Belge* announced in November 1903 that negotiations were taking place for the creation of a Belgo-German shipping line to take over the Antwerp–Congo run. Jones, alarmed at the rumour, approached the Foreign Office in December and pointed out that it would be undesirable for British trading interests if the Germans broke into the West African market. Foreign Office officials understood the danger, and ministers in the precarious Conservative government knew that Jones was an important Unionist, though they wondered if there was not possibly a connection with the fact that Casement's report had just been handed to them. It later emerged that there was never any danger of the Elder Dempster contract not being renewed.

The moral susceptibility of the United States was greatly to be feared and to forestall the spread of English language attacks, Leopold was thinking in the latter part of 1903 of visiting the United States himself. Various American millionaires responded enthusiastically and offered to place their luxurious houses, yachts and private trains at the disposal of the king.[6] Preparations were well advanced when the president, Theodore Roosevelt, informed Leopold that he would prefer the trip to be adjourned *sine die*. There was some talk of the danger to which the king would be exposed – it was soon after the assassination of President McKinley – but no convincing reasons were advanced.

While Leopold's reputation in England was tarnished and vulnerable in the United States in 1903, in Belgium, as a result of the vast programme of public building he had instigated, the king was enjoying, according to the British minister, 'at the present moment a popularity which he may at one time have forfeited, but which now is more general than at any previous period of his reign'.[7] But if in Belgium there was no desire to look too closely into the source of the new-found public affluence, in England parliamentarians and journalists were awaiting with great interest the Foreign Office decision on the Casement report.

The report had been delivered to the Foreign Office in mid-December 1903. Salisbury, Lansdowne and many officials were impressed by Casement's *exposé* and indictment of the Free State but they disagreed as to what should be done with it. The prime minister feared 'the possibility that those wretched blacks will still be worse used in consequence of publication', and he felt that it would be better to hand the report over to an international commission which would investigate the charges further.[8] 'If King Leopold would agree to this scheme, then the British government could delay publication of Casement's report until after the conclusions of the commissioners.'[9] Lansdowne disagreed and held that if the report were suppressed it would be believed that the British government condoned the state of affairs in the Congo. There would be great agitation in the House of Commons and throughout the country and, furthermore, it was exceedingly doubtful whether the king would sanction a commission which would meet British requirements.

Lansdowne's view prevailed, but there still remained a seemingly minor, though nevertheless critical, problem to be resolved. Casement had written in more sober terms than in his dispatches, much to the relief of Foreign Office officials who were uneasy with 'the exuberant diction for which Consul Casement has a weakness',[10] and the text itself needed little editing. However, he gave the names of those who had given evidence. The Foreign Office view was that they should be removed from the report. Casement insisted that as it was well known where he had been in the Congo, it would not protect them and that, without the names of witnesses, the report would lose impact. Both Salisbury and Lansdowne agreed with the official line.

The report was published on 12 February 1904 and a copy was sent to Leopold. But if he did not like what he saw, neither did Casement, who was furious. He wrote an eighteen-page letter – he was given to length as well as to colourful language – to the Foreign Office.

> You have issued a cooked and garbled report. I am ... a good deal disgusted at the whole thing – its obvious irresolution and futility and playing with a subject that calls for a clear thought-out plan.... By suppressing evidences of sincerity and altering dates (or suppressing them rather) and omitting names, the Foreign Office has certainly rendered the task of the Brussels people to confute me easier than it would otherwise have been.[11]

That may have been so. Nevertheless, the publication of the report posed serious problems for Leopold. The White Paper was prefaced by modified extracts from Cromer's damaging dispatch of the previous year on the EIC-controlled part of the southern Sudan. Casement's report began by paying tribute to the beneficial effects of 'energetic European intervention' and spoke highly of the well-built and well-maintained stations, the railways and the efficient fleet of river steamers which had opened up the centre of Africa. The compliments over, he then launched into an account of what he had seen in 1903, and the fact that he could compare conditions with those in the late 1880s added a great deal of weight to his analysis of the situation prevailing. Central to his case was the depopulation of the country which could not, he held, be accounted for by sleeping sickness. The native population had grown weak and unable to resist illness because of their excessive exertions in trying to comply with state demands and, in cases where they resisted, the impositions, undue punishments or military expeditions decimated their number.[12]

The report, which contained many particular examples of cruelty and murder, made an enormous impression on public opinion in England. Those who had in the past felt unsure as to the veracity of the horrifying reports from the Congo were convinced now that His Majesty's consul had confirmed the misgovernment of the Free State and called upon the British government to do something to put an end to such an invidious regime.

A rebuttal from Brussels of the Casement Report was expected and came a month later. The existence of forced labour was acknowledged but it was claimed that it was necessary to engender the work habit in the natives. The evidence of atrocities was based on untruthful Congolese and missionaries who were trying to further their own interests at the expense of the higher ones of the state. One particular case cited in the report which had attracted a great deal of attention concerned a boy called Epondo whom Casement had seen with a mutilated hand. The boy's hand, according to the EIC, had been bitten off by a wild boar. The state, however, accepted that odd cases of cruelty might have occurred. They would be looked into.

Even before the unsatisfactory reply had been issued, the Congo Reform Association had been created in England. The idea of forming a pressure group originated with Casement. He considered the Foreign Office cynical, mealy-mouthed and incapable of decisive action – a measure of how little he understood the limitations of diplomatic action. In December 1903 Casement had met a young journalist, Edmund Dene Morel, the founder and editor of the *West African Mail*, a weekly newspaper devoted to the thesis that the well-being of Africans and Europeans went hand in hand. A born campaigner, indefatigable and undeterred by setbacks, Morel was also an able journalist and good organizer. He was the ideal man to lead the campaign Casement envisaged to force the British government to take action on the Congo question by keeping the subject constantly before the public.[13]

The Congo Reform Association (CRA) was officially formed in March

1904 and during the next few months public meetings were held in various parts of the country at which well-known figures spoke. Morel wrote six pamphlets on the Congo in 1904 as well as editing the CRA's news-sheet, *Official Organ*, and in October 1904 he published a book *King Leopold's Rule in Africa*, a detailed attack on the EIC, though adding little to what was already known. In parliament questions were asked and in June 1904 Dilke, urged on by Casement, opened a second debate on the subject. The moral feebleness of the government was attacked from all sides; the government spokesman tried to pacify the House, assuring members that the EIC authorities had promised to institute an enquiry. If it did not, the British government would feel obliged to set up consular courts in the Congo to protect British subjects.[14]

Leopold's position was severely weakened by the British government's continued insistence that he should take steps to investigate the accusations made against the EIC. In addition, his position had weakened internationally. In Germany there was support in some quarters for the reform movement, even though the government would not align itself with England. But more important as regards Leopold's bargaining position was that the old bogey of France's right of pre-emption, could not be wielded in the face of the first enthusiastic flush of the *Entente Cordiale* in 1904. Leopold therefore found it impossible to manœuvre himself out of the promise he had made earlier in the year that he would investigate the state of affairs in the Congo. And while he was working out how to cede as little as possible to the bullying British, he found himself subjected to the first manifestations of pressure from within Belgium itself.

The British government was calling for a clearly impartial enquiry with sittings in public, the right to subpoena officials, full access to official documents and enough time at its disposal to study in depth conditions in the Congo. What emerged was less than what had been demanded, but considerably more than had been expected. By means of a ruse, A. J. Wauters, editor of *Le Mouvement Géographique*, and Félicien Cattier, a distinguished Brussels lawyer, both critics of the EIC, forced Leopold's hand. On 24 July the *Mouvement Géographique* announced that there was to be a commission of enquiry led by a Belgian judge, Emile Janssens, an Italian judge, Baron Nisco, and a third magistrate, either Swiss or Norwegian. The article went on to state that the enquiry would be conducted in the manner the CRA was calling for and that the reports of the proceedings would be published. Wauters and Cattier were in reality flying a kite but Leopold could not then announce a commission with a much more limited mandate without considerable loss of credibility.[15]

The three commissioners – the third was Doctor Edmund de Schumacher, a Swiss jurist – arrived in the Congo in October 1904 and remained there until February 1905. Leopold had asked for a copy of

Casement's original report, including the names of witnesses, and the British government had felt compelled to provide him with one. Armed with it the commissioners set off into the interior, knowing that the British government and the CRA were being kept informed of all that they did by English-speaking missionaries.

The absence of the commission of enquiry in the Congo provided some respite for Leopold and two incidents, discreditable to the Congo reformers, unsettled their confidence. Henry Fox Bourne, the aged and respected president of the Aborigines Protection Society which had refused to join up with the CRA, claimed that the secretary of the commission of enquiry was the brother of Leopold's private secretary. Fox Bourne's error was made public. A little later, in December 1904, L'Indépendance Belge published a story according to which an Italian employee of the EIC, Benedetti, claimed that he had been bribed by the CRA to fabricate allegations against the EIC. In fact Benedetti had volunteered information and the CRA paid his passage to Europe and compensation for loss of his job. The EIC authorities then outbid the CRA. This was not known at the time and the story as told in L'Indépendance Belge was accepted.

The commission of enquiry spent less time in the Congo than had been expected. Not that it shirked the task in hand. For the same reason that Casement had not visited all the areas planned, the commissioners decided after three months that they had seen enough. Two of the commissioners told the acting British consul in Boma that they were in agreement with Casement.[16] The consul went on:

> I learn from conversations with the members of the Commission that they were profoundly moved by the testimony of some of the Chiefs in the ABIR Concession, who in their childlike simplicity produced numerous twigs of various sizes, each representing a man, woman, or child, barbarously put to death under the arbitrary rule of those in power in that locality ... I gather from the Commissioners that the evidence in the Baringa district consisted of one long narrative of the most gruesome atrocities, which includes a lengthy list of murders, mutilations of limbs, acts of cannibalism, rape, and deaths caused by floggings administered with unexampled severity.[17]

In the ABIR area, where conditions were said to be worst, 'the Commissioners considered the charges against the ABIR fully proved, and the Director of the ABIR himself admitted the truth of those charges. The Director of the ABIR had every opportunity of disproving the evidence, but the utmost he could do was to attempt to explain away things and plead ignorance, but he did not succeed very well'.[18] As a result of their investigations in the ABIR area, they committed the local director for trial and appointed a judge to reside permanently in the area. 'It would thus appear,' wrote the British consul,

> that the attempts made by some of the responsible agents and others to discredit this evidence have, in some instances, failed to satisfy the Commissioners. The incredible theory that the serious allegations made before the Commissioners and substantiated by numerous native witnesses, who have individually testified to the loss of members of their own families and homesteads, are merely inventions devised by the missionaries for the attainment of their own mysterious aims, is not borne out by facts.[19]

The commission of enquiry returned from the Congo in February 1905 and during the following months rumours of its unfavourable findings were circulating throughout Europe. It would take some time, the EIC announced, for the commissioners to complete their report. The reformers in England for their part kept up the pressure in the interim. William Cadbury, the wealthy Birmingham chocolate-manufacturer, provided the CRA with much-needed funds and, through his ownership of the *Daily News*, placed an important newspaper at the reformers' disposal. Sixteen questions were asked in parliament and a further debate initiated in August 1905 with the aim of putting pressure on Leopold to publish the commission of enquiry's report.

But even in the House of Commons Leopold found some supporters. His press bureau in Brussels sent material to Catholic MPs portraying the reformers as Protestants hostile to the evangelical good work being done by Catholic missionaries and generally antipathetical to Catholic countries, such as Belgium. However, the Catholic MPs did not prove very enthusiastic defenders of the EIC and the *Catholic Herald* and the *Tablet* newspapers were unsuccessful in their attempt to arouse Catholic opinion in general in favour of the EIC. This was due to a large extent to the care the reformers took to avoid any denominationally contentious stands.

A more subtle attempt of Leopold's to combat the CRA in England was through the notorious ABIR Co., whose regime was responsible for much of the odium the EIC had incurred. In September 1905 Sir Alfred Jones informed the Foreign Office that Leopold was thinking of handing over the ABIR concession to a British company which he, Jones, would form. Jones was obliged to inform the Foreign Office. The Foreign Office were not taken in; as Lansdowne remarked, 'I cannot help doubting ... whether the offer is not merely a move on the part of the Congo Government intended to discount the Report of the Commission and to place us in an embarrassing position.'[20] Jones in fact abandoned the scheme of his own volition.

The British minister in Brussels, Sir Constantine Phipps, took a more sympathetic view of the EIC than others in the Foreign Office (though he was not the sycophant that Casement and Morel made out and enlivened Brussels' dinner parties with his mimicry of Leopold) and strong language was used in dispatches from London to make him put pressure on Leopold to publish the evidence and full report of the commission of enquiry. Suspicions were mounting in the autumn of 1905 because of the length of time that had elapsed since the commissioners returned to Belgium. It was known that they had finished their report by the end of August. It was finally published in November 1905.

At first sight the report of the commission of enquiry was not such a dramatic document as the Casement Report, as it was phrased in general terms. Careful perusal of it, however, showed it to be highly critical of the Leopoldian regime in the Congo. It began, as had Casement, by praising the work done by the EIC before dealing in the first instance with land tenure in the Congo.[21] The commission accepted that the state had the right to take over uncultivated land; nevertheless, the interpretation of vacant land had been much too narrow, to the detriment of the rights and welfare of the Congolese. The report recommended that considerably more land should be placed at the disposal of the native population. Following on from this they considered that they should be able to sell what they produced on their land to whoever they liked, that is, that the state and concessionaire monopoly should be ended. Furthermore, commercial transactions should be in money and not for barter.

As the Free State's was not a cash economy, it was necessary to raise revenue by taxing labour. This, the commissioners held – and it was their most important criticism – had led to many of the abuses brought to their attention. The fundamental injustice of the system was that even though the labour tax was in principle fixed at forty hours a week (before 1903 it had been variable), what the authorities considered the product of forty hours' work did not correspond with reality and natives were in many cases having to work for much more to comply with the demands of the state.

They went on to criticize the role of the concessionaire companies. The state had been wrong to allow the commercial companies to levy the labour tax as they were not supervised by the state and their employees had allowed commercial considerations to hold sway. They advised immediate government supervision and, in the longer term, the reopening of the country for free trade.

The report contained enough compliments for the official press to claim that it had exonerated the EIC and, because it did not describe particular atrocities, it did not make good copy for those newspapers hostile to Leopold. But among the influential sections of the population in Belgium it had great impact. Parliamentarians, lawyers, those in the universities, understood the indictment of the Leopoldian system and were shocked by what they read. The Casement Report may have been read in such circles but, although in England his report was accepted as impartial, in Belgium it had been seen as British retaliation for Belgian attacks on the conduct of the Boer War and a possible guise for an attempt by the colonially voracious British to take over the Congo.

As a result of the adverse report of the commission of enquiry, Leopold suddenly found himself confronted by widespread opposition in Belgium. The call was for fundamental reforms or annexation by Belgium. Men in the past who had supported him, such as Paul Janson the Radical leader, suddenly turned against him. Many Catholics who had given their backing because of the privileges given to Catholic missions were bitter and disillusioned.

If one takes a generous view one may allow that Leopold had not been convinced of the impartiality and veracity of the Casement Report; one cannot do the same after the report of the commission of enquiry – and the king was in possession of the evidence on which it was based. It was his duty of the most fundamental kind to institute the necessary drastic reforms or, if the task were too onerous, to hand over the Congo to Belgium before his death. The story of the next three years, the wresting of the Congo from Leopold by the Belgians, is not a pleasant one.

25 A Man Alone

'Leopold II could say with more justification
than Louis XIV, "L'Etat, c'est moi".'[1]

Félicien Cattier, 1898.

Early in 1906 Félicien Cattier published an *Etude sur la situation de l'Etat Indépendant du Congo*. Cattier, who had previously been a supporter of Leopold's regime, had become convinced of the case against the state. Basing himself on the findings of the commission of enquiry, he came to the conclusion that 'the Congo Free State is not a colonial power; it is a business enterprise ... The colony has not been administered either in the best interests of the indigenous population or those of Belgium. It has been run only for the financial benefit of the King-Sovereign.'[2] Reluctantly Cattier felt forced to hold one man responsible for the state of affairs in the Free State. 'Absolute monarchs have to bear the sole responsibility for the policies of their governments. I regret that this principle, and the facts before us, have obliged me to be highly critical of the personal policy of the King-Sovereign.'[3]

Fundamental reform of the whole organization of the Free State was necessary. This would entail spending a great deal of money on the colony and men with different attitudes would be needed. Cattier concluded:

> I firmly believe that the Congo is useful and necessary to Belgium, but also that the country cannot renounce her responsibilities without incurring a grave moral defeat and showing herself to be dangerously powerless. Immediate annexation seems to me to be the only honourable way out of the present situation. If we delay it will be imposed on us in disadvantageous conditions ... Today it can be effected without any danger.'[4]

Cattier was professor at the free-thinking University of Brussels and his book had most effect in Liberal circles. However, two months later a Jesuit priest, Father Arthur Vermeersch, professor of law and political science at the Catholic University of Louvain, published *La Question*

Congolaise in which he too criticized the EIC. He appealed to his fellow countrymen:

> Although officially we do not have to answer for the treatment meted out to Congolese natives, our honour and the good name of Belgium are at stake because the country is governed by our King and to a large extent administered by Belgians ... People are saying about us, 'These people whom we believed to be so independent-minded and generous-spirited ... a few tons of rubber are sufficient to deaden their consciences and show them as grasping and cruel' ... But what a magnificent mission could be ours.[5]

Though Cattier's study was a more substantial work, Father Vermeersch's book had in some respects more political effect because it was written by a Catholic and influenced many Catholics who had hitherto supported the king.

At the end of February 1906 the Belgian parliament debated the Congo. Cattier's book had received wide publicity and the report of the commission of enquiry was still fresh in the minds of deputies. As on previous occasions the subject was raised by the opposition and this time there was sufficiently widespread support for a sustained discussion to take place. Vandervelde, the Socialist leader, was impressive. It was not a political question in any partisan sense that they had before them; it was an humanitarian one and he called upon the Catholics, Liberals and Socialists to unite. The majority of his own party opposed annexation but the Liberals and many Catholics were prepared to give him their support. Beernaert judged the moment propitious for putting forward a moderate motion calling for re-examination of the 1901 bill which would provide the necessary legal framework for Belgian government of the Congo. Leopold told the chief minister, Smet de Naeyer, to make sure that the motion did not succeed. Smet de Naeyer told the king that the government would be brought down if it opposed the motion. It would be better to let it go through as it did not entail annexation of the Congo. Leopold was obliged to comply and the motion was duly passed. Nevertheless, the annexationists were disappointed at their slight victory. The Belgian parliament had shown that it did not wish to be tarred with the same brush as its monarch, but it was in no hurry to acquire the Congo.

Leopold had been in the habit of spending the winter months in the south of France for several years. In March 1906 he did not return, as was his custom, to Belgium. Furious at the assertive attitude manifested by the Belgian parliament, he remained at Villefranche and planned his stand against his obstreperous subjects. The failure of his Chinese projects and his defeat on the Nile, which took place at this time, in no way deterred him. He was going to fight hard to keep the Congo. But he was too much of a realist not to prepare at the same time an advantageous fall-back position.

The king had promised to initiate reforms in the EIC as a result of the recommendations of the commission of enquiry. It was a commitment he could not avoid, and they were announced in June 1906. In two respects they went further than the commission had advised, namely that the concessionaire companies were no longer to be able to levy or collect taxes. This was now to be the exclusive prerogative of the state and the taxes, instead of being denominated in terms of hours of labour, were given money values. In other respects, as expected, the decrees fell short and the domainal system was maintained. However, the twenty-four decrees were overshadowed by a covering letter to the secretaries-general from the king-sovereign. Defiantly Leopold proclaimed:

> My rights over the Congo cannot be shared; they are the fruit of my own labours and my own expenditure ... The adversaries of the Congo are pressing for immediate annexation. These persons no doubt hope that a change of regime would effectively sabotage the work now in progress and would enable them to reap some rich booty from the wreckage ... I consider myself morally bound to inform the country when ... I feel the moment is ripe for examining the question of annexation. I have nothing to say at present.[6]

But not only did the king issue an aggressive refusal to accept annexation; he declared in a further document that his will of 1889 bequeathing the Congo to Belgium no longer stood and he laid down new conditions according to which Belgium would have to undertake to respect all engagements entered into prior to annexation by the EIC with third parties, as well as all commitments concerning the *Domaine de la Couronne*, now publicly renamed the *Fondation de la Couronne*. Shortly expressed, Leopold was trying to ensure that large sums of money from the Congo would continue to flow into Belgium to maintain properties and lands he had previously left to Belgium. It made, he hoped, the Congo a less attractive buy for Belgium.[7]

The plan misfired. The reforming decrees passed unnoticed, while the king's arrogant attitude towards his countrymen was so insulting as to be totally unacceptable to opinion-formers in Belgium. *Pro rege saepe, pro patria semper*; after the 'royal manifesto' of June 1906 the Belgians were determined not only to annex the Congo, but to do so on their own terms and without further delay.

The British government, now a Liberal administration with Sir Edward Grey as foreign secretary, had adopted as its Congo policy advocacy of the 'Belgian solution'. Both Houses of Parliament discussed the subject in early July 1906; Grey had no difficulty in summing up. The EIC authorities had not shown themselves prepared to undertake the fundamental reforms that the commission of enquiry had recommended. The sovereign apparently considered himself the owner of private property. This in itself was unacceptable; 'even property', said Grey, 'has its duties as well as its rights; and every Sovereign of every State, though he has his rights, also has his obligations'.[8]

Although the CRA was by now advocating annexation by Belgium only on certain conditions, the reformers felt that substantial progress had been achieved now that the British government had come down squarely in favour of the 'Belgian solution'. Morel, in the autumn of 1906, published *Red Rubber*, which brought together the arguments advanced against the EIC during the previous two years. It was an immediate best-seller. He also organized a deputation, which was received by Grey, of parliamentarians, representatives of the churches, humanitarians and chambers of commerce. By the end of 1906 opinion in England was unanimous and constituted, according to *The Times*, 'the plainest warning yet addressed to King Leopold and, ... one which he will do well to heed.'[9]

In Belgium most parliamentarians also felt that immediate annexation was necessary and a debate lasting a full fortnight began at the end of November 1906. Following the 'royal manifesto', the government had accepted the inevitability of annexation but to forestall attacks on the king-sovereign, the conciliatory Smet de Naeyer opened the debate by outlining the government's policy and playing down the implications of the more provocative parts of the June manifesto. In vain; the hard-line annexationists could not be deflected. When Paul Hymans, the Liberal leader, summed up, he insisted that the government answer several pertinent questions. Were the conditions expressed in the 'royal manifesto' accepted by the government? Would the government demand full information from the EIC before drawing up a colonial law? And Beernaert wanted to know how soon an annexation bill would be presented.[10]

Behind the scenes Smet de Naeyer had been trying to persuade Leopold to attenuate the royal manifesto. The negotiations were tortuous and the result unsatisfactory. The chief minister did not want to set himself against the king; at the same time parliament was calling for annexation in no uncertain terms. Suddenly, out of the blue on 13 December – the day before Smet de Naeyer had to wind up the debate and reply to the questions posed – Leopold's secretary arrived with a message from the king saying that he agreed to annexation. Furthermore, it should take place as soon as possible.[11]

The reason for Leopold's amazing *volte face* was the threat of intervention by the United States. The king had from the earliest stages of the campaign against the EIC attached great importance to the maintenance of good relations with the United States government and receiving a 'good press' in America. Morel visited the United States in the autumn of 1904 and as a result an American branch of the CRA was established. About the same time Leopold secretly set up an American Congo lobby directed by Baron Moncheur, the Belgian minister in Washington, and run by probably some of the first professional public relations men, notably Colonel Henry Kowalsky, a lawyer specializing in electoral campaigns. While Kowalsky placed articles favourable to the EIC in the press, Henry Wack wrote a laudatory history of the Free State and many eminent men were approached and asked to support the civilizing cause. Leopold himself followed closely the activities of the American Congo lobby: on receiving the report on a dinner meeting in San Francisco he asked de Cuvelier to write to Kowalsky complimenting him on the work done but, 'you will not congratulate him on the menu which struck me as being horrible'.[12]

Apart from straightforward rebuttals of purported atrocities, the American Congo lobby made much of the fact that the United States had not signed the Berlin Act and therefore had no legal right to interfere in the running of the Free State. Another line emphasized the traditional American policy on non-intervention in European affairs and held that the Monroe Doctrine worked in reverse. The reformers had difficulty in combating these arguments and in February 1906 the American secretary of state for foreign affairs, Elihu Root, in answer to a senator's letter, gave the government view. He reiterated that the United States government had not signed the Berlin Act. In any case it was, Root held, questionable whether the act afforded its signatories the right of intervention in the domestic affairs of the Free State. As regards the atrocities, the United States government had no first-hand source of information in the Congo and could not therefore accept the reports placed before it. Furthermore, the EIC authorities had always shown themselves willing to deal with any complaints involving American interests brought to their notice.

Leopold saw to it that Root's letter was reprinted and widely distributed in the United States and Europe, and later in the year the king tried to consolidate his American position by the formation of the American Congo Company. Leopold persuaded a syndicate of American millionaires, including Daniel Guggenheim, to provide the money needed to develop 2,500,000 acres near the mouth of the river Kasai; in return for this they would be awarded a sixty-year concession.

Three other companies – the *Société Internationale Forestière et Minière du Congo*, the *Union Minière du Haut-Katanga* and the *Compagnie du Chemin de Fer du Bas-Congo et du Katanga* – were also formed at this time from capital put up by both American business interests and the EIC. By forming these companies Leopold hoped not only to receive the support of the American business lobby but more importantly, he had realized that sooner or later the Congo would be taken over by Belgium and he was trying to tie up as much as possible of the state's wealth in companies with foreign and *Société Générale* participation. He could then attribute his shares to his foundations and so continue to control the use of money from the Congo.

By the end of 1906, however, the tide had turned against Leopold in the United States. Mark Twain published a virulent satirical attack on the king, *King Leopold's Soliloquy*. In it words were put into Leopold's mouth. A 'madman wants to construct a memorial for the perpetuation of my name, out of my 15,000,000 skulls and skeletons, and is full of vindictive enthusiasm over his strange project ... Out of the skulls he will build a combined monument to me which shall exactly duplicate the Pyramid of Cheops ... He desires to stuff me and stand me up in the sky on that apex' and, 'if I am spared ten years longer there will be fresh skulls enough to add 175 feet to the pyramid making it by a long way the loftiest architectural construction on the earth'.[13]

The reformers stepped up their campaign: congressmen were inundated with letters and telegrams and the Senate Committee on Foreign Affairs came out against the Free State. It was known that the president, Theodore Roosevelt, had for some time been personally convinced of the case against the Free State, but in November 1906 a journalist known to be in Roosevelt's confidence published an article stating that the United States government was prepared to co-operate with Britain in attending any international conference convened to discuss the Congo Free State. This was a serious blow to Leopold, who until then had kept the British isolated. Neither France nor Germany would support him; when the Anglo-Saxon powers joined up his position was endangered.

The willingness of the United States executive to intervene – Root had changed his mind during the course of the year – was reinforced the following month when a newspaper, the *New York American*, on the basis of information provided by Kowalsky, who had been dropped, exposed the American Congo lobby.[14] It revealed, to the horror of Americans who were not prepared to countenance foreign interference in the workings of their system of government, that Kowalsky and others were in the king's pay. The following day, 10 December, Senator Henry Cabot Lodge, who had only a little while before been favourably disposed towards Leopold, tabled a resolution pledging the support of the Senate in any action the president might feel fit over the Congo. Backed now by the legislature, Roosevelt officially informed the British government that the United States would co-operate with them.[15] In the face of this united front, on 13 December 1906, Leopold decided to yield and to allow Belgium to annex the Congo.

With the king's consent Smet de Naeyer was therefore able to announce

at the end of the debate on 14 December that the government was committed to annexation and an all-party working party was set up, known
as the Commission of XVII, to draft a colonial law. It was to be under
the chairmanship of Frans Schollaert, president of the Chamber of Representatives. Schollaert, an independent-minded Catholic, was mildly
favourably disposed towards Leopold but when, as a good parliamen-
tarian, he chose representatives of each party reflecting the various shades
of opinion within the parties, the king protested. But no-one would support him.

Less than a week later Leopold submitted a draft Treaty of Cession
to the *chef du cabinet*. He wanted to get the whole horrible business out
of the way as quickly as possible. He did not like being subjected to international pressure and, now that he felt sure that he had successfully tied
up a great deal of money as to be able to continue his building programme, he was prepared to hand over.

The cabinet, however, did not want to rush annexation through parliament. In its opinion it was indispensable first of all to work out a suitable
system of government. This was the task of the Commission of XVII
which set to work in the new year. Soon afterwards, as expected, it asked
the government – the intermediary between the commission and the EIC
– for information regarding the Free State. The commission wanted for
a start full texts of all laws and 'regulations' operating in the Free State.
A curt reply telling them to refer to the *Bulletin Officiel* – available in
any bookshop – was received. It was common knowledge that many decrees had been issued and not published in the *Bulletin Officiel*.[16] When
the parliamentarians then asked for access to the state's accounts and
budgets, the government knew that trouble was in store and dispatched
the head of the Ministry of Foreign Affairs, Baron van der Elst, to the
south of France to frame as diplomatically as possible the request. Leopold received van der Elst on his yacht where he spent several days with
the king.[17] Leopold was charming and showed the baron round his
gardens at Cap Ferrat; but when van der Elst posed the question about
divulging EIC financial information, the king's mien changed. 'The Congo
Free State', he said, 'is unique in its kind. It has nothing to hide and no
secrets but it is not beholden to anyone except to its Founder ... No-
one has the right to ask for its accounts.'[18]

Parliament was becoming increasingly restive and the king was clearly
totally inflexible as to his 'recommendations' of 1906 which Smet de
Naeyer had hoped could be modified, and the chief minister felt his hold
on the Chamber growing weaker. Harassed on both sides, the government courted defeat in parliament (on a subject unrelated to the Congo)
and resigned.

The king's absence from Belgium did not make matters easy, as there was no obvious successor to Smet de Naeyer and the various factions in the Catholic party were manœuvring. Finally, after a few weeks without a government, Jules de Trooz formed a new administration, little different in substance from the outgoing government except that the new *chef du cabinet*'s relations with the king were better than Smet de Naeyer's had been of late. De Trooz was also more popular within the Catholic party and parliament in general than his predecessor.

Parliament was now demanding that matters move faster than they had been doing in previous months, and de Trooz's cabinet agreed that it was necessary to push ahead with annexation concurrently with the work of the Commission of XVII working out the terms of the colonial law. To this end in September 1907 a new colonial bill was presented to parliament which represented some advance on that put forward by Smet de Naeyer's administration. De Trooz was treading gently. Legislative and executive power was still to be vested in the crown, but with a minister of colonies assisted by a colonial council under him. Members of the council would be appointed by the crown but the Commission of XVII insisted on increasing their number from four to nine. However, Leopold's major concession was that although the colonial budget would be passed by the executive an annual report would be laid before parliament giving full financial information and parliament would be able to discuss the running of the colony. In addition loans could only be contracted with the cabinet's approval. For a short while it looked as though the process of annexation would now go through smoothly. But when Leopold announced that, while he accepted the draft Treaty of Cession, the *Fondation de la Couronne* was to be excluded, a head-on collision between king and parliament could not be avoided.

The *Domaine de la Couronne*, that part of the Congo – mainly east of Lake Leopold II in the central Congo – belonged exclusively to the sovereign and had provided Leopold with many millions of francs annually, which he was using for buildings and urban development in Belgium. It has been estimated that the *Domaine* produced about 40,000,000 francs worth of revenue between 1900 and 1907.[19] This figure may be on the low side as even Leopold was given cooked figures, EIC officials trying to underplay the extent of the revenue, in an attempt to keep some of the money for use in the Congo and to prevent the king from embarking on yet more ambitious schemes. The *Domaine* had been secretly constituted into the *Fondation de la Couronne* in about 1901, and later the king added a large portfolio of shares. In the following years it purchased a great deal of real estate in Belgium – Cattier calculated 18,000,000 francs worth – and many valuable properties in and around Cap Ferrat in the south of France.

For some time the magnificent public works to which the Belgian taxpayer did not have to contribute were admired and accepted in Belgium. But when the Belgians came to confront annexation this use of Congo money was seen differently. Parliament was for a start not prepared to commit itself to long-term projects involving large sums of money, and financed by a colony for which they were responsible; projects, moreover, over which they would have no control. And when it emerged that the EIC had handed over 30,000,000 francs to the *Fondation*, there was uproar in the Chamber of Representatives. The reply provided in answer to questions about the transaction was evasive and the state was rapidly compensated in property for the sum concerned.[20]

In the heated discussion over particular financial transactions which was taking place not only in parliament but in the press as well, the issue came to be seen in more general terms. Leopold had violated one of the major tenets of colonial theory, namely that the revenues of colonies should be managed in the interests of the colonies themselves. Belgians were forced to reflect on the organization of the Congo Free State; they saw that for years a poor African country had been exploited for the benefit of a rich European one. For some it was a question of principle; others saw its financial implications for Belgium. No money had been spent on the necessary administrative infrastructure in the Congo, economically nothing had been done to plan for the future. Wild rubber had been collected without planting new vines. Belgium would undoubtedly be called upon to provide large sums of money for the Congo while at the same time money would be flowing into Belgium from the Congo to maintain buildings and parks the Belgians had never asked for. There was also the constitutional aspect. The king was trying to exclude from Belgian sovereignty about a sixth of the Congo – and an area where some of the worst abuses had taken place. It would make a mockery of annexation if an important part of the colony was outside effective control by Belgian colonial authorities.

For Leopold the *Fondation de la Couronne* was the apotheosis of his colonial ambitions and his ambitions for Belgium. He could not understand how the country could want to turn down his gift of valuable properties, monuments, parks and wide tree-lined roads. He was over seventy and had worked without respite for fifty years to make Belgium richer and more beautiful. He had succeeded and in return his people turned on him. His bitterness at their ingratitude knew no bounds.

At the end of December 1907 de Trooz died. His obvious successor was Schollaert, chairman of the Commission of XVII and the only man who could hope to negotiate annexation through parliament. Leopold – the constitutional King of Belgium that he had always been – called upon Schollaert, who was now known to oppose the *Fondation de la Couronne*, to form a new government. By now there was no-one in whom the king could confide. Even his secretary Edmond Carton de Wiart was not in sympathy with his master, and Prince Albert, Leopold's heir, was known to be critical of his work.[21]

Schollaert was well known for his obstinacy and during the early months of 1908 he lived up to his reputation. He spent hours with the king in the latter's study without conceding anything. Leopold was authoritarian and given to bursts of rage if anyone disagreed with him. In such circumstances Schollaert left the king and waited in an adjoining room until Leopold subsided, and then went back and continued the discussion. The king was depressed and grumbled a great deal about those who were going to wreck 'his Congo'. He tried to give advice to Schollaert. 'I am going to explain to you how to put off annexation.' 'Sire,' replied the chief minister, 'I don't want to know.'[22] Carton de Wiart was thrown out of the room during one discussion with the king, and the door was slammed in his face.[23]

Alone, morose, filled with rancour towards everyone, in February 1908 Leopold capitulated and informed the government that he would abandon the *Fondation de la Couronne*. Old and isolated though he might be, Leopold had not lost all his previous verve and tenacity. He had had to give in over the *Fondation de la Couronne* but this did not entail his total capitulation. To keep his end up with the government he demanded military reforms the government had opposed as a *quid pro quo* even though, unbeknown to them, he had established another foundation.

In September 1906 Leopold had, to everyone's surprise, decided to attend the golden wedding celebrations of the Duke and Duchess of Baden and he had used the occasion to set-up a secret foundation based on the domain of Niederfullbach, which he had inherited from his father.[24] Paintings, jewellery and furniture to the value of 25,000,000 francs had been duly transferred to the new foundation in the following year; in addition, Leopold had reclaimed the 20,000,000 francs which he had made over to the EIC from his private fortune as a *fonds spécial* in the early financially uncertain days of the state, and secreted the money in Germany.[25]

The existence of the *Fondation de Niederfullbach* and its vast wealth was only revealed after Leopold's death; for the moment the government, feeling that it had dealt a hard blow to the old king, was prepared to temper his defeat by creating a *Fonds Léopold II* to undertake the sort of building works the king wanted. There was agreement in principle on both sides, until the sum involved was raised. Leopold asked for the gargantuan sum of 150,000,000 francs, roughly £125,000,000 in today's terms, to be taken from Congo funds, 100,000,000 francs to spend on Belgium and 50,000,000 on the Congo, although in his interpretation this included the Congo Museum at Tervuren and the World Colonial School he was planning to build there.[26] The sum was so ludicrously large that it is some measure of the government's attitude towards the king that it did not bother to express outrage at Leopold's pretensions. The balance of power had now shifted firmly in favour of the government and Schollaert proposed a scheme involving sums of a very different order of magnitude and with more precisely delimited objectives. From Belgian sources 45,000,000 francs would be provided to finish off those building works already begun; 15,000,000 for Laeken and 20,000,000 for Ostend. In addition the king would receive 50,000,000 francs 'as a mark of gratitude for all the great sacrifices he had made for the Congo'. This would be paid in fifteen annual sums and was to be used for purposes related to the Congo.[27] Schollaert also confronted the king with a revised colonial bill which Leopold could not but accept. The colonial council was to be increased from nine to ten, of whom the king could appoint six and parliament four but, much more important, the colonial budget was to be passed annually by parliament.[28]

After this Leopold was no longer an active party in the annexation process which was now in the hands of the government. 'I will do nothing to help annexation, I will do nothing to stop it, I just don't care about it,' he told his secretary.[29] It was now for Schollaert and his colleagues to contend with the parliamentarians and menaces from the United States and Britain. The British and American governments delivered strongly-worded documents to the minister of foreign affairs, Julien Davignon, insisting that annexation had to take place on terms such that would bring about genuine and profound changes in the system of government in the Congo. In particular they demanded that forced labour should be abolished immediately. Davignon pointed out that although the Belgian government intended to institute such changes, it could not declare itself so openly as it would be tantamount to public censure of the king and his administration. Furthermore, the Belgian government had consistently held that annexation would not cost the taxpayer anything and the abolition of forced labour would clearly entail additional expenditure.

The British and Americans accepted Davignon's reasons and decided to let annexation go through on the best terms the Belgian government could elicit, but to withhold recognition until it was possible to judge the reforms. For they appreciated another factor which Davignon did not mention, namely that elections for half the Chamber were to be held in May 1908 and those Catholics opposing annexation and many Socialists were waging a campaign based on the slogans 'annexation means doubling taxes' and 'annexation means sending your sons to their death in the Congo'. The Catholics remained in power as a result of the elections, though with a reduced majority. Discussion of annexation was therefore taken up again and Schollaert ably steered the bills through parliament. On 18 October 1908 the king signed the Treaty of Cession.

Leopold had failed in that Belgium had wrenched 'his' Congo from him against his will. At the same time he had succeeded in his youthful, if long forgotten, ambition to see Belgium become a colonial power.

26 An Old Man: a New Century

*'All that I have done for my country, I have
done without my country.'*[1]

Leopold II.

For the three decades from 1870 to 1900 Leopold II had virtually no private life; his work was his sole interest. Then in 1900 he met a young Parisian woman, Blanche Delacroix, who became his mistress. Estranged from his wife and two elder daughters, Leopold at this late stage in life discovered love and affection. He became devoted to the Baroness de Vaughan, as Blanche Delacroix came to be called (a courtesy title and without official foundation), and they remained together until the king's death in 1909. His attachment to Madame de Vaughan did not, however, keep him away from his work. If his pace slackened in his last years it was due more to problems with his health.

Leopold was already unpopular with his subjects and his liaison with Madame de Vaughan did not help matters, but it was his unkind, even cruel, treatment of his daughters and his mean provision for them in his will which were the main causes of his subjects' disapprobation at the time. Leopold had inherited 15,000,000 francs from his parents and he consistently claimed that although large sums of money had passed through his hands at various times his net fortune remained the same. It was this sum that Leopold wished to have considered as his fortune in his will in 1900; the enormous wealth – estimated to be 50,000,000 francs in 1908[2] – that he had in fact accumulated in Germany was only gradually discovered after his death (it was not therefore a reason for his unpopularity) and after many years of sordid legal wrangling with Leopold's daughters most of it went to the state.[3]

As Leopold had three children he was permitted by law to divide his assets into four, three-quarters of which he was obliged to leave to his children. In his draft will of 1900 he thus attributed 3,750,000 francs for each daughter and what he claimed to be property worth the same amount as a *Donation Royale* for Belgium.[4] It comprised the domains of Laeken, Ciergnon and Villers in the Ardennes, the Chalet Royal at Ostend, 400 hectares of land at Tervuren, the Jardin du Roi, the Duden Park and land at Nieuport; Clementine, the youngest daughter, the château and park of Ardenne, the château of Belvedere and some smaller properties at Laeken; and 'the two others', as Leopold contemptuously referred to Louise and Stephanie, the domain of Niederfullbach in Germany, the Freyr Forest, some houses at Ostend, small amounts of land at Tervuren and Laeken and some money. However, Leopold argued that the value of the estates he had given to Belgium was reduced by his veto on using the land for building and his insistence that the domains should be kept in their existing state which would involve heavy maintenance costs.

The draft will was not made public so that it was not known in 1900 what sums Leopold intended leaving to his daughters. It was, though, suspected that the quarter he wished the country to inherit was worth more than the king claimed. Distaste for Leopold's treatment of his daughters was already widespread and when, in addition, it was pointed out that the king's insistence on handing over the *Donation* before his death and *in toto* was illegal, there were ructions in parliament and the press. But in the end the offer proved too attractive to refuse and the *Donation Royale* was accepted by parliament. (The *Donation Royale* turned out to be the only one of Leopold's foundations to survive and is today a public institution responsible to the Ministry of Finance.)

Looking at Leopold's relations with his two elder daughters over the preceding years it is perhaps not surprising that he treated them so ungenerously – his will was merely a reflection of his feelings towards them and his life-long view that women were very second-class citizens. Louise's way of life in Vienna, her affairs and her unpaid debts, had for years been a source of international gossip, while her current infatuation with a Croatian army officer, Count Geza Mattachich, had resulted in his imprisonment and her committal to a lunatic asylum. Louise had wanted to marry Mattachich and had gone to Belgium to ask her parents for their support in applying for a divorce from Philip of Saxe-Coburg, but neither had consented to help. Despite his own unsuccessful marriage Leopold was not persuaded that royalty ought to be able to choose their spouses. If an arranged marriage brought unhappiness, *tant pis*; it was part of the duty of princes to establish and then maintain diplomatic alliances through marriages. Harried by the Austrian royal family – perhaps with the connivance of Leopold – to pay her outstanding debts, Louise had mistakenly returned to Vienna and begun divorce proceedings. Mattachich had been arrested and imprisoned for four years and she had been given the choice of returning to her husband or being certified insane – being a woman of spirit, whatever her faults, she had chosen the latter. (In 1902 Mattachich was released, Louise contrived to escape and the two lovers fled to Paris and eventually married.)

Stephanie was a very different character from her elder sister. She had been only twenty-five when widowed and for ten years after Rudolph's death she lived quietly with her daughter Elizabeth at Miramar. She maintained friendly relations with her father and visited Belgium from time to time, the last occasion being in 1899. Only a short time afterwards her engagement to Count Elmer Lonyay was announced in *The Times*, where Leopold learnt of it for the first time. There was a complete rupture between father and daughter as a result. It would appear that Stephanie realized that her father would not accept her remarrying beneath her previous rank and that she preferred to avoid a showdown by presenting him with a *fait accompli* in her absence. Stephanie found great happiness in her second marriage after her miserable and humiliating youthful experience, but in Leopold's eyes she was as reprobate as her elder sister. Stephanie inherited her father's determination but not his wilfulness, of which Louise had plenty. She was by all accounts intelligent and calm and much more attractive looking as a mature woman than as a young girl.

Two years after Stephanie's marriage Marie-Henriette died at Spa. The princess immediately went to her mother's death-bed and was with her when Leopold, who had been on holiday in Luchon with Madame de Vaughan, arrived. When he heard that Stephanie was in her mother's room, he refused to enter. The princess, who had hoped for a reconciliation with her father, was told to leave as he did not wish to see her. The incident became public knowledge and many in Belgium and elsewhere felt that the princess had not merited such treatment. Among those who considered that Leopold had behaved in a heartless way towards his daughter was Edward VII and he let his opinion be known. Leopold was irritated by his cousin's criticism but nevertheless tried to justify himself. 'Princess Stephanie,' the Grand Maréchal told the British minister, 'was now an absolute *déséquilibrée*. She had made a *sot mariage* without consulting her parents or even previously informing them.' And as regards the Spa affair: 'The Princess had never been told either to leave the Palace nor her mother's remains. The king simply could not "*se laisser forcer la main*" at such a melancholy conjuncture.'[5] In his reply to the British minister, Edward's secretary wrote tersely: 'The King thinks that whatever faults and imprudences she may have committed, she was treated with much harshness by her Father, and as the affair became a public one, H.M. has felt himself at liberty to express an opinion on it, like everyone else.'[6]

After Marie-Henriette's death the two elder princesses claimed part of their mother's fortune on the grounds that Leopold and Marie-Henriette had been married under the regime of *communauté de biens*. They lost their court case but even though Leopold won, the public squabbling between king and daughters was seen in Belgium as yet another unfavourable reflection on Leopold. It need hardly be said that the case deepened the schism between him and Louise and Stephanie.

Clementine, the youngest daughter, whose birth had been such a disappointment to Leopold, was the only one with whom the king remained on amicable terms. This she achieved by subjugating her own wishes to those of her father. Even before Marie-Henriette's death in 1902, but more so after it, she took the queen's place at public functions. In 1904 she told her father that she wanted to marry Prince Victor-Napoleon, the Bonapartist pretender who lived in exile in Brussels. Her father forbade the marriage on the straightforward political grounds that he could not afford to annoy his powerful neighbour, the French republic. An article, written in a distinctly Leopoldian style, appeared in *L'Indépendance Belge* reminding the princess of her duties to the dynasty and her father and, although over thirty by then, Clementine submitted to paternal authority.[7] (A year after Leopold's own death she married Prince Victor-Napoleon.)

Leopold was by 1900 a frequent visitor to Paris. At first his trips had been motivated by political considerations or business, but as he grew older Leopold came to enjoy worldly pleasures in a way unimaginable in the ascetic Duke of Brabant or the serious young king. He ate in smart restaurants, went to the Folies Bergère and took pleasure in wandering freely in the streets where he bought the many newspapers and magazines attacking him. There was a well-known Frenchman who bore a striking resemblance to Leopold and the king would jovially say, 'They're getting at Valère-Mabille again. How like me he is.'[8] It was on one such visit that he met Blanche Delacroix.

Over the years Leopold had had various passing affairs with women and it was claimed in the popular press that his mistress was a dancer at the *Théâtre de la Monnaie*, Cléo de Mérode. *Le Roi Cléopold* was a target for cartoonists and satirical journalists for some time. The story seems to have been contrived by Cléo de Mérode herself, for whom it provided good publicity.[9] However, whether justified or not, the King of the Belgians had by the turn of the century acquired an international reputation for concupiscence – a reputation that ironically Queen Victoria, but not her eldest son, was prepared to overlook. Sir Frederick Ponsonby notes in his memoirs that when Leopold had dinner with his cousin in about 1898, 'He seemed very nervous and frightened of her and sat twisting his hands like a schoolboy. It was curious that she should like him, because his morals were notorious, but the Queen seemed to over-look this.'[10]

The origins of Blanche Delacroix are far from clear. She was born in Bucharest of French parents either Blanche or Caroline, maybe both, and her surname was either Delacroix or Lacroix. She was about sixteen in 1900. Baroness de Vaughan has produced two volumes of 'autobio-graphy', *Quelques Souvenirs de ma Vie* (in which she acknowledges the help of a journalist) and *Presque Reine*. Both books, which are very repeti-tive, are so riddled with easily verifiable inaccuracies that the rather charming anecdotes recounted about her life with Leopold unfortunately lose credibility. What cannot be denied, however, is that the ageing monarch came to love the young girl and what probably started out as a casual sexual encounter developed into a very affectionate relationship. Madame de Vaughan was not a ravishing beauty. She was tall, large breasted even by the standards of the time and, according to those who knew her, pretty in a rather common way. She was outspoken to the point of vulgarity and was known to shout at Leopold from time to time. The imperious, authoritarian king, who would not stand for the slightest disagreement from his ministers, accepted these rebuffs. If he was cross with her she simply lit a large cigar and concentrated on puffing it.[11]

The young woman's head was understandably turned by the attentions of a king: she enjoyed being able to buy expensive dresses and being recognized in good hotels but she did not exploit Leopold as she might have done. He appreciated her youthful physical attractions but also her warmth of character, lack of guile and solicitude for his personal welfare and well-being. She awoke in Leopold the ability to feel and to reciprocate affection which had been dormant most of his life. Clear testimony of the Baroness de Vaughan's feeling for Leopold was her behaviour when he was known to be dying. The ministers and family were closing in and Madame de Vaughan must have known that as soon as Leopold was dead they would be only too pleased to throw her out. But she left her château in France when she learnt that the King was very ill and stayed by his side, giving what comfort she could. She was by then in possession of about 6,000,000 francs worth of financial assets so there was nothing material for her to gain by remaining with the moribund old man. She did not leave him until he was dead.

At first Leopold had tried to keep his mistress out of the public eye but after Marie-Henriette's death he gave up, although he kept her away from his official entourage, and his private secretary, with whom he worked most days, did not meet Madame de Vaughan until after Leo-pold's death.[12] When the king was in Belgium the baroness lived in the Villa van der Borght, close to the château of Laeken, and a footbridge was built connecting the villa with the château grounds. Each year, though, they spent several months on the French Riviera.

In the mid-1890s Leopold had visited the Riviera in his yacht and had found it so agreeable and the climate so beneficial to his health that he bought some land, the Passable Garden, on Cap Ferrat, giving on to the bay of Villefranche where he later built a small jetty and mooring facilities. He did not intend to build there, he told Queen Victoria, who like him had discovered the attractions of the south of France.[13] He enjoyed living on his yacht, 'my very modest camp' as he called it, for although the *Alberta* herself was luxurious, the king's quarters were simple.[14] When Baron van der Elst visited Leopold for a few days in 1907 he and the king worked together in Leopold's cabin. At lunch and dinner time their papers had to be cleared away for the same table to be laid for a meal. The food, wine and water were placed on it and they served themselves.[15]

The king still rose at five in the summer and six in the winter and worked most of the day. He had, however, acquired a taste for the tricycle, '*mon animal*' as he called it, and for a time enjoyed the exercise and sightseeing that cycling provided. As the years passed and his left leg caused him increasing trouble, he turned to the motor car and became a great automobile enthusiast. When in Paris he liked to visit the *Salon de l'Automobile* and possessed several high-powered Mercedes. There was a luxurious style of motor car interior at the time called King of the Belgians.[16] Leopold loved being driven fast and complaints were received in Belgium about the dangerous speed at which the king's vehicles were driven.

On his outings on his tricycle and in his cars Leopld came to know Cap Ferrat well and bought up virtually all that was for sale there. In 1900 he acquired the Villa Pollonais (in the name of his doctor), a large house above the Passable Garden. He planted cedar trees and renamed it the Villa des Cèdres.[17] It is certainly one of the most beautiful in a region well endowed with elegant houses. He later bought the Col de Caire at Beaulieu, now known as La Leopolda, a long, Italian-style stuccoed house, next door to Lord Salisbury's villa, though there does not seem to have been any political intent in the king's choice. Another neighbour was Joseph Chamberlain with whom Leopold liked to discuss colonial matters. The road on which these houses are found is now the avenue Léopold II and there are two monuments to Leopold on Cap Ferrat. The king bought several other properties and after a while he could not resist the temptation to build on the Passable Garden. In addition, as Leopold felt that the climate of the south of France was so salubrious, he built three villas there for retired EIC officers and those whose health had been damaged in the Congo.

In 1905 Blanche became pregnant and a child was born in February 1906 at the Villa des Cèdres. It was a boy and he was named Lucien after Doctor Lucien Thiriar, nephew of Leopold's physician who assisted at the birth, and registered in the name Delacroix. A year later she was again pregnant and in late 1907 a second son, Philippe, was born. To begin with Madame de Vaughan lived with her children in the Villa des Cèdres. A little later they were installed in the château of Lormoy in nothern France, conveniently placed for the king to visit them from Belgium, which Leopold rented. He later bought the château of Balincourt, closer to Paris for the children and their mother. The king, who was now over seventy, visited them as often as possible and seems to have derived great pleasure from his two young sons. (Philippe died at the age of ten and the fate of Lucien is unknown.)

In the Congo reform campaign Morel and others claimed that Leopold spent vast sums of money maintaining his mistress, and in Belgium it was said that the king went to the French Riviera to be with her. Both charges were untrue. The cost of some dresses from Vionnet was infinitesimal compared with the sums Leopold was spending on buildings in Belgium, and he had developed the habit of wintering in the south of France, not unreasonable for a man of his age, several years before he met Blanche Delacroix. To some his private life was more shocking and reprehensible than what was going on in the Congo and he was constantly and violently attacked in the press in Belgium, and in other countries, for maintaining a mistress and producing illegitimate children.

By means of the *Donation Royale* Leopold had effectively handed over to the Belgian government those properties he had inherited. But by 1900 his ambitions to embellish Belgium extended beyond the alterations and extensions he had made to royal residences and parks. By means of the revenues from the *Domaine de la Couronne* he bought much land in Brussels and elsewhere with the express intention of redeveloping it, and he financed the building of impressive national monuments.

Leopold had been greatly disappointed that the *Cinquantenaire* project had been left in abeyance for years, and as soon as he had enough money himself he paid for the replacement of the temporary exhibition halls and joined them up with a triumphal arch. However, the king did not want it to be known that he was providing the money and he called together some well-known figures and asked them to lend their names, without any financial contribution, as donors. The architect in charge of the project was by now dead and a French architect, Charles Girault, whose Petit Palais built for the 1900 Paris Exhibition had impressed Leopold, took charge. Without financial problems (the project cost 7,500,000 francs) and with the deadline of the seventy-fifth anniversary celebrations in 1905 as an incentive, the work was completed on time. Leopold was to inaugurate the monument at eleven in the morning of 27 September 1905. He went alone at dawn to examine at leisure his beloved project before returning later for the opening ceremony and to thank the generous contributors.

Before taking over personal control of the *Cinquantenaire* project, Leopold had embarked on a larger building programme at Tervuren. The château built at the end of the avenue de Tervuren for the Congolese section of the 1898 exhibition was soon found to be too small to house the rapidly-increasing collection, and the king decided that he wanted to build a new Congo museum at Tervuren. He asked Girault to produce a design similar to that of the Petit Palais but for a larger and more substantial building. Work began in 1904 and the main works, costing 8,700,000 francs, were finished in 1906. Set in a magnificent park, the museum is of good proportions and a more pleasing construction than the Petit Palais. It is perhaps the most aesthetically successful of Leopold's monuments.

The Congo museum, however, represented only part of Leopold's plans for Tervuren and after considering various ideas he decided to build a World School of Colonialism which, unique in the world, would provide a wide range of training for colonial administrators and the specialist skills needed for tropical medicine, engineering and trade development. Leopold laid the foundation stone of the World School of Colonialism in 1905. He had prepared a speech but was given so warm a reception that he was too moved to read it out.[18] He was not as immune to the opinion of others as he would have people believe.

The *Fondation de la Couronne* was again to be the source of finance, and when it was abolished Leopold lost his financial independence. He tried hard to preserve this scheme but the Belgian government was not sympathetic, and Leopold resigned himself to using the 50,000,000 francs indemnity he received on annexation of the Congo to continue the building of the World School of Colonialism. After his death the project was dropped even though work had begun. The builders were compensated to the extent of 7,000,000 francs.

During the early years of the twentieth century, the apogee of his building programme, Leopold also embarked on an extensive programme of works at Laeken and on a new façade for the Palais Royal.[19] His intention at Laeken was not to provide more spacious accommodation for the royal family but to make the château into a Palais des Nations where international conferences could be held. He also planned an underground railway linking Laeken with central Brussels.[20] The king followed the works closely; the story is told that on one occasion his nephew Albert accompanied him (Albert had been told that it would be tactful to show some interest in his uncle's projects). The prince made an effort to be impressed by the works being undertaken: 'But, Uncle, it will be a little Versailles!' he exclaimed. The king pulled himself up to his full height and snarled at the young man. 'Little?'[21] Albert was not on the same wavelength as the old king and Leopold knew it. Girault wanted to install a sumptuous Louis XIV style king's bedroom at Laeken, suitable for holding royal levées. Leopold vetoed it. 'It would never be executed. I'm almost at the end of my life and my successor sleeps in the same bedroom as his wife.'[22]

Works at Laeken did not advance as planned. Costs soared to about 12,500,000 francs from the 5,000,000 planned. The new wings were far from finished when the battle over the *Fondation de la Couronne* took place and Leopold laid great emphasis on the need to complete them. As previously mentioned, parliament reluctantly granted 15,000,000 francs to cover works which were already fairly well advanced.

In general Leopold's taste in architecture was for French classical – though Brussels was at this time the centre of Art Nouveau – and the exceptions to it are more a reflection of his political interests than a widening of his aesthetic sensibilities. He had been greatly impressed by a Japanese tower exhibited at the 1900 Paris Exhibition. He haggled over the price and then finally bought it.[23] The 130-foot-high wooden construction was dismantled, brought to Belgium (at a total cost of more than a million francs) and rebuilt on the edge of the royal park at Laeken, where for some years it was open to the public. It is now in an advanced state of disrepair.

The turn of the century was the high point of Leopold's 'Far Eastern period' and the Japanese Tower gave him the idea of building a Chinese pagoda at Laeken to go with it. With his business mind, he decided that the pagoda should be a restaurant. While still unfinished it was another casualty of annexation, and when the Belgian government took it over they could not find a restaurateur prepared to run it. It has since become, appropriately enough, a museum of Oriental art.

Not all Leopold's schemes for embellishing royal residences and their surroundings were so exotic. He considered that the Royal Chalet at Ostend and the area between it and the race course needed redeveloping in the interests of attracting tourism for, as he said, 'Seaside resorts in France and England have naturally beautiful sites, with cliffs, interesting landscapes and trees in abundance. Ostend does not possess such natural assets; it must make them.'[24] But although the land needed for the redevelopment plan had been acquired by 1907, by then the *Fondation de la Couronne* was under attack. Leopold asked Schollaert for 45,000,000 francs for Ostend. The chief minister was evasive; after the king's death the scheme was forgotten by the government.

Some schemes dear to the king's heart were not realized until after his death, others not at all. In the centre of Brussels the Montagne de la Cour, a steep slope covered with small streets and houses, between the Place Royale and the Grand' Place, was to be redeveloped with museums, a national library, a building for archives situated among terraced gardens – a Mont des Arts. Various designs were advanced. Houses were demolished and Leopold aimed to have new buildings ready for the World Exhibition to be held in 1910. But during the debate on annexation strong feeling against the king's 'sumptuous' building scheme had been provoked and it was claimed that the planned Mont des Arts would be out of proportion to the scale of buildings in the area. A temporary garden – which remained for forty years – was made to cover the rubble-littered area. The king also favoured the construction of a central station close to the Montagne de la Cour to link the North and South stations. This and the Mont des Arts were realized in the 1950s.

The mental energy and imagination that Leopold poured into his building and urban development projects is breathtaking. But what is more, he was physically active in implementing them. He not infrequently visited work sites at 6 am. In that way he avoided public notice and the knowledge that he might pass by kept those involved on their toes. During the demolition of the Montagne de la Cour, he had a special box erected, suspended from an adjacent building, from which he could get a good overall view. One of his equerries describes his obvious pleasure on entering Girault's office and discussing detailed plans; he listed what he intended doing on 23 August 1908 (at the age of seventy-three):

> Please ask the Minister of Public Works to be at the Palace at 9 a.m. I would like to go with him to the St. Gilles Park and to be there by 9.30 a.m. Then to the Cinquantenaire at 11.30. Then lunch at the Palace about 12.30, then to Laeken at 2 p.m. A stop at the canal on the Allée Verte on the way. At 3 Avenue van Praet and the Japanese Tower. At 4 Route de Meysse and Route du Heysel. The Minister could perhaps have someone there to talk to but without attracting attention. At 5 it would be a good idea to take a quick look at the works in the Church at Laeken. Please ask the Minister of Finance to come and see me at the Palace at 8.30.[25]

The Congo, China, urbanism. These three headings would seem more than enough to occupy a man nearly seventy. But Leopold was also involved in military politics. After thirty years of uninterrupted peace the danger of war was not one that weighed heavily on the minds of many in Belgium. The king's reiteration, whenever he had the chance to make a public speech, of the need for personal service, fell upon deaf ears.

Anglo-German relations were bad in 1903 and Leopold decided to take advantage of the anglophobia in Germany to re-establish more cordial relations between Belgium and Germany. But the kaiser was in no mood for discussions. He praised the greatness of the Dukes of Burgundy, Leopold's medieval predecessors, as rulers of the Low Countries. With effort Belgium could acquire French Flanders, Artois and the French Ardennes.[26] Leopold's eyes almost popped out of their sockets, according to William. Then he laughed nervously and said feebly that neither his ministers nor parliament would ever consider such ambitions. 'I then lost patience,' said the kaiser. 'I told him that I could have absolutely no respect for a monarch who held himself responsible in front of deputies and ministers and not in front of God. I also told him that I would not stand for any shilly-shallying. In a European war one had to be with me or against me. As a soldier I am of the school of Frederick the Great and Napoleon . . . If Belgium did not go along with me, I would be obliged to let myself be guided only by strategic considerations'.[27] Leopold looked pale and shocked, the atmosphere was strained and the king, unlike his usual self, hardly uttered a word.

Stunned to have heard from the kaiser himself that Germany would not hesitate to invade Belgium, Leopold's determination to make the Belgians wake up to the dangers of their vulnerable position was redoubled. The following year marked the seventy-fifth anniversary of the founding of Belgium and the king took advantage of his engagements throughout Belgium to try to awaken awareness of the dangers and to press the case for personal service. However, the Moroccan crisis of the same year had more effect in persuading Belgians of the need to improve their state of military preparedness. The kaiser's provocative visit to Tangier, instead of isolating France as intended, cemented the *Entente Cordiale*.

The French had got wind by this stage of the German plan – known to history as the Schlieffen Plan – to invade France from the north via Belgium, and Anglo-French military talks began at the end of 1905. Such an invasion, it was obvious, would entail passing through Belgium and the British offered to include Belgium in their contingency planning. The Belgian government willingly took up the offer, as it had been greatly disturbed by Belgium's increasing alienation from its traditional protector because of the Congo. The Anglo-Belgian military conversations concerned how many troops and where the British would land in Belgium in the event of a German invasion. They fizzled out in 1906 after the Conference of Algeciras when the war scare was over and for technical reasons the plans were soon out-of-date.[28]

From Leopold's point of view the awareness of the danger from Germany that the Moroccan crisis produced was all to the good and the government was prepared to strengthen the Antwerp fortifications in 1906 and several new guns were tried out by the army. A Krupp was chosen.[29] Leopold intended using the *Fondation de la Couronne* to finance the Belgian artillery, as the government was, as usual, penny-pinching, but annexation forestalled him.

By the end of 1908 annexation was out of the way and Leopold no longer had money to spend on public monuments. In 1909 he devoted most of his energies to one subject, defence, in particular to personal service. He felt it his most fundamental duty to make Belgium prepared to defend herself as best she could in the event of a European war. Only knowledge that he was dying persuaded the Belgians to adopt the policy Leopold had advocated for forty years.

For most of his adult life Leopold had enjoyed good health. Certainly he did all he could to maintain himself in good physical condition and in his seventies he made a point of talking to others at great length standing up until they showed signs of discomfort. Satisfied that they were physically inferior, he would then let them go.[30] Leopold was terrified of becoming ill and took great pains to avoid contagious illnesses and colds. He had a waterproof cover made for his beard to prevent catching cold in the rain because of it. If anyone sneezed his reaction was solely of alarm for himself. When his aides-de-camp and equerries felt in need of a break they let it be known that they had a cold. The king did not want to see them until they were well and truly over it.[31]

However, he had to confront increasing problems with his health and about 1905 he put on a great deal of weight. Leopold had been $13\frac{1}{2}$ stone but quickly went up to nearly 16 stone, an excessive weight even for a man over six feet tall.[32] His weight may have contributed to his major complaint, the increasing paralysis of his left leg. He tried to dissimulate his increasing lameness, and when obliged to lean on an equerry's arm in public, pretended that he was in private conversation.[33] His leg and foot were painful and he tried a treatment based on water under pressure in Nice. This failed and he embarked on electrical treatment in Paris which entailed frequent visits to the French capital.

Then suddenly at the beginning of December 1909 Leopold became ill. He was in France at the time and, returning immediately to Belgium, was installed in the Pavillon des Palmiers in Laeken. During the previous year he had preferred to live in this simple house at the far end of the greenhouses to the palace itself, with only a valet to look after him. He was suffering from severe abdominal pains and his physician Doctor Jules Thiriar, told him that he had a blockage in the large intestine that might well necessitate an operation. On learning this the king started working in a hurried, untypical manner, as though he realized that he was mortally ill, and turned over his remaining personal possessions to the *Fondation de Niederfullbach*. Those around him were shocked by the change in his appearance; he was ashen, so different from his normally fresh complexion. He also started falling asleep from time to time during the day, something he had never done before. The king's stomach became very bloated and he could not wear any of his day clothes. He lay in a dressing gown stretched out on chairs.

Madame de Vaughan had arrived from Balincourt on 7 December. She stayed at the Villa van der Borght to begin with but then moved into the Pavillon des Palmiers to be with the king all the time. The British minister believed that she had brought Lucien and Philippe with her.[34] On 12 December the king's condition deteriorated. Drugs had failed to dislodge the blockage and the doctors began to believe that there might be a knot or twist in the intestines.[35] Leopold was told that an operation was inevitable; and he asked for the Last Sacraments to be administered to him so that he might receive them while still in full possession of his faculties.[36]

There have been different opinions advanced as to what Leopold's genuine religious views were. Some claim that he was a non-believer who felt that as king of a Catholic country he ought to conform to the external manifestations of Catholicism. His private secretary held that he was genuinely religious even though he did not adhere to some aspects of Catholic dogma. Whatever Leopold may have thought during his life, in his last days he clearly felt the need for the comfort of religion. His well-known liaison with Madame de Vaughan though did not place him in a position to receive Extreme Unction.

It seems almost certain that sometime during his last few days a religious marriage took place between Leopold and his mistress, though for a marriage to be legal in Belgium a civil ceremony has to take place first, and it is a punishable offence for a priest to perform a religious ceremony before this has taken place. The king's priest, Father Cooreman, let it be known that 'all was in order'.

On 12 December the telegraph services in Brussels were told to maintain a full complement of operators on duty night and day, and at the Ministry of the Interior the details of Leopold I's funeral arrangements were brought out and studied.[37] The press announced that the king was dying and Louise and Stephanie came to Brussels in the futile hope of a reconciliation. Baron Auguste Goffinet, who was in charge of Leopold's personal affairs, was seen to remove wads of papers from the king's desk and packages were seen leaving the Villa van der Borght addressed to Balincourt.[38]

Clementine, Albert and his wife Princess Elisabeth, came to see the king, followed by Schollaert, who had a long conversation with his sovereign. For Leopold knew that he was dying but was determined to survive a little longer as the Senate was at that time debating an Army Bill which, if passed, would institute personal service (it had already gone through the Chamber). 'I can hold on for two days,' Leopold told him. 'I want to live just long enough to sign it.'[39] There was certainly greater support in parliament for personal service than before, but when on 14 December the Senate passed the bill and sent it to Laeken for the king's signature it was more as a last gesture of reconciliation with the king with whom they had such acrimonious battles than as an act of political volition. Leopold had been operated on that morning and was coming round from the anaesthetic when the bill arrived. With effort, but with a firm hand, he added his signature.

Leopold held on for another two days, then in the early hours of 17 December, the anniversary of his accession to the throne, he woke up gasping for breath. He died a few minutes later of an embolism. Madame de Vaughan in tears had to be forcibly led away. The king's testamentary instructions, written a month before, were then read out. 'I wish to be buried in the early morning, and without pomp. Apart from my nephew Albert and those closest to me, I forbid anyone to follow my cortège. Let God watch over Belgium and be merciful to my soul.'[40]

It was immediately decided to override the king's last wishes, on the grounds that such a burial might be interpreted as an insult to the late king by his successor and government. His body was transported to the Palais Royal in Brussels where it lay in state for two days and he was then given a state funeral. His power was indeed transient.

Notes

Abbreviations

AA	Archives Africaines
AGR	Archives Générales du Royaume, Brussels
AMAE	Archives due Ministère des Affaires Etrangères, Brussels
APR	Archives du Palais Royal, Brussels
ARSC	Académie Royale des Sciences Coloniales, Brussels
ARSOM	Académie Royale des Sciences d'Outre-Mer, Brussels
IRCB	Institut Royal Colonial Belge, Brussels
LSE	London School of Economics and Political Science
MD	Musée de la Dynastie, Brussels
MRA	Musée Royal de l'Armée et d'Histoire Militaire, Brussels
PRO	Public Record Office, London
RA	Royal Archives, Windsor
SOAS	School of Oriental and African Studies, London University

Note on Currencies

Evening out fluctuations in the price index, over the period 1865–1909 one franc was worth roughly seventy-five Belgian francs today. The French and the Belgian franc were fixed to the same gold parity. One pound sterling was equal to about twenty-five francs.

NOTES

Chapter 1

1 Dumont G.H., *Leopold II, Pensées et Réflexions* (Brussels, 1948), pp. 17–18.
2 Vandenbosch A., *Dutch Foreign Policy since 1815* (The Hague, 1959), p. 54.
3 De la Force, Duc, *Curiosités Historiques, Confidences des Princesses* (Paris, 1923), p. 244.
4 De Mérode-Westerloo, Comte, *Souvenirs* (Brussels, 1864), 2 vols, vol. II, p. 276.
5 *Letters of Queen Victoria* ed. Buckle G. (London, 1907), 1st series, vol. I, pp. 44–5.
6 De la Force, op. cit., p. 246.
7 Gaskell, Mrs, *Life of Charlotte Brontë* (Edinburgh, 1924), p. 241.
8 De la Force, op. cit., p. 246.
9 D'Ursel, Comte H., *La Cour de Belgique et la Cour de France de 1832 à 1852* (Paris, 1933), p. 299.

10 Ibid., p. 18.
11 *Lettres de Léopold I*, ed. Bronne C. (Brussels, 1943), p. 126.
12 D'Ursel, op. cit., p. 29.
13 RA Y62/12, Leopold I to Princess Victoria, 16 November 1835.
14 D'Ursel, op. cit., p. 289.
15 Bronne, op. cit., p. 146.
16 RA Y63/58, Leopold I to Queen Victoria, 29 July 1837.
17 RA Y65/21, Leopold I to Queen Victoria, 28 December 1838.
18 RA Y71/60, Leopold I to Queen Victoria, 25 April 1845; Y65/58, Leopold I to Queen Victoria, 12 July 1839.
19 RA Y90/27, Leopold I to Queen Victoria, 26 July 1841; Y65/58, Leopold I to Queen Victoria, 12 July 1839; Y68/5, Leopold I to Queen Victoria, 27 July 1841.
20 RA Y65/33, Leopold I to Queen Victoria, 15 February 1839.

21 Eg Wilson H.L., *Diplomatic Episodes in Mexico, Belgium and Chile* (London, 1927), p. 125.

22 RA Y63/8, Leopold I to Princess Victoria, 1 November 1836.

23 RA Y64/34, Leopold I to Queen Victoria, 27 March 1838.

24 De Ridder A., 'L'Education des Princes', *L'Eventail-Noël*, 1930.

25 Ibid.

26 RA Y90/27 Leopold I to Queen Victoria, 26 July 1841.

27 RA Y72/14, Leopold I to Queen Victoria, 24 October 1845.

28 Freddy G., *Léopold II Intime* (Paris, 1905), p. 27.

29 D'Ursel, op. cit., p. 290.

30 Published in Richardson J., *My Dearest Uncle* (London, 1961), p. 181.

31 D'Ursel, op. cit., p. 292.

32 'Pièces Rélatives à la Mort de la Reine Louise'. A collection of documents. Bibliothèque Royale, Brussels.

33 Ibid.

34 Laroche L., *Louise d'Orléans* (Paris, 1902), p. 153.

35 Ibid.

Chapter 2

1 Vandewoude E., 'Brieven van de Hertog van Brabant aan Conway in Verband met Egypte (1855)', *ARSOM*, 1964.

2 *Letters of Queen Victoria*, op. cit., 1st series, vol. II, pp. 330–1.

3 Catalogue of the *Exposition Léopold I et son Règne* (Brussels, 1965). Correspondence in the possession of HM King Leopold III.

4 Duchesne A., 'Les Leçons de l'Expérience de son Père, ont-elles entraîné Léopold II dans la voie de la Colonisation?' in *La Conférence de Géographie de 1876* (Brussels, 1976), p. 269.

5 *Letters of Queen Victoria*, op. cit., 1st series, vol. II, p. 406.

6 Ibid., p. 457.

7 *Lettres du Comte et de la Comtesse de Ficquelmont à la Comtesse Tiesenhausen* (Paris, 1911), p. 417.

8 Ibid., p. 419.

9 APR Fonds Comte de Flandre no. 6, Duke of Brabant to Count of Flanders and Princess Charlotte, 15 May 1853.

10 Dino, Duchesse de, *Chronique de 1831 à 1862* (Paris, 1909), 4 vols, vol IV, p. 112.

11 RA Z194/18 Queen Victoria to Leopold I, 28 May 1853.

12 RA Y78/56 Leopold I to Queen Victoria, 30 May 1853.

13 RA Y78/71 Leopold I to Queen Victoria, 19 August 1853.

14 RA Y78/59 Leopold I to Queen Victoria, 3 June 1853; and RA 78/5 Leopold I to Queen Victoria, 17 June 1853.

15 'Cérémonies et fêtes du Mariage du S.A.R. Mgr. le Duc de Brabant et de S.A.R. Madame Marie-Henriette-Anne, Archiduchesse d'Autriche' in the Bibliothèque Royale, Brussels.

16 RA Y79/5 Queen Victoria to Leopold I, 15 November 1853.

17 RA Y79/6 Leopold I to Queen Victoria, 18 November 1853.

18 RA Y79/9 Queen Victoria to Leopold I, 29 November 1853.

19 RA Y79/11 Queen Victoria to Leopold I, 6 December 1853.

20 RA Y79/18 Queen Victoria to Leopold I, 26 December 1853.

21 RA Y79/11 Queen Victoria to Leopold I, 6 December 1853.

22 RA Y43/1 Princess Feodora to Queen Victoria, 9 November 1861.

23 Reinach Foussemagne, Countess de, *Charlotte de Belgique* (Brussels, 1925), p. 41.

24 Vandewoude E., op. cit.

25 Ibid.

26 Jacobs E.A., 'Le Premier Voyage du Futur Léopold II en Orient', *ARSOM*, 1965.

27 Ibid.

28 Vandewoude, op. cit.

29 Ibid.

30 Ibid.

31 Ibid.

32 Ibid.

33 Hübner, Count, *Neuf Ans de Souvenirs d'un Ambassadeur d'Autriche à Paris* (Paris, 1902), 2 vols., vol. II, p. 346.

34 Ibid., p. 348.

35 Beyens, Baron E., *Le Second Empire vu par un Diplomate Belge* (Bruges, 1924), 2 vols, vol. I, p. 153.

36 The question of the *vol de l'aigle* continued – Napoleon III offered 200,000 francs a year which was not accepted.

37 Harry G., 'L'Impératrice Charlotte', *L'Eventail*, January 1927.
38 Stengers J., 'Léopold II et le Patrimoine Dynastique', *Académie Royale, Classe des Lettres*, 1971.
39 RA Queen Victoria's Journal Z261/4, 31 July 1857.
40 Decamps, Baron E., 'Le Duc de Brabant au Sénat', *Académie Royale*, 1903, p. 8.
41 Ibid., p. 14.
42 Ibid., p. 30.
43 Vandenpeereboom A., *Mémoires*, published in Garsou J., *Les Débuts d'un Grand Règne* (Brussels, 1931), vol. I, pp. 30–1.

Chapter 3
1 MRA Chazal Papers III/38, Duke of Brabant to Chazal, 2 January 1861.
2 Baudhuin F., 'Les Emigrations autrefois et aujourd'hui', *Revue Générale Belge*, 1956.
3 *L'expansion belge sous Léopold I* (Brussels, 1965), a collection of essays; and Leconte J.R., *Les Tentatives d'Expansion Coloniale sous Règne de Léopold I* (Antwerp, 1946).
4 Gooch B., 'Leopold I's relations with the USA up till 1846', *ARSOM*, 1964.
5 Gooch B., 'Belgian interest in Danish possessions under Leopold I', *ARSOM*, 1964.
6 Duchesne A., 'Léopold I et Santo Tomas de Guatémala', *ARSOM*, 1964, and Van Grieken., 'Un temoignage sur l'histoire de la Compagnie Belge de Colonisation', ibid., 1965.
7 Duchesne A., 'La Politique Coloniale de Léopold I', *Revue Générale Belge*, 1954.
8 MRA Chazal Papers III/17, Duke of Brabant to Chazal, 3 November 1859.
9 RA M15/79, Duke of Brabant to Queen Victoria, 20 September 1857.
RA Y164/47, Duke of Brabant to Queen Victoria, 14 October 1857.
10 Garsou J., 'Léopold I, le Duc de Brabant et la Chine 1859–60', *Archives Diplomatiques et Consulaires*, 1937.
11 Garsou, op. cit.
12 Ibid.
13 MRA Chazal Papers III/13, Duke of Brabant to Chazal, 4 October 1859.
14 MRA Chazal Papers III/18, Duke of Brabant to Chazal, 26 December 1859.

15 Ibid.
16 Stinglhamber G. and Dresse P., *Léopold II au Travail* (Brussels, 1945), p. 65.
17 Ibid., p. 66.
18 Vandewoude E., 'L'échec de la tentative de colonisation belge aux Nouvelles Hébridies, 1861', *ARSOM*, 1965.
19 Ibid.
20 Ibid.
21 AMAE Lambermont Papers Series, *Papiers laissés par le Baron Lambermont*, vol. V, no. 8, Duke of Brabant to Lambermont, 11 June 1861.
22 Daye, op. cit., p. 83.
23 Crokaert P., *Brialmont, Éloge et Mémoires* (Brussels, 1925), p. 132.
24 Ibid., p. 138.
25 Ibid., p. 131.
26 Ibid., p. 135.
27 AMAE Lambermont Papers, Carolus to Lambermont, 6 May 1863.
28 AMAE Copies of Austrian Archives, Hügel to Rechberg, 5 December 1863.
29 Infra, Chapter VI.
30 RA Y81/61, Leopold I to Queen Victoria, 27 May 1858.
31 RA Y82/47, Leopold I to Queen Victoria, 20 April 1860.
32 AGR Frère-Orban Papers, no. 356, Duke of Brabant to Frère-Orban, 27 September 1860. The paperweight can be seen at the Musée de l'Afrique Centrale, Tervuren.
33 RA Y85/23, Leopold I to Queen Victoria, 29 May 1863.
34 RA Y85/25, Leopold I to Queen Victoria, 8 June 1864.
35 RA Y86/27, Leopold I to Queen Victoria, 26 April 1864.
RA Y86/65, Leopold I to Queen Victoria, 19 September 1864.
36 Bronne, op. cit., p. 299.
37 *Letters of Queen Victoria*, op. cit., 2nd series, vol. I, p. 286.
38 Beyens, op. cit., vol. I, p. 387.
39 RA Q1/148, Leopold II to Queen Victoria, 19 December 1865.

Chapter 4
1 Beyens, Baron, *Le Second Empire vu par un Diplomate Belge* (Bruges, 1924), 2 vols, vol. I, p. 86.
2 *Annales Parlementaires Sénat, Chambre*, 17 December 1865.

3 Fulford R., *Your Dear Letter* (London, 1971), p. 50.
4 Vandenpeereboom, op. cit., vol. I, p. 22.
5 Daye, op. cit., p. 95.
6 Vandenpeereboom, op. cit., p. 23.
7 Ibid., p. 24.
8 Ibid., pp. 29–30.
9 Quoted in many works, eg Palmer A., *Bismarck* (London, 1976), p. 77.
10 *Origines Diplomatiques de la Guerre de 1870–1871* (Paris, 1910–32), 19 vols, vol. VII. Lefebvre de Behaine to Drouyn de Lhuys, 27 September 1865.
11 *Origines Diplomatiques*, op. cit., vol. IX. Benedetti to Drouyn de Lhuys, dépêche 3159, 26 July 1866.
12 Oncken H., *Die Rheinpolitik Kaiser Napoleons III von 1863 bis 1870* (Stuttgart, 1926), 3 vols, vol. II, pp. 87–8.
13 De Lannoy F., 'La Neutralité Belge et la Guerre de 1870', *Revue Catholique des Idées et des faits*, 1925.
14 RA Q1/169, Leopold II to Queen Victoria, 10 September 1866.
15 Ibid.
16 Published in *The Times*, 25 July 1870.
17 Letter of Devaux, quoted in Garsou, op. cit., vol. I, pp. 83–4.
18 Ibid.
19 Corti E., *Maximilian and Charlotte of Mexico* (London, 1928), 2 vols, vol. II, pp. 666–7.
20 Ibid., p. 667.
21 Hyde M., *The Mexican Adventure* (London, 1945), p. 211.
22 Reinach Foussemagne, op. cit., p. 295.
23 Corti, op. cit., pp. 685.
24 Hyde, op. cit., p. 226.
25 Haslip J., *The Crown of Mexico* (London, 1971), p. 421.
26 Reinach Foussemagne, op. cit., pp. 88–9.
27 Fulford, op. cit., p. 51.
28 Ibid., p. 230.
29 RA Q2/14, Leopold II to Queen Victoria, 12 March 1867.
30 RA Q2/18, Leopold II to Queen Victoria, 12 April 1867.
31 Lichtervelde L. de, *Léopold II* (Brussels, 1926), p. 64.
32 AGR Rogier Papers, no. 468, document 3, n.d. (April 1867?).
33 RA I71/232, Leopold II to Queen Victoria, 3 May 1867.
34 AGR van de Weyer Papers, no. 44, Grey to van de Weyer, 6 May 1867.
35 Ibid., no. 40.
36 AGR Rogier Papers, no. 468, document 9, de Jonghe to Rogier, 17 April 1867.
37 Van der Smissen E., *Léopold II et Beernaert, d'après leur correspondance inédite de 1884 à 1894* (Brussels, 1920), 2 vols, vol. II, p. 231.
38 Craig G., 'Great Britain and the Belgian Railways Dispute', *American Historical Review*, 1945.
39 Ollivier E., *L'Empire Libéral* (Paris, 1895–1912), 17 vols, vol. XI, p. 375.

Chapter 5
1 Gooch B., *Napoleon III, Man of Destiny* (New York, 1966), p. 104.
2 Bonnin G., *Bismarck and the Hohenzollern Candidate* (London, 1957), pp. 68–9.
3 Van Vracem P., 'La Neutralité Belge pendant la Guerre Franco-Allemande de 1870'. Unpublished thesis Louvain University 1952.
4 Vandewoude E., 'Leopold II en de Graaf van Vlaanderen tegen over de oorlog van 1870', *Revue Belge d'Histoire Militaire*, 1969.
5 Corley T.A.B., *Democratic Despot* (London, 1961), p. 330.
6 Ibid., p. 331.
7 RA Add A17/365, Prince of Wales to Princess Louise, 22 May 1870.
8 Demoulin R., 'Documents Inédits sur la Crise de 1870', *Académie Royale, Commission Royale d'Histoire*, 1957.
9 Vandewoude E., 'Plannen tot reorganisatie van de Belgische Artillerie 1866–71', *Revue Belge d'Histoire Militaire*, 1968.
10 MRA *Fonds Mobilisation de 1870*, File XXVII, Report of Minister of War.
11 Ibid.
12 Ibid.
13 Ibid., Files III and XXVII.
14 Ibid.
15 Demoulin, op. cit.
16 MRA *Fonds Mobilisation de 1870*, File XXVII.
17 Ibid.
18 Ibid., File CXXVIII.
19 Ibid., File CXXX.
20 MRA Chazal Papers, Count of Flanders to Chazal, 2 August 1870.

21 Buffin C., 'Napoléon III, Prisonnier de Guerre en Belgique', *Le Flambeau*, 1924, and Wilmet L., 'Napoléon III en Belgique', *Carnet de la Fourragère*, 1930.
22 Demoulin, op. cit.
23 Buffin, op. cit.
24 Buffin, op. cit.
25 RA Q1/67, Granville to Ponsonby, 27 December 1870.

Chapter 6
1 Van der Elst, Baron, 'Souvenirs sur Léopold II', *Revue Générale*, 1923.
2 RA M54/70, Duke of Brabant to the Prince Consort, 19 November 1857.
3 RA Queen Victoria's Journal, 5 May 1873.
4 Bronne L., *La Tapisserie Royale* (Brussels, 1959), p. 159.
5 Fulford, op. cit., p. 213.
6 This information was kindly brought to my attention by M.Emile Vandewoude who talked to Count Carton de Wiart.
7 AMAE Lambermont Papers 1851–1875, no. 137, Leopold II to E. de Borchgrave, 1 December 1866.
8 Vandewoude E., 'Een plan van Leopold II tot industriële prospectie van China en Japan 1863–73', *ARSOM*, 1967.
9 RA 94/156, Leopold II to Queen Victoria, 8 June 1876.
10 AMAE Lambermont Papers, 'Notes et Mémoires' vol. IV, Document 15, 'Tentatives d'Expansion Belge en Extrème Orient 1840–1890'.
11 AMAE Microfilm of d'Anethan Papers.
12 Greindl L., 'A la Recherche d'un Etat Indépendant: Léopold II et les Philippines 1869–1875', *ARSOM*, 1962.
13 De Trannoy, Baron, 'Léopold II et Jules Malou', *Revue Générale*, 1920.
14 Greindl, op. cit.
15 Ibid.
16 RA Q4/151, Note by General Ponsonby, 23 July 1875, for Queen Victoria based on information from Lord Derby.
17 Stengers J., 'Léopold II entre l'Extrème Orient et l'Afrique (1875–1876)' in *La Conférence de Géographie de 1876* (Brussels, 1976), p. 313.
18 Ibid.
19 RA Q4/150, Derby to Ponsonby, 23 July 1875.

20 PRO FO 10/595, Monson to Rosebery, 28 January 1893.
21 Roeykens A., 'Le Dessein Africain de Léopold II', *ARSC*, 1956.
22 Stengers, op. cit., p. 332.
23 Ibid., p. 341.

Chapter 7
1 Dumont, op. cit., p. 11.
2 Dumont, op. cit., p. 55.
3 Dumont G., *Pensées et Réflexions*, p. 12.
4 Stengers J., *Belgique et Congo: L'Elaboration et la Charte Coloniale* (Brussels, 1963), p. 98.
5 MRA Chazal Papers, Files LXVII and LXVIII.
6 Daye, op. cit., pp. 232–3.
7 Wilson, op. cit., p. 148.
8 Freddy, op. cit., p. 63. Much of what follows is based on Freddy and individual references will not be given.
9 Stinglhamber et Dresse, op. cit., p. 51.
10 Vandervelde E., *Souvenirs d'un Militant Socialiste* (Brussels, 1931), p. 71.
11 RA Add. A17/365, Prince of Wales to Princess Louise, 22 May 1870.
12 Daye, op. cit., p. 103.
13 Stengers J., 'Léopold II et le Patrimoine Dynastique' in *Académie Royale, Classe des Lettres*, 1971.
14 Ibid.
15 Ibid.
16 Louise of Belgium, *My Own Affairs* (London, 1921), p. 59.
17 Ibid., p. 59.
18 Ibid., p. 61.
19 Ibid., p. 69.
20 Haslip J., *The Lonely Empress* (London, 1965), p. 318.
21 Ibid., p. 317.
22 Ibid., p. 339.
23 Ibid., p. 25.

Chapter 8
1 AMAE Lambermont Papers Series, *Papiers laissés par le Baron Lambermont*, vol. V, no. 9, Leopold II to Lambermont, 22 August 1875.
2 McKay D.V., 'Colonialism in the French Geographical Movement 1871–1881', *Geographical Review*, 1933.
Stengers J., 'Textes Inédits d'Emile Banning', *ARSC*, 1955, p. 14.

4 Guillaume Baron, 'Comment le Roi Léopold II est intervenu au Congo', *L'Indépendance Belge*, 2 March 1918.
5 Banning E., in *L'Indépendance Belge*, January 1876.
6 Roeykens A., 'La Génie de Léopold II et la Conférence Géographique de Bruxelles de 1876', *La Conférence de Géographie de 1876* (Brussels, 1976), pp. 377 and 379.
7 Roeykens A., 'Le Dessein Africain de Léopold II', ARSC, 1956, p. 216.
8 RA Y160/33, Leopold II to Queen Victoria, 4 June 1876; and Q4/155, Leopold II to Queen Victoria, 26 May 1876.
9 Vandewoude E., 'De Aardrijksundige Conferentie (1876) Vanuit Het Koninglijk Paleis Gezien', *La Conférence de Géographie de 1876*, pp. 416–17.
10 RA Y160/33 Leopold II to Queen Victoria, 4 June 1876.
11 Vandewoude, op. cit., p. 422.
12 Ibid., p. 433.
13 Ibid., p. 437.
14 Banning E., *La Conférence Géographique de Bruxelles* (Brussels, 1877), pp. 123–4.
15 Roeykens A., 'Les Réunions Préparatoires de la Délégation Belge à la Conférence Géographique de Bruxelles en 1876', *Zaïre*, 1953.
16 Banning, op. cit., pp. 102–5.
17 APR *Fonds Congo* 100/1, Leopold II to Solvyns, 17 November 1877.
18 Shepperson G., *The Exploration of Africa in the 18th and 19th Centuries* (Edinburgh, 1971), p. 142.
19 AMAE Dossier, 'Afrique Centrale Conférence Géographique de Bruxelles 1876–1884', no. 32.
20 Franssens K., 'Nederland na de Aardrijkskundige Conferentie van Brussels (1877–1879', *La Conférence de Géographie de Bruxelles 1876*, p. 503.
21 APR *Fonds Congo* 55/1. According to Père Bontinck this letter was written in 1877. M. Emile Vandewoude considers that the projected visit was in 1883.
22 SOAS Mackinnon Papers, IBEA Co. File 1c.
23 RA Add. A/12, 359, Knollys to Ponsonby, 27 December 1876.
24 RA Y160/37, Leopold II to Queen Victoria, 14 January 1877.

Chapter 9
1 Camoens, *Lusiads*, vol. 2, translated by Sir Richard Burton.
2 Published many times, including Hall R., *Stanley, An Adventurer Explored* (London, 1974), pp. 90–1.
3 Vansina J., 'L'Afrique Centrale vers 1875' in *La Conférence de Géographie de 1876* for full discussion of the subject.
4 Rinchon P.D., *La Traite et l'Esclavage des Congolais par des Européens*, (Brussels, 1929), p. 133.
5 Greindl L., 'Quelques documents sur un projet d'expédition au Mont Cameroun en 1877', ARSC, 1959.
6 Roeykens A., 'Les Débuts de l'Œuvre Africaine de Léopold II', ARSC, 1955, p. 246.
7 Thomson R., *La Fondation de L'Etat Indépendant du Congo* (Brussels, 1933), p. 56.
8 Ibid., p. 55.
9 APR *Fonds Congo* 100/1, Leopold II to Solvyns, 17 November 1877.
10 Hird F., *Stanley, an Authorized Life* (London, 1935), p. 169.
11 Ibid.
12 Roeykens A., 'La Période Initiale de l'Œuvre Africaine de Léopold II 1875–1883', ARSC, 1957, p. 93.
13 Greindl to Sanford, 11 June 1878. Thomson R., 'Léopold II et Le Congo' in *Revue Congo*, 1931.
14 Greindl to Sanford, 18 September 1878. Ibid.
15 Sanford to Greindl n.d. Ibid.
16 Ibid.
17 Guebels L., 'Rapport sur le Dossier J. Greindl', IRCB, 1953, for publication of the statutes of the CEHC. There is disagreement as to whether Hutton and Mackinnon were among the original subscribers.
18 Hird, op. cit., p. 171.
19 APR *Fonds Congo* 10/2, Beaconsfield to Leopold II, 29 October 1878.
20 Hird, op. cit., p. 176.
21 Van Grieken E., 'H.M. Stanley au Congo (1879–1884) d'après le manuscrit de Ch. Notte', IRCB, 1954.
22 Ibid., pp. 2–6.
23 Ceulemans P., 'Les Tentatives de Léopold II pour engager le Colonel Charles Gordon au Service de l'AIA (1880)', *Zaïre*, 1958. Charles Chenevix Trench, in *Charley Gordon* (London,

1978), p. 163, says that Gordon considered that action should be taken in the Congo basin and Egypt.

Chapter 10

1 Hird, op. cit., p. 177.
2 Stanley H.M., *The Congo and the Foundation of the Free State* (London, 1885), vol. I, pp. 59–60.
3 Hird, op. cit., p. 176.
4 Ibid., p. 177, with correction Congo basin for Congo.
5 Ibid., p. 178.
6 Maurice A., *Stanley, Unpublished Letters* (London, 1957), p. 36. See also Stengers J., 'Quelques observations sur la correspondance de Stanley', *Zaïre*, 1955.
7 Stanley, op. cit., p. 154.
8 Maurice, op. cit., p. 34.
9 Ibid., p. 35.
10 Stanley, op. cit., p. 234.
11 Stanley to Strauch, 12 June 1881, published in Maurice, op. cit., p. 52.
12 Ibid.
13 Stanley to Strauch, 23 June 1881. Ibid., pp. 60–9.
14 Stanley, op. cit., p. 292.
15 Ibid., pp. 379–80.
16 Hird, op. cit., pp. 183–4.
17 Maurice, op. cit., pp. 130–7.
18 Hird, op. cit., p. 186.
19 Maurice, op. cit., p. 149.
20 Ibid.
21 Ibid., p. 152.
22 Ibid., p. 155.
23 APR *Fonds Congo* 128/6. Press cuttings of the quarrel.
24 Stanley, op. cit., p. 469.

Chapter 11

1 APR *Fonds Congo* 1/6, note by Leopold II for use by Mackinnon, 3 February 1883.
2 RA P19/128a, Memorandum by Sir Charles Dilke, 3 December 1884.
3 SOAS MP Private Correspondence File 66, Hutton to Mackinnon, 27 February 1883.
4 APR *Fonds Congo* I/25, Leopold II to Prince of Wales, 13 March 1883.
5 Hansard CCLXXVII HC 1284–96, 3 April 1883.
6 APR *Fonds Congo* 2/14, Sandford to Devaux, 27 May 1883.
7 Bontinck F., *Aux Origines de l'Etat Indépendant du Congo. Documents*

tirés d'archives américains (Louvain, 1966), p. 135.
8 Thomson, op. cit., p. 153.
9 Ibid., p. 151.
10 PRO FO 30/29/198, note by Anderson, 20 February 1884.
11 Ibid.
12 Quai d'Orsay, '*Correspondence Politique, Belgique*', 75, 8 March 1883.
13 Stengers J., 'Stanley, Léopold II et l'Angleterre', *Le Flambeau*, 1954.
14 RA P19/114, Leopold II to Queen Victoria, 27 January 1884, for his reply.
15 APR *Fonds Congo*, Dossiers 60 and 140.
16 Ibid., 136/2, Strauch to Ferry, 23 April 1884.
17 Ibid., 2/64, Ferry to Strauch, 24 April 1884.
18 Ibid., 61/3, Leopold II to Granville, 22 May 1884.
19 PRO FO 30/29/128, note by Anderson, 16 May 1884.
20 For relations between Gantier and Leopold II see APR *Fonds Congo* 56/1–102.
21 Thomson, op. cit., p. 175.
22 Bontinck, op. cit., p. 138.
23 Stengers J., 'Léopold II et la Fixation des Frontières du Congo', *Le Flambeau*, 1963.
24 Ibid.
25 Ibid.
26 Van Zuylen, op. cit., p. 96.
27 APR *Fonds Congo* 117/12, Von Bleichröder to Leopold II, 5 August 1884.
28 Stengers, op. cit.
29 Quai d'Orsay, *Correspondance Politique, Allemagne*, 58, 30 August 1884.
30 APR *Fonds Congo* 116/5, Bismarck to Leopold II, 4 September 1884.

Chapter 12

1 Stengers J., 'Leopold II et la Rivalité Franco-Anglaise en Afrique (1882–4)', *Revue Belge de Philologie et d'Histoire*, 1969.
2 Crowe S.E., *The Berlin West African Conference 1884–1885* (London, 1942), p. 29. For the whole of this chapter I am indebted to Miss Crowe's study.
3 Ibid., p. 31.
4 APR *Fonds Congo* 98/37, note by Leopold II, 8 November 1884.
5 PRO FO 84/1815, Lister to Malet, 19 November 1884.

6 *Economiste Français*, 7 December 1884.
7 PRO FO 84/1815, Lister to Malet, 19 November 1884.
8 Ibid., Minute, 20 November 1884.
9 APR *Fonds Congo* 141/5, Leopold II to Lambermont, 24 November 1884.
10 Ibid., Dossier 98.
11 Crowe, op. cit., p. 156.
12 Thomson P., 'Léopold II et le Congo', *Revue Congo*, February 1931.
13 Thomson, op. cit.
14 Ibid.
15 Crowe, op. cit., p. 191.
16 Van der Smissen E., *Léopold II et Beernaert d'après leur correspondance, inédite de 1884 à 1894* (Brussels, 1920), 2 vols, vol. I, p. 127.
17 Ibid., p. 128.
18 Ibid., p. 130.
19 *Annales Chambres*, *1884–1885*, *Chambre*, 28 April 1885.
20 *Mouvement Géographique*, 1910, p. 332.
21 Stengers J., *Léopold II et la Fixation des Frontières du Congo*, op. cit.
22 Ibid.

Chapter 13
1 Daye, op. cit., p. 374.
2 *Correspondance Léopold II, d'Anethan*. Published in Lichtervelde, op. cit., pp. 107–8.
3 Ibid. p. 110.
4 Ibid., p. 126.
5 Woeste C., *Mémoires pour servir de l'Histoire de la Belgique* (Brussels, 1927–37), 3 vols, vol. I, p. 113.
6 Maeterlinck M., *Bulles bleues* (Brussels and Paris, 1948), pp. 11–12.
7 *Histoire de la Belgique Contemporaire 1830–1914* (Brussels, 1929), vol. II, p. 144.
8 Lichtervelde, op. cit., p. 192.
9 De Trannoy, Baron, 'Léopold II et Jules Malou', *Revue Générale*, 1920.
10 Lichtervelde, op. cit., pp. 199–200.
11 Daye, op. cit., pp. 245–6.

Chapter 14
1 Dumont, op. cit., p. 68.
2 Worth 23,000,000 francs per annum in the 1830s and 1,365,000,000 francs in the 1880s. This was offset to some extent by freight payments to foreign carriers for Belgian exports as the country lacked ships. See Van Moeseke P., 'Profit Inflation and the Belgian Industrial Expansion 1830–1914' in *Tijdschrift voor Economie*, 1969.
3 Coal output in Belgium reached 17,000,000 tons in 1880, while France produced 19,300,000 tons: average annual output per blast furnace in Belgium was 12,000 tons and 9,150 tons in Britain. Between 1840 and 1880 imports went up by 819% in value, while exports rocketed by a 2,300% increase. Belgium was clearly highly competitive in world markets. Ibid.
4 For example, in 1890 a steel worker in the Ruhr earned on average 4.76 marks an hour, in Paris 4.64 marks, in London 6.48 marks and in Liège 2.90 marks. Ibid.
5 Pierson M., *Histoire du Socialisme en Belgique* (Brussels, 1955), pp. 80–1. It became the Belgian Socialist party after the Second World War.
6 Chlepner B.S., *Cent Ans D'Histoire Sociale* (Brussels, 1956), pp. 52–3.
7 Van der Smissen, op. cit., vol. I, p. 84.
8 Woeste, op. cit., vol. I, p. 325.
9 Van der Smissen, op. cit., vol. I, p. 84.
10 Lichtervelde, op. cit., pp. 291–2.
11 AGR Banning Papers, no. 88.
12 *Annales Parlementaires, Chambre*, 1 March 1887.
13 Van der Smissen, op. cit., pp. 175–6.
14 Ibid., p. 212.
15 Ibid., p. 213.
16 AGR Banning Papers, no. 91.
17 Lichtervelde, op. cit., pp. 303–4.
18 Van der Smissen, op. cit., vol. II, p. 68.
19 RA Q7/8, Count of Flanders to Queen Victoria, 27 March 1892.
20 Stengers J., *Textes Inédits d'Emile Banning*, op. cit., p. 72.
21 Woeste, op. cit., vol. I, pp. 445–6.
22 Daye, op. cit., p. 388.
23 *Histoire Contemporaire*, vol. II, p. 203.
24 Infra, Chapter XXVI.

Chapter 15
1 Stengers J., 'The Congo Free State and the Belgian Congo before 1914', in Duignan P. and Gann L.H. eds, *Colonialism in Africa*, 5 vols (Cambridge, Mass., 1968–70).
2 APR *Fonds Congo* 206/2, Ferry to de Borchgrave, 5 February 1885.
3 Van der Smissen, op. cit., vol. I, p. 138.

4 APR *Fonds Congo* 206/76, C de Roths-child to Leopold II, 9 January 1886.
5 Stenmans, op. cit., p. 52.
6 Infra, Chapter XVIII.
7 APR *Fonds Congo* 206/127, Telegram Beyens to de Borchgrave, 19 May 1888.
8 Ibid., 106/10, Lambert to Leopold II, 4 May 1887.
9 Van der Smissen, op. cit., p. 304.
10 APR *Fonds Congo* 12/24, Leopold II to Beernaert, 5 May 1889.
11 SOAS Mackinnon Papers, Private Correspondence, File 67, van Eetvelde to Mackinnon, 24 September 1885.
12 AMAE Strauch Papers, no. 510, Leopold II to Strauch, 20 December 1885.
13 Hird, op. cit., p. 209.
14 SOAS Mackinnon Papers, Private Correspondence, File 68, Hutton to Mackinnon, 16 September 1886.
15 Ibid.
16 Cornet R., *La Bataille du Rail* (Brussels, 1953), p. 74.
17 Ibid., p. 143.
18 Stenmans, op. cit., p. 32.
19 Ibid., p. 35.
20 Harry G., *Conversations avec Stanley* (Brussels, 1890).
21 PRO FO 84/2103, Kirk to Wylde, 24 April 1890.
22 RA P20/37, Leopold II to Queen Victoria, 29 June 1890.
23 RA P20/60, Leopold II to Queen Victoria, 19 October 1890.
24 APR *Fonds Congo* 102/29, Leopold II to Stanley, 22 October 1890.
25 Woeste, op. cit., vol. I, p. 473.
26 Ibid.
27 'Textes Inédits d'Emile Banning', ed. Stengers J., op. cit., p. 100.
28 Ibid., p. 101.
29 APR *Fonds Congo* 62/13, Leopold II to Greindl, 13 August 1892.
30 Ibid., 62/21, Greindl to Leopold II, 23 September 1892.
31 Wauters A.J., *Histoire Politique du Congo* (Brussels, 1911), p. 203.

Chapter 16
1 PRO FO 84/1775, Minute by Salisbury, n.d. (c. October 1886).
2 APR *Fonds Congo* 170/1, Stanley to Leopold II, 18 March 1886.
3 *The Times*, 29 October 1886.
4 PRO FO 84/1852, Enclosure, Emin Bey to Mackay, 9 April 1887.

5 *The Times*, 14 January 1887.
6 PRO FO 84/1852, Enclosure, Emin Bey to Mackay, 9 April 1887.
7 SOAS Mackinnon Papers, Private Correspondence, File 68. Memorandum by Hutton, 27 November 1886.
8 Ibid.
9 I am indebted to Iain Smith's *The Emin Pasha Relief Expedition* (Oxford, 1972), for much of this chapter.
10 Hird, op. cit., p. 222.
11 Ibid., pp. 222–3.
12 Ibid., p. 223.
13 SOAS Mackinnon Papers, Emin Pasha Relief Committee, Files 2, 3 and 4.
14 Ceulemans P., *La Question Arabe*, ARSC, 1959, p. 100.
15 Ibid., p. 103.
16 Stanley H.M., *In Darkest Africa* (London, 1890) 2 vols, vol. I, p. 374.
17 Ibid., p. 378.
18 Schnitzer E., *Die Tagebücher* (Berlin, 1917), p. 105.
19 SOAS Mackinnon Papers, Emin Pasha Relief Committee, File 20, Stanley to Mackinnon, 3 September 1888.
20 Stanley, op. cit., p. 392.
21 Hird, op. cit., p. 276.

Chapter 17
1 *Letters of Queen Victoria*, 3rd series, vol. II, p. 420.
2 Grosse Politik, vol. VIII, doc. no. 1678.
3 PRO FO 10/595 no. 21, Monson to Rosebery, 28 January 1897.
4 *Letters of Queen Victoria*, 3rd series, vol. I, p. 609.
5 AGR van Eetvelde Papers, no. 27, van Eetvelde to Leopold II, 29 April 1890.
6 AGR de Borchgrave Papers, no. 22, Leopold II to de Borchgrave, 15 January 1891.
7 PRO FO 10/597, Plunkett to Salisbury, 5 November 1893.
8 Collins R.O., *The Southern Sudan 1883–1893, A Struggle for Control* (New Haven, 1962), p. 96.
9 PRO FO 84/2200, Salisbury to Vivian, no. 24, 19 February 1892.
10 Collins, op. cit., p. 122.
11 Ibid.
12 Sanderson G., *England, Europe and the Upper Nile* (Edinburgh, 1965), p. 97. I owe a great deal to Professor Sanderson's study.

13 Langer E.G., *The Diplomacy of Imperialism* (New York, 1972 ed.), p. 122.
14 APR *Fonds Congo*, Gladstone to Leopold II, 30 September 1892.
15 MD de Cuvelier Papers, no. 3136, Leopold II to de Cuvelier, n.d.
16 PRO FO 10/595, Monson to Rosebery, no. 21, 28 January 1893.
17 PRO FO 10/597, Plunkett to Rosebery, no. 169, 26 November 1893.
18 APR *Fonds Congo* 169/1–5, June–July 1893.
19 Gardiner A.G., *Life of Sir William Harcourt* (London, 1923) 2 vols, vol. II, pp. 315–16.
20 Ibid., p. 313.
21 Sanderson, op. cit., p. 162.
22 He had already protested to Lord Dufferin, the British ambassador to France, on 1 June. Taylor A.J.P., 'Prelude to Fashoda', *EHR*, 1950.
23 Taylor, op. cit.
24 Hornik M.P., 'The Anglo-Belgian Agreement of 12th May 1894', *EHR*, 1942.
25 Ibid.
26 Stengers J., 'Aux Origines de Fachoda', *Revue Belge de Philologie et d'Histoire*, 1958.

Chapter 18
1 *The Poems of Jonathan Swift*, ed. Williams H. (Oxford, 1958), pp. 645–6.
2 Van Zuylen, op. cit., pp. 135–6.
3 AA AE 283 (256), Memorandum by de Grelle Rogier, 6 January 1892.
4 AMAE Strauch Papers, AF I–13 no. 592, 8 May 1886.
5 Supra, Chapter XV.
6 Sanderson, *England, Europe and the Upper Nile 1882–1889* (Edinburgh, 1965), pp. 125–6.
7 Generet J.M., 'La Question de l'Oubangi', unpublished thesis, University of Louvain, 1962, p. 141.
8 AA AE 283 (256) I, Leopold II to Beyens, 1 March 1892.
9 Generet, op. cit.
10 Ibid., p. 172.
11 AA AE 284 (256), note of Leopold II, 31 July 1892.
12 APR *Fonds Congo* 62/13, Leopold II to Greindl, 13 August 1892; and 62/20, Greindl to Leopold II, 13 September 1892.

13 AA (257) AE 289, de Grelle Rogier to Leopold II, 18 May 1893.
14 Infra, Chapter XVII.
15 Ibid.
16 Ibid.
17 Van Zuylen, op. cit., pp. 179–80.
18 RA P20/42, Leopold II to Queen Victoria, 27 July 1890.
19 Ceulemans P., op. cit., p. 167.
20 Ibid., p. 339.
21 Ibid., pp. 310–11.
22 Ibid., pp. 319–20.
23 Ibid., p. 347.
24 Slade R., *King Leopold's Congo* (Oxford, 1962), p. 110.
25 Michaux O., *Carnet de Campagne* (Namur, 1913), p. 178.
26 Slade, op. cit., p. 110.

Chapter 19
1 Verbeken A. and Walraet M., 'La Première traversée du Katanga en 1806', *IRCB*, 1953.
2 Cornet R., *Katanga* (Brussels, 1943), p. 38.
3 Ibid., pp. 38–9.
4 Arnot F., *Garanganze or Seven Years' Pioneer Mission Work in Central Africa* (London, 1889).
5 Van Zuylen, op. cit., p. 202.
6 PRO FO 84/2086, Leopold II to Lord Salisbury, 12 July 1890.
7 Oliver R., *Sir Harry Johnston and the Scramble for Africa* (London, 1959), p. 194.
8 Ibid.
9 Robert M., *Géologie et Géographie du Katanga* (Brussels, 1956), p. 319.
10 Martelli, op. cit., p. 133.
11 Moloney J.A., *With Captain Stairs to Katanga* (London, 1893), p. 194; and Crawford D., *Thinking Black* (London, 1912), p. 307. The accounts vary somewhat.
12 Cornet, op. cit., pp. 207–8.
13 Cornet, op. cit., p. 243.
14 Robert, op. cit., p. 336.
15 Strage M., *Cape to Cairo* (London, 1977), p. 185.
16 Robert, op. cit., p. 337.

Chapter 20
1 *Letters of Queen Victoria*, 3rd series, vol. III, p. 349.
2 Infra, Chapter XXIII.
3 RA P21/107, Salisbury to Bigge, 7 December 1895.

4 *Letters of Queen Victoria*, 3rd series, vol. III, pp. 24–5.
5 Gallagher etc., *Africa and the Victorians*, p. 350.
6 Quoted in various works eg Sanderson, op. cit., p. 245.
7 Quoted in many works eg Langer, op. cit., p. 558.
8 Chatlin L.N., 'Vers le Nil 1890–1906' in *Le Congo Belge* ed. Franck L. (Brussels, 1930) 2 vols, vol. II, pp. 107–14.
9 For full discussion see Ranieri L., 'Les relations entre l'Etat Indépendant du Congo et l'Italie', *ARSC*, 1959.
10 Ranieri, op. cit., p. 90.
11 Ibid., p. 105.
12 Ibid., pp. 104–5.
13 PRO 2/216, Plunkett to Sanderson, 29 May 1899.
14 APR *Fonds Congo* 157/12, Annex de Borchgrave to A. d'Anethan, 2 February 1899; 157/15, A. d'Anethan to de Borchgrave, 8 February 1899.
15 Collins R.O., *King Leopold, England and the Upper Nile* (New Haven and London, 1968), p. 59.
16 PRO FO 78/5024 no. 211, Cromer to Salisbury, 11 December 1899.
17 Collins, op. cit., p. 76.
18 Ibid., p. 133.
19 PRO FO 10/785 no. 57, Lansdowne to Phipps, 17 June 1903.
20 Collins, op. cit., p. 157.
21 LSE Morel Papers, F.4, Dilke to Morel, 13 August 1903.
22 Collins, op. cit., p. 220.
23 Ibid., pp. 228–9.
24 Ibid., p. 230.
25 Ibid., p. 238.
26 Collins R.O., 'The Anglo-Congolese Negotiations 1900–1906', *Zaire*, 1958.
27 For full text see either of Collins's appendices.
28 Collins, *King Leopold, England and the Upper Nile*, p. 270.
29 APR *Fonds Congo* 157/36, Enclosure Hardinge to van Eetvelde, 9 June 1906.
30 Ibid. 157/39, Carton de Wiart to de Favereau, 20 November 1906; 157/40, de Favereau to Carton de Wiart, 20 November 1906.
31 Collins, op. cit., p. 299.
32 Infra, Chapter XXV.
33 PRO FO 371/245 no. 39529, Hardinge to Grey, recd. 2 December 1907.
34 Carton de Wiart, *Souvenirs des Dernières Années* (Brussels, 1944), p. 141.

Chapter 21
1 Dumont, op. cit., p. 19.
2 APR *Fonds Congo* 243, Whetnall to de Borchgrave, 29 May 1885.
3 Ibid., 124/2, Whetnall to Leopold II, 4 March 1887.
4 Ibid., 244/6, Report by Lahure, 2 December 1888.
5 Duchesne A., 'Léopold II et le Maroc', *ARSOM*, 1965, p. 56.
6 Ibid., p. 73.
7 Van der Smissen, op. cit., vol. I, p. 394.
8 Ibid.
9 Duchesne, op. cit., p. 96.
10 Ibid., p. 111.
11 Ibid., p. 122.
12 Ibid., p. 124.
13 Ibid., p. 133.
14 Ibid., p. 142.
15 APR *Fonds Congo* 46/17, Devolder to Leopold II, 29 December 1899.
16 Ibid., 50/5, Empain to Leopold II, 15 January 1904.
17 Ibid., Empain to Carton de Wiart, 11 August 1906.
18 Ibid., 365/1, Leopold II to Verhaeghe de Naeyer, 10 July 1898; and AMAE Lambermont Papers, 1897–1913, no. 36. Note by Leopold II, 12 December 1898.
19 APR *Fonds Congo* 365/2, Verhaeghe de Naeyer to Leopold II, 19 August 1898; and 365/26, de Borchgrave to Verhaeghe de Naeyer, 28 November 1898; and 365/27, Verhaeghe de Naeyer to de Borchgrave, 3 December 1898.
20 Willequet J., *Le Congo Belge et la Weltpolitik* (Brussels, 1962), pp. 37–9.
21 De Selliers de Moranville, Chevalier A., 'Léopold II', *Bulletin de la Fédération des Industries Belges*, 1970.
22 Mackay P., *Pioneers for Profit* (Chicago, 1970), p. 32.
23 Dumoulin M., 'La Présence Belge en Perse', *Revue Belge d'Histoire Contemporaire*, 1977.

Chapter 22
1 Kurgan-van Hentenryk G., *Léopold II et les Groupes Financiers Belges en Chine (1885–1914)*, Académie Royale, Mémoires de la Classe des Lettres (Brussels, 1972), p. 308. Madame

Kurgan's superb study provides the basis for this chapter.

2 Daye, op. cit., p. 419.
3 Ibid., p. 420.
4 Kurgan, op. cit., p. 93.
5 Ibid., p. 97.
6 Ibid., p. 121.
7 Ibid., p. 123.
8 Ibid., p. 127.
9 Ibid., p. 136.
10 Ibid., p. 139.
11 Ibid., p. 277.
12 Ibid., p. 279.
13 Ibid., p. 282.
14 Ibid., p. 262.
15 APR Fonds Congo 253/13, China Exploration Company to Bunge, 25 May 1899.
16 Daye, op. cit., pp. 422–3.
17 Kurgan, op. cit., p. 200.
18 Ibid., pp. 235–6.
19 Ibid., p. 247.
20 Ibid., pp. 255–7.
21 Duchesne A., Un projet d'expédition contre les Boxers (Brussels, 1948), p. 3.
22 MRA 'België-Buitenland', B7 XIX/31.
23 Ibid., B7 XIX/30.
24 Willequet, op. cit., p. 36.
25 Duchesne, op. cit., p. 93.
26 Kurgan, op. cit., p. 381.
27 Ibid., p. 392.
28 Ibid., p. 444.
29 Ibid., p. 459.
30 Ibid., p. 460.
31 Ibid., p. 464.
32 AGR van Eetvelde Papers no. 78, Leopold II to van Eetvelde, 25 September 1902.
33 Kurgan, op. cit., p. 495.
34 APR Fonds Congo 253/27, note by Leopold II, 3 April 1904.
35 Kurgan, op. cit., p. 515.
36 Ibid., p. 526.
37 Ibid., p. 531.
38 Ibid., p. 538.
39 Ibid., p. 545.
40 Carton de Wiart E., Souvenirs des Dernières Années (Brussels, 1944), p. 115.
41 Lichtervelde, op. cit., p. 285.
42 Kurgan, op. cit., p. 611.
42 Ibid., p. 563.

Chapter 23
1 Acton, Lord, Historical Essays and Studies (London, 1907), p. 504.

2 Stengers J., 'La Première Tentative de Reprise du Congo par la Belgique', Société Royale de Géographie, 1949, p. 49.
3 PRO FO 10/595, Monson to Salisbury, 28 January 1893.
4 Stengers, op. cit., p. 102.
5 APR Fonds Congo 219/31, A. D'Anethan to de Burlet, 29 May 1895.
6 In 1890 100 metric tons of rubber were exported; in 1896 exports reached 1,300 metric tons; in 1898 the figure was 2,000 and in 1901 6,000 metric tons. In 1890 the state had received 150,000 francs from its domains; in 1901 18,000,000 francs. See also graph, p. 235.
7 Stengers J., Belgique et Congo: l'Elaboration de la Charte Coloniale (Brussels, 1963), p. 48.
8 Cookey S.J.S., Britain and the Congo Question 1885–1913 (London, 1968), p. 36.
9 Ibid., p. 26.
10 APR Fonds Congo 102/100, Stanley to Leopold II, 16 September 1896.
11 Letter published in La Nation Belge, May 1931.
12 PRO FO 123/429, Phipps to Lansdowne, 31 May 1903.
13 PRO FO 403/399, Beale to Grey, 6 September 1907.
14 PRO FO 403/364, Mackie to Lansdowne, 11 March 1905 annex 2.
15 PRO FO 10/801, Lansdowne to Phipps, Draft May 1903.
16 Gwynn S. and Tuckwell G.M., The Life of the Rt Hon. Sir Charles Dilke (London, 1917), vol. II, p. 380.
17 PRO FO 10/665 no. 150A Africa, Plunkett to Salisbury, 14 June 1896.
18 PRO FO 10/754, Davidson to Gosselin, 16 May 1900.
19 Willequet, op. cit., p. 46.
20 PRO FO 10/801, Cromer to Lansdowne, 21 January 1903.
21 AGR van Eetvelde Papers no. 34, Leopold II to Liebrechts, 3 January 1899.
22 Taylor A.J.P., Essays in English History (London, 1976), p. 212. A reprint of his review of Brian Inglis's Roger Casement in 1973.
23 RA W43/145, Knollys to Phipps, 4 November 1903.
24 PRO FO 10/804, Lansdowne to Phipps, 21 May 1903.

Chapter 24

1   LSE Morel Papers. F.1.
2   Louis W.R., Roger Casement and the Congo, *Journal of African History*, 1964.
3   PRO FO 10/773 no. 71, Phipps to Lansdowne, 20 September 1902. It should be pointed out that there is no record in the archives of the Palais Royal of this meeting.
4   Inglis B., *Roger Casement* (London, 1973). (Paperback edition 1974 references used), p. 61.
5   Cookey S.J.S., *Britain and the Congo Question* (London, 1968), p. 85.
6   Carton de Wiart E., *Souvenirs des Dernières Années* (Brussels, 1944), p. 60.
7   RA W43/110, Phipps to Lansdowne, 18 July 1903.
8   PRO FO 10/807, Salisbury to Lansdowne, 26 January 1904.
9   PRO FO 10/807, note by Villiers, 21 December 1903.
10 Louis, op. cit.
11 PRO FO 10/808, Casement to Farnhall, 20 February 1904.
12 Accounts and Papers, 1904 (cd. 1933).
13 LSE Morel Papers, F. 8, Casement to Morel, 25 January 1904.
14 Hansard, House of Commons, 9 June 1904. CXXXV 1236–90.
15 LSE Morel Papers, F.8, Fox Bourne to Morel, 26 July 1904. First brought to light by Cookey, op. cit., pp. 122–3.
16 PRO FO 403/364, Mackie to Lansdowne, 11 March 1905.
17 Ibid.
18 Ibid. Report by E. Stannard, Bolobo, Annex 3.
19 Ibid. Mackie to Lansdowne, 11 March 1905.
20 PRO FO 403/364, Lansdowne to Sanderson, 10 September 1905.
21 Stenmans, op. cit., p. 298 et seq.

Chapter 25

1   Cattier F., *Droit et Administration de l'Etat Indépendant du Congo* (Brussels, 1898), p. 134.
2   Cattier F., *Etude sur la Situation de l'Etat Indépendant du Congo* (Brussels, 1906), p. 341.
3   Ibid., pp. iii–iv.
4   Ibid., p. iii.
5   Vermeersch Fr A., S.J., *La Question Congolaise* (Brussels, 1906), pp. 360–3.
6   Stenmans, op. cit., p. 333.
7   Cookey, op. cit., p. 167.
8   Cookey, op. cit., p. 163.
9   *The Times*, 21 November 1906.
10 Stengers J., *Belgique et Congo: l'Elaboration de la Charte Coloniale* (Brussels, 1963), pp. 84–5.
11 Stengers J., 'Quand Léopold II s'est-il rallié à l'annexation du Congo par la Belgique', ARSC, 1952.
12 MD de Cuvelier Papers, no. 3115, Leopold II to de Cuvelier, 23 January 1905.
13 Twain M., *King Leopold's Soliloquy* (New York, 1906), 1961 ed., pp. 54–5.
14 Cookey, op. cit., p. 176.
15 Ibid., p. 177.
16 Stengers J., *Belgique et Congo: l'Elaboration de la Charte Coloniale*, p. 127.
17 Van der Elst, Baron, 'Souvenirs sur Léopold II', *Revue Générale*, 1923.
18 Ibid.
19 Stengers J., 'Combien le Congo a-t-il coûté à la Belgique', ARSC, 1957.
20 Daye, op. cit., p. 520.
21 Carton de Wiart, op. cit., p. 182.
22 Stengers, op. cit., p. 167.
23 Carton de Wiart, op. cit., p. 188.
24 Willequet, op. cit., p. 183.
25 Stengers J., 'Note sur l'histoire des finances congolaises: "le trésor" ou "fonds spécial" du Roi-Souverain', IRCB, 1954.
26 MD de Cuvelier Papers no. 3131, Leopold II to de Cuvelier, 21 February 1908.
27 Stengers, op. cit., pp. 171–2.
28 Ibid., p. 174.
29 Carton de Wiart, op. cit., p. 190.

Chapter 26

1   Stenmans, op. cit., p. 9.
2   Stengers J., 'Léopold II et le Patrimoine Dynastique', op. cit.
3   After their father's death the two elder princesses sued, claiming that the assets of the *Fondation de Niederfullbach* were part of the king's personal fortune. The lawyer for the Belgian state held that the *fonds spécial*, which formed the basis of the foundation, was originally the EIC treasury and therefore belonged to Belgium by right

of annexation. The latter won the case, although the princesses received 25,000,000 francs to be divided among them. Posthumously, Leopold was successful in handing over the greater part of his fortune to Belgium rather than his daughters. See 'Succession de Léopold II. Documents produits par l'Etat Belge and Plaidoirie de Mᶜ Henry Jaspar pour SAR Madame la Princesse Louise de Belgique, 1911', for details of the suit brought by the Princesses Louise and Stephanie after their father's death.

4 Buisseret A., 'Un Fondation de Léopold II. La Donation Royale', *Revue Générale*, 1932; Lefébure R., 'La Donation Royale', *Revue Générale Belge*, 1952.

5 RA W43/144, Phipps to Edward VII, 31 October 1903.

6 RA W43/145, Knollys to Phipps, 4 November 1903.

7 Paoli X., 'The Late King of the Belgians', *Contemporary Review*, 1911.

8 Ibid.

9 Daye, op. cit., p. 479.

10 Ponsonby, Sir Frederick, *Recollections of Three Reigns* (London, 1951), p. 55.

11 Paoli, op. cit.

12 Carton de Wiart, op. cit., p. 222.

13 RA Y162/22, Leopold II to Queen Victoria, 6 November 1897.

14 APR *Fonds Congo* 5/5, Leopold II to Renkin, 3 March 1909.

15 Van der Elst, op. cit.

16 Weightman C. and Barnes A., *Brussels: Grote Markt to Common Market* (Brussels, 1977), p. 197.

17 I am very grateful for the help of M. Albert Duchesne, Conservator of the Musée de l'Armée et d'Histoire Militaire, Brussels, as regards Leopold II's properties in the south of France.

18 Ranieri, op. cit., p. 145.

19 Ibid., p. 155.

20 Ibid., p. 192.

21 Stinglhamber and Dresse, op. cit., p. 256.

22 Ibid., p. 254.

23 De Raymond, Count, *Léopold II à Paris* (Bruges, 1953), pp. 111–13.

24 Ranieri, op. cit., p. 241.

25 Carton de Wiart, op. cit., p. 177.

26 Von Bülow, Prince, *Mémoires* (Paris, 1930) 2 vols, vol. II, p. 111.

27 Ibid.

28 Vandaele F., 'Les Conversations anglo-belges d'avant Guerre (1906 et 1912)', *Revue des Livres, Documents et Archives de la Guerre 1914*, 1932–3.

29 APR IIE E45e, Minister of War to Leopold II, 19 December 1905.

30 Wilson, op. cit., p. 147.

31 Paoli, op. cit.

32 Stinglhamber and Dresse, op. cit., p. 302.

33 De Raymond, op. cit., p. 99.

34 RA W55/67, Hardinge to Grey, 14 December 1909.

35 RA W55/68, Hardinge to Grey, 14 December 1909.

36 Ibid.

37 RA W55/66, Hardinge to Grey, 12 December 1909.

38 Daye, op. cit., p. 555.

39 Davignon J., 'La Mort de Léopold II et L'Avènement de Albert I', leaflet MD.

40 Lichtervelde, op. cit., p. 360.

Sources

Archives of the Palais Royal, Brussels

Dossiers Cabinet Léopold II, in particular *Fonds Congo*. See Vandewoude E., *Inventaire des Archives Relatives au Développement Extérieur de la Belgique sous le Règne de Léopold II* (Brussels, 1965), for details.

Royal Archives, Windsor

Victorian Archive and Victorian Additional Archive.

Ministry of Foreign Affairs, Brussels

Correspondance Politique, Guerre de 1870.
Neutralité, Indépendance, Défense Militaire.
Conférence Géographique de Bruxelles.
Association Internationale du Congo.
Conférence de Berlin.
Etat Indépendant du Congo.
Conférence Anti-esclavagiste de Bruxelles.
Series AR 1, 1–43 (relating to the Congo).
Lambermont Papers.
Strauch Papers (half).

Archives Générales du Royaume, Brussels

Rogier Papers.
Van de Weyer Papers.
Banning Papers.
Frère-Orban Papers.
Van Eetvelde Papers.
De Borchgrave (E) Papers.
Schollaert-Hellputte Papers.
See Cosemans A., 'Les Archives Générales du Royaume au point de vue de la documentation historique coloniale', *IRCB*, 1954.

Archives Africaines, Brussels

See Van Grieken-Taverniers M., 'Inventaire des archives des affaires étrangères de l'Etat Indépendant du Congo et du Ministère des Colonies 1885–1914', *ARSC*, 1955.

See also reports on individual dossiers in the bulletins of the *IRCB*, *ARSC* and *ARSOM*.

Musée de la Dynastie, Brussels

Strauch Papers (half)
De Cuvelier Papers
See de Selliers de Moranville, Chevalier A., 'Un fonds d'archives nouveau pour l'histoire du Congo', *ARSOM*, 1963.

Musée Royal de l'Armée et d'Histoire Militaire, Brussels.

Chazal Papers
Fonds Mobilisation de 1870.
België–Buitenland (China)
See Duchesne A., 'Le Musée Royal de l'Armée et d'Histoire Militaire au point de vue de la documentation historique coloniale', *ARSC*, 1958.

School of Oriental and African Studies, London University

Mackinnon Papers. See catalogue.

London School of Economics and Political Science

Morel Papers

Public Record Office, London

FO 2   Africa
FO 10   Belgium
FO 27   France
FO 30   Germany
FO 63   Portugal
FO 84   Slave Trade
FO 123 British Legation, Brussels
FO 367 Africa
FO 371 Belgium (political correspondence)
FO 403 Africa, confidential prints
FO 800 Lansdowne, Grey, Papers
GD/29   Granville Papers

OFFICIAL PUBLICATIONS

Annales Parlementaires.
Bulletin Officiel de l'Etat Indépendant du Congo.
Documents Diplomatiques Francais 1871–1914, 41 vols (Paris, 1929–60).
Die Grosse Politik der Europäischen Kabinette 1871–1914, 40 vols (Berlin, 1923–7).
Moniteur Belge.

Origines Diplomatiques de la Guerre de 1870, 19 vols (Paris, 1910–32).
Succession de S.M. Léopold II. Documents produits par l'Etat Belge.
For the pleas of the lawyers of the Princesses Louise and Stephanie see *Tribunal de Première Instance de Bruxelles* and *Cour d'Appel de Bruxelles*.

UNPUBLISHED THESES

Genneret M.J., 'La Question de l'Oubangi. Litige entre la France et l'Etat Indépendant du Congo, 1885–1894' (Katholieke Universiteit, Leuven, 1962).
Michielsen, K., 'De Kongokwestie in 1906. De opinie van pers parlement en Koning' (Katholieke Universiteit, Leuven, 1969–1970).
Ranieri L., 'Lambermont et Banning, collaborateurs de Leopold II' (Université Libre de Bruxelles, 1951).
Van Vracem P., 'La neutralité belge pendant la guerre franco-allemande de 1870' (Katholieke Universiteit, Leuven, 1952).

BIBLIOGRAPHIES

Belder J. de and Hannes J., *Bibliographie de l'Histoire de Belgique 1865–1914* (Louvain, 1965).
Cosemans A. and Heyse T., *Contribution à la bibliographie dynastique et nationale. Règne de Léopold II 1865–1909* (Brussels, 1957–8).
Duchesne A., 'Bibliographie des Tentatives de Colonisation et d'Expansion Belge sous le Règne de Léopold I', *ARSOM*, 1964.
Heyse T., *Bibliographie du Congo Belge et du Ruanda-Urundi* (1946–53).
Heyse T., *Bibliographie de H.M. Stanley 1841–1904* (Brussels, 1961).
Simpson D., 'A Bibliography of Emin Pasha', *Uganda Journal*, 1960.
Walraet M., *Bibliographie du Katanga* vols 1 and 2 (Brussels, 1954–6).

Select Bibliography

Anstey R., *Britain and the Congo in the Nineteenth Century* (Oxford, 1962).
Anstruther I., *I presume* (London, 1956).
Aronson T., *The Coburgs of Belgium* (London, 1969).
Ascherson N., *The King Incorporated* (London, 1963).

Bagnuenault de Puchesse G., 'La Neutralité Belge pendant la Guerre Franco-Allemande (1870–1871)', *Revue d'Histoire Diplomatique*, 1902.
Banning E., *L'Afrique et la Conférence Géographique de Bruxelles* (Brussels, 1877).
  L'Association Internationale Africaine et le Comité d'Etudes du Haut Congo (Brussels, 1882).
  La Conférence Africaine de Berlin et l'Association Internationale du Congo (Brussels, 1885).
  Réflexions Morales et Politiques (Brussels, 1889).
  Les Origines et les Phases de la Neutralité Belge (Brussels, 1927).
  Mémoires Politiques et Diplomatiques (Brussels, 1927).
Barker N., 'Monarchy in Mexico: Harebrained scheme or well-considered Prospect?' *Journal of Modern History*, 1976.
Barnes A. and Weightman C., *Brussels: Grote Markt to Common Market* (Brussels, 1976).
Bauer L., *Leopold The Unloved* (London, 1934).
Bernard H., *Par la Paix Armée vers la Guerre Totale. Compléments d'Histoire Contemporaine 1871–1939* (Brussels, 1951).
Bertrand L., *Léopold II et son Règne 1865–1890* (Brussels, 1890).
  Le Scandale Congolais (Brussels, 1908).
  Souvenirs 2 vols (Brussels, 1927).
Bethune L. de, 'L'Etat Indépendant du Congo et l'Opinion Anglaise', *Revue Générale*, 1903.
Beyens, Baron, *Le Second Empire vu par un Diplomate Belge*, 2 vols (Bruges, 1924).
  'Souvenirs de Léopold II et de la Cour de Belgique', *Revue Générale*, 1932.
Binkley R.C., *Realism and Nationalism 1852–1871* (New York, 1935).
Biographie Coloniale Belge, 6 vols (Brussels, 1948–67).
Blanc J., *Le Droit de Préférence de la France sur le Congo Belge (1884–1911)* (Paris, 1921).

Blanchard G., *Formation et Constitution Politique de l'Etat indépendant du Congo* (Paris, 1899).

Bonnin G. ed., *Bismarck and the Hohenzollern Candidature for the Spanish Throne* (London, 1957).

Bontinck F., *Aux Origines de l'Etat Indépendant du Congo, Documents tirés d'Archives Américaines* (Louvain, 1966).

'L'Autobiographie de Hamed ben Mohammed el Murjebi Tippo Tib'. Translation from Swahili *ARSOM*, 1974.

de Borchgrave E., *Souvenirs Diplomatiques de Quarante Ans (1863–1903)* (Brussels, 1908).

'Les Origines de l'Etat Indépendant du Congo', *Académie Royale de Belgique, Bulletin de la Classe des Lettres et des Sciences Morales et Politiques*, 1919.

Boulger D., *The Reign of Leopold II*, 2 vols (London, 1925).

Bronne C., *Léopold I et Son Temps* (Brussels, 1942).

Lettres de Léopold I (Brussels, 1943).

La Tapisserie Royale, Faits et Portraits Léopoldiens (Brussels, 1952).

'Léopold II et le Comte Smet de Naeyer: Lettres inédites du Roi', *Revue Générale Belge*, 1966.

Bruhat J., 'Léopold II', in *Les Politiques d'Expansion Imperialiste* (Paris, 1949).

Brunschwig H., *La Colonisation Française* (Paris, 1949).

Le Partage de l'Afrique Noire (Paris, 1971).

Mythes et Réalités de l'Impérialisme Colonial Française (Paris, 1960).

'La Colonisation Belge et le Congo', *Revue Historique*, 1957.

Buffin C., *La Jeunesse de Léopold I* (Brussels, 1914).

La Tragédie Mexicaine (Brussels, n.d.).

'Napoléon III, prisonnier de guerre en Belgique', *Le Flambeau*, 1924.

Buisseret, 'La Donation Royale', *Revue Générale*, 1932.

Burton R., *Two Trips to Gorilla Land and the Cataracts of the Congo* (London, 1876).

Calmes C., 'Malaise et annexionisme belge en 1867', *Hemrecht*, 1969.

Cameron V.L., *Across Africa*, 2 vols (London, 1877).

Carton de Wiart, Comte E., *Souvenirs des Dernières Années* (Brussels, 1944).

Beernaert et son Temps (Brussels, 1945).

'Léopold II', *L'Eventail-Noël*, 1930.

Cattier F., *Droit et Administration de l'État Indépendant du Congo* (Brussels, 1898).

Etude sur la situation de l'Etat Indépendant du Congo (Brussels, 1906).

Cérémonies et fêtes du Mariage de SAR Mgr. le Duc de Brabant (Brussels, 1855).

Ceulemans P., 'Les Tentatives pour engager le Colonel Charles Gordon au service de l'Association Internationale Africaine, 1880', *Zäire*, 1958.

'La Question Arabe et le Congo, 1883–1893', *ARSC*, 1959.

Chatlin L.N., 'Vers le Nil', in Franck L., *Le Congo Belge*, 2 vols (Brussels, 1930).

Chenevix Trench C., *Charley Gordon* (London, 1978).

Chlepner B.S., *Cent Ans d'Histoire Sociale en Belgique* (Brussels, 1956).
  'Esquisse sur l'Evolution bancaire en Belgique', *La Revue de Banque*, 1953.
  'Belgian Banking and Banking Theory' (Brookings Institution, 1943).
Clough S. B., *A History of the Flemish Movement in Belgium* (New York, 1930).
Cocks F.S., *E.D. Morel: the man and his work* (London, 1920).
Collins R.O., *King Leopold, England and the Upper Nile 1899–1909* (New Haven, 1968).
  The Southern Sudan 1883–1898: a struggle for control (New Haven, 1962)
  'The Anglo-Congolese negotiations 1900–1906', *Zaïre*, 1958.
  'Origins of the Nile Struggle', in Gifford P. & Louis W.R., *Britain and Germany in Africa* (New Haven, 1967).
  ed. *The Partition of Africa: Illusion or Necessity* (New York, 1969).
La Conférence de Géographie de 1876, Recueil d'Etudes, ARSOM, 1976.
Conrad J., *The Heart of Darkness* (London, 1902).
Cookey S.J.S., *Britain and the Congo Question* (London, 1968).
  'Tippu Tib and the Decline of the Congo Arabs', *Tarikh*, 1966.
Corley T.A.B., *Democratic Despot: A Life of Napoleon III* (London, 1961).
Cornet R.J., *La Bataille du Rail* (Brussels, 1953).
  Katanga (Brussels, 1943).
Cornevin R., *Histoire du Congo* (Paris, 1966).
Corti, Count E., *Maximilian and Charlotte of Mexico*, 2 vols (London, 1928).
Cosyn A., *Laeken Ancien et Moderne* (Brussels, 1904).
Craig G.A., 'Great Britain and the Belgian Railways Dispute of 1869', *American Historical Review*, 1945.
Crokaert P., *Brialmont Eloge et Mémoires* (Brussels, 1925).
Crowe S.E., *The Berlin West African Conference 1884–1885* (London, 1942).

Daye P., *Léopold II* (Brussels, 1934).
Demoulin R., 'Guillaume I et l'Economie Belge', *Le Flambeau*, 1938.
  Documents inédits sur la Crise Internationale de 1870 (Brussels, 1957).
  'Léopold II et le grand-duché de Luxembourg au printemps 1867', in *Mélanges offertes à G. Jacquemyns* (Brussels, 1968).
Depage H., 'Note au sujet de documents inédits relatifs à deux expeditions de H.M. Stanley en Afrique 1874–1877, 1887–1889', *IRCB*, 1954.
Descamps E., 'Le Duc de Brabant au Sénat de Belgique', *Académie Royale de Belgique*, 1903.
Dhondt J. ed., *Geschiedenis van de Socialistsche Arbeidsbeweging in België* (Antwerp, 1960).
Discailles E., *Charles Rogier 1800–1885*, 4 vols (Brussels, 1892–5).
Duchesne A., *Quand les Belges devaient partir pour la Chine. Un projet d'expédition contre les Boxers* (Brussels, 1948).
  'La politique coloniale Léopold I', *Revue Générale Belge*, 1954.
  'Appréciations françaises sur la valeur de l'armée belge et les perspectives de guerre de 1871 à 1914', *Carnet de la Fourragere*, 1961.

'L'Armée et la politique militaire belge de 1871 à 1920 jugées par les attachés militaires de France à Bruxelles', *Revue Belge de Philologie et d'Histoire*, 1961–2.

'La Pensée expansionniste du Duc de Brabant à travers sa correspondance avec le Général Chazal (1859–1861)', *ARSOM*, 1963.

'Les aspects diplomatiques au projet d'expédition belge en Chine en 1900', *Revue Belge de Philologie et d'Histoire*, 1954.

'Léopold II et le Maroc', *ARSC*, 1965.

'Léopold I et Santo Tomas de Guatémala, un témoignage inconnu', *ARSOM*, 1965.

'Les leçons de l'expérience de son père ont-elles entraîné Leopold II dans la voie de la colonialisation?' *La Conférence de Géographie de 1876, Recueil d'Etudes* (Brussels, 1976).

'Si Balincourt nous était conté ...', *Vieux Papiers* (Paris, 1978).

Duignan L.P. and Gann L.H. eds, *Colonialism in Africa*, 5 vols (Cambridge, Mass., 1968–70).

Dumont G. H., *Léopold II: Pensées et Reflexions* (Liège, 1948).

La vie quotidienne en Belgique sons le règne de Léopold II (Brussels, 1974).

Eickhoff F., *Essai sur les Origines Diplomatiques de l'Etat Indépendant du Congo* (Brussels, 1936).

Expansion Belge 1831–1865: Recueil d'Etudes, ARSOM, 1965.

Fage J.D., *An Atlas of African History* (London, 1963).

A History of West Africa (London, 1969).

Le Febve de Vivy L., 'Documents d'histoire précoloniale belge 1861–65. Les idées coloniales du Duc de Brabant', *ARSC*, 1955.

Foot M.R.D., 'Great Britain and Luxembourg, 1867', *English Historical Review*, 1952.

Forbath P., *The River Congo* (New York, 1977).

Fox Bourne H.R., *The Other Side of the Emin Pasha Relief Expedition* (London, 1891).

Civilisation in Congo-land (London, 1903).

Franck L., *La Nationalité belge et le mouvement flamand* (Brussels, 1931).

ed. *Le Congo Belge*, 2 vols (Brussels, 1930).

de Franqueville B., 'Léon XIII et la Belgique pendant la lutte scolaire', *Revue Générale*, 1910.

Freddy G., *Léopold II Intime* (Paris, 1905).

Frochisse J., *La Belgique et la Chine; relations diplomatiques et économiques 1839–1909* (Brussels, 1936).

Galbraith J.S., *Mackinnon and East Africa 1878–1895* (Cambridge, 1972).

Gallagher J. and Robinson R., 'The Imperialism of Free Trade', *Economic History Review*, 1953.

Garsou J., *Les Débuts d'un Grand Règne*, 2 vols (Brussels, 1934).

L'Evolution du Parti Libéral 1841–1939 (Brussels, 1939).

Le Général Chazal 1808–1892 (Brussels, 1945).
Les Relations Extérieures de la Belgique 1839–1914 (Brussels, 1946).
'Léopold II et la défense nationale', *Le Flambeau*, 1935.
'Léopold I et la Chine', *Archives Diplomatiques et Consulaires*, 1937.
'Léopold II et d'Anethan. Lettres inédites', *Revue Générale Belge*, 1948.
with Olschewsky S., *Léopold II, Roi des Belges* (Brussels, 1905).
with Van Leyenseele H., *Frère-Orban: le Crépuscule 1878–1896* (Brussels, 1954).
Gerady P. (attributed), *Les Carnets du Roi* (Paris, 1903).
Gifford P. and Louis W.R. ed., *Britain and Germany in Africa* (New Haven, 1967).
France and Britain in Africa (New Haven, 1971).
de Golesco H. and de Weisme A., *Marie-Henriette, Reine des Belges* (Brussels, 1944).
Gooch B.D., *Europe in the 19th century* (London, 1970).
ed. *Napoleon III: Man of Destiny* (New York, 1966).
Gossart E., *Emile Banning et Léopold II 1867–1892* (Brussels, 1920).
Gottschalk M., 'Le Pouvoir d'achat et la consommation des ouvriers belges à différentes époques', *Revue Internationale de Travail*, 1932.
Grand Carteret J., *Popold II: Roi des Belges et des Belles* (Paris, 1908).
Greindl L., 'Léopold II et les Philippines 1869–1875', *ARSOM*, 1962.
Guillaume, Baron, 'Souvenirs intimes: Comment le Roi Léopold II est intervenu au Congo', *L'Indépendance Belge*, 2 March 1918.
Gwynn S. and Tuckwell G., *The Life of the Rt. Hon. Sir Charles Dilke*, 2 vols (London, 1917).

Hall R., *Stanley: an Adventurer Explored* (London, 1974).
Hammond R.J., 'Economic Imperialism. Sidelights on a Stereotype', *Journal of Economic History*, 1961.
Hargreaves J.D., *Prelude to the Partition of West Africa* (London, 1963).
Haslip J., *The Lonely Empress* (London, 1965).
The Crown of Mexico (London, 1971).
Hautcler G., 'L'Armée Belge, face à la Crise de Sedan', *Revue Internationale d'Histoire Militaire*, 1959.
Heenen G., 'Les Finances au Congo Belge' in *Histoire des Finances Publiques*, vol III (Brussels, 1955).
Helly D. O., 'Informed opinion on Tropical Africa in Great Britain 1860–1890', *African Affairs*, 1969.
Helmreich J.E., *Belgium and Europe: a study in small power diplomacy* (Amsterdam, 1976).
Hertslet E., *The Map of Africa by Treaty*, 3 vols (London, 1909).
Hinde S., *The Fall of the Congo Arabs* (London, 1897).
Hird F., *H.M. Stanley: the Authorized Life* (London, 1935).
Histoire de la Belgique Contemporaine, 3 vols (Brussels, 1928–30).
Histoire des Finances Publiques en Belgique, 3 vols (Brussels, 1950–5).

Hornik M.P., 'The Anglo-Belgian agreement of 12 May 1894', *English Historical Review*, 1942.

Howard M., *The Franco-Prussian War* (London, 1961).

Huisman M., 'La Belgique et les Pays Bas pendant la crise de 1870', *Le Flambeau*, 1928.

Hyde H.M., *The Mexican Empire* (London, 1946).

Hymans P., *Frère-Orban*, 2 vols (Brussels, 1905–10).

Inglis B., *Roger Casement* (London, 1973).

Jacobs E.A., 'Le premier voyage du future Léopold II en Orient (1854–5), d'après des documents inédits', *ARSOM*, 1965.

Julien C. ed., *Les Politiques d'Expansion Impérialiste* (Paris, 1949).

Julin A., 'The economic progress of Belgium from 1883 to 1908', *Journal of the Royal Statistical Society*, 1911.

   'L'Ouvrier belge en 1853 et en 1886 d'après les budgets de famille', *La Reforme Sociale*, 1891.

Keith, Sir A.B., *The Belgian Congo and the Berlin Act* (Oxford, 1919).

Kurgan-van Hentenryk G., 'Une tentative de pénétration économique belge en Chine. La mission Fivé, 1898–1900', *ARSOM*, 1962.

   'Jean Jadot: Artisan de l'Expansion belge en Chine', *ARSOM*, 1965.

   'Léopold II et les groupes financiers belges en Chine (1895–1914)', *Académie Royale, Classe des Lettres*, 1972.

Laboulaye P. de, 'Souvenirs de ma mission en Belgique 1870–1871', *Revue de Paris*, 1938.

Landes D.S., 'Some thoughts on the nature of economic imperalism', *Journal of Economic History*, 1961.

Langer W., *The Diplomacy of Imperialism*, 2 vols (New York, 1935), 1972 ed. 1 vol.

Lannoy F. de, 'La neutralité belge et la guerre de 1870', *Revue Catholique des Idées et des Faits*, 1925.

Laroche L., *Louise d'Orléans, première Reine des Belges* (Paris, 1902).

Leconte L., *Les Tentatives d'Expansion Coloniale sous Léopold I* (Antwerp, 1946).

Lefébure R., 'La Donation Royale', *Revue Générale Belge*, 1952.

Lichtervelde, Comte L. de, *Léopold II* (Brussels, 1926).

Liebrechts G., *Léopold II, Fondateur d'Empire* (Brussels, 1932).

Lord R., *The Origins of the War of 1870* (Cambridge, Mass., 1924).

Louis W.R., 'Great Britain and the Stokes case', *Uganda Journal*, 1964.

   'Roger Casement and the Congo', *Journal of African History*, 1964.

Louise, Princesse, *My Own Affairs* (London, 1921).

Luwel M., 'Organisation de l'Exploration Scientifique du Congo 1889–1894', *ARSC*, 1955.
'Histoire du Musée Royal du Congo Belge à Tervuren', *Congo-Tervuren*, 1960.

MacColl R., *Roger Casement* (London, 1958).
Martelli G., *Leopold to Lumumba* (London, 1962).
Martens M. ed., *Histoire de Bruxelles* (Brussels, 1976).
Masoin F., *Histoire de l'Etat Indépendant du Congo* (Namur, 1912–13).
Maurice A., *Stanley: Unpublished Letters* (London, 1957).
Mazenot G., *La Likouala-Mossako, histoire de la pénétration du Haut-Congo 1878–1910* (Paris, 1970).
Miracle M.P., 'Trade and Economic Change in Katanga, 1850–1959', *West African History*, 1969.
Moiné W., 'Résultats des élections belges entre 1867 et 1914', *Bulletin de l'Institut Belge de Sciences Politiques*, 1970.
Morel E.D., *King Leopold's Rule in Africa* (London, 1904).
   Red Rubber (London, 1906).
   Great Britain and the Congo (London, 1909).
   History of the Congo Reform Movement (ed. Louis W.R. and Stengers J., Oxford, 1968).
Mutwale-Myimbwe, 'Les Sources publiques de financement de l'Etat du Congo 1885–1907', *Cahiers de CEDAF*, 1973.

Norton W.B., 'A Belgian Socialist Critic of Colonialism, Louis Bertrand (1856–1943)', *ARSOM*, 1965.

Oliver R., *Sir Henry Johnston and the Scramble for Africa* (London, 1957).
Ollivier E., *L'Empire Libéral*, 17 vols (Paris, 1895–1915).

Palmer A., *Bismarck* (London, 1976).
Panneels E., *De Diplomatieke activiteit van Koning Leopold II* (Brussels, 1970).
Paoli X., 'The Late King of the Belgians', *Contemporary Review*, 1910.
Peemans J-P., 'Capital accumulation in the Congo under Colonialism: the role of the State' in Duigan and Gann, *Colonialism in Africa*, vol. 4 (Cambridge, Mass., 1970).
Peeters M., 'L'Evolution des salaires en Belgique de 1831 à 1913', *Bulletin de l'Institut de Recherches Economiques*, 1939.
Pierson M., *Histoire du Socialisme en Belgique* (Brussels, 1955).
Pirenne H., *Histoire de la Belgique*, 6 vols (Brussels, 1909–26).

Ranieri L., 'Les relations entre l'Etat Indépendant du Congo et l'Italie 1876–1908', *ARSC*, 1959.
   Léopold II Urbaniste (Brussels, 1973).

Raymond, Comte G. de, *Léopold II à Paris* (Bruges, 1950).

Reinach-Foussemagne, Comtesse de, *Charlotte de Belgique, Impératrice du Mexique* (Paris, 1925).

Richardson J., *My Dearest Uncle* (London, 1961).

Ridder A. de, *Le Mariage de Léopold II d'après des documents inédits* (Brussels, 1925).

'Le traité Benedetti', *Revue Catholique des Idées et des Faits*, 1926.

'Education des princes', *L'Eventail-Noël*, 1930.

Ritter G., *The Schlieffen Plan* (London, 1958).

Robert M., *Géologie et Géographie du Katanga* (Brussels, 1956).

Robinson R., Gallagher T. and Denny A., *Africa and the Victorians* (London, 1961).

Roeykens A., 'Les Réunions préparatoires de la délégation belge à la Conférence Géographique de Bruxelles (1876)', *Zaïre*, 1953.

'Banning et la Conférence Géographique de Bruxelles, 1976', *Zaïre*, 1954.

'Les Débuts de l'œuvre africaine de Léopold II (1875–1879)', *ARSC*, 1955.

'Le dessein africain de Léopold II', *ARSC*, 1956.

'Le Baron L. de Béthune et la politique religieuse de Léopold II en Afrique', *Zaïre*, 1956.

'La période initiale de l'œuvre africaine de Léopold II', *ARSC*, 1957.

'Léopold et la cónference géographique de Bruxelles (1876)', *ARSC*, 1958.

'Léopold II et l'Afrique (1855–1880)', *ARSC*, 1958.

'Jules Malou et l'œuvre congolaise de Léopold II', *ARSOM*, 1961.

'L'initiative africaine de Léopold II et l'opinion publique belge', *ARSC*, 1964.

'La génie de Léopold II et la Conférence Géographique de Bruxelles de 1876' in *La Conférence de Géographie de 1876, Receuil d'Etudes* and *ARSOM*, 1976.

Rowntree B. Seebohm, *Land of Labour: lessons from Belgium* (London, 1910).

Sanderson G.N., *England, Europe and the Upper Nile* (Edinburgh, 1965).

'Leopold II and the Nile Valley': *Proceedings of the Sudan Historical Association*, 1955.

Schaloff S., *Reform in King Leopold's Congo* (Richmond, Va, 1970).

Selliers de Moranville, Chevalier A. de, 'Léopold II', *Bulletin de la Fédération des Industries Belges*, 1970 (special number).

Shepperson G., *The Exploration of Africa in the 18th and 19th centuries* (Edinburgh, 1971).

Simar T., 'Léopold II et l'Erythrée', *Revue Congo*, 1924.

Slade R., *King Leopold's Congo* (London, 1962).

'English missions and the beginning of the anti-Congolese campaign in England', *Revue Belge de Philologie et d'Histoire*, 1955.

'English speaking missions in the Congo Independent State 1878–1908', *ARSC*, 1959.

Smith I., *The Emin Pasha Relief Expedition 1886–1890* (Oxford, 1972).

Stanley H.M., *Through the Dark Continent*, 2 vols (London, 1878).
  The Congo and the Founding of the Free State, 2 vols (London, 1885).
  In Darkest Africa, 2 vols (London, 1890).
  The Autobiography of Sir H.M. Stanley ed. Dorothy Stanley (London, 1914).
Stengers J., 'La première tentative de reprise du Congo par la Belgique (1894–1895)', *Bulletin de la Société Royale Belge Géographique*, 1949.
  'La place de Léopold II dans l'histoire de la colonisation', *La Nouvelle Clio*, 1950.
  'Le rôle de la Commission d'Enquête de 1904–1905 au Congo', *Annuaire de l'Institut de Philologie et d'Histoire Orientale et Slave de l'Université Libre de Bruxelles*, 1950.
  'Quand Léopold II s'est-il rallié à l'annexation du Congo par la Belgique?' *IRCB*, 1952.
  'Rapport sur les dossiers "Reprise du Congo par la Belgique" et "dossier économique"', *IRCB*, 1953.
  'Note sur l'histoire des finances congolaises: le "trésor" ou "fonds spécial" du Roi-Souverain', *IRCB*, 1954.
  'Stanley, Léopold II et l'Angleterre', *Le Flambeau*, 1954.
  'Textes inédits d'Emile Banning', *ARSC*, 1955.
  'Quelques observations sur la correspondance de Stanley', *Zaïre*, 1955.
  'Combien le Congo a-t-il coûté à la Belgique?' *ARSC*, 1957.
  'Prélude de Fachoda', *Revue belge de philologie et d'histoire*, 1958.
  'L'Impérialisme colonial de la fin du XIXᵉ siècle: mythe ou réalité?' *Journal of African History*, 1962.
  Belgique e Congo: *L'Elaboration de la Charte Coloniale* (Brussels, 1963).
  'Léopold II et la fixation des frontières du Congo', *Le Flambeau*, 1963.
  'L'anti-colonialisme libéral du XIXᵉ siècle et son influence en Belgique', *ARSC*, 1965.
  'Léopold II et la Rivalité Franco-Anglaise en Afrique (1882–1884)', *Revue Belge de Philologie et d'Histoire*, 1969.
  'The Congo Free State and the Belgian Congo before 1914', in Duigan and Gann, *Colonialism in Africa*, vol. 1 (Cambridge, Mass., 1968).
  Académie Royal, Bulletin de la Classe des Lettres et des Sciences Morales et Politiques, 1972.
  'Léopold II entre l'Extrême Orient et l'Afrique (1875–1876)', in *La Conférence de Géographie de 1876, Recueil d'Etudes*, ARSOM, 1976.
  'Léopold II et le patrimoine dynastique', *Académie Royale, Classe des Lettres*, 1971.
  'Léopold II et le modèle colonial hollandais', *Tijdschrift voor Geschiedenis*, 1977.
Stenmans A., *La Reprise du Congo par la Belgique* (Brussels, 1949).
Stephanie, Princess, *I was to be Empress* (London, 1937).
Stinglhamber, Col. G. and Dresse P., *Léopold II au Travail* (Brussels, 1945).
Stokes E., 'Late 19th century colonial expansion and the attack on the theory of economic imperialism, A case of mistaken identity?' *Historical Journal*, 1969.
Strage M., *Cape to Cairo* (London, 1973).

Tardieu A., 'Léopold II et son Règne', *Revue des Deux Mondes*, 1910.

Taylor A.J.P., *Essays in English History* (London, 1976 ed.).

'Prelude to Fashoda', *English Historical Review*, 1950 (included in above 1976 edition).

Terlinden, Comte C., *Histoire Militaire des Belges* (Brussels, 1931).

Thibaut W., *Les Républicains Belges 1787–1914* (Brussels, 1961).

Thomson R.S., *La Fondation de l'Etat Indépendant du Congo* (Brussels, 1933).

'Léopold II et la Conférence de Berlin', *Revue Congo*, 1931.

'Léopold II et le Congo', *Revue Congo*, 1931.

Townsend M., *The Rise and Fall of Germany's Colonial Empire 1884–1918* (New York, 1930).

Trannoy, Baron de, 'Les Philippines avant le Congo', *Revue Générale*, 1920.

'Léopold II, Jules Malou et la crise financière de 1870', *Revue Générale*, 1921.

'Léopold II et Jules Malou – La révocation du Ministère d'Anethan 1871', *Revue Générale*, 1926.

Tuckey J.K., *Narrative of an Expedition to explore the river Zaïre* (London, 1818).

Twain M., *King Leopold's Soliloquy* (New York, 1906, 1971 ed.).

Ursel, Comte C. d', 'Souvenirs d'une mission diplomatique en Chine', *La Revue Nouvelle*, 1950.

Ursel, Comte H. d', *La Cour de Belgique et la Cour de France de 1832 à 1850* (Paris, 1933).

Vandaele F., 'Les conversations anglo-belges d'avant-guerre (1906 et 1912)', *Revue Belge des Livres, Documents et Archives de la Guerre 1914–1918*, 1932–3.

Van den Heuvel, J., 'Léopold II', *Le Correspondant*, 1910.

Vandenpeereboom A., Mémoires in Garsou J., *Les Débuts d'un Grand Règne* (Brussels, 1933).

Vandeplas A., 'Quelques mesures de précaution de Léopold II en 1883', *Revue d'Histoire de Colonies*, 1956.

Van der Elst, Baron L., 'Souvenirs sur Léopold II', *Revue Générale*, 1923.

'Léopold II et la Chine', *Revue Générale*, 1924.

Van der Smissen E., *Léopold II et Beernaert, d'après leur correspondance inédite de 1884 à 1894*, 2 vols (Brussels, 1920).

Vandervelde E., *Le Parti Ouvrier Belge 1885–1925* (Brussels, 1925).

Les Dix Dernières Années du Règne de Léopold II (Brussels, 1910).

Mémoires d'un Militant Socialiste (Brussels, 1939).

Vandewoude E., 'Brieven van Hertog van Brabant aan Conway in Verband met Egypte', *ARSOM*, 1964.

'Lettres de Jules Devaux au Roi Léopold II relatives au Congo (octobre-novembre 1883)', *Archives et Bibliothèques de Belgique*, 1964.

'L'échec de la Tentative de Colonisation belge aux Nouvelles-Hébrédes', *ARSOM*, 1965.

'Plannen tot reorganisatie van de Belgische artillerie 1866–1871', *Revue Belge d'Histoire Militaire*, 1968.

'Een plan van Leopold II tot industriële prospectie van China en Japan (1868–1873)', *ARSOM*, 1967.

'Leopold II en de Graaf van Vlaanderen tegen over de oorlog van 1870', *Revue Belge d'Histoire Militaire*, 1969.

'Leopold II en het domein van Tervuren', *Afrika–Tervuren*, 1969.

'De aard rijkskundige conferentie (1876) vanuit koninlijk Paleis gezien' in *La Conférence de Géographie de 1876, Recueil d'Etudes, ARSOM*, 1976.

Van Grieken E., 'H.M. Stanley au Congo (1879–1884), d'après le manuscript de Ch. Notte', *ARSC*, 1954.

Van Hecken J.L., 'Betrekkingen van België met China onder Leopold I in de Belgische Pers van 1858 tot 1865', *ARSOM*, 1964.

Van Houtte, 'Le Sentiment national belge au XIX⁰ siècle', *Revue Générale Belge*, 1961.

Van Kalken F., *Histoire de la Belgique et de son Expansion Coloniale* (Brussels, 1954).

Van Leyneseele H., 'Léopold et les Philippines en 1898', *ARSC*, 1956.

Van Moeske P., 'Profit, Inflation and Belgian Industrial Expansion 1830–1914', *Tijdschrift voor Economie*, 1963.

Van Zuylen, Baron P., *L'Echiquier Congolais ou le Secret du Roi* (Brussels, 1959).

Vaughan, Baroness de, *Quelques Souvenirs de ma Vie* (Paris, 1936).

Presque Reine (Paris, 1944).

Verbeken A., 'Contribution à la Géographie historique du Katanga', *IRCB*, 1954.

'La révolte des Batela en 1895', *ARSC*, 1958.

with Walraet M., 'La Première Traversée du Katanga en 1806', *IRCB*, 1953.

Verhaegen, Baron G., 'Les Institutions militaires belges' in *Histoire de la Belgique Contemporaine*, vol. 2 (Brussels, 1929).

Vermeersch A., *La Question Congolaise* (Brussels, 1906).

Victoria, Queen, *Letters of Queen Victoria*, 1st series, 3 vols (London, 1907); 2nd series, 3 vols (London, 1926–8); 3rd series, 3 vols (London, 1930–2).

Walraet S., 'L'œuvre des Belges au Siam à la fin du XIX⁰ siècle', *IRCB*, 1954.

Ward H., *Five Years with the Congo Cannibals* (London, 1891).

Wauters A.J., *Histoire Politique du Congo* (Brussels, 1911).

Wehler H.U., 'Bismarck's Imperialism 1862–1890', *Past and Present*, 1970.

Willequet J., *Le Congo Belge et la Weltpolitik (1894–1914)* (Brussels, 1962).

Le Baron Lambermont (Brussels, 1970).

'Appréciations allemandes sur la valeur de l'armée belge et les perspectives de guerre avant 1914', *Revue Internationale d'Histoire Militaire*, 1959.

'Les dossiers "Belgique" de la Wilhelmstrasse 1900–1914', *Archives Bibliothèques et Musées de Belgique*, 1961.

'Jules Greindl; une grande figure dans notre diplomatie', *Revue Générale Belge*, 1968.

Wilmet L., 'Napoléon III en Belgique, d'après les souvenirs des témoins oculaires et les archives du Musée Royal de l'Armée', *Carnet de la Fourragère*, 1930.

Wilson H.L., *Diplomatic Episodes in Mexico, Belgium and Chile* (London, 1927).

Wissmann H. von, *My Second Journey through Equatorial Africa from the Congo in the Years 1886–1887* (London, 1891).

Woeste, Comte C., *La Neutralité belge, La Belgique et la France* (Brussels, 1891).

A travers dix années 1885–1894, 2 vols (Brussels, 1895).

Mémoires pour servir à l'histoire contemporaine de la Belgique, 3 vols (Brussels, 1927–37).

Wullus-Rudiger J., *La Belgique et l'Equilibre Européen. Documents inédits* (Paris, 1935).

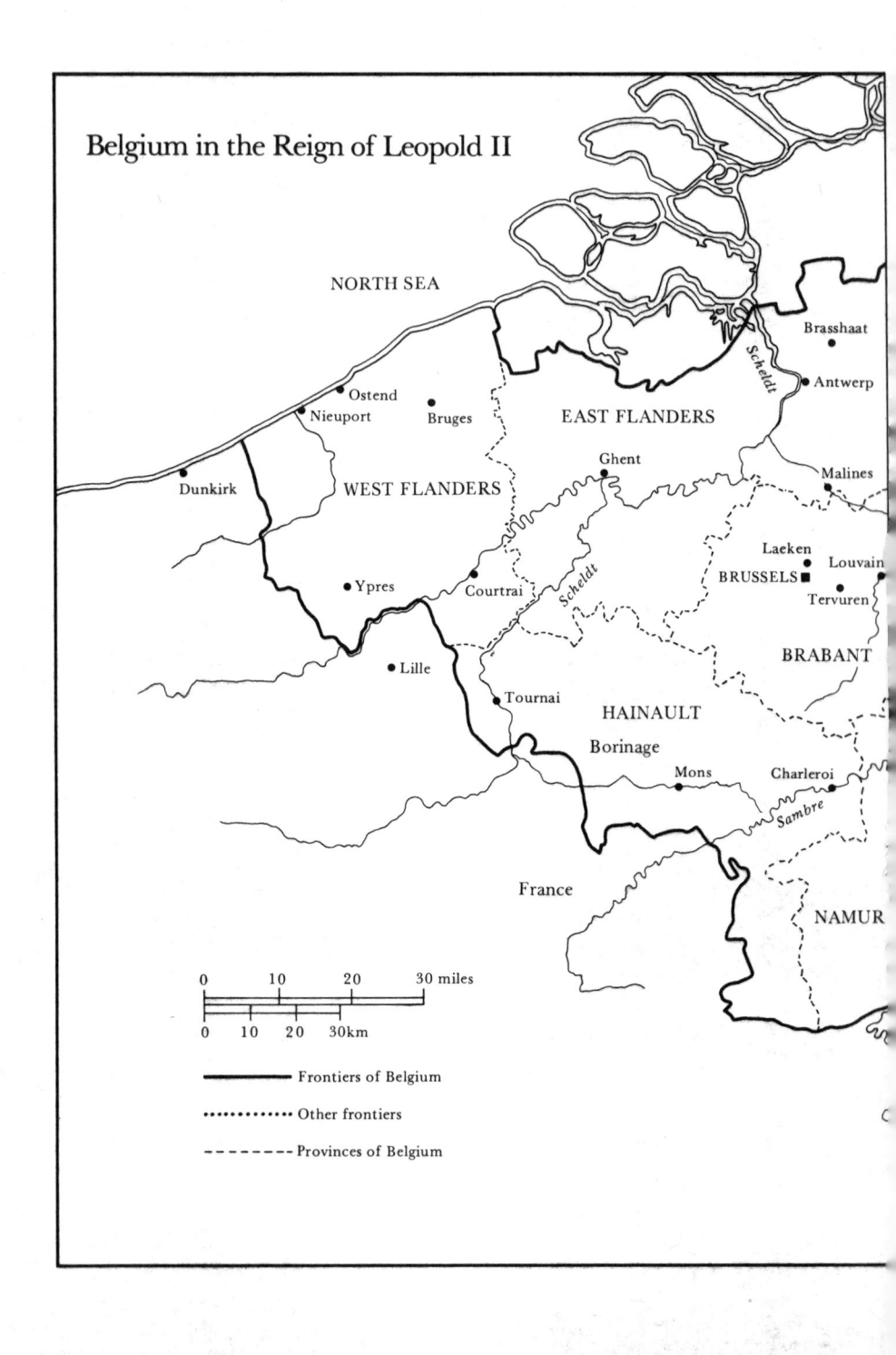

Belgium in the Reign of Leopold II

NORTH SEA

Brasshaat

Antwerp

Ostend
Nieuport

Bruges

EAST FLANDERS

Malines

Scheldt

Dunkirk

WEST FLANDERS

Ghent

Laeken
Louvain

BRUSSELS

Tervuren

Ypres

Courtrai

Scheldt

BRABANT

Lille

Tournai

HAINAULT

Borinage

Mons

Charleroi

Sambre

France

NAMUR

0   10   20   30 miles

0   10   20   30km

——— Frontiers of Belgium

•••••••••• Other frontiers

– – – – – Provinces of Belgium

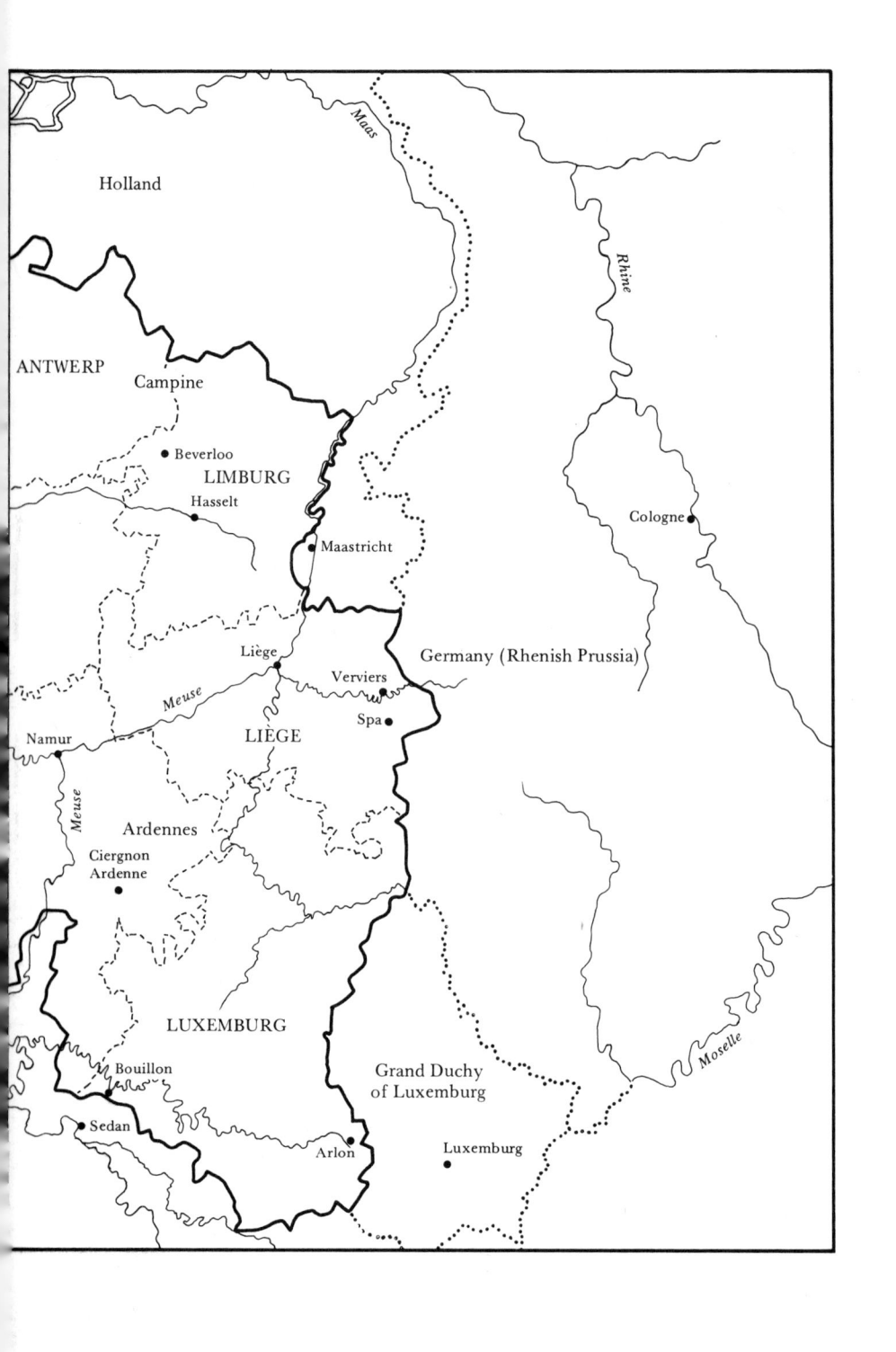

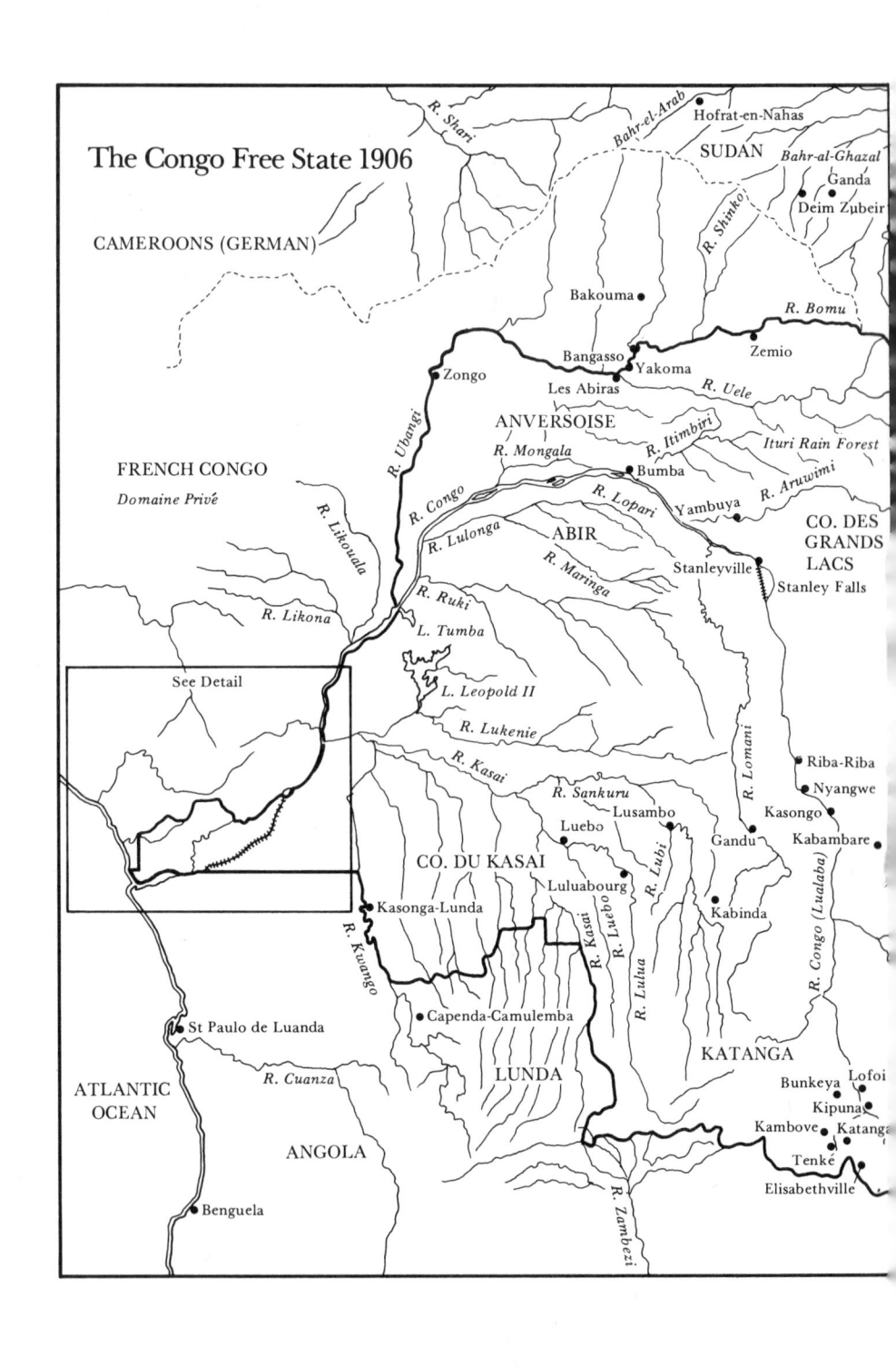

The Congo Free State 1906

CAMEROONS (GERMAN)

SUDAN

R. Shari

Bahr-el-Arab

Hofrat-en-Nahas

Bahr-al-Ghazal

Ganda

Deim Zubeir

R. Shinko

Bakouma

R. Bomu

Zemio

Bangasso

Yakoma

Zongo

Les Abiras

R. Uele

FRENCH CONGO

Domaine Privé

R. Ubangi

ANVERSOISE

R. Mongala

R. Itimbiri

Ituri Rain Forest

Bumba

R. Lopari

R. Aruwimi

R. Congo

Yambuya

CO. DES
GRANDS
LACS

R. Likouala

R. Lulonga

ABIR

Stanleyville

Stanley Falls

R. Maringa

R. Ruki

R. Likona

L. Tumba

See Detail

L. Leopold II

R. Lukenie

R. Lomani

Riba-Riba

Nyangwe

R. Kasai

R. Sankuru

Kasongo

Lusambo

Luebo

Gandu

Kabambare

CO. DU KASAI

Luluabourg

Kabinda

R. Kwango

Kasonga-Lunda

R. Kasai

R. Luebo

R. Lubi

R. Congo (Lualaba)

St Paulo de Luanda

Capenda-Camulemba

R. Lutua

KATANGA

ATLANTIC
OCEAN

R. Cuanza

LUNDA

Bunkeya

Lofoi

Kipuna

Kambove

Katanga

ANGOLA

Tenké

Elisabethville

Benguela

R. Zambezi

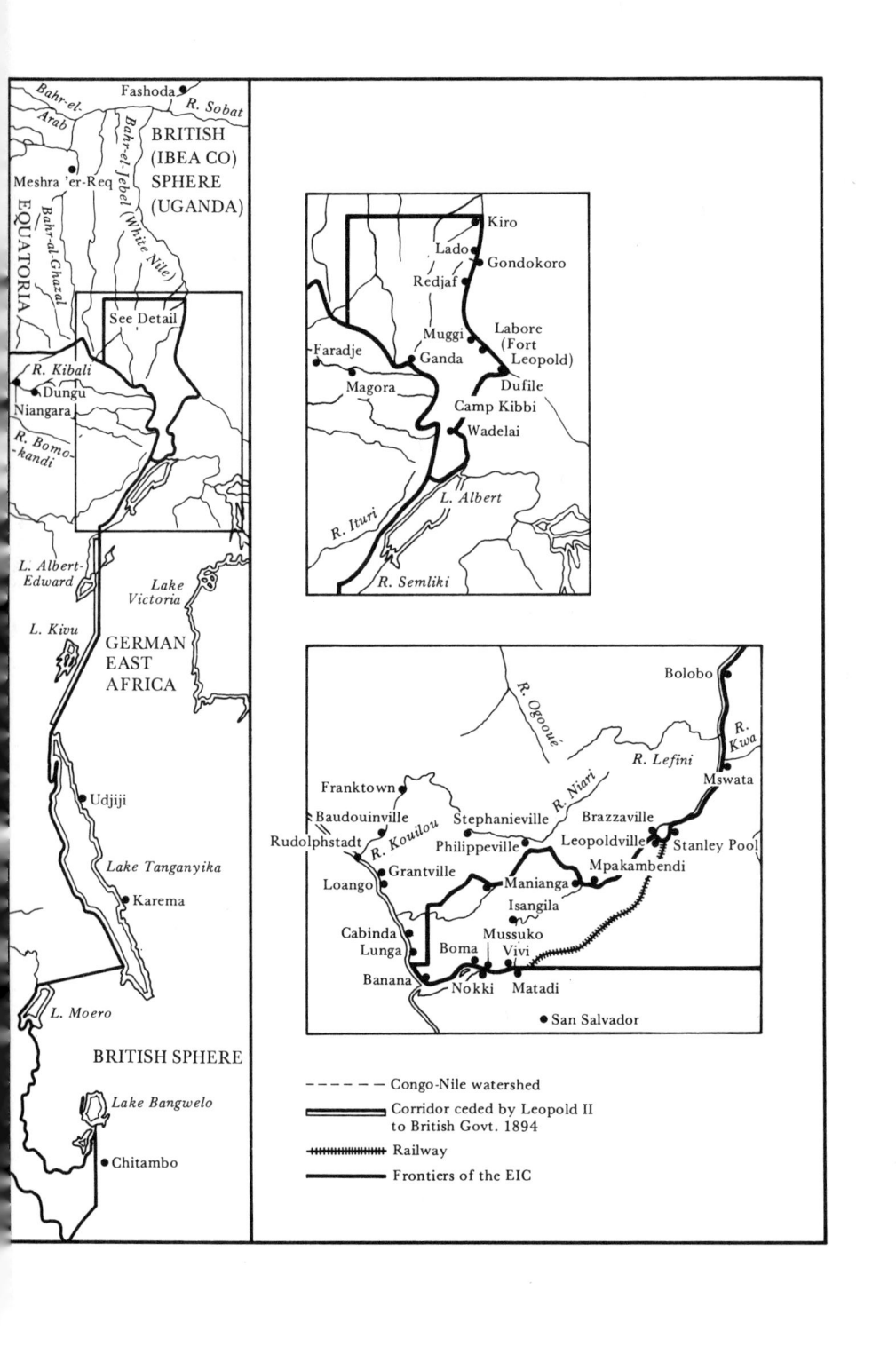

Fashoda
R. Sobat
Bahr-el-Arab
Bahr-el-Jebel (White Nile)
Meshra 'er-Req
BRITISH
(IBEA CO)
SPHERE
(UGANDA)
EQUATORIA
Bahr-al-Ghazal
See Detail
R. Kibali
Dungu
Niangara
R. Bomo-kandi
L. Albert-Edward
Lake Victoria
L. Kivu
GERMAN
EAST
AFRICA
Udjiji
Lake Tanganyika
Karema
L. Moero
BRITISH SPHERE
Lake Bangwelo
Chitambo

Kiro
Lado
Gondokoro
Redjaf
Muggi
Labore
(Fort
Leopold)
Faradje
Ganda
Magora
Dufile
Camp Kibbi
Wadelai
R. Ituri
L. Albert
R. Semliki

Bolobo
R. Ogooué
R. Kwa
R. Lefini
Mswata
Franktown
Baudouinville
Stephanieville
R. Niari
Brazzaville
Rudolphstadt
R. Kouilou
Philippeville
Leopoldville
Stanley Pool
Loango
Grantville
Manianga
Mpakambendi
Isangila
Cabinda
Mussuko
Lunga
Boma
Vivi
Banana
Nokki
Matadi
San Salvador

- - - - - Congo-Nile watershed
▭▭▭▭ Corridor ceded by Leopold II
to British Govt. 1894
▮▮▮▮▮▮▮ Railway
▬▬▬▬ Frontiers of the EIC

Index

In this index L = Leopold II